P9-BZB-740

We
Killed

We Killed

THE RISE OF WOMEN IN AMERICAN COMEDY

Yael Kohen

SARAH CRICHTON BOOKS

FARRAR, STRAUS AND GIROUX   NEW YORK

SARAH CRICHTON BOOKS
Farrar, Straus and Giroux
18 West 18th Street, New York 10011

Distributed in Canada by D&M Publishers, Inc.
Printed in the United States of America
First edition, 2012

Library of Congress Cataloging-in-Publication Data
Kohen, Yael, 1980–
    We killed : the rise of women in American comedy / Yael Kohen.
      p.   cm.
    Includes index.
    ISBN 978-0-374-28723-8 (alk. paper)
    1. Stand-up comedy—United States.   2. Women comedians—United States—
Biography.   3. Women comedians—United States—Interviews.   I. Title.

PN1969.C65 .K65 2012
792.7'6028092520973—dc23
[B]

                    2012018565

Designed by Abby Kagan

www.fsgbooks.com

10 9 8 7 6 5 4 3 2 1

For my daughter, Adele

Contents

Cast of Characters

SYBIL ADELMAN was a comedy writer who wrote for *The Mary Tyler Moore Show* and *Maude*, among other programs. Adelman has also written for Lily Tomlin.

CHRIS ALBRECHT was a co-owner of New York's Improv comedy club from 1975 to 1980. He left to become an agent at International Creative Management (ICM), where he stayed for five years before landing at HBO, where he rose through the ranks, eventually becoming president of original programming and, in 2002, chairman and CEO. He remained at HBO until 2007. He is currently the CEO of Starz.

LOUIE ANDERSON is a stand-up comedian who created the Emmy Award–winning animated series *Life with Louie*. He later hosted the second revival of the game show *Family Feud* for three seasons.

IRVIN ARTHUR is a talent agent who booked a variety of fifties- and sixties-era nightclubs (including the hungry i in San Francisco and the Playboy clubs). At various points in his career, Arthur has represented comedians such as Professor Irwin Corey, Mort Sahl, Woody Allen, and Ellen DeGeneres, among others.

SANDY ARTHUR is the wife of Irvin Arthur and made the club rounds with her husband. During the 1960s, the two briefly ran a club called the RSVP, which she managed. Sandy Arthur was also a partner in Irvin Arthur Associates, which opened in 1971.

JOANNE ASTROW   was a stand-up comedian who cut her teeth at the Comedy Store during the 1970s. Astrow went on to manage comedians such as Kathleen Madigan and Lewis Black. She is married to Improv co-owner Mark Lonow and is the mother of comedian and comedy writer Claudia Lonow.

GARY AUSTIN   is the founder and original director of the Groundlings, an improvisational comedy school and theater in Los Angeles.

JULIE BARR   is a stand-up comedian who circulated in the Boston comedy clubs throughout the 1980s and 1990s; today she works cruise ships.

ANNE BEATTS   was the first female editor at the *National Lampoon*. She is best known as a writer on *Saturday Night Live*, where she worked from 1975 to 1980.

JOY BEHAR   is a stand-up comedian and a co-host of *The View*.

GREG BEHRENDT   is a stand-up comedian who served as a consultant on *Sex and the City*. He is best known for cowriting the bestselling dating manual *He's Just Not That Into You*.

SHELLEY BERMAN   was a member of the fifties-era sketch theater the Compass Players who went on to perform solo shows as a stand-up. Berman's 1959 record *Inside Shelley Berman* is credited with being the first comedy record to become a gold album, selling over a million copies.

SANDRA BERNHARD   is a stand-up comedian best known for her breakout role in Martin Scorsese's *The King of Comedy* and later for her role on *Roseanne*. Bernhard was, at one point, famously rumored to be dating Madonna.

MATT BESSER   is a founding member of the Upright Citizens Brigade sketch comedy troupe. He later cofounded the Upright Citizens Brigade Theatre in New York.

LINDA BLOODWORTH-THOMASON is a comedy writer and producer who got her start penning scripts for *M*A*S*H* (with partner Mary Kay Place). Bloodworth-Thomason went on to create *Designing Women,* among other series.

STU BLOOMBERG was ABC vice president of comedy development from 1982 to 1989. Bloomberg also served as ABC Entertainment's executive vice president of prime time from 1989 to 1997 and ABC Entertainment Television cochairman from 1997 to 2002.

PATRICIA BRADFORD was a talent coordinator on *The Tonight Show Starring Johnny Carson* from 1969 to 1973.

MARSHALL BRICKMAN is an Academy Award–winning comedy writer best known for cowriting *Annie Hall* and *Manhattan* with Woody Allen. Brickman has also written for *The Tonight Show Starring Johnny Carson* and *The Dick Cavett Show*. He's written and directed a handful of his own films, including *The Manhattan Project,* and most recently he cowrote the Broadway musicals *Jersey Boys* and *The Addams Family.*

LOIS BROMFIELD is a stand-up comedian who wrote for the ABC sitcom *Roseanne* and was a producer on the Brett Butler sitcom *Grace Under Fire.*

CAROL BURNETT is a comedienne best known for her Emmy Award–winning variety series, *The Carol Burnett Show.*

ALLAN BURNS was a co-creator of *The Mary Tyler Moore Show.*

ZANE BUZBY was a sitcom director whose credits include *Charles in Charge, My Two Dads,* and *Blossom.* Buzby also directed the first episode of HBO's *Women of the Night* comedy special.

CINDY CAPONERA is a Second City alum and a former writer-performer for the sketch group Exit 57, and was a *Saturday Night Live* writer from 1995 to 1998. Caponera has written for a variety of sitcoms, most recently Showtime's *Shameless* and ABC's *No. One Son,* the latter of which she created. She is co-creator and executive producer of a new show starring Sherri Shepherd.

MARCY CARSEY was senior vice president for prime-time series at ABC from 1974 to 1980. Carsey went on to cofound Carsey-Werner Productions, where she produced top-ten hits like *The Cosby Show* and *Roseanne*, among the most groundbreaking sitcoms in television history.

MARGARET CHO is a stand-up comedian best known for her concert comedy tours *I'm the One That I Want* and *Notorious C.H.O.* Cho has starred in several television sitcoms, including the short-lived *All-American Girl*, presumably based on her stand-up, and most recently *Drop Dead Diva* on Lifetime. Cho has also had memorable cameos on such shows as *Sex and the City* and *30 Rock*.

CINDY CHUPACK is a comedy writer and producer best known for her work on *Sex and the City*. She has also written and produced for such programs as *Everybody Loves Raymond* and *Modern Family*, among others.

DAVID CROSS is a stand-up comedian who co-created and costarred in the HBO sketch comedy series *Mr. Show with Bob and David*. Cross spent three seasons on the Fox cult classic *Arrested Development*, and has made numerous appearances on various television shows and in movies.

WHITNEY CUMMINGS is a stand-up comedian who first gained notoriety as a panelist on *Chelsea Lately* and the Comedy Central Roast of Joan Rivers (she later roasted David Hasselhoff and Donald Trump). In 2011 Cummings went on to create two network sitcoms, the CBS show *2 Broke Girls* (which she co-created with *Sex and the City* mastermind Michael Patrick King) and NBC's *Whitney*, in which she also stars. She is also producing and starring in her own talk show, *Love You, Mean It with Whitney Cummings*, on the E! network.

JOAN DARLING began her career as an actress at the sixties-era New York improv theater the Premise. Darling later became one of the first women to direct television sitcoms, including Norman Lear's *Mary*

Hartman, Mary Hartman; The Mary Tyler Moore Show; Rhoda; and *M*A*S*H*, among others.

ELLEN DeGENERES is a stand-up comedian who famously came out on her nineties-era sitcom, *Ellen.* DeGeneres went on to host her own Emmy Award–winning daytime talk show, *The Ellen DeGeneres Show,* and has hosted the Academy Awards and *American Idol.*

PHYLLIS DILLER was a stand-up comedian best known for playing a comedic foil to Bob Hope: Diller appeared alongside the great comedy legend in three movies and twenty-nine NBC comedy specials, making Diller Hope's most frequent guest.

PAUL DOOLEY was a stand-up comedian in the fifties and sixties. Dooley is best known, however, as an actor who has appeared in a number of television series and movies, including *Curb Your Enthusiasm, Grace Under Fire,* and *My So-Called Life,* among others.

RACHEL DRATCH is a Second City alum and former *Saturday Night Live* performer who appeared on the program from 1999 to 2006.

TOM DREESEN is a stand-up comedian who opened regularly for Frank Sinatra and has made numerous appearances on the *Tonight Show* and *The Late Show with David Letterman.*

NORA DUNN is a Second City alum and was a *Saturday Night Live* cast member from 1985 to 1990. Dunn continues to make appearances in a variety of television and film roles.

SUSIE ESSMAN is a stand-up comedian best known for playing foul-mouthed ballbuster Susie Greene on HBO's *Curb Your Enthusiasm.*

MARK FLANAGAN is the owner of the Largo nightclub in Los Angeles, where in the late nineties the Monday comedy night became one of the hottest tickets in town.

BARBARA GALLAGHER was a comedy writer who wrote for *The Mary Tyler Moore Show, Maude,* and a Lily Tomlin special. Gallagher went on to become associate producer at *Saturday Night Live* when it debuted in 1975.

JANEANE GAROFALO is a stand-up comedian who first gained recognition on MTV's *The Ben Stiller Show* and then shot to national fame in the Generation X–defining film *Reality Bites*. Garofalo later starred in *The Truth About Cats & Dogs* with Uma Thurman and has made numerous cameo appearances on television and in film.

ANA GASTEYER is a Groundlings alum who went on to become a *Saturday Night Live* performer from 1996 to 2002. She had a supporting role in the Tina Fey–written film *Mean Girls*, and now appears on the ABC sitcom *Suburgatory*.

WHOOPI GOLDBERG is a stand-up comedian and actress who won an Academy Award for her part in *Ghost*. Goldberg is currently a co-host on the daytime talk show *The View*.

LORRAINE GORDON was the wife of Max Gordon, co-owner of the Blue Angel nightclub and the Village Vanguard in New York.

KATHY GRIFFIN is a stand-up comedian who had a supporting role on the NBC sitcom *Suddenly Susan*, and is best known for *My Life on the D-List*, the Emmy Award–winning Bravo reality series based on her life. She hosts *Kathy*, a talk show on Bravo.

MARY GROSS is a Second City alum and former *Saturday Night Live* performer who appeared on the program from 1981 to 1985. Gross is best known for costarring in a number of eighties-era comedies, including *Troop Beverly Hills* and *Feds*.

ARGUS HAMILTON is a stand-up comedian who has been a Comedy Store fixture since the 1970s.

CHELSEA HANDLER is a stand-up comedian best known for hosting her own late-night talk show *Chelsea Lately*, on the E! network. Handler has also written four bestselling books.

TED HARBERT was a longtime ABC executive who climbed the network's ranks, eventually landing top programming jobs at ABC Entertainment, including vice president of prime time from 1988 to 1989; executive vice president of prime time from 1989 to 1993; president, a position he held until 1996; and finally chairman of the board in 1996. In 1999, Harbert was named president of NBC Studios, the network's production arm. In 2004, he left to become head of Comcast's E! network and in 2010 he became chairman of Comcast's new acquisition, NBC Broadcasting. He famously dated Chelsea Handler.

VALERIE HARPER is a Second City alum best known for her role as Rhoda on *The Mary Tyler Moore Show* and the MTM spinoff *Rhoda*.

BARBARA HARRIS was a member of the Compass Players and the original Second City. Harris went on to a successful Broadway and film career. Her stage credits include *Mother Courage* and *The Apple Tree*; in film she starred in *A Thousand Clowns* and *Plaza Suite*.

SUSAN HARRIS is a comedy writer best known for creating the NBC series *The Golden Girls*.

CAROLINE HIRSCH is the owner of the comedy club Caroline's on Broadway.

MELANIE HUTSELL was a *Saturday Night Live* performer from 1991 to 1994.

VICTORIA JACKSON was a *Saturday Night Live* performer from 1986 to 1992.

ANJELAH JOHNSON is a stand-up comedian who appeared on the thirteenth season of *MADtv*; she later broke out as a YouTube sensation with two viral videos, the first reaching twenty-five million views, the second garnering fifty-five million.

BARRY KATZ is the former owner of the now-defunct Boston Comedy Club in New York. Katz has managed such stars as Dane Cook, Jay Mohr, and Whitney Cummings.

MARTA KAUFFMAN is an Emmy Award–winning writer who co-created the NBC sitcom *Friends*.

ELLIE KEMPER is a sketch comedian who trained at the Upright Citizens Brigade. She became a regular on NBC's *The Office* and went on to costar in the blockbuster female-driven comedy *Bridesmaids*.

ROBERTA KENT is a stand-up comedian best known as a comedy writer and opener for Barry Manilow.

LAURA KIGHTLINGER is a stand-up comedian who wrote for and performed on *Saturday Night Live* during the 1994–1995 season. She has also written for *Roseanne*, *Dennis Miller Live*, and *Will & Grace* (for which she was also a consulting producer).

KAREN KILGARIFF is a stand-up comedian who appeared on the HBO sketch series *Mr. Show* and later was head writer on *The Ellen DeGeneres Show*.

ANDY KINDLER is a stand-up comedian best known for appearing on *Everybody Loves Raymond* and for giving the Annual State of the Industry address at the Montreal Just for Laughs Festival.

JEN KIRKMAN is a stand-up comedian and a writer on *Chelsea Lately*, where she also makes appearances as a roundtable panelist.

MARCI KLEIN is a coproducer of *Saturday Night Live*.

ROBERT KLEIN is a Second City alum and stand-up comedian best known for his 1972 album *Child of the Fifties*.

LISA KUDROW is a Groundlings alum who is best known for her role as Phoebe Buffay on the NBC sitcom *Friends*. Kudrow also costarred in the cult comedy *Romy and Michele's High School Reunion*. She now stars in the Showtime series *Web Therapy*, which was developed from a popular Web series.

LISA LAMPANELLI is a stand-up comedian best known for her use of racial and ethnic slurs and as a regular participant in Comedy Central's roasts. She goes by the moniker "the Queen of Mean."

BETH LAPIDES is the cofounder of the hot nineties-era Los Angeles comedy showcase Un-Cabaret.

LOUISE LASSER is an actress best known for her starring role in the Norman Lear–produced soap opera parody *Mary Hartman, Mary Hartman*, which debuted in 1976. Lasser was also married to Woody Allen and appeared in several of his films, including *Bananas, Take the Money and Run*, and *Everything You Always Wanted to Know About Sex* (But Were Afraid to Ask)*.

NATASHA LEGGERO is a stand-up comedian best known for being a roundtable regular on *Chelsea Lately* and for acting as a judge on the seventh season of *Last Comic Standing*.

CAROL LEIFER is a stand-up comedian best known for writing on *Seinfeld* and for being the inspiration for the show's female character, Elaine Benes.

KELLY LEONARD is executive vice president of Second City.

EMILY LEVINE is a stand-up comedian and writer who's worked for various television shows, including *Designing Women* and *Love and War*.

RICHARD LEWIS is a stand-up comedian best known for his various late-night talk show appearances and television and sitcom work. His most recent claim to fame is acting as himself on Larry David's HBO series *Curb Your Enthusiasm*.

WENDY LIEBMAN is a stand-up comedian best known for her comedy club work.

WARREN LITTLEFIELD was the president of NBC Entertainment from 1993 to 1998; before that, he was the executive vice president of prime time at the network. In a twenty-year career at NBC, Littlefield was responsible for developing top programs, including *The Cosby Show*, *The Golden Girls*, and *Seinfeld*, as well as creating the network's blockbuster Thursday night lineup, "Must-See TV." He currently runs the Littlefield Company, a production company.

CLAUDIA LONOW is a stand-up comedian and comedy writer who most recently created the short-lived CBS sitcom *Accidentally on Purpose*. She is the daughter of JoAnne Astrow and stepdaughter of Mark Lonow.

MARK LONOW has been a co-owner of the Improv comedy chain since 1979. He is married to JoAnne Astrow and is the stepfather of Claudia Lonow.

LONI LOVE is a stand-up comedian who's best known as a regular panelist on *Chelsea Lately*.

MERRILL MARKOE is a comedy writer who co-created *Late Night with David Letterman*.

PENNY MARSHALL is an actress and director best known for appearing in the 1970s and 1980s sitcom *Laverne & Shirley* and for directing box office successes such as *Big* and *A League of Their Own*.

JAMIE MASADA is the owner of the Laugh Factory comedy club in Los Angeles.

ANNE MEARA is a sketch comic best known for being one half of the popular sixties-era comedy team Stiller and Meara with husband Jerry Stiller. The duo got their start at the St. Louis offshoot of the Chicago theater group and Second City precursor the Compass.

BETTE MIDLER is a comedian and Grammy Award–winning singer who made her name in New York City's cabarets and bathhouses during the 1970s. Midler was twice nominated for an Academy Award for her roles in *The Rose* and *For the Boys*.

GREG MILLER is a co-creator and founding producer of Un-Cabaret. He is married to Beth Lapides.

MARILYN SUZANNE MILLER is a comedy writer who wrote several episodes of *The Mary Tyler Moore Show* and then went on to become a staff writer for the original cast of *Saturday Night Live* and again from 1980 to 1982 and from 1992 to 1995.

LAURA MILLIGAN is a comedian who created the nineties-era Los Angeles alternative comedy showcase Tantrum.

MO'NIQUE is a stand-up comedian known for her role on the UPN sitcom *The Parkers* and for hosting *Showtime at the Apollo*. She won an Academy Award for her role in the 2009 film *Precious*.

PAUL MOONEY is a stand-up comedian best known as a mentor to Richard Pryor, serving as head writer on the 1977 sketch series *The Richard Pryor Show*. Mooney also mentored Sandra Bernhard.

MARY TYLER MOORE is an actress best known for appearing in two of the most popular sitcoms of all time: *The Dick Van Dyke Show* and *The Mary Tyler Moore Show*.

SETH MORRIS is a former member of the Upright Citizens Brigade in New York. Morris went on to become the artistic director of the Upright Citizens Brigade Theatre in Los Angeles. Today he is a writer and producer at FunnyorDie.com.

LARRY MOSS is an acting coach who began his career performing in revues at the Upstairs at the Downstairs.

LORI NASSO was a *Saturday Night Live* writer from 1995 to 1999.

RICK NEWMAN was the owner of the now-defunct Catch a Rising Star comedy club in New York.

DIANE NICHOLS is a stand-up comedian who was a regular at the Comedy Store.

BOB ODENKIRK is a comedy writer and performer who costarred in HBO's sketch comedy series *Mr. Show with Bob and David* with David

Cross. Among other programs, Odenkirk has written for *The Ben Stiller Show, Late Night with Conan O'Brien,* and *Saturday Night Live* from 1987 to 1995.

CHERI OTERI is a Groundlings alum and was a *Saturday Night Live* performer from 1995 to 2000.

GAIL PARENT is a comedy writer who got her start writing revues at the Upstairs at the Downstairs. Parent went on to write for *The Carol Burnett Show* and *The Golden Girls,* among other programs.

ROD PARKER was an executive producer of the CBS sitcom *Maude.*

SHELDON PATINKIN is the former manager and director of Second City. He is currently the company's artistic consultant.

PAULA PELL has been a writer for *Saturday Night Live* since 1995.

CHELSEA PERETTI is a stand-up comedian who went on to write for Comedy Central's *The Sarah Silverman Program* and later NBC's *Parks and Recreation.*

GENE PERRET is a comedy writer who got his start writing jokes for Phyllis Diller. Perret went on to write for variety stars such as Carol Burnett and Bob Hope.

IRENE PINN is a former manager of Lily Tomlin.

AUBREY PLAZA is a sketch comic who trained at the Upright Citizens Brigade. She is best known for her role in the Judd Apatow dramedy *Funny People* and now the NBC sitcom *Parks and Recreation.*

PAULA POUNDSTONE is a stand-up comedian best known for her club work. Today she is a panelist of NPR's *Wait Wait . . . Don't Tell Me!*

DAVE RATH is a comedy manager and founding partner of Generate Talent Management.

CARL REINER is an Emmy Award–winning comedy writer, actor, and producer who wrote and appeared on Sid Caesar's *Your Show of Shows* and *Caesar's Hour* and created *The Dick Van Dyke Show.*

CAROLINE RHEA is a stand-up comedian known for her role as Hilda on *Sabrina, the Teenage Witch*, for hosting the first two seasons of *The Biggest Loser*, and for replacing Rosie O'Donnell on her syndicated talk show, which was aptly renamed *The Caroline Rhea Show.*

JOAN RIVERS is a stand-up comedian who shot to fame on *The Tonight Show Starring Johnny Carson*, becoming that show's first permanent guest host. She left abruptly in 1985 to start her own rival late-night program, *The Late Show Starring Joan Rivers*, and when that failed she resurrected her career years later as a red-carpet insult comic on E! In recent years, she's made headlines by winning Donald Trump's NBC reality contest show *Celebrity Apprentice* and for being the subject of a well-received documentary film about her career.

ROSEANNE is a stand-up comedian best known for her groundbreaking ABC sitcom *Roseanne.*

RITA RUDNER is a stand-up comedian who made frequent appearances on various programs, including *Late Night with David Letterman*, the *Tonight Show, Hollywood Squares*, and on HBO comedy specials. Today she draws a healthy crowd to her popular Las Vegas stand-up show.

MAYA RUDOLPH is a Groundlings alum and former *Saturday Night Live* performer who appeared on the show from 2000 to 2007. In 2011 she costarred in the female-driven blockbuster comedy *Bridesmaids* with *SNL* costar Kristen Wiig and landed a starring role on the fresh NBC sitcom *Up All Night.*

LAUREN SACKIN is the daughter of Nat Sackin, former owner of the Bon Soir nightclub in New York.

BERNARD SAHLINS is a cofounder of Second City.

KRISTEN SCHAAL is a stand-up comedian best known for her appearances on the HBO comedy series *Flight of the Conchords*, on Jon Stewart's *The Daily Show*, and on *30 Rock*.

GEORGE SCHLATTER is a television producer and writer best known for creating *Rowan & Martin's Laugh-In*.

SHELLY SCHULTZ is a former talent coordinator and writer for *The Tonight Show Starring Johnny Carson* from 1962 to 1970.

DAVID SHEPHERD is the founder of the Compass Players.

ILIZA SHLESINGER is a stand-up comedian best known for being the first woman—and youngest comic—to win the stand-up comedy contest *Last Comic Standing*, in 2008. She is now host of the syndicated reality dating program *Excused*.

SAMMY SHORE is a stand-up comedian who founded the Comedy Store, then turned it over to his soon-to-be-ex-wife Mitzi Shore.

ROSIE SHUSTER is a comedy writer who has written for Lily Tomlin and was a staff writer for *Saturday Night Live* from 1975 to 1980 and again from 1982 to 1988. She is the ex-wife of *SNL* creator Lorne Michaels.

SUSAN SILVER is a comedy writer best known for her work on *The Mary Tyler Moore Show*.

FRED SILVERMAN was vice president of programs for CBS from 1970 to 1975, president of ABC Entertainment from 1975 to 1978, and president and chief executive officer of NBC from 1978 to 1981.

TREVA SILVERMAN is a comedy writer who cut her teeth writing revues at the Upstairs at the Downstairs during the 1960s. She went on to a successful career in television writing, contributing to variety programs and sitcoms, including *The Mary Tyler Moore Show* and *Rhoda*.

JEFF SINGER was a booker for the popular New York comedy show

"Eating It" at the Luna Lounge. He has been an executive consultant for the Just for Laughs Festival in Montreal since 2000.

BOBBY SLAYTON is a stand-up comedian who has appeared on the *Tonight Show, Politically Incorrect,* and *Comic Relief.*

JOYCE SLOANE was a Second City fixture for forty-nine years, serving as an associate and executive producer, and was a producer emeritus until she died in February 2011.

LINDA SMITH is a stand-up comedian who has written for the syndicated daytime talk show *The Rosie O'Donnell Show.* Smith now teaches classes on comedy at Caroline's on Broadway.

MARGARET SMITH is a stand-up comedian who was also a writer and producer of *The Ellen DeGeneres Show,* for which she has six Daytime Emmy Awards.

CARRIE SNOW is a stand-up comedian who was also a story editor on *Roseanne.*

SUZANNE SOMERS is a former actress best known for playing Chrissy Snow on the seventies-era sitcom *Three's Company.* She later starred in the ABC sitcom *Step by Step.*

EMILY SPIVEY is a former Groundling who wrote for *Saturday Night Live* from 2001 to 2011. She is the creator of the NBC sitcom *Up All Night.*

DAVID STEINBERG is a stand-up comedian and Second City alum best known for appearing on *The Smothers Brothers Comedy Hour* and, during the 1970s, for making the late-night rounds, including several stints guest-hosting on the *Tonight Show.* Steinberg went on to become a sitcom director, working on shows such as *Seinfeld, Friends, Designing Women,* and *Curb Your Enthusiasm.*

ALLAN STEPHAN is a stand-up comedian who also was an executive producer on *Roseanne* and a writer for HBO's *Arli$$.*

BRANDON STODDARD is a former ABC executive who began his career with the network in 1970, rising through the ranks to become president of ABC Entertainment from 1985 to 1989. He remained head of ABC Productions, the network's in-house production arm, until 1995.

HOWARD STORM is a former stand-up comedian who made the rounds in sixties-era New York. Storm went on to a successful career directing television sitcoms.

LISA SUNDSTEDT is a stand-up comedian and founder of the L.A. showcase Pretty, Funny Women. Sundstedt was a writer during the first two seasons of *Chelsea Lately*.

MARLO THOMAS is an actress turned women's rights activist. Thomas created and starred in the sixties-era sitcom *That Girl*. She is the daughter of comedian Danny Thomas, best known for his role on the fifties-era sitcom *Make Room for Daddy*.

ADRIANNE TOLSCH is a stand-up comedian who was the first woman to emcee at the New York comedy club Catch a Rising Star, where she was a regularly featured comedian.

LILY TOMLIN is a comedian who shot to fame on the NBC series *Rowan & Martin's Laugh-In* in 1969, and became one of the most groundbreaking and pivotal comedians to emerge in the 1970s.

THEA VIDALE is a stand-up comedian who's been featured on several comedy specials and is best known for starring in her own short-lived sitcom, *Thea*.

JANE WAGNER is a writer who has worked with Lily Tomlin since the early 1970s, helping to develop the comedian's most groundbreaking material.

JAN WALLMAN is a former nightclub manager of the Upstairs at the Duplex.

FRED WEINTRAUB was founder and a former owner of the Bitter End club in New York during the 1960s.

KRISTEN WIIG is a Groundlings alum and former *Saturday Night Live* performer who appeared on the show from 2005 to 2012. Wiig cowrote and starred in the blockbuster comedy *Bridesmaids*.

ROBIN WILLIAMS is a stand-up comedian turned Academy Award–winning actor best known for his roles in the films *Good Will Hunting, The Fisher King, Dead Poets Society*, and *Good Morning, Vietnam*, among many others.

CASEY WILSON is an Upright Citizens Brigade alum who became a featured player on *Saturday Night Live* from 2008 to 2009. Wilson co-wrote the 2009 movie *Bride Wars* and is now a regular cast member on the ABC sitcom *Happy Endings*.

LIZZ WINSTEAD is a stand-up comedian best known for co-creating *The Daily Show* on Comedy Central in 1996, two years before Jon Stewart assumed the anchor chair.

JO ANNE WORLEY is a comedian best known for performing on the NBC variety program *Rowan & Martin's Laugh-In* from 1968 to 1970.

CHARLYNE YI is a stand-up comedian best known for portraying a pothead in the 2007 Judd Apatow blockbuster *Knocked Up*. Yi is also the cowriter and star of the independent film *Paper Heart*.

CHRISTINE ZANDER is a former writer for *Saturday Night Live* who worked on the show from 1986 to 1993. Zander left *SNL* to write and produce a number of sitcoms, including *3rd Rock from the Sun, Nurse Jackie*, and *Raising Hope*.

ALAN ZWEIBEL is a comedy writer best known for his work on *Saturday Night Live* from 1975 to 1980, where he often collaborated with sketch comedy legend Gilda Radner.

Author's Note

After writing an oral history about women in comedy for the April 2009 issue of *Marie Claire* magazine, I decided there was more to this story than could be covered in just a few pages. Women in comedy had become a hot topic again—most of it centered on the old argument that women aren't funny. While that seemed a worthy conversation to dive into—and certainly one can't write a history of women working in this male-dominated field without exploring the argument—what interested me more was taking a broader look at how women have fit into the history of American comedy as a whole. So I gathered the interviews I had conducted for the magazine and decided that with the addition of even more interviews (from comedians and their managers, as well as club owners, network executives, and male colleagues), they could be expanded into an in-depth history. This book draws from more than two hundred interviews I conducted between late 2008, when I started writing about the subject for *Marie Claire*, and mid-2012. Getting the interviews wasn't an easy task; there are several comedians whom I would have loved to talk to, but who declined my requests. To those comedians who did agree to speak to me, I say "Thank you."

The interviews included in this book were conducted in person or on the phone, were recorded, and ranged in length from about thirty minutes to three hours. One of the interviews, and several follow-ups, were conducted by e-mail. The interviews were then condensed and edited for clarity, but their language and the meaning and context of what each person said remains the same. Meanwhile, portions of some of the interviews have appeared in subsequent articles in *Marie Claire* and *The Daily Beast*.

To create the narrative structure, I was guided mainly by my interviews, but a few books were particularly helpful when it came to background and insights. These were *Seriously Funny: The Rebel Comedians of the 1950s and 1960s*, by Gerald Nachman; *The Compass: The Improvisational Theatre That Revolutionized American Comedy*, by Janet Coleman; *Something Wonderful Right Away: An Oral History of the Second City and the Compass Players*, by Jeffrey Sweet; *I'm Dying Up Here: Heartbreak and High Times in Stand-up Comedy's Golden Era*, by William Knoedelseder; and *Live from New York: An Uncensored History of* Saturday Night Live, *as Told by Its Stars, Writers, and Guests*, by Tom Shales and James Andrew Miller. Gratitude must go to these authors, who have written fascinating histories of American comedy.

We Killed

Introduction

You've heard it before: Women aren't funny. The opinion has been appearing and reappearing in various guises for decades. John Belushi said it to Gilda Radner; Johnny Carson said it to *Rolling Stone*; the *National Lampoon*'s founding editor, Henry Beard, said it to his magazine's first female editor, Anne Beatts; Del Close, the Upright Citizen's Brigade guru, listed it as number thirteen on the list of comedy rules he circulated back when he was at Second City; and Jerry Lewis told an audience at the Aspen comedy festival that "a woman doing comedy doesn't offend me but sets me back a bit . . . I think of her as a producing machine that brings babies into the world." Behind the scenes, the comment has been made by comedy club owners, bookers, fellow comedians—male *and* female—and television executives. Then, in 2007, to incendiary effect, Christopher Hitchens wrote an essay in *Vanity Fair* about it. But few assertions are easier to disprove than this one. It's as simple as saying that women make us laugh. And right now, at the start of the second decade of the twenty-first century, there are plenty of women who do.

Evidence from the past ten years alone is abundant. Tina Fey emerged as a major comic icon, with a shelf full of Emmys and the honor of being the youngest person ever to win the prestigious Mark Twain Award for American Humor. Chelsea Handler had four bestselling books and a highly rated late-night talk show anchoring the E! network. The cofounder of the now-ubiquitous Upright Citizens Brigade Theatre, Amy Poehler, anchored one of the most respected sitcoms on television, *Parks and Recreation*. Joan Rivers reignited her career by upstaging Donald

Trump on his own show, *The Apprentice*, and then starred in a riveting documentary about her life as a stand-up. Sarah Silverman unleashed YouTube videos with millions of hits and garnered an Emmy for her video *I'm Fucking Matt Damon*. Kathy Griffin's hit reality show earned her two Emmys. Ellen DeGeneres, with her own hit daytime talk show, was dubbed the new Oprah. Wanda Sykes spent 2009 with a reputation for being the most controversial comic of the year after a provocative performance at the White House Correspondents' dinner. And three out of five of *The View*'s hosts are stand-up comedians: Joy Behar, Whoopi Goldberg, and Sherri Shepherd. Funny up-and-coming ladies can be seen all over prime-time, daytime, and late-night TV; they come in a variety of shapes, ages, sizes, and colors; pretty and plain; lesbian and straight.

Then, in May 2011, the success of these women seemed to culminate when *Saturday Night Live* star Kristen Wiig did what, despite all these successes, was still considered the impossible: lead an all-female cast to blockbuster success. *Bridesmaids*, the bawdy comedy that Wiig cowrote (with a female partner) and starred in hauled in $26 million its opening weekend, just behind the action extravaganza *Thor*. By its fifth week the movie had surpassed the ticket sales of another benchmark comedy, *Knocked Up*. It didn't just make bank: the movie was hailed by critics as groundbreaking—it proved that women could pull off a good fart joke as well as the next guy, and was nominated for two Golden Globes and, amazingly, two Oscars. By the fall of 2011, the four major networks had given the green light to nine female-driven comedies, and the networks continue to bet on women to fill their lineups. The success of *Bridesmaids*, it seemed, was a watershed moment, a film we could all point to as final proof that Hitchens's infamous diatribe "Why Women Aren't Funny" was history.

And yet, annoyingly, it remains unlikely that all these successes will be the last word on the "Are women funny?" debate. For one thing, funny women continue to face challenges in the comedy arena. Out of one hundred and forty-five writers working across ten late-night shows, sixteen writers are women (five of them for *Chelsea Lately*); out of twenty-four writers on *Saturday Night Live*, six are women; and out of fourteen performers, four are female. Female stand-ups continue to be left off major stand-up lineups; and Comedy Central, which has a *woman* as president, targets male audiences eighteen to thirty-four years old. Perhaps even more important, though, it seems no matter how many times women buck the conventional wisdom, the debate continues to rage. The question "Are women funny?" is older than Phyllis Diller, and has been nagging at women on and off—mostly on—for the past sixty years. Didn't Tina Fey drive the final nail in that coffin when she skewered vice presidential candidate Sarah Palin back in 2008? Or how about when Poehler joined Fey as co-anchor on *Saturday Night Live*'s Weekend Update desk in 2004? Or when Whoopi Goldberg donned a nun's habit in the box office success *Sister Act* in 1992? Or when Roseanne took the first season of her self-titled sitcom to the number one spot in the ratings over *The Cosby Show* in 1988? Or the time Joan Rivers became the first permanent guest host on *The Tonight Show Starring Johnny Carson* in 1983? Or when *Private Benjamin*, a movie starring Goldie Hawn and written by Nancy Meyer, was nominated for three Academy Awards in 1980?

Women have always been funny. It's just that every success is called an exception and every failure an example of the rule. And as each generation develops its own style of comedy, the coups of the previous era are washed away under the set of new challenges a younger group of women inevitably face. And yet, despite all the hecklers, boys' clubs, and old-school notions about women in comedy, the result is always the same: They kill.

1

. . . .

Mothers of Invention

Among the politically charged, foulmouthed, and confessional comics who revolutionized the entertainment establishment in the 1950s and early 1960s were two women who upended the image of the traditional comedienne: Phyllis Diller and Elaine May. In style and substance, neither woman had much to do with the other. Diller was a stand-up who built her act around seemingly trivial husband barbs and self-deprecating housewife jokes; May was an improvisational sketch artist who injected her vignettes with highbrow intellectualism and sharp, incisive observations about middle-class life. And yet, both women laid the groundwork for a new kind of female comic. Until Diller and May hit the New York nightclub scene in 1957, comediennes were expected to sing and dance. But that all changed. Diller—the prototypical female stand-up—proved that women could tell jokes "just like a man," while May—the mother of sketch comedy—introduced the country to improv. While each woman practiced different comedic art forms, both set future generations of funny ladies on one of these two separate but equally important paths to comedy success. And rather than make their names on the vaudeville circuit like many of the best-known comediennes of the past, Diller and May shot to national prominence from a group of small clubs in New York that were slowly changing the face of entertainment.

SHELLY SCHULTZ, talent coordinator and writer, *The Tonight Show Starring Johnny Carson* In New York at that time, you had the Copacabana, you had the Plaza Hotel, you had the Empire Room in the Waldorf, you had the Latin Quarter. And the Copacabana was the kind of place that had a line of dancing girls, it had an orchestra, and it had a big-name act and a supporting act and you could eat there. The Latin Quarter was more of a Las Vegas-y kind of thing, also had a line of girls, but they did more production. Barbara Walters's father owned that: Lou Walters. And then the smaller clubs were the Bon Soir and the Blue Angel, and they had the hipper acts. And the Bon Soir and the Blue Angel were very similar. They were both small, they both sat maybe a hundred people, they both had little tiny tables and a cover charge of five, six, or seven dollars. Food was secondary: couldn't get a meal there, really. People came to drink and watch the show. But you had some jazz clubs; you had piano bars. I mean, there was just tons of nightlife, just tons of nightlife. And in those days an agent would need to be out four or five nights a week or more.

JAN WALLMAN, manager, Upstairs at the Duplex   I was from St. Paul, Minnesota. I was married very young and widowed very young at the end of World War II and I came to New York because I wanted to get away from everything out there and I just wanted to go out every night and hear the music. Somebody called me the walking *Cue* magazine, which was kind of the *Time Out* of its day. I could always tell you who was performing here, who was performing there. And there were loads and loads of small clubs and big clubs. People went until four in the morning and everybody was out having a good time.

PAUL DOOLEY, actor and comedian   In the late fifties, I was acting and trying to break in as a comedian and I got this dream job, which, to most people, would just be a dumb job: I was helping seat people in a nightclub. But it was the famous Village Vanguard, which is still going in Greenwich Village. It's a jazz room basically and my friends would say to me, "You mean for free you get to see Miles Davis and Dizzy Gillespie?" and on and on. And I said, "No, I don't get to see them for free, I get to see Mike Nichols and Elaine May, Shelley Berman, Lenny Bruce, a guy named Professor Irwin Corey." There were about half a dozen comics who played in that club with these jazz greats. They would open the show and do about thirty or forty minutes and then Charles Mingus or Thelonious Monk or whoever—they were all famous jazz people—would come on and do their thing for maybe an hour or so. But for me, this was a clinic where I could study all these comedians, and get paid $5 a night to do it.

VARIETY, January 18, 1956 "New York is becoming a city of small cafés and intimeries. The economics of night clubs are such that the postage-stamp sized rooms are a feasible development in the present era. Large rooms, it's felt, have become victim of their own particular brand of economics. The public apparently cannot support more than three in the style to which the large spots have become accustomed. Many regard the present time as an era of shrinkage in niteries and therefore the small spots have a better chance of catching on.

"In the forefront of the small room development are the Blue Angel, Le Ruban Bleu and the Bon Soir, which are prosperous operations . . . The Village Vanguard and the Blue Angel also provided the push that helped many toward name status.

"Many regard the intimeries as a means of resuscitating the nitery biz . . .

"Many also feel they do better in a small room entertainment-wise, because of the informality of the proceedings and the absence of a regular show."

MARSHALL BRICKMAN, writer Every generation that comes up likes to define itself by its own movies or its own music. With us it was with the movies and people like Woody Allen and Mort Sahl and Elaine and Mike. They weren't cheesy Aqua-Velva-scented Vegas kind of cigar-chomping comedians. They were more sensitive, more aware, more cosmopolitan, more cultured, more intelligent. But oddly enough that didn't limit their impact.

HOWARD STORM, comedian We didn't want to be labeled a Borscht Belt comic, so we started working in the Village. We still did the Catskills in that period—those of us who were able to—because it was a way to make money. In the Village, you didn't make any money. But the Bon Soir was the club to work in in the Village. It was considered fancy and high-class, kind of a step below the Blue Angel. The Blue Angel was the epitome of the chichi clubs.

JAN WALLMAN In 1959, this was a time when comedy was going through a change. And it was tough for the guys in that era, because the stand-up guys that had done pretty well had worked in the [Catskill] mountains, which were very active in those days. They told jokes basically and they had a hard time switching over to that first-person conversational kind of comedy. It wasn't telling jokes. It was just being funny. It was a lot more cerebral, if you will, and much more intellectual.

PAUL DOOLEY The Blue Angel was one of these rooms in New York where these hard-core joke-telling guys would never play. The acts that played the Blue Angel were very discreet, intelligent, hip, and the audience, instead of being noisy and rude and drunk, would just stop and listen to them.

JAN WALLMAN The Blue Angel had panache; it had a European feel. When I was running the Upstairs at the Duplex I went to the Blue Angel at least every other week on my night off. If I went with another woman who was a friend of mine, they would pick up our check, they'd treat us like princesses. If we came with guys, if we had dates, they'd make them pay for it. I modeled what I was doing at the Duplex after the Blue Angel, which was my idea of the greatest place in the world. The Bon Soir was quite wonderful too. I hung out at those places before I had a thing of my own to do. But Herbert Jacoby of the Blue Angel was really my mentor and he used some of the acts that started with me. Mine was a room where people started and moved on.

LAUREN SACKIN, daughter of Nat Sackin, owner of the Bon Soir in the 1960s The Bon Soir was very dark and very small. When you went from West Eighth Street downstairs there was quite a steep set of stairs. It was how you would imagine a speakeasy to be. When you went down, there was a gentleman at a small podium, and I don't know what he was there for—maybe he was a bouncer, maybe he was to greet important customers. When you walked in there was a very tiny stage in the front. It was very dark, very gently lit with candles on each table. And there was a little tiny bar in back, a very tiny bar, and that bar was completely gay. Gay men, totally. Straight men did not hang out at that bar, gay women did not hang out at that bar. It was exclusively gay men who hung out at the bar. The nightclub was predominantly straight, but the bar in the back was three or four gay men deep.

PHYLLIS DILLER, comedian We used to call them discovery clubs. There was a group of discovery clubs, small boîtes: Mr. Kelly's, Bon

Soir, Blue Angel, Purple Onion, the hungry i. They all had a gay bar. And it's just where you could work more chicly. You could do some very, very esoteric stuff. And you're working for about, oh, $1,500 a week. But you weren't anybody till you worked the Copa, right? In those days the Copa was for the big boys: Sid Caesar, Carl Reiner, Jerry Lewis, Martin and Lewis. No female comic had ever played the Copa until this agency booked me for $3,000. You played for $3,000, then you'd get $5,000 for the next time you played, and then $7,000. That's a three-play deal. I played the $3,000 and told them what they could do with five and seven. I went back to the Blue Angel for $2,000. I did it for my career; I was on the wrong course at the Copa. If I was doing it only for the money I would've played the three, five, and seven. But I was not right for that room. 'Cause the audiences were that bad! They were rag people: rag salesmen. They needed titties, and boobs, and dancing girls. They wanted male comics who were sort of Borscht Belt circuit-y; they just needed music and the girls. The gay guys, they were chic. *That* crowd, that Copa crowd, was un-chic. They didn't care for smart material. If you want to be successful, you better stay with the gay crowd. Joan Rivers, to this day, just tells you that right out.

In her platinum fright wig and garish frock, waving a long-stemmed cigarette holder, Phyllis Diller hit the stage like a machine gun, shooting out joke after joke, every few lines punctuated with a blast of a cackle that was so infectious audiences keeled over in laughter. Diller was manic—and hilarious, a caricature of the prim 1950s housewife so idealized in Ike's postwar America. Certainly, there were brilliantly funny women who preceded her, but Diller, unlike her predecessors, didn't launch her career on the vaudeville stage but in the hot new clubs that were changing the face of comedy, emerging as the first female stand-up to garner mass, mainstream appeal. And while Diller's humor was not intellectual in the manner of her contemporaries—her delivery was always the joke-joke-joke rhythm of Bob Hope—she rode the wave of desire for a new kind of act.

PHYLLIS DILLER   I was a housewife with five children. And we reached the bottom. My husband, Sherwood Diller, said, "You're gonna have to get a job." And I immediately looked for a job and got it at a newspaper in Oakland, California. For five years, I was writing newspaper advertising, and if an advertiser would allow me, I would write a funny ad. That led to radio. But my husband kept nagging me and telling me I had to become a comic. It was his idea. He thought I was funny. And of course he was thinking of the money.

I met a guy, Lloyd Clark, who was coaching the writer and poet Maya Angelou for the Purple Onion nightclub. He was sitting next to me at a little bar where they had a jazz group, and I said, "I've been looking for someone to coach me." Lloyd knew about demeanor onstage. And he knew about attitude. He's the one that gave Maya that queenly, regal entrance. And he liked me. I was skinny (I only weighed about 110 pounds), and I was well-spoken, and he was glad to have a new client. So I started preparing for the audition. There was no such thing as an open mic but since he knew all the club owners in the North Beach [San Francisco] area, and they all knew him, he got me my own audition. And the whole time during my audition, which I did very seriously, all dressed up and everything, they were ordering Chinese food. I don't think they heard it at all. So I did it, and they said, "Thank you." And that was it. They had just hired a male stand-up comic by the name of Milt Kamen two weeks before and they didn't have room for me. But when Milt was offered a two-week stint in radio he begged them to let him go to New York for two weeks. Since I had just had my audition, they called me on a Friday night and said, "Could you open Monday?" And I said, "Yes." And in the two weeks that I worked, they watched me improve day by day by day. Milt got back, and I'd had two weeks onstage at the Purple Onion, which was as long as he'd worked there before he left. So they had to decide: Which one of these two, the man or the woman, were they gonna keep? They couldn't decide, so they kept us both.

LORRAINE GORDON, wife of Max Gordon, nightclub owner   Phyllis Diller played at the Blue Angel and she was a howl. She would come out from the wings with a leotard. Not great legs but a leotard anyway, and there was a big baby grand piano and they put the top down for her and she came out and she jumped and slid across the top of the piano and put her face and elbow like that and looked at the audience. It was such an entrance everybody broke up because she almost didn't make the piano. She wound up on top of that baby grand. She was very funny about her husband, Fang. She made terrible fun of him. We didn't believe it was a real husband, she just used that as a hook.

IRVIN ARTHUR, talent agent   She was definitely a new personality in the field of comedy for women. She was funny, and she was likable. People could identify with her. I thought she was one of a kind and she was offbeat. When I booked her in the Bon Soir, I booked Phyllis with Barbra Streisand. And I think Phyllis was the headline, and Barbra opened for her. Phyllis gave Barbra tips on how to dress.

SANDY ARTHUR, talent agent   And I must tell you that the first time that we saw Phyllis Diller at the Purple Onion she looked like she was wearing rags.

ARTHUR GELB writing in *The New York Times*, March 13, 1961   "Phyllis Diller, who is installed for a four-week run at the Bon Soir in Greenwich Village, is the leading member of that rare breed of nightclub entertainer—the female stand-up comic.

"Unlike the routines of such cabaret comediennes as Kaye Ballard, Dorothy Loudon or Jane Connell, who do what is known as 'special bits'—funny songs, skits, satirical takeoffs and so forth—Miss Diller's act consists of an hour or so of rapid-fire, out-and-out gags.

"The most taxing of all nightclub formulas, it is used by only two or three other women on the cabaret circuit; few have the tenacity to stick with it and develop into first-rate performers in demand across the country, as Miss Diller now is.

"Her patter, which she writes herself, combines the ingredients of a number of prominent male nightclub comics—part topical, part 'sick,' part blue (pale blue)—but the performer she most closely resembles in style is Bob Hope."

PAUL DOOLEY   Phyllis Diller was around at the same time that the change in comedy was happening, but she wasn't part of that movement. She didn't do that realistic, subtle Second City–influenced kind of throwaway humor. She always was and remains the person who got up and told jokes. She didn't make observations—well, I can't say it's not observational, because she wrote jokes about her life. But she made up a husband and she was mostly self-deprecating. Phyllis Diller wasn't subtle but she was new inasmuch as there weren't that many female comics. I can see why they would want to put her in the Blue Angel just as a novelty. A person who had become a successful female comic—there weren't that many around.

JAN WALLMAN   Most of the women in comedy that I worked with in those days were singer-comediennes, who were in either a revue that I did or they had a one-woman show where they sang—like Jo Anne Worley or Ruth Buzzi. Most of the male comics I worked with were just pure stand-up, like Woody Allen, like Dick Cavett, like my favorite, Howard Storm, and Rodney Dangerfield.

PHYLLIS DILLER   There's the actress, the comedi*enne*, and the comic. There've always been comic actresses in the movies but most of them couldn't possibly, ever, do stand-up. Lucille Ball was mainly a comic actress. Carol Channing is a perfect example of [a] comedienne [because she could sing and dance]. But stand-up is the ultra-final funny. You don't sing, you don't dance, you talk. It's just brain to brain.

SHELLY SCHULTZ   Phyllis was very hip—*very* hip. She was fresh and new. She was not a Borscht Belt comedian. That's not what Phyllis was. Phyllis Diller was more intimate—they use to call them *intime*. She played smaller rooms. She also came out of the [Purple Onion], which was a very hip club in San Francisco. She was never this kind of brassy broad that Totie Fields* was. She didn't get risqué but she did material that was off-center. She was a thinking person's comedian. And she was so far from being Jewish. Phyllis Diller's act didn't have anything to do with a Jewish mother, or an Italian mother. She was totally American and WASP. There was no religion attached to it, none of that heritage. You could see why Bob Hope adopted her, because she was white bread.

GENE PERRET, writer   Comedy at one time was Henny Youngman: "I haven't spoken to my wife in two years—I didn't want to interrupt . . . I wanted to buy a new car, my wife wanted a fur coat. So we compro-

---

* Totie Fields was a stand-up and singer who sometimes wove songs into her act. She emerged in the late 1960s, and her persona as a four-foot-nine 190-pound yenta made her a popular guest on programs like *The Ed Sullivan Show* and at venues like the Copacabana. Fields died in 1978 after complications due to plastic surgery.

mised. We bought a fur coat and we keep it in the garage . . ." It's that kind of stuff. It was mostly male-oriented and it had a kind of swagger to it. I think Phyllis opened that up. She said, I'm a woman, I'm home doing housework, I'm home taking care of the kids, and maybe my husband is not so great. She was doing jokes about her life. And she did good jokes about the husband: "He drank so much that one day, when he cut himself shaving, he bled so much his eyes cleared up." That's what the change was: We have a life of our own and it's different from yours. A man does certain things and complains about certain things; a woman does other things and has her own complaints. But we'd never heard them before. And now we're starting to hear them. Here was a woman complaining about a husband rather than a husband complaining about the woman or the mother-in-law and I think that was the big switch. We have a life too and it's fun and it's funny and we can make fun of ourselves and you, but from our side of the fence and not from yours. That was the big difference in comedy.

RICHARD LEWIS, comedian Her jokes really were an extension of many of the horrors in her real life. And the thing about her in particular— because I know her and I can speak about her—she's incredibly brave about using humor to explore all her pain. She had an unbelievably dark past, particularly with men. And there's a reason why she did a whole thing about Fang, because that represented the horrors that she had gone through as a woman.

BETTE MIDLER, comedienne It really was like someone who had been chained to an ironing board for years just said, "You know what? I'm too smart for this—let me out." And I think that in the days that she was working, it was a real relief for people, especially other homemakers.

PHYLLIS DILLER When I first started, I didn't know what I was. My coach was pointing me in a certain direction. He was gay and he was taking me to all these wonderful nightclubs to see all these female impersonators, drag queens. And he felt they were great actors—they probably were—but he was pointing me in a chichi direction. He wanted me to be *chic*. That's what they were doing—they were trying to be chic women. They would do Bette Davis. They would do Tallulah Bankhead. He wrote some wonderful stuff for me. When I started, he had written a parody of "Monotonous" from 1952's *New Faces*, and I did Eartha Kitt slithering and sliding all over the top of the piano in a black leotard—half cat, half snake. And I did a pretty good imitation of her voice. I can't tell you what a great opener that was. But if I had continued that way, that would've prevented me from being a stand-up comic. When I started writing, I was going housewife, because I was going where the laughs were. I learned from the audience where they wanted me to take 'em. I'd work off the audience's reaction: I see what's getting laughs, I see what's tickling them. They wanted me to talk about the kids at home: "How do you know they're growing up? Well, the bite marks are higher . . . How do you go about looking younger? Rent younger children . . ." I took it down the suburban road, where most of the people lived.

HOWARD STORM   She was not an attractive woman, and she had that weird wardrobe and that feather boa.

PHYLLIS DILLER   It helps a stand-up comic to have something wrong—to either have buck teeth, no chin, weigh five hundred pounds, have funny hair, or be too skinny or too tall or too something. Like, for instance, a guy comes out and he weighs five hundred pounds, and he says, "I haven't eaten in ten minutes," something like that. To refer to oneself in a negative way is always a good way to say hello to an audience. So right away, you come out and kiss ass. And the reason I developed things like [wearing a bag dress] was because I had such a great figure. So I had to dress so that they couldn't see any figure because I wanted to make jokes. I had 'em convinced that underneath whatever I was wearing, I was a skeleton, an ugly skeleton—and that's what I wanted. My legs were really thin. Model thin. I stuck out what was thin and covered up what wasn't, and everyone thought I was flat-chested.

SHELLEY BERMAN, comedian   And she used to just knock me out with that terrible dirty laugh of hers.

ANNE MEARA, comedian   I know where Phyllis's big guffaw came from. That was a save in case the audience wasn't laughing. But she didn't have to worry that much, because the audience was usually laughing with her ninety-nine percent of the time.

GENE PERRET Phyllis Diller and Bob Hope are basically the same style of comedian. They do setup, joke; setup, joke. They never waste any time. Phyllis was adamant about that. You go out and you tell jokes. You don't do other stuff—you don't ask how you doing or where you from. You just tell jokes. And Phyllis, like myself, idolized Bob Hope. He was the ultimate as far as jokes go. From our point of view, he had funny jokes and they were good on paper. Certainly the delivery added to it, same as with Phyllis—she adds that laugh to those jokes and she can pull laughter from the audience. So she respected him and felt, "This is a guy I can learn from." So he was a mentor, in that sense. And he was encouraging to her.

GEORGE SCHLATTER, creator and producer, *Rowan & Martin's Laugh-In* What we don't realize with Phyllis is not only the enormity of the talent, but also the vast skills that she had. She understood the joke. There is a science to joke telling. You have to have the attention of the audience, you have to have the intellectual as well as physical participation of the audience, and you must have an audible indication of their acceptance of you, and if you don't hear that every ten seconds, you're dying. Singers need applause once every three minutes; comics need to hear you love them every ten seconds. The joke is like a little play. It has three parts—a beginning, a middle, and an end. It has to have a story, it has to have a rhythm, it has to have construction. And what makes you laugh has to be at the end of the sentence. That's the same for men and women. For Phyllis, each joke had a plot, had a cast, had characters, had a beginning, a middle, and an end. You *knew* Fang.

PHYLLIS DILLER Wrong! A joke has *two* parts—setup, payoff. Forget this bullshit in the middle. The quicker you get to the payoff, the better. My idea is edit. If one word can do the work of five, now you're talking. And there are other rules. The joke ends, preferably, on an explosive consonant—like *cut*. Certain numbers work in certain places when you're writing a joke. You'll have to find just the right number—whether it's eight or eleven. Every word. No one realizes what a science it is. Of course, by now it's second nature.

SHELLY SCHULTZ She was able to put her evening together with a bunch of jokes. If six worked and the seventh didn't, it didn't bother her; she went on and did five more. She was a machine and she was just superb. A craftsman, a real craftsman.

PAULA POUNDSTONE, comedian The thing about Phyllis Diller is that she's like a windup toy. I was on a bill with her years ago, and she'd go out, she'd tell her joke, and it wasn't even a particularly funny joke, and it wouldn't go very far. And then she'd tell another one. And it was sort of the same thing—people kind of chuckled mildly. And then she'd tell another one, and it would just go and go and go and go. Eventually, what became funny was the fact that she is a bulldog and just wouldn't stop. And eventually you're laughing in spite of yourself. And it's not that they're all uninspired, unfunny jokes—they're not; many of them are very funny. But it doesn't matter when she's telling it. It doesn't matter if it's funny or not funny. It's Phyllis Diller telling it. And eventually you break down.

In the late fifties, Elaine May established herself as an outré new voice in comedy. She was whip-smart and sexy; her sense of humor tended toward verboten aspects of modern life. She and Mike Nichols, performing as Nichols and May, emerged as national stars in 1959. Their dynamic was sharp, neurotic, and unabashedly intellectual, marking a strong departure from the era's other major duos. They developed highly improvisational sketches that poked fun at middle-class mores. Their subjects, like adultery and psychoanalysis, had been deemed unfit for mass consumption by previous generations. But along with Mort Sahl and a handful of other contemporaries, Nichols and May were improvising their way to broader horizons—and audiences, in ever larger numbers, were listening.

PAUL DOOLEY The influx of Nichols and May and comedians like Shelley Berman and Bob Newhart brought into the comedy world people who were primarily actors—not joke tellers, not comedians per se—and it became so popular it began to change comedy. A Milton Berle or an Alan King would sort of be acting like funny people rather than doing scenes. With the new group, a kind of realism entered into comedy. Just telling jokes was no longer the only way to do comedy.

MARSHALL BRICKMAN Their act wasn't jokey. There were no jokes that could be taken out of context and then repeated at a dinner party.

TREVA SILVERMAN, writer To me, Nichols and May personified the new way of thinking. It was a breath of fresh air. Elaine was hysterically funny and brilliant, and besides that, a real beauty. That was a revelation to me. She didn't put herself down, she didn't do self-deprecating humor like Phyllis Diller and the others. She didn't strain to make a lack of self-esteem seem funny—she was light-years away from anything like that. She did characters. Fully developed characters who might be intellectual, or silly, or gorgeous, or whatever was called for. And they were people who were really talking like people talked. It was a whole different head trip. And it was really the beginning of the changeover of comedy.

TIME magazine, June 2, 1958 "The fastest-sharpening wits in television belong to dark, disheveled Elaine May and blond, carefully tailored Mike Nichols, both twenty-six, whose dry dialogues are as lethal as cold gin on a hot day.

"'It's not what they do,' says Milton Berle, who caught their nightclub act 'sixty or more times' in Manhattan. 'It's how they do it, and they always do it different.'"

PHYLLIS DILLER I thought they were absolutely sensational. *Sensational.* They were totally different than all comics. It was really deeper and very gentle humor. No slam bang thank you ma'am. None of that. It was just really subtle and gentle and based on things that were really highbrow. Like the rocket scientist whose mother wants to know why her son doesn't call. And, of course, there was a Jewish slant to their humor because they were both Jewish.

TREVA SILVERMAN In the movies and plays that I was raised on, a lot of times there was the star, who was beautiful, and then there was her best friend, who was funny. It was kind of divided up like that. Rarely were both characteristics embodied in the lead actress, as if being funny was okay as long as it was relegated to the second banana. Kind of an afterthought. So here on the landscape comes this gifted comedian-actress who is both dazzlingly attractive and stunningly hilarious. Wow! My world turned upside down.

MARSHALL BRICKMAN What was interesting is that Nichols and May came out of a political theater in Chicago. And they made assumptions about the range of knowledge and interest of the audience that were totally fresh and different from the set of assumptions that traditional comedians made. And of course that assumption worked to select out their audience from the general population, but it turned out to be a much bigger audience than you might have guessed. So they would do improvisations where they'd say, "Give us an author," and somebody would say, "Jane Austen." "All right, give us another author." "Uh, Friedrich Nietzsche." And then, "Give us a premise." You know, "Guy comes home and finds his wife in bed with somebody else." So a lot of their stuff carried the assumption that higher culture was fair game for humor in a popular art form. It was very audacious.

To fully grasp the shift that was taking place in New York comedy, one must understand the 1950s Chicago theater company the Compass Players, from which the art of improvisation and Nichols and May first developed. The Compass Players was a theater group primarily made up of University of Chicago alums. It was founded by David Shepherd, a Harvard-educated East Coast intellectual who dreamed of establishing a new kind of theater in Chicago, the middle of America. Unlike New York's theater scene, which he felt was overly influenced by European traditions and dependent on the works of dead English and French playwrights, this one would spring out of American culture and be geared toward the American working class. Ironically, though, Shepherd drew inspiration from the commedia dell'arte troupes who toured the towns of Renaissance Italy performing scriptless shows. Commedia troupes often injected their scenario plays with popular references, and they were often satirical. Shepherd's vision was to present loosely scripted, theme-based "scenario" pieces in which key events were planned but the dialogue was spontaneous. The theater wasn't supposed to be funny, but it was supposed to be accessible to all audiences, blue- and white-collar alike.

When Shepherd arrived in Chicago, he fell in with Paul Sills, a young director at the University of Chicago whose mother, Viola Spolin, had developed improvisational games while working at Hull House in the mid-1920s. The games were devised to teach people to drop their inhibitions onstage by focusing their attention on their partners rather than "performing." These games proved to be a perfect tool to help Shepherd realize his idea, at least in part.

The Compass made its debut on July 5, 1955. When the theater closed two years later, Nichols and May made their way to New York, while the handful of Compass members who stayed behind went on to create the famed Second City, an eventual launching pad for sketch comedy greats.

DAVID SHEPHERD, founder, the Compass Players I went to Chicago because I thought that the Midwest had more vitality than the East Coast. I felt that the East Coast was dominated by European formats. Cabaret in New York City might have a German groove to it or be based on what was going on in the Catskills. I was not interested in the Catskills. I was interested in mainstream Chicago culture. I also wanted to do a cabaret theater that would contradict the three-act play, so I joined this group of people who were surrounding Paul Sills and Charlie Jacobs. They wanted to do repertory theater, so I said, "Okay, we'll do repertory theater." And I did it for three years with them. I put a lot of money in it and then when it collapsed, I took the people I'd gotten to know well down to the South Side, near the university, and we did the cabaret theater that *I'd* wanted to do.

BARBARA HARRIS, member of the Compass Players and Second City David Shepherd took a bunch of us aside and discussed what he called a "working-class theater," where his idea was to go into different neighborhoods where nobody was interested in theater or Shakespeare, and go into bars, set up a stage, and do improvisational-type performances with a scenario of what we felt people who frequented bars and such would catch on to. And we would get to know the neighborhood and what the sociology of the neighborhood was and then do scenes and pack seven acts—however brief—of what he and everyone thought would enlighten the people of the neighborhood. The scenes weren't even supposed to be funny.

DAVID SHEPHERD It had nothing to do with comedy at all. We were not interested in comedy. We were interested in erasing the three-act play and the institution that goes with it, what we considered to be very stilted constructions and stilted characterizations. The scenarios had very funny twists in them because in all life there is both comedy and tragedy. So we were taking from life to improvise on the stage.

BARBARA HARRIS   But we couldn't really stick with that premise because most of the people in the audience were in fact intellectuals from the University of Chicago. I don't know how we managed to do it, but we found a space that connected to a bar that was frequented by all the University of Chicago people. And they would come into our room—where we were funny or not funny—trying to do this thing that everybody seems to do so easily now, which is to create scenes that are funny.

SHELLEY BERMAN   As improvisationists, we were confined to play as much to our lives as we could. We could only draw from our own experiences, or from the experiences of others, and by relating to the other person. We were trying to live a life in each moment.

BARBARA HARRIS   Actors didn't have to act. They had to know what they were talking about. We had a very nervous lawyer there: we put him onstage—he had never acted—so he talked about how to catch a tax evader or how to evade your taxes. We had something called "living chess" and then we had two of the best chess players from University of Chicago play a one-second chess game onstage. Then the lights would come on. And people were laughing.

DAVID SHEPHERD   [During the early days of the Compass Players] our format was based in stories, and Elaine May, who had come by way of California and was close to Paul Sills, had dozens of stories. And they were not the normal funny stuff about a normal life. She wrote a very strong piece called "Georgina's First Date." That tracked the desire of a mother to get her chubby daughter into the social set, which she did. I think the daughter was raped in the process. It's not totally clear. But that was a strong scenario. So she did one after another. There was another scenario called "The Real You," which was about a new form of human potential training that she wanted to satirize. And she did it by showing several people answering a radio ad for it and going to the workshops, which were run by a guy name Bob Coughlan from the University of Chicago, and then going back home and practicing what they had learned and completely wrecking their lives—one after another. It was a very cynical scenario but it was strong and it was successful.

SHELDON PATINKIN, former manager and director, Second City The material was always reflective of the audience. And the University of Chicago audience, which would become the Second City audience as well, already had their degrees. They were doctors, lawyers, many many psychiatrists and analysts. They were wealthy, upper-middle-class, and well educated. And over time, the Compass morphed to the format that is still the basic Second City format—a two-act revue of material that is set. The set piece often came from audience suggestions during the previous show, but the show was set. And then there were usually one or two pieces done on the spot in each show. And there still are.

JOAN RIVERS, comedian Second City defined intelligent comedy at that time. It was very snobby. Half of them were University of Chicago graduates and if you know anything about the University of Chicago, you know they look down on Harvard, Yale, and Princeton.

SHELLEY BERMAN This style that came out of the Compass Players had not been a style before. Whatever that style was—it had not been a style before.

Even from her earliest days at the Compass, Elaine May stood out as a particularly expert writer and improvisationist. And when Nichols and May arrived in New York in late 1957 with an act, their rise to national prominence was quick. By January 1958, three months after they rolled into town, Nichols and May appeared on the television show Omnibus *and shot to stardom.*

LORRAINE GORDON They opened at the Village Vanguard. They were brought in one night by their agent. They had never played anywhere except in the Midwest. I was in that room, standing in front of the red velvet curtain. The place was packed with people. Nichols and May got up on the stage. They were auditioning live. They had never been there. Well, Max, my husband, he came up to me and said, "Please don't laugh so loud. The agent is in the room and the price is going to go up." I buckled my mouth.

PAUL DOOLEY I saw Nichols and May open their show down at the Vanguard and they were such a hit that within a week or two they were taken uptown to the Blue Angel. That's where Mike and Elaine started getting national recognition. Then they did the *Tonight Show*, they did some Sunday afternoon shows, and pretty soon they did a two-person show on Broadway, *An Evening with Mike Nichols and Elaine May*.

BERNARD SAHLINS, cofounder, Second City I think everyone was skilled in entertaining the bourgeoisie but she was a tremendous actress. I think it's often forgotten that to succeed, that kind of comedy requires acting talent. It isn't a matter of punch lines, gags, but it's personifying the targets.

MARSHALL BRICKMAN She had the ability to inhabit a character, a situation, and bring endless inventive changes on it so that if you set up a situation for her, whatever it might be, she could keep going for an hour or a day. And actually if you listen to the albums you see that it's Mike who is shaping it a little bit and bringing it to a conclusion. She was an endless fountain of invention and insight, a lot of which, I suspect, is not by design, it's just intuitive. She had some path between her various levels of unconsciousness. She was a great, great actor—but she was not only acting but writing at the same time.

The screen is split: on the right is Mike Nichols, blond and baby-faced; on the left is Elaine May, in dark-rimmed glasses and a classic housewife apron. They hold telephones to their ears.

"Hello, Arthur? This is your mother. Do you remember me?" May says, aggrieved and long-suffering.

"Mom, I was just going to call you. Isn't that a funny thing? You know that I had my hand on the phone—"

"You were supposed to call me last Friday . . ."

They haggle over why the son failed to call his mother on Friday, Saturday, or Sunday . . .

"Mother, I was sending up a rocket! I didn't have a second!"

"Well, it's always something, isn't it? You know, Arthur, I'm sure that all the other scientists there have mothers. And I'm sure that they all find time after their breakfast, or before their countoff—"

"—down . . ."

"—to pick up the phone and call their mothers . . . And you know how I worry. I read in the paper that you're still losing them [rockets]—"

"Mother, mother, I don't lose them—"

"—I nearly went out of my mind. I thought, 'What if they're taking it out of his pay?' . . ."

Arthur tries to change the subject, so he asks his mother how she is.

"I'm sick."

"What's wrong?"

"Nothing . . . Well, you know what it is, Arthur, it's the same thing it's always been. It's my nerves. And I went to the doctor and he tells me, he said, 'Listen, Mrs. White, you are a very nervous, very high-strung woman—'"

"God knows that's true."

"'And you cannot stand the slightest aggravation.' I said, 'Doctor, I know that, I do I know that.' You know I do, I know that. I said, 'But you see, Doctor, I have this son. And he's very busy—and it's the truth, he is, he's busy.' I said, 'You see, Doctor, he's too busy to pick up the phone and call his mother.' Arthur, when I said that to him, that man turned pale. He said, 'Mrs. White, I have been a doctor for thirty-five years, and I've never heard of a son too busy to call his mother.' That's just what he said to me, Arthur. And that man is a doctor.*"*

May continues to torture her son with guilt. She tells him she's going to be in the hospital for a while—so they can "X-ray my nerves." She fusses over a hangnail he had recently. He tells her not to worry.

"Arthur, I'm a mother . . . Someday, honey, you'll get married, and you'll have children of your own. And, honey, when you do, I only pray that they make you suffer the way you're making me suffer. That's all I pray, Arthur. That's a mother's prayer."

Head in hand, the rocket scientist gives up. "Okay, Mom, thanks for calling."

"You're very sarcastic . . . I'm sorry. I'm sorry that I bothered you when you were so busy. Believe me, I won't be around to bother you much longer. And listen, I hope I didn't make you feel bad."

"Are you kidding? I feel awful!"

"Oh, honey," May says, in controlled (and controlling) triumph. "If I could believe that, I'd be the happiest mother in the world."

MARILYN SUZANNE MILLER, writer I heard a recording of them, *improv*-ing the scenes that became the sketches. And it felt to me, when I was listening to some of this stuff, that Elaine was taking the lead in creating the setups for Mike to follow. When I heard that, I couldn't believe it. She had something in mind, she had a place to go that he didn't know, and she would lead him there and then he'd figure it out. Boy, she was absolutely my idol. I couldn't imagine anything more desirable than to do whatever it was that she was doing.

ROBIN WILLIAMS, comedian*   Elaine would throw out the idea. She'd say, "Okay, let's try this." And Mike would literally say, "Okay, that works. That works. That works. That doesn't." And really kind of shape it. Sometimes he'd really cut away, and sometimes he'd say, "I need a little more there," and it was wonderful. But he would just tell her, she would bring it in, and most of the times it was great, and when it wasn't, he would just say, "Let's lose that." You know, he would kind of look at it, he wouldn't have to say much, he would just raise an eyebrow and go, "Okay, cut." Sometimes she would know before he would even say it. And it was great to see that she was available to do that with him. I think they had that shorthand as performers.

DAVID SHEPHERD   When we were at the Compass, if she saw that you didn't make any sense, she'd tell you right out: "You're not making any sense; you're being sentimental." I don't know where she got this tendency, but I remember being wilted by her comments sometimes. And I was supposed to be the producer of this new group. She didn't give a shit. She'd tell me what she thought.

PAUL DOOLEY   I used to hear bad press on her. Like, she's very tough. Men who would work with her think of her as tough. I wanted to work with her but I thought if she didn't like what you were doing she would be a bitch on wheels. But [years later, when I got to work with her], I didn't find that at all. She wrote a play called *Adaptation*. We rehearsed it four weeks, then it was dropped; about six months later it was revived and we did it in Greenwich Village. We rehearsed again for three or four weeks and it played for four or five months and in all that time I never saw her be anything but terrific with the actors. I thought she was a total sweetheart. She was helpful and informative and helped us

* Robin Williams worked with Nichols and May on the 1996 movie *The Bird Cage*. May wrote the script, with Nichols directing.

find ways to make things funnier. So I don't know what people are talking about.

LOUISE LASSER, comedian   I revered her as a person. I wouldn't say we were close as best friends, but I knew her over the years and I revered her. I thought she was so hip. And she would smoke cigars. Her husband was a psychiatrist and she was married a few times before and broke everybody's heart. I thought that was great! A total heartbreaker.

PAUL DOOLEY   She doesn't like to be interviewed. She doesn't like publicity. She doesn't like all that stuff. I remember *The New York Times* wanted to interview her. She says, "I'll do this but you have to let me interview myself!" So she wrote an interview where she did the questions and she did the answers. And she wrote, "What's most important to you as an actress?" And she says, "Good grooming." And it was hilarious, because she's the last person in the world who cares about good grooming. When I worked with her on our play, every day she wore the same thing: a sailor's peacoat. And she was so concentrated on what she was talking about that when she would smoke, the cigarette in her mouth would grow a very long ash and then as she would talk the ashes would fall off on her jacket. But she was so concentrated on what she was thinking and saying that she paid no attention to the ashes on her clothing. So when she said in the interview "Good grooming," I thought, "Boy, that's funny." She doesn't care anything about that. The actors used to go out for lunch and they'd say, "Elaine, come on, let's go to lunch. You want to go out to lunch with us?" And she'd say, "I have to talk to the lighting man." "What can we bring you?" And she'd say, "Bring me a Ding Dong or a Yodel." It was always some little dinky lunch. A little cheap cake. Not even a nice dessert— just something you'd buy at the candy store. "Bring me a soda, a Dr Pepper." She just didn't care about the things most people care about.

And she's not a person who cares so much about fame. Elaine has doctored a lot of stuff. She worked on *Reds* uncredited for Warren Beatty. She worked on *Tootsie*. A lot of them—because she's uncredited, we don't know about them all.

MERRILL MARKOE, writer and co-creator, *Late Night with David Letterman*   I watched the movie *A New Leaf* [written, directed by, and starring

May] three times in a row once, just marveling at how well she milks comedy out of her own behavior. For example, there is a scene where she can't get into a one-shouldered Roman toga, and another one where she is trying to apply eyeliner and can't see well enough without her glasses so she keeps holding her glasses in front of the mirror to try to see her eye. I kept thinking to myself, Why was she not as big a comedic actor as, say, Will Ferrell or Adam Sandler? And the question remains to this day. I think the unfortunate answer is that women just don't get as far being hilarious as men do. Period.

By the 1960s, the influence of Nichols and May, and improvisational contemporaries like Shelley Berman, had infiltrated the stand-up crowd, among them Woody Allen, a comic who was becoming best known for the way he blurred the line between his onstage persona and the real person. The comic wasn't just telling jokes; he was airing his dirty laundry. The first woman to join the new confessional wave was Joan Rivers, a Barnard-educated self-declared Jewish princess from Larchmont, New York. When Rivers first took the stage in the mid-1960s in Greenwich Village, she wasn't the caustic celebrity insult comic that we know so well today. Instead, Rivers, dressed in her little black dress and pearls, presented herself as the pathetic single girl who couldn't fulfill her mother's dream: to nab a husband. Like Allen, she shared personal thoughts and stories in front of a live audience. But in style, she seemed to teeter between the worlds of Diller and May, filling her act with a series of self-deprecating jokes but delivering them attractively dressed and in the fresh, new, breakthrough talk style.

JOAN RIVERS I wanted to be an actress. And when I would make the rounds to the agents, I would always make the secretaries laugh so they'd remind the agent about me. Then someone said, "You can make a little money, you're funny. A friend of mine is a stand-up, they make $8 a night. You should go down and be a stand-up." And I thought, "How great, I can do that at night and make the rounds during the day." And that's how I started in comedy.

In those days you used to make the rounds on foot. The B&G was one of those little coffee shops you'd always hang out at between appointments, talking to other comedians, and there was a telephone there, so you could use the phone, and you got to know the people in the business, and you could hear tips—"Oh, this one's looking for this," and "This one is a good Catskill agent." But in the beginning, when [bookers] sent you out, they sent you to these horrible places. They didn't know you and you didn't know who the hell you were, and you worked wherever they needed somebody. I worked the Catskill Mountains, which was a nightmare because they surely didn't get me. And I was doing stolen material at that point and it wasn't working.

It was just years of trying to find yourself. You worked on your material, you tried things, and you would get all excited: "Oh, I'm going to try this," and then you'd do it and half the time it didn't work. And it was very competitive even at the lowest level. It was a struggle and it was total rejection. And for every audience that did like you, there'd be six shows where they just didn't.

IRVIN ARTHUR   I was never a fan of her performance. I'm still not. But I liked her and I would go downtown to see what she was like. I was quite frank with her. I said, "You are [in] poor taste and I wouldn't know what to do." But there was no doubt that she was determined. She had such a determination to make good. I don't think I've ever encountered anyone with the flair she had and the fire in her belly to fight to become something. I think she would have killed somebody to make it.

JOAN RIVERS   It was all about a place in Greenwich Village called the Duplex. That's where I started, and Woody started, and Dick Cavett started, and Linda Lavin started, and Bill Cosby. It was a little dumpy place, upstairs, on Bleecker Street. It had a little bar along the left-hand side of the room. And there was no dressing room. There were four performers on the bill and we just stood outside in the hallway and waited.

JAN WALLMAN   Joan sang in her act in the beginning. Or it was her opinion that she sang. In my opinion, she was not a singer, and as soon as I could, I disabused her of that notion and took the piano player away from her. But she was doing some singing comedy in a coffeehouse on Bleecker Street and this guy named Bob Waxman was playing there. And he brought her to me along with a couple of guys who had a song-and-dance-man kind of act that I worked with and he said he thought she was really a funny lady. She had to audition for me—nobody went on my stage that didn't audition for me—and Bob played for her and she sang a song written by a guy I knew named Ronnie Ax called "I'll Never Forget What's His Name." At that time, I had three acts on a bill and I'd usually start with musical comedy or a boy singer, then have stand-up comedy in the middle, and a strong girl singer to close. And at first I wouldn't hold Joan the whole three acts, I'd hold her over one or two or none, changing every few weeks. And then I brought in John Wallowitch, who later became a famous songwriter, and I told Joan he has to play intermission piano and he has to play for two other acts and if you want the stand-up spot in the middle you have to stop singing and just talk.

HOWARD STORM   Jan allowed you to fail. And that was the beauty of it. Rodney Dangerfield decided to try to make a comeback and the way he did it was in the Duplex. He got up there every night. That was the thing that was so great. You got up and you tried anything you wanted to try. I remember I would take the subway downtown, and while on the subway I would start to write a piece of material, something I saw, something that someone did, and I'd get up and talk about it. And that's what Joan did.

IRVIN ARTHUR   Joan Rivers was my secretary. We had an office on Seventh Avenue and at night she would be doing stand-up down in the Village at the Bitter End or at a place called Upstairs at the Duplex. What was funny is, people would call me, people who were well known and who she thought could help her, and she would do her act on the phone before she would turn the phone over to me. Like, I was doing work for Woody Allen, trying to get Woody Allen some stand-up jobs, and Jack Rollins [the legendary comedy manager] would call, and she'd tell him her name and do a monologue on the phone. And *then* she would tell me, "Jack Rollins is calling." And he would say, "Who's this dame? All I want to ask is, are you going to go down to the club tonight?"

In 1961, Rivers joined Chicago's Second City, which had been started two years earlier by Compass Players alumni. She was replacing Barbara Harris. While Rivers's stint at Second City was brief—she was, at heart, a solo act—the experience was fundamental to her development as a stand-up.

JOAN RIVERS Second City was very frustrating because I really couldn't do what I wanted to do, and while I was there, I would work at night afterward as a single. But being at Second City gave me enough confidence to really go off on my own. It all gelled there. And it was great in Chicago. But smart little kid that I was, I said, "This is wonderful, I'm going back to New York."

CHARLES L. MEE, JR., in *The New York Times*, October 31, 1965 "Though Miss Rivers does not consider herself a 'product' of Second City, the experience counted crucially. She learned to rely on improvisation, to turn autobiography into comedy. And with that she joined the ranks of the New Comedians, for if Joan Rivers is a new talent, alone and apart, she is also a prime example of what is new in comedy.

"The style is conversational, suited to television 'talk' programs. It may take the form of Bill Cosby's colloquial stories or Woody Allen's self-analysis or Mort Sahl's intellectual nervosities. But it is not Jack Benny. Benny may be a tightwad onstage and a philanthropist off. Not so with the new comedians. They write their own jokes and are expected to live them offstage as well as on."

MARSHALL BRICKMAN The thing about those days was that the comedy became much more personal. I was in a folk-singing group in those days, and when I first saw Woody, when he was our opening act, he was talking about his analyst and his wife and sexual problems and things like that. It was very startling to hear somebody actually get up and sort of reveal themselves.

FRED WEINTRAUB, former owner, the Bitter End Joanie, basically, was a girl who hung around the club, watching Woody a lot. She was just full of all that energy, which she still has today. There were three Jewish girls in the back room; sometimes they'd sit around talking. There was Carly Simon, Naomi Cohen—who became Cass Elliot—and Joan Rivers. And I always wondered what their mothers thought of them, the three of them just sitting in the back there.

EUGENE BOE, in *Cue* magazine, March 2, 1963 "Joan 'Second City' Rivers . . . is a very funny femme in search of an act. Her unmeasured monologue contains some of the sharpest, smartest talk to proceed out of the mouth of a babe since Elaine May. Female comics are usually horrors who de-sex themselves for a laugh. But Miss R. remains visibly—and unalterably—a girl throughout her stream-of-consciousness script."

TREVA SILVERMAN   What made her so different was, first of all, she was young and pretty attractive. Her whole thing is "Nobody wants me." But she was really an attractive woman and pretty adorable. Her early stuff was quite attitudinal and quite personal. What she's doing now isn't so much about her as her opinions. Then it was more about her.

JOAN RIVERS   I was talking about having an affair with a married professor and that wasn't a thing a nice Jewish girl talked about. And I was talking about my mother, desperate to get my sister and me married. I was talking about my gay friend Mr. Phyllis, and you just didn't talk about that. It sounds so tame and silly now but my act spoke to women who weren't able to talk about things. How nice it was to have a girl that's fairly attractive stand up and say, "My mother wants me to get married but I don't want to," or "I hated this date." And when I heard Lenny Bruce I suddenly realized, I'm absolutely on the right track here. I had seen Lenny Bruce very early on when I was on a date. He just was talking about the truth: he wasn't doing mother-in-law jokes, because he didn't have a mother-in-law. He was talking from his life experiences. I thought to myself, "My God, he's doing what I'm doing." I was talking about things that were really true.

JAN WALLMAN   She was an instant success at the Duplex. And her act was rough and it was raw. When I say raw I don't mean bad taste. It wasn't refined. She was single and she was talking about her own life and it was highly personal. But she was the hardest-working act I've ever worked with. She wasn't a drinker. She wasn't a chaser-arounder. She was focused on what she was doing. She worked with a real tape recorder, a great big thing that she had to carry in and set up in the club. And she'd tape the show every night and worked on it the next day, and the next night it was sharper and better and different.

HOWARD STORM   Jan was very nurturing. And I would say that sixty to seventy percent of the audience was gay. And they were great audiences and it was a great place to work. And as you went on, you got braver and braver.

JOAN RIVERS   I wouldn't be here without the gay audience, absolutely wouldn't be here. They were the ones that laughed and encouraged and thought you were wonderful and therefore gave you the impetus to move on, and go, "Ooh, if they liked that, let me try this."

PATRICIA BRADFORD, talent coordinator, *The Tonight Show Starring Johnny Carson*   She wore a little black dress primarily. She didn't try to look like a comedian. Phyllis Diller was taking the I'll-look-strange kind of road and Joan always tried to look attractive, which was unusual. Up until then women comedians were kind of dependent on looking funny and Joan really didn't. Although she did do a lot of her act about not being able to get a date, not finding a man. Of course, when she got married she went into bad-marriage jokes.

PHYLLIS DILLER   I always was very careful to keep it separate: there was a husband Sherwood Diller and there was Phyllis Diller's Fang. But Joan talked about a real husband: *Edgah*.

JOAN RIVERS   One of us always had an agent who was bringing somebody from the *Tonight Show* down to the Duplex since the *Tonight Show* was always looking for young, unknown comedians to introduce. So someone from the *Tonight Show* saw me at the Duplex and then brought me up for eight different auditions. But they never booked me. Finally Bill Cosby got on the *Tonight Show*—he was really white-hot at that moment—and the comedian they had on the show with him bombed. And Bill said to them, "You might as well use Joan Rivers, she can't be worse than who you had on tonight." And they put me on.

SHELLY SCHULTZ   Let me say something about Joan Rivers. Joan rewrites history as she remembers it from time to time. Many performers do. She wrote a memoir some years ago and I was in it and I read the story and it had nothing to do with what happened. She did not audition eight times. There is no way she could have auditioned eight times and missed me. Impossible. I'm telling you *impossible*. Now, let me tell you this story. She had a manager by the name of Roy Silver. Roy Silver and I were buddies. He had two acts: the Mamas and the Papas and Bill Cosby. And I put Bill Cosby on the *Tonight Show* for the first time. Roy called me six months before that and said, "Come down and see my guy, please." I got down there and it turned out that two or three people from my staff had been down there and didn't like him. And I saw him and fell in love with him, so I came back and told our producer in a staff meeting, "I'll put my career on this one." Well, he was *phenomenal*. So much so that we brought him back the next night with Johnny and he was *phenomenal* again, and then, the next day, he got called by Sheldon Leonard and they asked him if he would do a series and that was *I Spy* and it was off and running. So Roy was over the top and I was all excited for them, so Roy and I became really close buddies and he called me and said, "I've got somebody for you again." I said, "Okay." And I went down to the Bitter End and I saw Joan and I just loved her. She was adorable. She was just wonderful. She was cute and Brooklynese and she was funny and she had style. And I thought she was vulnerable and I thought Johnny would love her. And I said, "Okay, we're going to do this." And I sat down and helped her craft her spot. And she came on and it was the same thing. Bingo!

JOAN RIVERS   I remember, on the show I was doing this whole bit about my wig being run over by a car. I was saying that I was in an old car and that my wig blew out and somebody ran over the wig. So I was walking down the West Side Highway with a dead wig in my arms that said Firestone across it. Okay, it doesn't sound funny now. But I also remember talking about being single, that my mother had a sign up in Larchmont, New York, that said, "Last girl before highway." That was the kind of stuff, single-girl stuff, that I was doing. And on the air, Carson said, "You're going to be a star." The next day I went into a bank and asked the woman if she'd mind holding the check—in those days, you could ask them to hold the check. She sees me, and says, "I saw you last night! Of course, no problem. God, you were funny." And I thought to myself, "My life has changed." After I got on the the *Tonight Show*, I said to my agent, "My God, you know what this means?" He says, "This means you'll always make at least $300 a week." I couldn't believe that. Wow.

2

. . . .

Lily of the Underground

The same year Joan Rivers got her break on the Tonight Show, *Lily Tomlin made her New York debut, embracing the ethos of 1960s countercul-ture in ways that get-the-ring Rivers never did. Social consciousness was beginning to penetrate New York's comedy scene, and Tomlin, whose performances featured a variety of personas, seemed to have picked up where Elaine May, who by then had quit stage performing, had left off. Tomlin's characters were based on people she'd known growing up in a racially diverse blue-collar neighborhood of Detroit. As May had, she gently mocked the establishment and the conventions of the time. But unlike May, whose act was geared toward an educated middle class, Tomlin favored material that focused on the working class and the poor. In some ways, the differences between the two comics was genera-tional. Tomlin came of age during one of the most tumultuous times in U.S. history: the country was mired in an unpopular war, the civil rights movement was in full swing, and the sexual revolution was changing gender dynamics. In addressing these topics with disarming frankness, Tomlin became, alongside Richard Pryor, one of the most dangerous and revolutionary comedic performers to emerge in the 1970s.*

LILY TOMLIN, comedian   I went to New York in '62 to study mime after college. This is because I had got a bit in *The Madwoman of Chaillot* and it became a big success. I did a little improv and people screamed, and thought it was fantastic, and I thought, "Oh, this is great." And then the next thing I knew, I got into a variety show. Everything they were doing was so sophomoric—parodies of *Gunsmoke* and stuff—but I did my first real monologue. It was an interview with a Grosse Pointe [Michigan] matron and it was about Grosse Pointe being segregated. And I got *such* a response from it, because it was the only thing that had any relevance. And I went on all the local TV shows and did it. I'd show up at the studio dressed as the character and try to pass her off as real. So then I said on spring break, "Well, I'm gonna go to New York."

I had the idea that a mime was considered purer, because in the part of the culture that I identified with, to be an actress was seen as being kind of affected or narcissistic. It wasn't seminal. You weren't a poet. You weren't a writer or a composer. You were an interpreter of the art, not a creator of the art. But it was *really* male dominated. And in those days, a female, unless she was a real feminist or a lesbian, they were mostly child-bearers; they rolled the joints. And they kind of supported their old man and he would, like, stay up all night and go to the coffee-houses or wherever. It was that old bohemian tradition. That's how it felt in that downtown, underground, bohemian, just-transitioning-to-hippie kind of culture. Anyway, I only studied mime for a short time—maybe a month or two months—because it was so arduous. And there were no words, so it was too anonymous, too limiting.

So I went back to Detroit because I didn't really know what to do. I'd never auditioned, I'd never done anything. In Detroit I started working in the coffeehouses. I had begun to develop sketches and to develop characters, bits and stuff. And then at some point in '64 I visited New York. My brother was living there then, and I took my brother down to the Cafe Au Go Go or the Bitter End, one or the other, I can't remember now, because they were looking for English comedians. I hadn't taken my mother's name yet but my mother's name was Lily. And my brother's name is Richard, but my dad's name was Guy. So we thought Lily and Guy Tomlin sounded very English. So we went down and pretended we were English and did a couple of old bits that I guess we'd done in Detroit. And it involved a lot of mime, and the guy who was doing the mime show just happened to be there! And so the English revue never got done, but the guy who saw me doing all this physical stuff in the sketch with my brother hired me for the mime show. And I was introduced as Lily Tomlin, and I got my equity card.

I moved to New York permanently in 1965 when I opened for Louis St. Louis and Jackie Aloysio at the Cafe Au Go Go. They were never well known but they had grown up in Detroit, and for some reason,

I guess the Au Go Go had a dark week, because Louis and Jackie wouldn't be anybody that would be at the Cafe Au Go Go. They were more the Copa. They called me up and asked me to open for them. I came back and I didn't leave again.

CHRIS ALBRECHT, former co-owner, the Improv in New York Lily wasn't a stand-up comic. She could be a solo performer, but she wasn't someone who sat around and wrote jokes. Lily did characters. You rarely saw her onstage as herself. She told her stories and her monologues through the veil of a character other than who she was.

MARSHALL BRICKMAN Lily Tomlin was more in the tradition of Elaine May and Second City—a brilliant actress with a point of view and a bit of social insight about her characters.

DAVID STEINBERG, comedian Carol Burnett was already making a name for herself on television in the sixties. She was a remarkable sketch comedian, but in terms of a live act, Lily's act was just incredible, totally unique. No one did characters like that. They were edgy and not necessarily optimistic, goofy, Pollyannaish. She was able to take dark things and make them very light for the audience, but they had a depth that you'd never seen before.

LILY TOMLIN I grew up in an old apartment house in a black neighborhood in Detroit. My mother and dad were Southern. I spent my summers on the farm and I just saw too many different kinds of people not to be infatuated with them all. I was forever imitating a neighbor or my parents or my relatives and seeing the world as cultural types—how people expressed a certain slice of something that was going on.

I wasn't particularly divided between men and women, because I was very sympathetic to my father too. He was a factory worker. I was a working-class kid who just saw the culture from a certain perspective. I saw what politics did to people, what money or lack of it did to people. I saw the confusion around fear and ignorance. And yet I saw everybody really adorable too, how funny they could be, and how likable and how sad, all of them at the same time. Nobody was that different, and yet they were outwardly quite different.

LARRY MOSS, actor, the Upstairs at the Downstairs She was like an attractive Olive Oyl from Popeye. She was tall and gangly and she used to do a monologue about a lady—she called her the Hat Lady—who would go to a funeral and look at the corpse and say, "Oh my God, he looks awful! Give me that wig off your head." And she would appall the audience! She would pick up the corpse and make like a ventriloquist, and then she would put the wig on the corpse. It was all mime, but sometimes the audience would look at her like she was insane. And sometimes they would get it and they would roar.

BETTE MIDLER It turned the world upside down. The standard way that women were supposed to be funny was no longer true. It wasn't yucky. It wasn't guffaws. She gave women brand-new ways to be funny. It was thoughtful and provocative and very funny, but funny mostly through observation. People would walk out of the show and say, "Yeah, why do people treat women like that?" I think she changed the culture in a lot of ways.

PATRICIA BRADFORD I saw Lily audition once for a *Dick Cavett Show*. She was appearing at the Upstairs at the Downstairs and she and somebody else did a bit that was a takeoff on Mike and Elaine, who used to do a Pirandello play in their routine, where you couldn't tell when the play ended and reality took over, and it ends in a big fight. And Lily Tomlin and some other person did a skit and then they started picking on each other and before you knew it they were having an argument onstage and I will never forget her saying, "I have people here watching me tonight from *The Dick Cavett Show*." And you are just sitting there, you are cringing, because you absolutely bought into it. And then they turned around and they said, "We are doing Mike and Elaine doing Pirandello." Well, unfortunately they had made everyone in the audience so uncomfortable that they were just like, "Nah, we don't want to book her." And they didn't.

JAN WALLMAN When Lily Tomlin auditioned for me, I loved characterization comedy, but I didn't book her because I knew I couldn't sell her to one of those shows. And for a long time she thought that I just didn't like her—or didn't like her act. I thought she was brilliant but I had plenty of people who could do what the shows were buying and that's what I was trying to promote at that point.

IRENE PINN, former manager for Lily Tomlin   When she was still in the revue at the Upstairs, she had had something like twenty-one interviews with the *Tonight Show* and they just didn't get it.

LILY TOMLIN   The Improv was the first place I was seen in any kind of aboveground way. I'd become friendly with a couple of guys that wrote for Ron Carey and somehow I found my way to the Improv when it was over there on Forty-fourth Street way on the West Side. It had a big plate glass window. And because I had a sense of theater I had a lot of antique clothes from the thrift shop. Anybody could get up to sing or do whatever they did, but for comedy someone had to vouch for you. So I must have had a couple of friends who had seen me do something. Anyway, I got a spot on a particular night and I told Budd Friedman [the owner of the Improv] I had to do it between such-and-such a time. And what I picked was a time during theater time, because the limos would hang out around the theaters waiting for their clients, and many times you could pick up a limo for a few bucks. So I was all dressed up in a big ol' dress and some really bad furs that I had gotten at the thrift shop—ones that looked good at night, like white fox or something— and I paid a limo driver $5 or something to take me over to the Improv, and wait for me outside the big plate glass window. I pulled up, swept in, did five minutes, swept out, and drove away. That made kind of a big splash. After that, I'd go to the Improv once or twice a week to do a set and start trying to develop things.

IRENE PINN   You didn't get paid at the Improv in those days. But the biggest problem with the Improv was that they didn't get Lily. They had no idea what she was doing. And I can't say I really got her, either. But I knew it was something—and I knew it was something terrific.

LILY TOMLIN   Madeline Kahn saw me at the Improv one night and sent me a note saying to call Rod Warren at the Upstairs because somebody was leaving the show—I think it was Fannie Flagg; I think Fannie was leaving to do *Candid Camera*—and they needed a girl in the show.

So I wrote Rod, or called him, and I auditioned and I got into the revue. That was the summer of '66. I got into a show called *Below the Belt*, with Madeline Kahn and Dixie Carter.

At the Upstairs there was a certain revue style. It was all specialty material that would be written by many different people: a lot of satirical songs about the city, stuff like that. Very New York-y.

LARRY MOSS Madeline Kahn used to do a wonderful parody on a Bertolt Brecht–Kurt Weill song, like from *Three Penny Opera*, and it was called "Das Chicago Song." She did a takeoff on Lotte Lenya, the great German singer who was married to Kurt Weill, and she brought the house down every night playing this German cabaret. It was like when she did Marlene Dietrich with a terrible German accent in *Blazing Saddles*. It was just fucking hilarious. I mean, Madeline doing a comedy song based on a Kurt Weill–Bertolt Brecht song, that's very sophisticated. First of all, you'd have to know Brecht and Weill to get the satire. There was always a sense of "I'm performing for people who I assume are educated."

LILY TOMLIN In the fall of '68, Irv Haber, who owned the Upstairs at the Downstairs, asked me to come back to the revue and I said I would come back if I could do at least one of my own monologues. I didn't get to do it that first time, in '66, because they said, "Oh it's not in our style." But when I went back in '68, I got do to Madame Lupe, the world's oldest living beauty expert, and I got a big review in *The New York Times* from Vince Canby. He was doing nightclubs then. And that's how I kind of got started, because Irene Pinn, a young Englishwoman who had been a publicist, saw this review in the *Times*. And she came and said she wanted to try to work with me, and I told her, "I don't want to be famous. I want to work in New York." I don't know what was in my head.

VINCENT CANBY, in *The New York Times*, March 9, 1968 "Miss Tomlin's abilities are particularly evident in two monologues she wrote for herself. There is a poignant and funny bit about computer matchmaking ('This is my third date tonight,' the misfit announces triumphantly as she flicks her cigar ash neatly into her nose corsage), and another in which an ageless beauty, who could be Coco Chanel or the

Duchess of Windsor or even Edna Wallace Hopper, demonstrates how to rub in cold cream, 'Soothing and smoothing away those scowl lines, tea stains and aluminum pot marks,' she says encouragingly."

More than her female predecessors, Tomlin was a driving force behind the countercultural group that would usher television into the modern era. When Tomlin first arrived on television in 1969, Phyllis Diller was spending most of her on-air time goofing alongside Bob Hope; Elaine May had retreated behind the scenes; and Rivers, who by the 1970s was regularly featured on the Tonight Show, *was morphing into a catty joke-teller best known for skewering celebrities. Tomlin, however, found stardom on* Rowan & Martin's Laugh-In, *NBC's dizzyingly untraditional variety series that was part of a new group of programs set to revolutionize television.*

When Laugh-In *debuted in 1968 on NBC, the show was a breath of fresh air for Americans bored with the decades-old variety format of* The Lawrence Welk Show *and* Ed Sullivan. *It debuted six months after* The Smothers Brothers Comedy Hour, *which had given the country a taste of the counterculture with in-your-face political commentary and antiwar stances but was booted from the air in 1969. Contentwise,* Laugh-In *was never as bold, but it nevertheless upended the form. In many ways,* Laugh-In *was a bridge show that combined old-school devices—tuxedoed comedy duo Dan Rowan and Dick Martin; blackouts that originated in burlesque; jokes that packed a one-two punch—with fast-paced and zany sketches that captured the psychedelic and go-go feelings of the 1960s. It made veiled references to drugs and sex, and poked fun at hippies, politicians, and newscasters. From the beginning,* Laugh-In *was a ratings blockbuster, and after its success television variety was never the same.*

LILY TOMLIN In the fall of '66 I went on *The Garry Moore Show*. But they dropped my option after only three episodes 'cause I was always arguing about material—something I didn't want to do, or wouldn't do. I would just flat out say, "I'm not gonna do this; it's unintelligent." And then they'd bring in some really, really fine character actress, and I'd hear her in the room with them for *hours* trying to make this thing work. I remember when they called in Charlotte Rae at one point to do this bit which was totally stupid. And it didn't work. And I said, "What happened to Charlotte?" and they said, "Well, the bit's been cut from the show," and I said. "Well, you didn't have to put her through that to find that out, did you?" I was incorrigible that way—I'm not bragging about it. After I got fired from *Garry Moore*, I thought, "Oh God, well, that's it, I've had my chance."

GARY AUSTIN, founder, the Groundlings   The variety shows I would see—*The George Gobel Show* and all the musical shows too—had comedy in them like Eddie Fisher and Dinah Shore. The comedy was sort of square, sort of dumb, with a lot of stupid patter between star and guest that was supposed to be funny and wasn't. Of course, George Gobel was hilarious. I mean, the comedy stars were great. But it was just a different form.

LILY TOMLIN   *Smothers Brothers* went on CBS mid-season in '67, and *Laugh-In* went on NBC in the fall of '68. So they were like the new variety. And *Smothers Brothers* was identified more as counterculture.

DAVID STEINBERG   The Smothers Brothers shifted television away from a Catskills circuit kind of humor, with sketches that were subtly political. At the time, society was broken up into the establishment and the antiestablishment. And the antiestablishment were all of us, and the establishment was everyone who had come before us. The Smothers Brothers had Leigh French on. She sort of parodied hippie culture, playing a great hippie character with long hair. She was portraying an aspect of society that most of the establishment didn't even know was around.

  Laugh-In was different; *Laugh-In* wasn't political. It was just very commercial but with incredible talent.

GARY AUSTIN   *Laugh-In* changed the world of comedy. Things like the blackout wall, or whatever it was called, where they stick their heads out to say one line—none of that had ever been done before.

TIME magazine, October 11, 1968   "Wacky, rapid-fire comedy is not new to TV. Indeed, *Laugh-In*'s attack has touches of the late Ernie Kovacs, smatterings of early Sid Caesar and Steve Allen, and a pie-in-the-face splat or two of Soupy Sales. But on *Laugh-In*, the calculated aim is to create a state of sensory overload, a condition that audiences nowadays seem to want or need. Blackouts, slapstick, instant skits, pinwheel before the eyes; chatter and sound effects collide in the ear. Other TV variety shows can be dropped intact onto a theater or nightclub stage, but *Laugh-In* would be impossible anywhere but on television. For one thing, each show is stitched together from about 350 snippets of videotape. Some of them—a flash of graffiti, for example, or a mugging face—last only an eighth of a second."

GEORGE SCHLATTER *Laugh-In* came from my own somewhat minimal attention span. It looked like a pinball machine. We would do a hard joke—a political joke—and then we would do a silly one, then we would do a sexy joke, then we would do more politics. And it was political but, see, the politics was bracketed—we would do a political joke and then somebody would go through a trap door or somebody would get hit with water.

For instance, we did a joke once on "News of the Future," which was twenty years from then, so 1989: "With marriage in the Church now an accepted practice, the archbishop and his lovely bride, the former Sister Mary Catherine, both announce this time it's for keeps. If only for the sake of the children." But on both sides of that joke we had "Sock it to me, sock it to me." We had silly little things, so by the time you thought about what you heard you were on to the next joke. The secret was in the speed. And the fact that it got away from them. We had a fifty percent share—today you're lucky if you get a two. This meant that half of everybody was watching. And with that big a rating we were autonomous.

JO ANNE WORLEY, comedian, *Laugh-In* It was like a game that you were all in on and they weren't. They would put the red herring in the script to draw attention away from the joke that was kind of iffy.

GEORGE SCHLATTER When I put Goldie on the show, she was a dancer. She had been on *The Andy Griffith Show* and she had a little part on a thing on ABC. Goldie never auditioned for anybody—they had told me about her and she came in and sat in this big overstuffed leather chair that I had, and I just couldn't believe it. I hired her after our first meeting. I said, "I want you to do the show." She said, "When is it?" I said, "I want you to do all of them." She said, "What do you want me to do?" I said, "I don't have the slightest idea. I know I just want you there." I was mesmerized by her. And we put her on the show. And then I realized that Goldie could be easily distracted. The secret of Goldie Hawn was to divert her attention, and if she ever realized she was losing it, she would giggle. So I would do terrible things to her. We rewrote the cue cards and inverted all the words because I wanted to get that giggle. I would have my fly open with my shirttail out. Ruth Buzzi would make rude noises. And Goldie was trying to get it, and when she realized she wasn't going to get through it, she giggled. Now, Goldie was wide-eyed, but she was a long way from being a dumb blonde—she was one of the brightest members of that cast. Goldie knew where the joke was.

NORA DUNN, comedian, *Saturday Night Live*, 1985–1990   There were all these women on *Laugh-In*—Ruth Buzzi and Goldie Hawn and Lily Tomlin. They were equal to the men. As a kid, I did characters. So did my sister; my brother Brian had several. We would just be these people, and we'd ask each other questions in these characters; I didn't realize that adults did that too. So when I saw Lily Tomlin doing Edith Ann I was like, "Oh my God, this is . . ." It was like seeing a baseball pitcher and going, "Oh, I can be a pitcher too. I can be in the majors."

Lily Tomlin arrived at Laugh-In *in 1969, during the show's third season.*

IRENE PINN   [When I first became Lily's manager] the first thing I did was get Lily on *The Merv Griffin Show*. And they liked her and the audience liked her so much on the Griffin show that she became a regular. She was on every month. And every month I would buy the tapes and send them to CMA [her agency] on the West Coast, but nobody ever looked at them. She did nine *Griffins*, I believe. And finally I said, "Lily, nobody on the West Coast is looking at these tapes, so we've gotta go out there. I'll take two weeks off. I'll go for two weeks and you come for the second week and hopefully I'll have stuff set up for you."

I made an appointment with the head of the variety department at CMA and he was this kindly, elderly gentleman by the name of Shep Fields. He was the brother of Freddie Fields, who was one of the founders and owners of the agency. I walked into his office, and I saw how kind and grandfatherly-like he was, so I started crying. I just blubbered away and said, "What am I gonna do? I can't get anybody to look at these tapes and this is an incredibly talented woman." So he said, "Be there at nine o'clock the next morning and come to the conference room." And I did. And every agent in the variety department was there. And we watched the tapes, and they actually were impressed and started sending her out on auditions—and one was *Laugh-In*. The agent at the time told her that he'd set up a meeting with George Schlatter and that Schlatter was a weird kind of duck and he liked to be surprised and he liked people to be somewhat audacious. So she went on the interview in a trench coat and nothing underneath, or that's what she told me and that's what she told him.

GEORGE SCHLATTER   When I was doing *Laugh-In* I saw a tape of Lily Tomlin doing a routine about a rubber freak. She ate rubber—she just loved rubber. She went to a psychiatrist and was telling her problems. She knelt down in front of him and ate his rubber-sole shoes and ate the tip on his cane. I saw that and just loved it. It's even too weird for her to do today. That first day I met Lily, we sat there for three hours.

IRENE PINN   So we got an offer from *Laugh-In* and at the same time we got an offer from a show called *Music Scene*. She wanted to do *Music Scene*. She was scared that it would be too competitive at *Laugh-In* and that she would be wiped out.

LILY TOMLIN   *Laugh-In* was an enormous success. But television wasn't something I wanted to be a part of at that moment. In those days television was very disrespected by the counterculture. If you were on TV, you were a sellout. I thought it was square and it just wasn't artistic enough, in my pretensions, to being an artist or whatever I thought I was. I'm making it sound like I was about to go out and strap explosives to my body or something. But I just didn't wanna be on television. I didn't wanna go to California, either. I'd never been there and I had that New York snobbism about California. But I did go for *Music Scene* in '69 because I thought *Music Scene* was very hip. It had a tie-in with *Billboard* magazine and we did concerts with Jimi Hendrix and Janis Joplin and anybody that was really current. It was like a precursor to *Midnight Special*.

DAVID STEINBERG On *Music Scene*, they were trying to re-create Second City. And Lily was, I think, the only woman in that. It was Lily, myself, and, like Second City, a group of four people. It was like an early *Saturday Night Live*. But eventually they fired everyone except for Lily and me.

IRENE PINN *Music Scene*, which was an experimental show, got killed by the critics. Lily got really good reviews but the show got universally panned. So even though ABC had committed to thirteen episodes, of course they were dropping the show after that. So the show was canceled almost immediately. Lily did Ernestine on that show, but it wasn't the Ernestine that we know. I mean, this Ernestine was in a business suit, working at the phone company. They never aired it. So when it was obvious that *Music Scene* was not gonna make it, which was immediate, I called her agent and said, "Call George Schlatter and see if he still wants her." And he did. I got her lawyers to negotiate as part of her contract that Lily owned her characters. The characters that Lily brought to the show she owned.

LILY TOMLIN [I created the characters but] they wrote them on the show. But if there was something that I objected to politically I would usually call George at night or something and I'd say, "Can't we change this? Can't we do this?" And he was totally like a big teddy bear. I'd go to him sometimes on Friday when we used to read the new draft. We'd have Thursdays off and then we'd be dead tired and Friday we'd drag in, and that's when we'd see who the guest star was going to be. Like, Rita Hayworth might be sitting there. And so I'd go to George after the read-through, and I'd say, "George, I can't say this, I don't want to say this"—it'd be something sexist or homophobic or something. And he'd say, "Babe, you don't have to say this!"

THE NEW YORK TIMES, November 8, 1970 "Lily herself is well ensconced in the pantheon of zanies whose mad, mad antics keep viewers laughing at 'Laugh-In.' Lily made her mark with two comic characterizations that caught the public's fancy almost at once. One was Ernestine, a horse-faced telephone company hatchet woman whose wheedling and bullying of subscribers, punctuated by whinnies of smug superiority, obviously appealed to some deep-seated public hostility toward corporate bungling. The other characters was the Fast Talker, a sweet young thing afflicted with a galloping sense of double-talk and thus unable to make sense, at great length, on any topic whatsoever."

LILY TOMLIN   No one wanted Edith Ann at the beginning. They thought she was too bratty. But I had this other old character, Suzy Sorority of the Silent Majority, which would be like the Tea Party now. I hadn't really developed her yet but just had this little bit. And they wanted Suzy Sorority, so I said, "I'll do Suzy Sorority if I can do Edith Ann," so they let me do her. And I had to do her out of a cardboard box to try to hide her size. I used a big old refrigerator box like kids would use when they make a fort out of a cardboard; I would just stick my head out of a flap on the box. They didn't build the rocking chair for her until maybe four or five weeks later. I don't know why, but she caught on right away.

And then I brought Ernestine and I brought her Veedle monologue with me. I had developed that with Jim Rusk and in a matter of weeks after Ernestine aired, she was so phenomenally popular that AT&T came to me to asked me to do commercials. And I burst into tears. Irene came backstage and she was hyperventilating because it was so much money at that time. And it probably had the potential to make a lot more money. [But I didn't want to do it.] Irene said, "The phone company wants Ernestine to do commercials." And you fancy that you're gonna make some significant movement in society, that you're gonna somehow have the revelation and you're gonna impart it to everyone. So I was just crushed.

After I got on *Laugh-In* and I got so absolutely literally famous overnight, I came back and I was gonna play at the Bitter End, and I can remember my friends saying, "Well, what are you gonna play the Bitter End for?" And I'd say, "Where should I play?" And they'd say, "Well, we thought maybe you'd play at the Plaza Hotel," where Vegas-y kind of people play. Five years before, I couldn't have been hipper, but now, just because I was on TV . . .

Tomlin emerged from Laugh-In *a star. And riding that wave of success, Tomlin brought her character-driven solo act to sold-out tours across the country, and created a Grammy-winning comedy album,* This Is a Recording, *based on her work as Ernestine. When she was working on her next album, Edith Ann material titled* And That's the Truth, *she brought in a writer, Jane Wagner, with whom she had a romantic relationship, to help her shape and add depth to her monologues. (Tomlin and Wagner have been together ever since.) Together they transformed Tomlin into one of the most revolutionary comedians of her time, on par with comic legend Richard Pryor. In 1973, CBS offered Tomlin her own special, which was followed by a second special and eventually two more on ABC. Today, the only place to see Tomlin's specials are in museums and special collections. But those specials, in particular her second CBS program—for which Lorne Michaels would win his first Emmy and Richard Pryor would win his only one—capture the underground sensibility that would eventually take off on* Saturday Night Live.

MARILYN SUZANNE MILLER When Lily showed up—and Richard Pryor before Lily—they were like the first people that represented that group that was analogous to the sixties people who I had gone to college with. They were in trouble with the network. Not to say that other people weren't—Norman Lear and Jim Brooks and Allan Burns, they were too. But this group, they really wanted to do sketches that weren't funny, among other things, and I thought that was just fine, because I thought of TV as an art form, a form of theater.

ROSIE SHUSTER, writer There was a real revolution happening in other media: there were all these Jack Nicholson movies coming out that reflected that sensibility of the sixties that television never reflected; and in music there was Jimi Hendrix and Janis Joplin, the Stones and Beatles. But television was still stuck in some time warp that was more like the fifties. I think Lily, and to an extent her friendly exposure to Richard Pryor, brought home that there was a revolution about to happen in television. And certainly Richard Pryor had that dangerous flavor and Lily had her own version of that. She wasn't just going for the laugh; she wasn't just going for crowd-pleasing entertainment.

MERRILL MARKOE Lily and Richard Pryor were subversive. They were artistic outsiders. Carol Burnett—and Joan and Phyllis—were all mainstream show business, which never really resonated with me. The material she did in her own shows was full of a combination of sharp, incisive observational humor—cerebral, yes—and clear-eyed observations about the world, American behavior, politics, the middle class.

DAVID FELTON, *Rolling Stone*, October 10, 1974   "Richard Pryor and Lily Tomlin are not a comedy team although they have performed together on television and seem to share a mutually high respect for each other's talents. Independently they have developed their art along similar lines. Both are exceptional actors and mimes. Both are astute observers of so-called reality—their private lives, experiences of friends and strangers, the news of the day—drawing from it material which they present onstage with minimal alteration. They don't tell jokes, they seldom indulge in hyperbole or commentary—traditional tools of most comedians.

"Instead, they have introduced a version of comedy which goes way beyond laughter, certainly way beyond the escapist entertainment we are used to seeing in nightclubs and on television. It is real theater, a theater of the routine, the blemished, the pretentious, the lame—the common affairs and crutches of common people. Watching Lily and Richard perform is like watching yourself and all the victims of human nature onstage; it can be painful and it can be exhilarating."

RICHARD PRYOR, in *Time* magazine, March 28, 1977   "We are soul mates. I mean the characters we do literally take possession of us. You're O.K. as long as you keep an eye on what's happening, as long as you don't get scared and tighten up. Because then you lose control over yourself and the character takes over completely. I've never seen it happen to any other entertainers but Lily and me. You can see the physical change take place when she's working. It is eerie."

JANE WAGNER, writer   We were at odds with the network executives, CBS and ABC. There was not total acceptance with us, certainly not from the suits. But we had a feeling that wonderful comedy was breaking through. Certainly Joan Rivers was around, and Phyllis Diller. And they were great and I loved them all, but they weren't talking about social issues much. We were able to do that. I mean, that was our natural inclination, but we pushed ourselves onto the network. They felt they were going to get more Ernestine, and of course we wanted to do everything but. I don't know why we got so many specials.

LILY TOMLIN   We thought variety television was pretty much going to die soon, because it was just too hokey. But it's not that you're saying,

"Well, out with the old and in with the new!" You're going to follow your sensibility, and our sensibility was not to sweeten the show—which they made us do anyway.

JANE WAGNER   We just instinctually did certain things. We didn't always analyze why; we didn't say, "Well, now we're gonna deconstruct the variety show format." I just felt that the old variety format was very presentational. You had a curtain, you'd come out, you smiled to the camera, all of that. And I guess we were sensing that the camera would eventually move all around, rather than the camera being so big that it couldn't move. We knew what we wanted to do, but it was really hard to do it a lot of times. At first, I just figured, well, why couldn't we take a sketch and do it more like something that you would see off-Broadway, rather than on a variety show. And we tried not to have a laugh track, and that was a fight too.

MARILYN SUZANNE MILLER   They wanted us to write real things from our lives, instead of what I used to see on *The Brady Bunch* or on *Leave It to Beaver* or *Father Knows Best*. You have to understand how close we were to that stuff. It used to be, TV was one big lie. A whole bunch of people with blue eyes and blond hair and turned-up noses acting like everything was fine. And we wanted to do people we really knew and things that had really, truly happened to us. We wanted to use music that we were familiar with, which was rock and roll.

JANE WAGNER   During the Juke and Opal sketch, we wanted to use jukebox music so it would seem real—you know, music from the jukebox, which was part of the set, instead of music over, which would not seem like it was coming from the source. That's what they usually did. And it was really hard to get that music. Now everything is done with wall-to-wall music—from the highest shows to the lowest. But at that time, to use a piece of popular music just wasn't done.

IRENE PINN   I'm not sure that the executives at CBS ever really watched Lily's stuff, other than on *Laugh-In*. And when Goldie Hawn left and Lily hit, Lily was like the new Goldie. She was essentially the star of *Laugh-In*. But I think they were totally unaware [of Lily's sensibility].

They really thought they were going to get something closer to *Laugh-In* kind of humor.

Actually, none of these were deals for specials; they were all pilots for series. But Lily and I both knew that there was no way she could do a series the way we worked on these specials. I mean, we had an inordinate number of writers. We would do preproduction for three months, which was unheard-of. We went over budget. Not the first time—the first time we were absolutely fine, because we hooked up with Bob Precht, and it was a coproduction. He's Ed Sullivan's son-in-law, and it was a coproduction between him and Omnipotent, which was Lily's company. But after that I made Lily autonomous—she was the boss. And in many ways that was a mistake at the time. She owned the specials. Omnipotent produced the specials, so we didn't have a financial partner, somebody who was financially responsible, which Precht was. We were financially responsible and it was too soon, because we went over budget every single time.

But the reason we got the second special was because Fred Silverman [the head of programming at CBS] thought that the first one was close enough to being a series, but not completely, and he wanted to take another shot. So what did we do? We went further out. I mean, I can't say that we just sat down and said, "Okay, fuck him," but again we did know that we didn't wanna be a series. And I would have these lunches with Sam Cohn [the talent agent] and Freddie Silverman and he'd be talking about a series and I'd be going along with it as much as I had to. Now, Sam did know that I didn't believe we could do a series, nor did Lily want to. But they kept programming us after Streisand. There'd be a Streisand special and then us. And the Streisand specials were fantastic, they were phenomenal, but nobody watched them. I mean one of our specials on CBS got better ratings than she did. But it wasn't what they wanted for a series, thank God. And we knew that. And the first special, I think, was not as intense as the second one. Then the two ABCs were, I believe, less intense again. To me the second CBS was the most intense, the most controversial. It's also the one that won the Emmy, which is amazing when you think about it.

LILY TOMLIN The first special I did was phenomenally successful ratings-wise because I came off of *Laugh-In*. And I was crazy about

Richard Pryor, so I got Richard on the show right away. I sought him out and hung out with him to get him to come on the show. But they made me have a partner for that show. They gave me Bob Precht, who was Ed Sullivan's son-in-law. He was very much a company guy, but a nice guy, nice enough. But the show didn't please me. I wasn't crazy about the show because they sort of picked the personnel, because I had never produced television. But I got such a high rating, they didn't want to let me go, so they gave me another special. And I said, "Okay, we'll do another one if we don't have to have a partner!" But they insisted that I get some tried-and-true executive producer, like Norman Lear or Grant Tinker. I went and met with a few people—I don't know how many—whoever was a top comedy producer at that time. So I went and met with [the groundbreaking sitcom producer] Norman Lear. I did that country singer, Wanda V. Wilford, and he said, "I don't understand the country singer, what was that about?" And I said, "Well, it's not that it's about something, it's a poem." And he said, "A poem!" And I thought, "As good as Norman is and everything he's done, he's not the guy for me." And then, when I went to Grant Tinker, he didn't have too many opinions.

IRENE PINN Richard Pryor wrote a piece for the first special that never got on the show. It was about a suburban woman who comes out into the backyard and is looking for her son because it's dinnertime. And she's calling for him and there are planes flying overhead and she's ducking and there are mines in the backyard. It's obviously an antiwar piece, and against toy guns, things like that. It was hysterically funny. She finds her son, and she says, "Where is your arm? You think arms grow on trees? Go find it." It's just black, black humor.

LILY TOMLIN The piece was about Mrs. Beasley, who appeared elsewhere on that first special. She was doing a hidden-camera-type laundry detergent commercial. She finds lipstick on her husband's collar and has a breakdown on camera. We kept that bit, but after that certain bit was over, she went out the back door and down into her yard, where there was a war going on—'cause the Vietnam War was still going on. And it was a little enactment of that: the kids are playing war, but they're playing war with real weapons and the yard's all shot up, and burned, and the swing sets are all twisted. And then she finally sees Billy, and she says, "Where's your leg?" and all that business. It was meant to be a companion piece to this detergent commercial. And, well, we were able to keep the commercial, but they would not let us do "War Games."

IRENE PINN   They wouldn't even let us tape it. I mean, we had to take that out of the script. So the second special we put it back in, and it was actually a red herring for the diner [Juke and Opal] piece, because we wanted to get that on the show. But this time they allowed us to tape the woman in the backyard and the deal was, we would check the audience before we taped it. Because they kept saying that we had a subversive audience, that we had hippies and druggies out there. So I walked out into the theater with the CBS executive responsible for the show and I said, "Okay, is this *your* audience or *our* audience?" It was very clearly a CBS bus tour audience. And the piece got a standing ovation. But having agreed it was their audience, CBS still wouldn't let it on the air. But we got the drug piece on—I mean the diner piece, which in actual fact was a drug piece. It wasn't as good as it should've been, because I made a fatal mistake and called Richard Pryor into work too early that day and he had to sit around. And when he sat around he would be drinking and drugging and stuff like that. It was designed to be in the middle of the show. There was a piece with Alan Alda and Lily, where their alter egos dance. They're exes, and they wind up in the same dining room sitting at opposite tables, and their alter egos leave their bodies and dance together. That was designed to end the show, but CBS made us put it in the middle. We had to do that, and then we did the monologue, and one piece with Richard Pryor and Lily where his wino and her tasteful lady were stuck in an elevator together. And we did the monologue and the elevator sketch with an audience. But the diner, the alter ego, and there was a country-western sketch too, we did not do before an audience. And CBS had a fit. I was sitting in my office when our lawyer called saying he'd gotten a call from CBS's lawyer saying this was the worst thing they'd ever seen in television, they weren't gonna air it, they especially weren't gonna air it after Streisand without a laugh track. And they were gonna put the laugh track on, and Lily and I were not allowed anywhere near where the laugh track was being put on. So I called Lily and I said, "Look, this is what's going on. I think I can get CBS to let us put the laugh track on, and we will do it a hell of a lot more mildly and gently than they will." So she said, "Okay, let's try to do that." I mean, she was not a happy camper, and trust me, I wasn't either. Still, I went back to the lawyer, he called CBS, and CBS agreed. When it came to doing it, Lily wouldn't go anywhere near it. I had to do it, which was big trouble for me. So off I went to put the laugh track on. We were on the road, we were just about to start a tour. And we were actually visiting Lily's mother when the show aired. She sat in a chair, I sat on the floor, and I'm telling you, you could barely hear the laugh track. But all I know is, she didn't talk to me after she saw it. That was the second one at CBS, the one that won the Emmy.

VARIETY, November 5, 1973 "Something important was being said on the Lily Tomlin special, something wise and picking at the dark edges of truth. The humor disguised some bitterness, at times successfully, at others not. In any case, it was what the public has asked for for some time: Something fresh, and of all things, innovative."

ROSIE SHUSTER You could just see that she took it to another level. It wasn't the sketch comedy that I was used to. She did scenes and she didn't go for jokes and she certainly didn't go for the lowest common denominator. She went for these deeper caricatures. Everything had a beautiful sense of authenticity: if there was supposed to be radio playing it wasn't just a cue from the booth, they would actually get a radio on; or if bathwater was running, she made sure the bathwater was running. She really went out there on a limb to create scenes with their own ambience. She was really an artist.

It wasn't what you would call normal television. It was much more "out there." It felt like there was something in the air, that a revolution really could happen in television. I think it had a lot to do with the seeds of what was finally coming with *Saturday Night Live*.

IRENE PINN We hired Lorne Michaels, and about ten days into Lorne working on the show Lily came into my office and said, "I want you to fire him." I said, "Okay, but what's the problem?" And she said, "Well, as you know, he comes in late every day, and then he talks to everybody so none of the writers are writing, they're all talking." So I said, "Okay." I said, "but you know we hired him for a reason, so does the reason still apply if I can get him to stop this?" And she said, "Yeah, I would keep him." So I called Lorne into my office and I said, "Okay, Lily wants me to fire you, why shouldn't I?" He was in my office for three hours and I kept saying, "Look, Lorne, if you don't change your ways you're gonna be gone, and neither Lily nor I really wanna fire you."

In general, he brought a different kind of humor. I mean, he was Canadian. I don't remember exactly what everybody that we hired brought, except we were looking for different aesthetics. Lorne wrote some of the more charming monologues. Jane wrote the edgy pieces. And I think that Lorne and Jane are very different aesthetically, or they were. Lorne was political, but in a lighter way, and Jane is political in a heavier way. Jane is totally brilliant. But I think Lorne knew how to tap into a broader audience. We weren't able to do that. And the thing is: we didn't really try to do it, either.

JANE WAGNER When *Saturday Night Live* did imitations they were almost always of celebrities. What we did was to try to create culture types that were original. Like, Mrs. Beasley exists somewhere in every Midwestern town. We did people other than celebrities—and that was always a weakness. Not a weakness aesthetically, but in terms of accessibility, of people understanding what we were doing. They didn't always get it.

LILY TOMLIN Lorne's father-in-law at that time was in one of the big Canadian comedy teams, and Lorne had a lot of showbiz savvy. I can't say we absolutely shared a sensibility. I don't want to get into this, but Jane was always ahead, and Jane said, "We've got to convince the network to do a live show," because nobody is going to buy variety anymore that's taped and edited. So we would often talk and argue about this. And Lorne was very much on the side that there will never be a live show again; that with the advent of tape, there'll just never be another live show.

FRED SILVERMAN, former head of programming, CBS Lily and her manager thought the specials were groundbreaking, but I didn't share the enthusiasm because I ordered the special, and I didn't think it was a very good show. I thought it was inconsistent, and it just didn't work. It didn't work. The show went on the air in a very good time period and nobody came. If you are a die-hard Lily Tomlin fan, then it was a very good show. But objectively, as a special, it failed. At least in terms of what we were looking for. And we were not PBS. In order to make the

CBS schedule, the show had to be very, very attractive, and it had to be the kind of show that would attract a large audience or else there just wasn't any room for it. I enjoyed Lily personally, and I loved her on *Laugh-In*. But she's an artist, and she had a whole hour to fill, and it just veered off in so many directions that were too esoteric for a general audience. It was the wrong kind of show. But that's a creative judgment. And a lot of people disagreed with me, because it won all sorts of awards.

3

. . . .

Prime Time

Network television has always been a conservative medium, and while the 1960s may have marked the start of the women's movement in America, it wasn't until the 1970s that the changing roles of the American woman received any real notice on the small screen. Since the first sitcoms began appearing in 1949, women had been depicted primarily as housewives (Lucy Ricardo), mothers (June Cleaver), or schoolteachers (Connie Brooks). Along the way, a few characters with less-traditional lifestyles slipped through. There was Sally Rogers, the late-night comedy writer who was one of the boys (albeit with a bow in her hair) on The Dick Van Dyke Show, and then there was Ann Marie, that girl of That Girl, the first show to feature a single woman living not with her parents but in an apartment of her very own. But while worth noting, neither role was particularly revolutionary. It would take until 1970, with the advent of The Mary Tyler Moore Show, for the roles of women on television to really begin to reflect cultural shifts. Mary Tyler Moore, the first show to depict a single, independent career woman who would, as the theme song said, "make it on her own," sent the first signal that female-driven television was on a new track, a signal that was underscored when Norman Lear launched Maude. With that, the 1970s became the most prolific decade for women in television, and not simply because writers and producers were ready to tackle modern-day subject matter (birth control, infidelity, abortion), but also because, for the first time, women were beginning to emerge as writers, directors, producers, and creators of their own programs.

FRED SILVERMAN   Up until the 1970s most of the women in television shows played very familiar roles—housewives, nurses, teachers. But there were very few career women.

BARBARA GALLAGHER, writer   The shows I grew up with in the fifties and early sixties were family-oriented, had a moral to the story; fathers and mothers were respected and children learned from their mistakes.

MARLO THOMAS, actress and creator, *That Girl*   Lucille Ball couldn't sleep in the same bed with her husband even though they were really married in real life. My dad, Danny Thomas, and Marjorie Lord slept in different beds on the set of his show. That's so ridiculous! Married people do sleep in the same bed! It's not a sin.

CARL REINER, writer   We couldn't say "pregnant"!

PENNY MARSHALL, actress and director   When I first started my career, television was full of perky girls, like Sally Field in *The Flying Nun*. I'm not that type. I had been married, had kids, was divorced. These girls were all saying, "Let's go for a hoagie and a Coke," and I was saying, "How far do we have to walk?" We were working-class, and we'd do anything to make the rent. My attitude was not that of the happy-go-lucky person.

MARLO THOMAS   The funny part about it all was that in the sixties we were free love, no bras, Woodstock—and on television, it was reflective of nothing. On my show, the network was very concerned that Ann Marie [my character on *That Girl*] not look like she was sleeping with her boyfriend, Donald, so the show usually had to end with him leaving the apartment.

TREVA SILVERMAN   The thing that's generally said about *That Girl* is that it was the forerunner to *Mary Tyler Moore*, and in some ways it was, and in some ways it wasn't. How it was the forerunner is: here's an attractive woman making her way in the world who doesn't consider herself a failure or inferior in any way because she doesn't have a husband and family at her age, which at that time, pretty much you were supposed to have gotten married. Where it wasn't a forerunner of *Mary* is that with the very first episode Mary wanted a job with responsibility. She wanted to work and she wanted to be good at her work, whereas in *That Girl*, Ann Marie wanted to be an actress—as in, well, who doesn't? But she didn't really make inroads with that. She would have auditions and she was taking temporary jobs to support herself (and her wardrobe). It was like no temp job could pay for those clothes, but we all forgave her because she looked so great.

MARLO THOMAS I wanted to be a comedy actress. And I knew when I got the opportunity that I wanted to play the person that had the problem, not the person who assisted the person with the problem. I could see very clearly that I didn't want to be the wife of somebody, or the secretary of somebody, or the daughter of somebody. I wanted to carry the story as opposed to just being an appendage of the story, which is what women were on television.

So when I did the pilot for a show called *Two's Company*, I screen-tested for it. And I got the part. It was a very cute show about a couple who had just been married for a week or so. So when the pilot didn't sell, the head of the network called me in and said that the network felt that I could be a television star and that Clairol already wanted to sponsor me in a show. At the same time, Ed Scherick, the head of ABC programming, sent me some other ideas for scripts and stories. I called him and said, "You know, if I could be so bold as to say, these are really old-fashioned, where the girl is the daughter of or the wife of or the secretary of. Have you ever considered the girl to be the somebody?" And he said, "Would anybody watch a show like that?" I said, "I think they would."

And so I gave him the book *The Feminine Mystique*, and he read it and kind of became convinced. There was also a woman at the time named Rena Bartos. She was the one of the first female vice presidents of J. Walter Thompson, and she was going after the female consumer, trying to explain to the ad agency, and to the advertisers themselves, that women are buying cars, women are buying home appliances. She said this great thing: "If you want to hit a moving target, you have to aim at where it's going, not at where it's been." I took that phrase, which I had read in the paper somewhere, to ABC and said, "This is the fact. I am not my mother at all and neither are any of my friends. We want a completely different life." And so that is what I think convinced him to let us make the pilot.

When I spoke to Ed Scherick about this idea, I told him I'd like to do a show about a girl like me, who wanted to be an actress, who graduated from college, whose parents wanted her to get married, whose father was terrified she was losing her virginity, and who wanted to live on her own. I thought that that would be a great story to tell. And I called the show *Ms. Independence*, which was my nickname when I was a kid.

After we made the pilot they screened it. They had already decided to put it on, and the advertiser, Clairol, was thrilled—they had a new young woman they could advertise to. So as they were gearing up for it, they did what they always would do—have what they called an "intention to view." They don't do that anymore. But in the "intention to view," they surveyed the audience with a list of questions. And what became clear from this audience was that it was not interested in a young woman who didn't have a family unit. [So Clairol decided] I should move in with an old-maid aunt. I said, "But nobody would do that. Nobody goes to New York and brings their aunt along." Then they said that no one was interested in a girl that was in show business, because people felt that show business was kind of like chorus girls and they didn't like that. And nobody was interested in somebody named Marlo Thomas who nobody'd ever heard of. So there was nothing that was going to be appealing to the audience. So the "intention to view" was very low on the show. I kept thinking we'd just hear this gigantic click as the whole country turned the TV off. But it was this big hit the first night.

The whole time, we had to have Ann Marie look somewhat normal. I mean, who's she connected to? She's not connected to her parents. She's moved out. She's got to have a boyfriend. But we didn't want her to look like a slut, right? So we had to have her have *a* guy. And she needed a foil. And it was Donald. It gave the audience and the show some kind of anchor. She couldn't just be this girl that had nothing. And I think having a boyfriend gave it a normalcy. We understood her better. She looked like girls everywhere. Girls have boyfriends. And then we needed some kind of romantic movement, because you felt, well, she's not gonna be a star. So that's why we let there be an engagement. I was always a little queasy about it but I thought, "Okay, it's just an engagement; engagements can be broken." But then at the end, when Clairol wanted a wedding and ABC wanted a wedding, I said, "No. No wedding. There will be no wedding." I said, "First of all, it's a betrayal to all the young women who have been following this show and finding their own independence. If we get married in the last show, what we're saying is that's the only happy ending there is. That is dangerous." I said, "And that, as far as I'm concerned, will really make everyone angry with all of you." I was so passionate about it. It wasn't a capricious thing. "This is the girl that I've invented, that I want to play, and I don't want to get married either, so this is completely against the story that I want to tell." They were passionate conversations. The talks went on for a year.

MARILYN SUZANNE MILLER *Barefoot in the Park* came out in 1967, and in that play Neil Simon chose to characterize the new woman of that period, and one of the things that was happening then was an awareness by writers that there were what they referred to as "kooky girls." The title, *Barefoot in the Park*, was in reference to the fact that the Jane Fonda character, at least as played in the movie, was so kooky that she wanted to walk barefoot in Washington Square Park. This kind of kooky girl was the first representation of an independent woman that I can remember in the arts. And even though Jane Fonda was married to Robert Redford's character, the play hinges on the fact that he's a lawyer and very straight and has to get up and go to work, while she just wants to go to every kooky foreign restaurant and wear a lot of very short skirts and Courrèges boots, which all contributed to the notion of the kooky girl. And Ann Marie in *That Girl* was the kind of woman who embraced those things. She got a lot of money from home and she had that Robert Redford-ish respectable boyfriend in Ted Bessell [the actor who played Donald Hollinger], who was always in a suit and tie. And if she just wasn't so kooky, then she would settle down. This whole idea of a kooky girl really preceded the idea of an independent woman. And there's a big difference between a kooky girl and an independent woman.

In the beginning, The Mary Tyler Moore Show *seemed to have little chance of getting a fair shot on CBS, least of all getting the coveted Saturday night time slot it eventually landed. From the get-go the show's creators had to circumvent network executives who were gunning for yet another rural TV show of the kind that CBS was then known for:* The Beverly Hillbillies, Petticoat Junction, *and* Hogan's Heroes. *In fact, were it not for a corporate shake-up that ousted CBS honcho Michael Dann,* Mary Tyler Moore *might have been buried alive. When Fred Silverman arrived at CBS in 1970, his mission was to bring more upscale, sophisticated shows that would attract advertisers who were looking for a younger, wealthier, and more urban audience. The* Mary Tyler Moore Show *was exactly what he needed.*

ROD PARKER, producer and writer, *Maude* Mary Tyler Moore was a woman who was starting out and trying to be her own person but she was never very political or very feminist. She was just semi-running a television station. She was still pretty much Miss Goody Two-shoes but she was a symbol for young women—yes, you can go out and throw your hat in the air and get a job and make it work and put up with a cranky boss.

MARY TYLER MOORE, actress Some of the shows that have been very successful have come from no truth whatsoever—as in *Three's Company*—but they are all larger-than-life and almost comedic versions of soap operas and some of the nighttime series. I did not want to be that. I wanted to take my chances with the real version of comedy, the eloquent approach to the funny aspects of what a person is in real life.

LANCE MORROW, *Time* magazine, March 14, 1977 "In *MTM*, Mary Richards—Moore's character—gave a humanely plausible version of American women—some American women—in the early and mid-'70s. Not many, of course, are as lovely as Mary or as funny. She was single, independent, pursued her career, was interested in men but not in an obsessive, husband-trapping way. Many women in the audience felt happier with themselves because of her."

FRED SILVERMAN The show was scheduled first and foremost because Mary Tyler Moore was an enormous star. She was coming off *The Dick Van Dyke Show*, and everybody at CBS believed she had the goods to do her own show, so you have to start there.

MARY TYLER MOORE I did a special with Dick called *Dick Van Dyke and the Other Woman* and it was regarding his experiences with his own wife. After that show aired, it got very good ratings and very good reviews, so CBS asked me if I would consider doing my own series. They said, "You can make it anything you want." It was up to me what kind of show it was going to be, and so my then husband, Grant Tinker, and I sat down with Allan Burns and Jim Brooks and talked with them about what would be a good choice of characters for me.

ALLAN BURNS, co-creator, The Mary Tyler Moore Show We had never met Mary when we were hired to do the show. Grant Tinker came to us. We were doing *Room 222*, which was produced by Twentieth Century Fox, and Grant at that time was the vice president at Fox in charge of television. He saw what we were doing on *Room 222*, which was about what was going on in inner-city schools that were racially mixed. And we did a lot of research on it. Every time we did a show the writer would spend time at the school we used and try to soak up the atmosphere. Grant saw that and I think he just wanted us because he thought we were not going to turn around and do *The Lucy Show*. I mean, I love *The Lucy Show*, but that's not something I can write. I think he saw in us two guys who would give it a very contemporary feeling.

It was completely up to us whatever we wanted to do and so Jim and I went to work, trying to come up with a good format for her. We didn't want to do a show where she was going to be a wife again because she had done that with Dick and she was not anxious to do that again. Although we never really discussed it—we just assumed that. Where was that magic likely to happen again as between the two of them? It's harder than you think when you can do anything. Sometimes it's nice to be told, "We want to do a show about Mary doing this or doing that," but when you're hearing, "Well, it's all open, whatever you want to do," that's the hardest kind of thing to go into. So it took us a while to come up with a format for this, and what we originally came up with was something that every writer that we knew wanted to do. Maybe this is because so many writers are divorced, but we wanted to do a show about a divorce that was an amicable divorce. If you can believe this, in 1970 there had never been a series where one of the characters was divorced. It was a taboo subject.

What do you call it when it's a leg person for a columnist? Somebody who does all the research while the columnist takes the credit for it? We thought that would be her job and that she would be coming off this divorce. We went to New York with this concept. Unfortunately, Grant wasn't with us, because he couldn't be. He was still working at Twentieth Century Fox. This show was going to be done for CBS through Mary and Grant's own company, but Grant did not have an active role, at least a visible role, so he couldn't go with us. We went to New York with a man who was Mary's manager and who was going to be the vice president of MTM, which was the company they formed. We were ushered into a room at CBS at Black Rock [CBS headquarters] in New York that was out of Kafka, a room that had, I swear, either very dark brown or black fabric on the walls with no windows. And we were in there with spotlights shining down on us from the ceiling and in a semicircle, talking to CBS brass. The head of programming for CBS at that time was a man named Michael Dann. He had been very, very successful as their head programmer. And Michael hated this idea, hated it. And he had a guy from CBS Research there—he was kind of a sweaty, heavyset man—and he said, "We have found that there are four things that American television audiences won't accept: men with mustaches, people who live in New York, Jews"—he actually said this—"Jews, and divorce."

We just sat there with our mouths hanging open. Of course, it would explain why Tom Selleck was never a star, you know—the mustache part. The Jewish part we actually see now—how about Seinfeld and the gang? The New York part—most shows seem to come from New York. And then divorce being the other one. We said, "Well, but why? I mean, we'll make it very clear that this divorce will not be Mary's fault. We have two characters in the format that are the ex-husband's parents who love her and think he's a schmuck for having lost her." And so we thought we were prepared for every argument [we thought they would use against us]: that everybody understood divorce in America and, like it or not, it was a fact and et cetera, et cetera, et cetera. And Mike Dann just stared at us and said, "Okay, well, I guess the meeting is over."

Now, they had a deal that was a firm commitment to go on the air and Grant and Mary liked this idea very much. Both of them were divorced from other people and so they understood it. And Mary was very excited about it. We told the CBS brass that, but it didn't make any difference. We were dismissed. And as we were leaving, Mike Dann said to the guy we went in with from Hollywood, Mary's manager, "Arthur, can you stay behind? There are some business things I want to talk to you about." Arthur came out ten or fifteen minutes later and he was just ashen, and he said, "Fellas, can you think this over at all?" And we said, "But, Arthur, this is a good idea and we'll do it right." And he said, "They'll put the show on. They have to put a show on. But they won't like it. They'll be against it from the beginning, and if there's something you can do to tweak it a little so it isn't throwing it right in their faces, you should."

So we took a very long flight back to Los Angeles from New York thinking, "You know, it isn't worth it, we'll quit." Jim already had *Room 222* on the air. I was working on screenplay development at the time. And we said, "Why don't we just do that and get out of here right now, because it's going to be miserable." And then we said, "Nah, we can't do that. Mary and Grant have been so decent through this whole process and so supportive. If we quit, it'll look like a disagreement with them, so let's think about it some more." That's when we came up with this format where she wasn't divorced but had been living with some guy at the beginning. In the pilot it was quite clear that she had been living with some guy and that she was breaking up with him and that she had had an affair with him for a long time. Somehow they accepted that. I don't know if it was that they were just so relieved to get rid of the divorce that they would accept anything; I don't know. This was odd to us, that they would accept this, but they did. And actually the idea was, for us, even realer than the divorce idea—the idea that people have these long affairs with the man or woman they think will be the love of their life, and it turns out not to be, and they end up alone again, which became the overriding issue, I think, on the show. This woman who finds that she's not alone, that she's got this family of people whom she works with.

We had the benefit of working with the preeminent casting director in television; her name was Ethel Winant. Ethel was the vice president of talent for CBS, which meant that she was the head of all casting directors. She was also a woman's voice in a predominantly male business at CBS. There were no other executives who were women at that time. And Ethel did something very unusual. She would usually just assign a casting director to a new show and she would oversee it, but she would not be there for readings and things like that. But Ethel read our first script and loved it, and for about six months she was our only defender at CBS, because even after we made those changes for CBS, they still didn't like the show. They didn't like the scripts they were reading. They hadn't seen the shows yet, but they didn't like the scripts. Ethel did. Ethel got it and she defended us. She defended us to the point where she started to annoy the other executives and her superiors for saying that this is good stuff. And they kept saying, "You don't understand, Ethel. We don't like this stuff. Why are you defending it?" She told me later on that she was very much in jeopardy of losing her job at one point for taking our side, so she took great pains to get this show cast correctly.

I remember having a meeting with a man named Perry Lafferty, who was the vice president of CBS in Hollywood, and when he read our first script, he called us up and said, "Guys, does she have to be thirty? Do we have to say she's thirty?" We said, "Yeah. Yeah, she clearly is." I think Mary was thirty-two or thirty-three at the time. And we said, "What's so bad about that?" And he said, "We had Doris Day on the air for years without ever saying how old she was and we had Lucille Ball." And we said, "That's fine . . . if that's what they wanted, because they wanted to hold on to their youth forever, but we've got to come to this with some degree of reality here and we think it's interesting."

And when we shot our first episode, unbeknownst to us, CBS took it and tested it. They do this audience testing and we got the worst, absolute worst possible comments. That Mary—because she was thirty and unmarried—was a loser. They presented us that with great pride, because it showed they were right as far as they were concerned. That Valerie was too Jewish and too abrasive. That Phyllis was just a pain in the ass and we should rewrite accordingly. All these women who didn't have men—except Phyllis, who was in an unhappy marriage—were depressing to people. I don't think they were picking on women, in particular. They didn't like Ed Asner, either. They didn't think he was funny. That went away when he won the Emmy that year for comedy.

We had a terrible time slot when the schedule was announced. They were burying the show. It was awful. We were against *The Mod Squad*, which was a number one show in the country at the time, and a new show starring Don Knotts, which was supposed to be a big hit. They were going to kill us off, there's no doubt about it. They were going to kill us off—thirteen episodes and we'd be gone.

FRED SILVERMAN   It was scheduled on a Tuesday night between, I believe, *The Beverly Hillbillies* and *Hee Haw*. Now when you think about scheduling, it looks pretty stupid. A sophisticated show like *Mary Tyler Moore* in between these two shows. But the fact of the matter is, that's what CBS had available to work with.

ALLAN BURNS   CBS's attitude about the show changed, completely changed, when Mike Dann left CBS in a dispute with the new president of CBS, Bob Wood, who became our hero, because Bob Wood hired Fred Silverman to be his new vice president in charge of programming. [Silverman was just a] young guy, very young, just barely thirty, I think. Freddie came in and viewed our first episode with Ethel Winant. He had come in from New York to look at the new product. He had been hearing about this show that was a big problem, the *Mary* show. So they went down to the screening room late one afternoon, Ethel and Freddie and the male executives out here, and there was no laughter in the room. None. And Ethel thought, "Uh-oh." The half hour ended, the lights came up. Fred said to his assistant, "Get me Bob Wood in New York," and she thought, "Here it comes. The ax." He gets on the phone. It's nine o'clock in New York. He gets Bob at home and Ethel hears, "You know this *Mary Tyler Moore Show* that everybody hates so much? It's exactly what we want." And she thought, "Oh my God. He *gets it*."

FRED SILVERMAN   When I came into CBS we canceled all those shows like *The Beverly Hillbillies* and *Hee Haw* because they really weren't sellable and we were a national advertising medium. We were getting enormous ratings in the C and D counties and dying in the big cities where we owned television stations. And on top of this geographical disparity, those shows appealed to *really* old people. So that was a lethal combination—old and rural. We really had to change the face of CBS or die! Really, it came down to that. Because there is no point in shows that get thirty-five to forty percent like *Hee Haw* if you can't sell them, because after all it is a business. So we made a very difficult decision, because we canceled over a dozen shows with a combined audience share of—I think it was 38, which is unheard-of. You got a 38 share today, you'd be the highest-rated show in the world.

So *Mary Tyler Moore* was one of the first shows that moved up in that more sophisticated, big-city, younger demographic appeal. Incidentally, the [original] scheduling never took effect, because before the start of the broadcast season that year we moved the show to Saturday night and saved it from what I know would have been an untimely death in that time period.

MARILYN SUZANNE MILLER   They looked at every kind of woman on that show. Every kind of woman except a happily married woman, which was great. That was the first time that ever happened.

FRED SILVERMAN   It was just one of those shows that clicked. Every aspect. The casting was great, the writing was superb, the directing was Jay Sandrich. Just every element of the show worked, and ultimately, over the period of a year, it ended up, at nine o'clock, getting 40-plus shares. It was always in the top ten and in its own way, in a very quiet way, made a statement about the women's movement and the fact that women are more than housewives and mothers and nurses and they can do anything a man can do. And it made its point comedically. But first and foremost, it was a terrific half-hour comedy show. We didn't put it on to broadcast a message. But it came through loud and clear.

ALLAN BURNS   It was unusual to have three or four women in one series. Later, *The Golden Girls* is a good example of multiple women in a cast, or *Sex and the City*. But at that time, that was very unusual. And I think that was largely due to Mary's generosity—that she didn't want to be the whole show; that she had seen that for the good of the show, it was better that she surround herself with people who were as good as she was, and let them have the limelight too. And it was. Mary used to say, "Wouldn't this line be better coming out of Rhoda than me?" and it was a laugh line. She did it because it seemed to work for the good of the show.

VALERIE HARPER, actress   Even just the Jewishness of Rhoda was a step forward. Other than the Goldbergs, which was way back in the fifties, was there any other leading Jewish character? Rhoda was more New Yorker than Jewish, but Morgenstern, there's no question about it. It's funny, I knew a lot of Yiddish and they didn't want to use it at all. They said, "Absolutely not." They said, "We don't wanna get into some ghettoized cartoon." They had such good taste. They had such a touch for what was over the line. And Charlotte [Brown, who wrote on *Mary Tyler Moore* and *Rhoda*] used to tell me they'd sit in the writers' room and there was a thing—"TR" they called it—that meant a joke was too rough. You know, it would be late, one in the morning, and they'd start getting filthy. "What if Phyllis says this to Rhoda?" And they'd say, "Yeah, TR, too rough." Meaning it was too vulgar.

MARILYN SUZANNE MILLER There was a *Mary Tyler Moore* episode where Phyllis's brother came to town and was staying with Phyllis upstairs and Rhoda was over at Mary's house. And the brother and Rhoda met, and decided to go to the theater together, and they began dating. Well, Phyllis, who hated Rhoda, was, needless to say, just hysterical. And her hysteria grew through the whole episode. And finally, at the very end, what Rhoda did was turn to Phyllis, who was about to just say, "Hands off," and say, "Phyllis, your brother, he's gay." And Phyllis said, "Thank God." What was great about that was, again, there was a bit of politics. What they were saying was: Who gave a shit if he was gay?

TREVA SILVERMAN At the beginning Mary was described as an incredible reactor. If everybody around her is funny and she reacts, she's the *us* seeing insanity in something. But as time went on, we all started to appreciate that she didn't always have to be that. There was so much more to her and I think everybody started to give her truly comedic scenes, and she changed and developed and matured so much. She went through a whole transformation. At the beginning it was "Ask Grant." And if you're going to lean on somebody, Grant Tinker is one of the best. He's dear and he's smart and he respects writers and he respects the process. But I don't think she was the same person at the end of *Mary Tyler Moore* as she was in the beginning.

SUSAN SILVER, writer I identified with Mary because I was from Milwaukee and she was from Minneapolis. Even though she was the Goody Two-shoes version of me. In fact, at one point, in one of the stories, I said to them, "Don't you think it's time that she has a little sex?" She was like asexual. So my script was the first time she kissed a guy. She took a class from Michael Tolan and she got a C-plus in writing, and so she went out with him and he raised the grade to a B. And then he became a little bit of a recurring character, so she had a little sex life.

TREVA SILVERMAN   When we were in preproduction, I didn't know what Valerie looked like. Of course I knew what Mary looked like from *The Dick Van Dyke Show*—very slender. But because the sidekick nearly always looks the opposite of the lead, when I was writing my first episode, I wrote about Rhoda being on a diet and needing to lose weight. After I finished the script I thought to myself, "Uh-oh, suppose you're not right? Suppose Valerie's thin too?" So I called Jim and Allan's assistant and said, "Is Valerie Harper fat?" And she said emphatically, "No, she's not fat." And my heart sank. Then she added, "She's more . . . zaftig." And *zaftig* is an affectionate way of saying "pleasantly plump," so my world got right again.

What started happening was that I really took to the Rhoda character. And as I got to know Valerie more and more and we became close friends, Rhoda became even more interesting for me to write. I began layering in aspects of Valerie's personality with Rhoda's personality and sometimes throwing in a bit of myself.

The *Mary* show went on the air in 1970, about the time when the women's movement was just starting. The first feminist book I read was Kate Millett's *Sexual Politics*, where she wrote about the misogyny of Norman Mailer and Henry Miller. And I had this huge revelation: no wonder I didn't like them! All the brightest guys in college were always talking about Mailer and Miller and I simply didn't enjoy reading them. I had never thought in those terms before. But now, through my friendship with Marlo Thomas, I was becoming immersed in women's rights—joining women's groups and going to ERA fund-raisers. I went to small dinner parties where I met Bella Abzug, Gloria Steinem, and a lot of other activists, and I never saw life the same way again. And I remember, the agent I had at the time, Gary Nardino, flew in from New York, where his office was. I hadn't seen him in several years, and at the end of our meeting he said, "You really have changed." And I said, "What do you mean? How?" And Gary said, "This is the first meeting I've had with you where you haven't put yourself down." I was stunned.

That started showing in my work. Rhoda started getting more self-esteem, and she stopped putting herself down. I remember a lot of the time saying, "No, no, no, that insinuates Valerie would go out with *anybody*. She wouldn't." It was a time of my own—I hate this expression, but—personal growth and the women's movement, and I was responding to it through my work. Oh God, does that sound arrogant!

ALLAN BURNS Betty White had been famous for doing these kind of Goody Two-shoes parts where she was just all sweetness and light. And she had a number of early successes in early television playing this sweet, upbeat character. And Ed. Weinberger and Stan Daniels had become partners and they wrote a script featuring "the Happy Home-maker," in which they described the character as being a Betty White type. And it was a very funny script about somebody who has a *Happy Homemaker* show on WJM, their television station, who hangs around and flirts in the newsroom and has a sort of lovely trampy quality about her. And that's the other side—the happy homemaker being the happy home-breaker, since she is having an affair with Phyllis's husband. It was a hilarious script. Anyway, they started trying to cast it. Casting made everything. And they saw every sort of middle-aged woman comedian and nobody seemed quite right. And again Ethel Winant comes in, and says, "They're having trouble casting this part that's 'like Betty White.' Have you ever thought of Betty White to play it?" And we thought, "That's interesting." Because we knew Betty had kind of a bawdy sense of humor off camera, and we thought, "Well, that's real interesting," but she was also one of Mary's best friends in real life and we thought, "But what if she comes on the show and it doesn't work? That's really going to be sticky." And we said, "Well, we don't have anybody else. What the hell, let's do it." And Ethel said, "That's what I was hoping you'd say."

I remember going down to see the first run-through of the show. You read on Monday, and Tuesday we'd go down to see a sort of rough run-through of what they were doing. We get to the soundstage and Mary meets us at the door and she says, "Guys, you don't realize just how funny this woman is," and "We've got to figure out a way to get her on the show every week." Now here she is again, wanting to reach out to other actors and make them a part of this process.

We saw this run-through and we were on the floor laughing at her. It was just wonderful. She brought so much stuff to it. Physical business. There was a scene where she was trying to get something out of the oven that was a soufflé or something, and both hands were busy, so she just took her knee and whacked the oven shut. Betty just did that on her own, and it's one of the bigger laughs in the show. Just the way she did it—it was so unladylike for this prissy woman who was "the Happy Homemaker." It was the perfect way to tell you who Sue Ann

Nivens really was, that she wasn't going to let the fact that her two hands were busy stop her from closing that damn oven. And we realized Mary was right, and started writing Betty in a little more each week. We started because we were maybe four or five weeks ahead on scripts, and we started revising the scripts just to get her in. She and Murray, the newswriter, had this wonderful caustic relationship, this back-and-forth that worked so well for us. We just went to town on that.

A year after Brooks and Burns debuted Mary Tyler Moore, *Norman Lear upended almost all television taboos with the groundbreaking* All in the Family. *While that show, which began airing on CBS in 1971, tackled racism and class, it paid little attention to sexism. That changed with 1972's* Maude, *another Norman Lear creation, starring Bea Arthur as a forty-seven-year-old feminist firebrand—a sort of liberal response to* All in the Family's *racist and domineering Archie Bunker.*

Between Mary Tyler Moore *and* Maude, *the course of female-driven sitcoms was changing. And yet, no two characters could have been more unalike. Mary was the feminist ideal incarnate, a young, attractive, single woman who supported herself by working in an office and spent her downtime hanging out with girlfriends. Maude was a thrice-divorced housewife struggling to find her place in the world as she took care of a fourth husband, a grown daughter, and a grandson. Both shows tackled the burgeoning women's movement in the style of their creators, and their successes led to an outpouring of programs that reflected the diversity of real women, among them Lear's* Mary Hartman, Mary Hartman, *Susan Harris's* Soap, *and Garry Marshall's* Laverne & Shirley.

ALLAN BURNS *Maude* was a very political show and we tried to avoid that kind of stuff on *Mary Tyler Moore*. We weren't trying to make points. If they were made, fine, but we didn't say, "Let's do a show about . . ." I can think of one that Jim and I wrote about equal pay, and we did it just because it made for a funny show. Another time we did an episode where Mary had a breakthrough with her father. He was a doctor and a little tight, and they never had an easy way of talking to one another. And Mary's mother was delivering her father over to Mary's apartment so they could have an evening alone, which Mary was dreading. And as her mother is leaving, she says the line "Don't forget to take your pill." Now, she's talking to the father. But Mary answers, "I won't." It got a good laugh, as I recall. It was an episode about her parents, but it was the 1970s and she was over thirty and we just wanted to make sure that people knew that she had a sex life. It wasn't that we were trying to score points.

So Norman's shows and our shows were extremely different in their approach. Jim would always say, "We're getting too political with this one, let's pull back a little bit. We don't want to be teaching people the lesson of the week." I agree with him. Unless it is funny in its own right, don't do it.

SUSAN HARRIS, writer Norman Lear was always taking on causes and he really, I think, was responsible for a sea change in television comedy. Before *All in the Family*, sitcoms were about nothing. They were inane. But Norman was always pushing boundaries and making statements. Norman's very political and never one to avoid a confrontation and a fight if it had anything to do with principle. And after the success of *All in the Family* he had a lot of power.

FRED SILVERMAN Maude was a guest shot in *All in the Family* and, believe it or not, I think I was the only person on earth who didn't know who Bea Arthur was. I said, "She is terrific, she could run her own show!" And I called Norman up and the first thing he did was laugh at me. He said, "What, you don't know who Bea Arthur is? She's a big Broadway star." I didn't know. But I had to beg him to do a bookended guest shot, which was like a pilot of sorts, on *All in the Family*, where we were with Archie and Edith for a second and a half and then with Maude. He was reluctant to do it. He loved *All in the Family* but he got talked into doing *Maude*, he got talked into doing *Good Times* [a spin-off of *Maude* that centered around an African-American family]. He was always "Oh, I don't know if I want to do this now." But *Maude* was terrific—it was [CBS chief executive] William Paley's favorite show.

***TIME* magazine, October 1, 1973** "If Actress Arthur is not exactly garden-variety glamorous, Maude is even less likely as the heroine of a TV situation comedy. In a medium that until a few years ago shied from portraying divorced women and left politics to the 6 o'clock news, Maude is on her fourth husband and her umpteenth outspokenly liberal cause. She bullies her family and neighbors with the steamroller self-assurance of a Marine sergeant marshaling a troop of Cub Scouts, and when that fails, she invokes the aid of the Deity. 'God'll getcha for that,' she warns those who cross her. She is a fighter who takes on city hall, featherbedding repairmen and department-store complaint departments. She can deck an adversary with an arch of a single brow as surely as with an adder-tongued retort like last week's explanation of a black eye: 'I was jumping rope—without a bra.' "

MARLO THOMAS   Don't forget the wife in *All in the Family* was twenty-seven steps backward and the daughter was living at home. I mean, it's almost like Norman Lear owed us *Maude*, because the women in *All in the Family* were just steps backward. "Stifle yourself, Edith"? I mean, every now and then she'd burst out of it, but basically it was a really bad marriage.

ROD PARKER   With *Maude*, Norman Lear wanted to do with liberals what he did with Archie Bunker, who was a right-winger. He wanted to do a show about a liberal. And as far as women went, Bea became a symbol of women's rights because of her strong personality. All sorts of things happened to Bea. We made her a manic-depressive; even though she was middle-aged, she and her husband Walter still had sex—not too many middle-aged couples on television did. We even made Walter an alcoholic, and making a leading man an alcoholic hadn't been done before in a comedy. We gave her a black maid named Florida, and Maude would just go overboard with her white liberal guilt, and then Florida would knock her down, and Maude always took it. Bea was also, by the way, the first woman in a comedy to say, "You son of a bitch." With that episode, Norman took the master tape and put it in the trunk of his car so CBS couldn't get to it until he convinced [Standards and Practices to let them air it].

Then, when we had John Wayne [known as a staunch conservative] on the show, everybody wondered, "Oh boy, is Maude gonna take care of John Wayne?" He had agreed to do to the show, and Maude was going to tell off John Wayne for his political leanings [and he was going to respond]. But when he came in he said, "I can't do this." I said, "Why?" He said, "Because I'm John Wayne: I wouldn't speak to a lady this way. If I were playing another character, okay, but I'm playing myself." So we had to go back and do a lot of quick rewriting. We made it funny, but the feminists were a little bit unhappy with the show. The abortion, though, that was the big thing. And actually, that came about almost as an accident. We hired Susan Harris to write the show.

SUSAN HARRIS   I had written some *All in the Family*s for Norman and then he screened *Maude* for me, and I just naturally went over and did some *Maude*s for him. He had a male staff—at that time there weren't a lot of women writers in television—I'm sure he wanted a woman's point of view, and he liked the way I wrote. And [the abortion episode] was their idea. They wanted Vivian, the next-door neighbor, to be the one who was pregnant and who was going to have an abortion.

ROD PARKER   Originally it was supposed to be about Walter saying he was going to get a vasectomy. And what happened was that he had lied about getting one. And in that episode we introduced a character named Vivian—played by Rue McClanahan—as a middle-aged woman who got pregnant. But when the first drafts came in from the script, Norman asked me, "How was it?" I said, "The wrong woman is funny."

But the question was, how can we make Bea pregnant? We couldn't have her have a miscarriage, because Sally [Struthers] had just done that on *All in the Family*. And we couldn't have her have a false pregnancy, because that's not honest. But a woman having an abortion on television was unheard-of—so we made it a two-parter.

SUSAN HARRIS   All the sponsors pulled out.

ROD PARKER   I got some of the worst mail in the world. You know, pictures of fetuses and all of this stuff.

FRED SILVERMAN   There was a lot of hubbub about it, particularly at the broadcast Standards office. My feeling always was with Norman Lear on all his shows: Go for it. I wasn't into standards. I just wanted it to be funny, and if it had a good point to make, go ahead and do it. The Standards department had to worry about the FCC and a lot of other considerations, so most of the arguments were between him and them, not with me. But I loved the idea and I thought the two-parter was one of the best shows the series ever did. I thought they were going to burn Black Rock down in New York. It was very controversial.

And there were some advertisers who didn't want to have anything to do with it. But I think by and large we had no trouble selling that show. It was a very, very good show, very well done. Got great ratings, won all sorts of awards.

Even though Mary Tyler Moore *and* Maude *proved that women-driven shows dealing with real female problems could draw an audience, network executives still worried about overstepping the bounds of traditional values. In 1975, for example,* Fay, *a series starring Lee Grant about a woman in her forties who gets divorced after twenty-five years of marriage, starts a new job, and starts dating, was yanked after eight episodes. Even* Laverne & Shirley *had to tread lightly.*

SUSAN HARRIS *Fay* was ahead of its time. They didn't want me to do a show about a divorced woman. We had all kinds of problems in casting and doing an episode about a woman sleeping with a man outside of marriage. Things had changed enough so that we could show that women could live alone and be independent, but there were barriers that couldn't be crossed yet. And it took quite some time for that to happen.

They loosened up for me with *Soap* [a 1977 series that centered around two sisters and their families]. The times were changing; we were in the middle of change. I wrote the script and we had a lot of fans at ABC who were pushing for it. We had a gay character, who I think was the first gay character on television, and one of the daughters was sleeping around and in love with a priest. Fred Silverman was there then and he had guts and he wanted it on the air. We had a lot of problems with prepublicity. Before people even saw the show, sponsors were pulling out. There was this article in *Newsweek* months before *Soap* was screened, about what you could expect, and how shocking it was, and how appalled they were. Of course, half the things they mentioned in the article were never even on the show. So we started at a disadvantage, with a lot of prepublicity we didn't want and a lot of misinformation. But seeing that it was causing such a commotion and knowing that we'd get a pretty big audience up front, we just went ahead and did a two-parter and did whatever we could get away with. We were always pushing and making deals with Standards and Practices, and insisting that we could do more. We had fights on absolutely every level.

PENNY MARSHALL My brother [Garry Marshall] called and said, "What are you doing? We need two fast girls on *Happy Days*. You can play opposite Henry Winkler or Ron Howard, it doesn't matter. Is Cindy [Williams] around?" And I said, "Yes, she is." We weren't looking for a series. But I guess we scored as the fast girls, Laverne and Shirley, in a scene in Fonzi's apartment over the garage. And after the *Happy Days* shot we did another scene, and my brother did a presentation for a series called *Laverne & Shirley* to Fred Silverman, and they bought it around Thanksgiving and by January we were on the air. We premiered number one for some reason and we stayed up there for a very long time. But our characters had to change, because the show was on during family hour and so we couldn't say we did it. When we were on *Happy Days* we were fast girls who put out—then we had to become virgins.

We did that for a long time. And people seemed to like working-class girls who were friends trying to make a dollar—and that was the basis of the show. We dared to be stupid or silly. We weren't a class show in the industry. We weren't *Mary Tyler Moore* or *Rhoda*. We were lower-class so we really didn't exist. David Lander, Squiggy, used to say "Only the public likes us." We weren't groundbreaking. We were just old-school comedy.

While shifts in subject matter and character development were among the biggest changes to happen to women on television in the 1970s, a more profound if less visible shift was taking place behind the scenes. Jim Brooks and Allan Burns brought on board an unprecedented number of female television writers to help bring the women characters of Mary Tyler Moore *to life. That, in turn, led to the hiring and mentoring of women at shows created by the powerful men who spent the decade transforming the sitcom: Norman Lear, Larry Gelbart (M*A*S*H), Garry Marshall (*The Odd Couple*), and Carl Reiner (who had created the first visible female comedy writer:* The Dick Van Dyke Show's *Sally Rogers.)*

VALERIE HARPER The comedy writer used to be a guy with a polo sweater and a cigar saying, "That's funny." That guy kind of moved away.

In the seventies you had a lot more people, younger men with a different sensibility, and women.

MARLO THOMAS [When I was developing *That Girl* in the late 1960s] I was hunting out female writers and only coming up with women who wrote in teams with a man, which was fine, because when we sat down we, the female and I, would get to the core of what we thought a girl would say. But it was difficult to be in a room of all men on my team. The producer, the two executive producers, the story editor, the associate producer, all the directors, they were all men. So we'd sit in a meeting— and I was in every meeting—and I would say, "I don't think a girl would say that to her father," or "I don't think a girl would say that to her friend." And so it was like I was the only girl authority in the room, and after a while it's like being the only anything: they kind of gang up on you.

TREVA SILVERMAN Jim and Allan really broke a lot of barriers, be- cause then it became very hip to hire women. Not immediately. But I went to live in Europe in 1974, and stayed for two and a half years. When I left, I was one of the few women writing. When I came back, there were a lot more—and a lot more women executives too.

LINDA BLOODWORTH-THOMASON, writer All the big guys were hir- ing women. And there weren't many women. When I first started I was working with an actress who was thinking she wanted to be a writer named Mary Kay Place. And Norman Lear was our mentor, Jim Brooks was our other mentor, and Larry Gelbart was our other mentor. So there were three. They all gave us jobs immediately. It was just like a fairy tale. We were so lucky. We were the first women to write for *M*A*S*H*. But right out of the gate, everything I wrote I wanted to have female power in it.

SUSAN HARRIS I got into writing because I had to make a living. I had a baby and the story is true that I was watching television one night and I said, "I think I can do that," and did it. At that time there weren't a lot of women writers in television. There was Treva Silverman, there was me, just a handful.

TREVA SILVERMAN   When I was writing revues at the Upstairs at the Downstairs, Bob Banner, who owned Carol Burnett's production company, had seen the show a few days before and wanted Carol to see the show before any offer went out to me. So Carol saw the show, we met each other, I fell in love at first hug, and was hired. And the show was then called *The Entertainers*, and it also had Dom DeLuise, John Davidson, and Bob Newhart. And I was the kid and the only woman on it. By then, I had already been turned down by the Johnny Carson show because they said that there is no way Johnny's going to work with a woman around, that the men would not feel comfortable. So during the first production meeting that we had, I thought, "Okay, I'm going make these guys feel comfortable"—and they were all older men, seasoned veterans. So I'm saying the "fucking" this, the "son of a bitch" that, and "motherfucker" and thinking, "Oh, I'm really accomplishing a lot here." And one of the sweet men came over to me and said, "Treva, please don't curse. It makes me feel embarrassed." And really, everybody was very accepting and very nice.

After that, I did *The Monkees* [1966–1968], and it was a big deal then because I was the only woman writer working alone in episodic comedy. And after I left *The Monkees* I partnered up with a lovely writer named Peter Myerson. Somebody read our work, so we went in for a pitch session, and when we walked in, the man said, "Oh, I didn't realize Treva was a woman's name. So, what, Treva, you do the story and the structure but Peter does the comedy?" So there was an assumption about a woman writer.

SUSAN SILVER   I was working in casting on *Laugh-In* and the guys on *Laugh-In* worked in a motel. And I said, "Couldn't I be a writer on the show too?" And George Schlatter said, "No, because the guys swear a lot and fart and do other things, and we can't have a woman in there."

GAIL PARENT, writer   [When I started my career in the 1960s] I had a writing partner named Kenny Solms who I worked with at the Upstairs at the Downstairs because I was up for shows like *The Smothers Brothers* and they said, "We really can't have a woman on the staff, it'll ruin the guys being able to curse." Well, you know that's not true, I can have a filthy mouth. So after I got two turndowns, the offer came from

Carol Burnett [for *The Carol Burnett Show*]. And it was just glorious, unbelievable. We met her at a hotel and we said, "Let's get on our knees when she opens the door." And she was on *her* knees when the door opened. There were ten writers, and I was the only woman for the five years that I was there. But at least they knew that I could play with the boys.

CAROL BURNETT, comedian We had mostly men writers. We had two women, Mitzie Welch and Gail Parent. Mitzie and Kenny Welch came on board and wrote a lot of the special material that we did and then went on to write all of the specials I did with Julie Andrews and Beverly Sills and Plácido Domingo. They wrote those shows. And then we had Gail Parent and Kenny Solms. Then the rest were pretty much men.

VALERIE HARPER I know that Jim Brooks and Allan Burns actively sought female writers. Actively. I remember Jim saying to me one day, "You know, Val, Al and I, we're married. But we don't do that pantyhose and nail polish stuff very well. I know there is a wealth of comedy in my wife's purse, but I can't access it." And so they brought on female writers.

ALLAN BURNS A wave of feminism was just starting, really, and we didn't realize what we would be able to mine until we got into it. We were fortunate enough to have two extremely good woman writers on our staff. One of them was a woman named Treva Silverman and the other was Sue Silver—oddly enough, two Silvers—and they really pushed us in the right direction with what women were feeling and helped us with our misconceptions.

TREVA SILVERMAN I did a bunch of shows and then I did some *Room 222*s with Jim Brooks and Allan Burns. And when they were doing *The Mary Tyler Moore Show* Jim called and said, "We're so excited we're writing for Mary Tyler Moore, and if anything happens we want you aboard." Once it was picked up he called me: "What are you doing?" And I said something like "I'm about to wash my hair." And he said, "No, no. In your career and your work. We just want you to come here and write as many *Mary*s as you want." It was simultaneously very comforting and scared the hell out of me. You know, that ambivalent thing of "Oh, that's great, they believe in me—isn't that wonderful!" and "Oh, I'll never do what they want! I'll never be as good as they think that I am. I'll be found out." The famous I'll-be-found-out syndrome that everybody on earth has. When I was on *Mary* it was the first time a woman had been an executive on a comedy show. It was a big deal. Big deal. This was 1970. And when I won the Emmy for *Mary Tyler Moore*, it was the first time that a woman had ever won without a partner.

SUSAN SILVER I had gone out with a guy who was married to Iris Rainer Dart, who wrote the movie *Beaches*, and I ran into him when I was with my husband and he said, "Oh, you should meet my wife, because she wants to be a writer too." So she and I teamed up. Garry Marshall used to run a group of young writers, and he was our manager. And then she, I think, had a baby at the time, or her husband didn't want her to work, whatever it was. Anyway, I said, "I just saw this show *Mary Tyler Moore* and I can do this show." She and I had done a *Love, American Style* together, and that was the only thing we had done. And I said, "I can do this *Mary Tyler Moore Show* if you can get me a meeting there." So they got me a meeting and they said, "If we get picked up for the next thirteen, we'll give you some shows."

And I did only stories from my own life, because I didn't know we were allowed to make things up. I know that's crazy, but that's what I thought. I don't know why. So the first one I pitched was the Twinks episode, where Mary has to stand up for her old camp mate's wedding. And she hated her in camp and she hates her now. She's at the station and her name is Twinks and she's overly friendly, and she had the Bo Peep gown and all that. Well, that was from my own life. But of course every girl has gone through this; something like this has happened to every girl. But they thought I was like some kind of a genius or something.

Another show that I did was when Rhoda lost her job and there was one available at the station but Mary didn't want her to have it, because that's her own territory. And the guys thought that was like, "Oh my God, what an incredible story." But every girl will tell you, you want your own nest. You want your own place.

TREVA SILVERMAN Jim and Allan really wanted insights. Take for instance *The Monkees*, which was the least insightful show. That was one part of my humor, which is off-the-wall stuff, but the thing that I care most about is character-based stuff. And if something happened to you, Jim and Allan would say, "Put it in the show, put it in the show." The first thing I ever wrote for them, I was telling them anecdotally over lunch, or maybe it was our first story meeting; I said, "Something happened to me where somebody came over and said, 'Thank you, ma'am.' I said. 'Ma'am. Wait a minute. I'm honey or sweetie but I'm not ma'am.'" So that was the very first thing that I wrote for them. Mary had been called ma'am and was going out of her mind.

SUSAN SILVER Nobody else worked like they did. Nobody. They had Lorenzo Music and David Davis and Allan and Jim sit in a room with you and spend a whole day listening to your pitches, breaking down your stories. Then you'd go home and you'd follow their outline and you could use their jokes. It was a real collaborative thing.

It was a totally different work experience than any other show. I'd go to another show and they'd give you twenty minutes, you'd walk out, you wouldn't know where you were or what you were doing, and then the scripts would come back and they'd say, "Well, we didn't have this in mind." On *Mary Tyler Moore* it was just a very friendly, nurturing atmosphere.

TREVA SILVERMAN Also, no talking about those times would be complete without talking about grass and coke. I think pretty much every comedy writer I know, at that time, was always smoking dope—always, always, always. And we would get complaints: "Listen, guys, smoke your dope, but it shouldn't be in the corridors when guests come in." Some of the *Mary Tyler Moore* type people got into a lot of trouble. I remember hearing that somebody only hired their assistant if they could really roll up a joint. I mean, they talk about *Saturday Night Live* with everybody on coke. But I think at that point in Hollywood all the comedy writers I knew were on grass. There was a lot of smoking going on. I would bake brownies and bring them in for myself. I took to heart that "we don't want it in the corridors." But everybody was always stoned.

MARILYN SUZANNE MILLER Jim's real interest was to find out all the way down at the bottom of your soul who this person would end up being. What choice would they end up making? He gave the same attention to every episode of that show as he would, I think, to writing a play. And in those days they really did farm out the episodes. They would write a few in-house episodes but they would also really farm out episodes to outside writers. And if you said something that they didn't understand, Jim would say, "Well, is that like a girl joke?" I was often tempted to lie and go, "Yeah." Just to get it in. But if it really was a girl joke, if it was really something that was understood among women and you said that, he'd put it in for that reason. "Oh, I don't get this because it's a girl joke and therefore it should be in, therefore we will put it in."

VALERIE HARPER I remember, there was a joke where the boys, Jim and Allan, had said something like "I have a date tonight, I better look under 'B' for blonde, 'BR' for brunette, and 'R' for redhead." And it was a joke, and everyone laughed. I'm not structuring it properly but it was an actual laugh line. And Mary is standing there. And Treva said, "Guys, guys, you can't leave that. Take Mary out of the shot, but Mary can't hear that and not comment or have a rejoinder." And so she did. And it was funny, so there was a double laugh. So they were making a consciousness moment for everybody.

MARILYN SUZANNE MILLER I was sort of discovered by Jim Brooks. I applied to the University of Iowa in writing, but that wasn't gonna start until September and meanwhile I was sitting at home and I was watching TV. And I had watched *The Mary Tyler Moore Show* a lot in college too. And I thought, "You know, maybe I could pay for grad school," because that was a big fear. It was three years for an MFA. Now, after three years of law school or med school, you had a job. When you left writing school, you could go live in a garret, whatever a garret was. So I said, "Maybe I could sell a script to *Mary Tyler Moore*." So I read the credits and I called CBS and asked for Jim Brooks, and for reasons neither of us to this day know, he took the call. And I had written a script. And I said, "Hi, my name is Marilyn Miller. I live in Monroeville, Pennsylvania. I'm twenty-two years old and I have a script. Would you read it?" And he said, "Yes." This is an unreal story. It's a real Lana Turner story. And I sent it to him, and within two weeks he had given it to all his friends, to Garry Marshall, and it was a small world, the world of comedy out there then. And Garry Marshall and Jim had talked, and arrangements were made to fly me out to California in two weeks. And first I was a junior writer on *The Odd Couple*, meaning that I got to whisper and if it was any good Garry would say it aloud. And then I got my first assignment, with a partner who was the sister of Garry's partner, Jerry Belson. She went on to write with Albert Brooks. And I was so young: believe it or not, twenty-two was very young in those days to be working out there. And they wanted Monica Mc-gowan Johnson and me to work as a team and that's how I got my first *Mary* assignment.

BARBARA GALLAGHER   I was working for Norman Lear as a production assistant on *Maude*. And I credit my experience with Norman in how to learn comedy timing, because I was handling the scripts and I was on the floor and working with the director. And so one day my girlfriend Sybil Adelman, who was Carl Reiner's secretary, said to me, "Why don't we write a *Mary*?" And I looked at her as if she had fourteen heads. I said, "What? I don't know how to write. What are you . . . ?" She said, "No, no, you worked for Norman. You can write." I said, "Yeah, right."

SYBIL ADELMAN, writer   One day somebody in the office said something about Sheldon's old biddy, and they were referring to Sheldon Leonard's secretary. I thought, "That's going to be me." I loved working for Carl but that was not my goal, to be Carl's old biddy. The women's movement had just raised all of our aspirations but not our ability to do anything, just awareness that this might just not be it. So I had to figure out a career very quickly, and I was in group therapy and thought I'd go back to school and become a therapist. And I didn't get in. I didn't know what to do. So I was just flashing, looking around for a career, and one night Barbara and I were watching *The Mary Tyler Moore Show* and I said, "We can write this." I said, "I have an idea for a story." And Carl had just started to do television at the time—he had been doing movies and plays while I was working for him—and I saw the scripts being dropped off and they weren't as scary for television. The TV scripts came in looking a little more approachable and accessible. So that was where we got the nerve to try to do it.

BARBARA GALLAGHER   We sat down and we did a spec *Mary* [an unsolicited script]. We enjoyed it. And Carl Reiner read it. And Carl said, "You really should submit this. This is really good." We couldn't believe it. He said, "Show it to the *Mary* people." But at that time *Mary* was on hiatus, and so Sybil and I decided to write another script for a pilot series that Carl Reiner was doing with Danny Arnold. We thought, "Well, we'll write this script and if Carl's really serious he'll give us work if he likes our writing." So we did it, and we didn't tell him we were doing it. Carl kept saying, "What are you doing? What is going on here?" So Sybil said, "We wrote this script and we would love for you to read it." So we give it to him. It's a Friday. And we're standing there and he said, "You want me to read it *now*?" We said, "Well . . ." And he said, "I'm not gonna read it now while you're sitting there." So we were kind of disheartened, and we went into our office and he beeped in and he said, "Well, tell Barbara to wait. I'll read it." So he read it and he came in and he was nonplussed. He said, "This is amazing." He said, "I've never read a spec script like this. I want you to come in with some ideas for *Van Dyke*," because he was doing *The Dick Van Dyke Show* at the time—the second one with Hope Lange—"and come in with some ideas for Dick, and if we get a go-ahead on the show, we're gonna see if we can get you a multiple on this." So we were kind of stunned. We couldn't believe it, as you can imagine.

So we did come in with some ideas for *Van Dyke*, and we had one of the most controversial shows. It was a show about the little girl—their daughter—walking in on them in bed. Carl had sent around the script without our names on it to get a feel because it was controversial. What was so funny is that I was at Carl's office and I pick up the phone and it's Norman Lear. Well, first of all, he couldn't believe I picked up the phone. He said, "Is this Barbara?" I said, "Yeah." He said, "What are you doing there?" I said, "Oh, my friend is Carl's secretary. Is there anything I can help you with?" He said, "Probably not but . . ." I said, "I can relay the message." He said, "Well, Carl sent us a script and we wanna know who wrote it." And it was that script. And I was kind of embarrassed, I said, "Well, um, my friend and I did." He said, "What?" I said, "Well, my friend and I wrote it." He started laughing. He could not believe it.

The network didn't wanna do it. And Carl said, "We're gonna do it anyway." So he and Dick footed the bill. And we had all the brass from CBS sitting around the table, listening to the reading. This is a Monday morning reading, and they couldn't find anything wrong with it. And they went back, reported to Bob Wood, who was at that time the president of CBS, and he still wouldn't do it. So they came to the studio when we shot the show and the audience went crazy. They loved it. But the brass still wouldn't air it. So it's a show that only got aired in Canada. But we got a reputation. Everybody had heard about us. We got over to the *Mary* show. We wrote a show. And then Norman and Bud Yorkin sent us to interview Jane Alexander in New York to do a pilot. It just escalated. It was such fun. And we wrote various pilots and half hours for a few years together. The last thing we wrote together on was *The Lily Tomlin Show*. We won an Emmy. And that is where I met Lorne Michaels.*

SYBIL ADELMAN   The way the women were depicted on the shows and the way we were being responded to in real life matched up in an interesting way. The first show that Barbara and I wrote was *The New Dick Van Dyke Show*. Hope Lange played his wife, and she often complained that all she did on the show was "I only pour coffee, I only pour coffee." That seemed to correlate with what was happening to me. I was working on a show, and they weren't used to any women. I walked into the producer's office and he didn't look up, he just said, "Honey, could you get me a cup of coffee?" And I thought, "Still I have to get coffee?" I thought I didn't have to get coffee anymore! But you couldn't get confrontational. So I said to him, "Don't you think I'm being paid a lot? If you want the coffee, I'll get it, but it seems like you're paying a high price to get this cup of coffee." And then he realized that he hadn't looked to see who he was talking to, he just felt a female come in.

MARCY CARSEY, producer, Carsey-Werner Productions   By the way, women watch sitcoms more than men do. That was part of the reason I became head of comedy at ABC. ABC was smart enough to put women in the jobs where the purpose of the job was to turn out programming that mostly women watched. So movies, mini-series, daytime, all that.

---

* In 1975, Gallagher became an associate producer for *Saturday Night Live*.

When I got to ABC, I was almost thirty and pregnant. Obviously, there were steps along the way before I got there. But it was great, because Michael Eisner hired me pregnant. This was 1974. I've always loved Michael since then. I mean, he was a great boss, but also I thought it was great of him because I was three months pregnant. You couldn't tell, and I said, "Michael, I'm pregnant, I have a job that I like. You wanna hire me after I have the baby?" And he said, "Well, Jane and I are pregnant too. I'm coming back to work. Are you coming back to work?" And I said, "Sure." "Then, well, why are we talking about this?"

Then, I used to bring my babies to work! Not every day, but whenever I could. People remember my kids, when they were little, running around the floor. Lana was the receptionist; she was a wonderful woman. She was there for a long time and her desk faced the elevator, and I would say, "Lana, just make sure the kids don't get on the elevator."

JOAN DARLING, sitcom director   I was "the first woman director" in Hollywood, which was not literally true at all. Elaine May had directed films, and a woman named Dorothy Arzner had directed, and Ida Lupino had directed a couple of things. But I was the first woman in this era that got up every day and got dressed and went to work as a director, and then a lot of women began to follow. But Norman Lear is really the one who made me a director and gave me *Mary Hartman*, which was the first thing I directed.

How it happened was that I had gone to see Norman because I had been on a television series as an actress on *Owen Marshall: Counselor at Law* [from 1971 to 1974], and I knew the series was winding down but I still had what they call TVQ. In the old days, they had a rating system for how recognizable a person was from being on TV and whether people liked them or not. The result of that was called your TVQ, or television quotient. And I knew Norman because I had done some writing for him, and I knew him socially. So I went to try to convince him to do a ninety-minute movie on the life of Golda Meir from the time she was sixteen to sixty, starring me. I had this whole story worked out. And as I was telling this to him, he said, "Wait a minute, I want you to tell this . . ." and he called in his second-in-command, a man named Al Burton, and said, "Tell him what you have in mind." And I'm thinking to myself, "Oh boy, he's going to do it and I'll get to act the part." And when I finished telling him, Norman said to this guy, "I think she's the one." And Al said, "I think you're right." And Norman turned to me and said, "You wanna be a director?" I said, "What?" He said, "That's what I think you really are." He had known that I'd been a teacher; I had been teaching as well as acting for a long time. And he gave me the script for *Mary Hartman*. I said, "I have no idea whether I can do this." I read it and I remember I flew back out to L.A. to see him, and I said, "Here's what I think: When I first read these I thought, 'I don't know what this is.' And then my second thought was 'This is something so unique that I've never seen it before.'" And then I said to him, "I don't know if I'm a director. If I did direct, I would have to be doing my own concept. I don't know if I could direct, somebody else's concept." So I told him what my idea for the show was, which was that I felt it was not a satire on a soap opera, but a satire on what was going wrong in the United States of America, based on what was happening to us with television. I meant specifically that the values that were killing Mary Hartman were all coming through the media at her. You know, "Don't have any waxy yellow buildup . . . My toothpaste has added whiteners . . . My underarms are so dry that they're flaking . . . Why won't Tom sleep with me?" So what I really felt lay underneath that story was this media assault and this American materialism that was coming at us through that media assault, which was killing us. He said, "If you can do it, great!"

The first year of directing, after I did the *Mary Hartman* pilot—but before *Mary Hartman* was on the air—I got a call to do a season at MTM, the Mary Tyler Moore company, and I took it. I didn't want to, particularly. I still wasn't ambitious to be a director, but I agreed to do it because I thought that there was no woman director and I knew without a doubt that I could do all the things that they thought women couldn't do, like lead a crew and get the work done on time. I knew I could do that. So I said, "Well, I'm gonna do it for one year to establish that idea." And what happened was the second show I directed for them was the Chuckles Bites the Dust episode, and that was such a huge success and phenomenon—*The New York Times* called it the funniest half hour ever on television—that suddenly I was a very valuable commodity, because if somebody hired me they got press for it, and I could also deliver Emmy-nominated shows. The fact that I was out there, and that my name was out there nominated for awards and things like that, kind of made it fashionable to hire women. And a lot of women who really wanted to do it, had prepared themselves, and were very good at it came out of that era.

CAROL BURNETT

When The Carol Burnett Show *debuted on CBS on September 11, 1967, no one suspected that it would become one of the best, most memorable variety shows of all time. At first, CBS didn't really want the series; they ordered it simply to fulfill a clause in Burnett's contract. And Burnett's show came at a time when the form was in flux. The Smothers Brothers Comedy Hour* debuted that same year, giving the country a taste for a new kind of political variety show. NBC followed up with Rowan & Martin's Laugh-In, *which had a quick-paced, go-go feel that upended the old form. By the time the 1970s rolled around, Lily Tomlin and* Saturday Night Live *were pushing television limits even further by creating subversive satirical shows for the first generation to grow up on television. Other than the fact that Carol Burnett was the first woman to host her own variety show, there was nothing particularly new about* The Carol Burnett Show, *a musical-variety program that had traces of vaudeville and elaborate stage productions that drew big laughs with broad jokes and slapstick. The show was successful simply because of the wildly talented Burnett and her hilarious cast mates: Vicki Lawrence, Tim Conway, Harvey Korman, and Lyle Waggoner. The show picked up twenty-five Emmys during its run. But Burnett was also the last music-variety performer of her kind. When her show ended in 1978, its brand of singing-and-dancing comedienne disappeared from television with her.*

CAROL BURNETT   It came about by sheer accident, really. I had signed a contract with CBS [where I had been a regular performing on *The Garry Moore Show*] for ten years at a certain amount a year, which

meant I would have to do two guest shots on a CBS show and one special a year. In the first five years, if I decided I wanted to do a weekly
variety show, all I had to do was pick up the phone and push the button
and say, "I'd like to do a variety show," and it would be thirty shows
that they would either pay or play, which was unheard-of.

So it's that week between Christmas and New Year's that fifth year.
My husband and I had one baby, then another one on the way, and we
had moved to California and neither one of us really had a steady job.
And we looked at each other and I said, "You know, I guess maybe we
ought to push that button." So we picked up the phone and called CBS
in New York and got Mike Dann on the phone. And he was one of
the heads of CBS. And he said, "Hi, Carol"—he had a voice—"how are
you, dear? Merry Christmas." I said, "Hey, Mike, I'm calling because
the five years is almost up and I think I really want to do a variety
show." And there was a dead silence. He had totally forgotten. He said,
"What do you mean?" I said, "Well, it's in the contract that if by this
time, before the five years are up, if I want to do a variety show . . ." and
I repeated it. And he said, "Oh, great. Well, let me get back to you." I
said, "Okay." So you know they called all the lawyers in and they probably pored over the contract that night. And the next day he called me.
He said, "Look. You know variety is more of a man's field: Sid Caesar
and Jackie Gleason and Milton Berle and Dean Martin." He said,
"We've got a great pilot that you could shoot. It's a sitcom and it's called
Here's Agnes." I could just picture what it would be, right? "Heeeeere's
Agnes . . ." Oh God.

So I said, "I want to do a show the way Sid did his show. I want to
have a rep company and I want to have music. I want to do sketches
and I want to have guest stars." Well, they had to put it on the air. So I
remember Joe flew back, 'cause he was producer, to talk to Mike about
what we were gonna do and who we were gonna look for to cast and so
forth. And Mike had a bulletin board behind his desk that announced
the shows in ink and everything—what was gonna go on Monday
nights at ten, what was gonna go on Tuesday nights at nine, so forth, so
forth. And our show was booked for Monday nights at ten. That's *The
Carol Burnett Show.* And then it went to February and in that slot was
a big question mark. Which meant they weren't thinking we were gonna
run and that they would have to replace us. But nonetheless, they would
still have to pay us for thirty full hours. I said, "We're just gonna have

to go and do it and have fun and not worry about pleasing anybody but ourselves." And I must say CBS left us alone.

Then we proceeded to hire the cast. And my beloved Harvey, we had seen him on *The Danny Kaye Show*. He was a second banana there and then *Danny* went off the air just as we were gonna be going on. And I remember practically attacking Harvey in the parking lot. We were walking to our cars and we kind of knew each other and I ran up to him and I said, "Oh, please. You've gotta be on our show. Please, please, please . . ." So we got Harvey and we discovered Vicki and then we auditioned for the good-looking announcer, Lyle, and we were off and running.

I started out as the goofy nerd. Zany, kook. And I would swoon over Lyle and make faces and so forth. After I think about the fourth year I started to grow up—on the show—and not be kooky but still be funny. And so I think our sketches got funnier, and some more sophisticated. Some still very slapstick, which I love too. And we got Tim, and of course that was such gold, with Tim and Harvey. And things just kind of developed and then the writers started coming up with some really wonderful, interesting stuff like "The Family" with Eunice, and Ed, and those were pretty heavy sketches that we did and they were fun. They were more acting sketches. There were no jokes written for those particular sketches; it was all character and situation. Then there was Tim and me doing Mrs. Wiggins and Mr. Tuddball. And also, I was raised by my grandmother and we lived a block north of Hollywood Boulevard, and when we saved our money we could go see movies. And movies were my salvation. And then when I got my own show, aside from doing some of these other things, I said "Gee, I'd love to be Betty Grable" or "I'd love to be Joan Crawford. Let's do a takeoff on *Mildred Pierce*." And in three or four weeks I'd be doing that, with costumes and lighting and orchestrations and the whole thing. It was a grown-up fantasy come true. And then of course the classic *Gone With the Wind* sketch. I mean, that's one of the longest laughs in history—that sight gag of Scarlett coming down the stairs wearing the curtain rod. And as long as we got the ratings, they didn't come in and try to tell you how to do it.

The writers were mostly men. We had two women. A lot of them moved out from New York to be with us who were on *The Garry Moore Show*. To me, it never became to me a boys' club. But on the other hand Sid Caesar or Gleason might go in and say, "Hey, guys. This stinks . . .

Let's make it better. It ain't working." But I would call the writers down to the rehearsal hall and I'd say, "Gee, I don't know, I think we need some help here. I'm not getting this as well as I should." I would go in the back door. I just didn't want to castrate anybody because a woman doing that in those days would be considered bitchy. Whereas a man would be assertive.

I remember Lucille Ball was on our show. And this was, gosh, in '68 or '69. . . . And it was a rehearsal night for the orchestra and we'd already done our blocking, so during the break I took her across to the Farmers Market, where they had a little Italian restaurant. So she and I sat and we were talking, and she always called me "kid." And she said, "So, kid, you're really lucky you got Joe to run the show for you and all of that." She says, "It's great. So you can just come in and be Carol." And she said, "That's the way it was with me and the Cuban." I said, "Oh, well what do you mean?" She said, "Well, I never worried about the script. Desi would do all of that. He would talk to the writers if it wasn't right. He'd tell them what was wrong. And so on Monday morning I'd come in and everything would be perfect and I could just be funny Lucy." She said, "And then we got divorced. And so this one Monday I came in and read the script and I was horrified. It was terrible and I didn't know what to do, what to say to the writers. I'd never been in that position before. So I went into my office and I thought and I thought and I thought. I've got to do something or we're not going to be able to continue this way." So she said she went back after lunch and she said, "I told the writers what I thought, and, kid, that's when they put the *s* on the end of my last name."

Anyway, our show was a well-oiled show from the very first week, because we patterned it after what we did on Garry's show: the rehearsal schedule, when we would have the dance numbers staged, when we would have this, when that would happen, when we'd have our run-through, how we would do our camera blocking. It was just very smooth.

And we went for eleven years, and I felt it was time to cash it in. CBS wanted us for a twelfth season. But I just felt it was classier to leave before they knocked on the door and said, "Stop doing this."

4

· · · · · · · · · · ·

Saturday Night Live: The Boys' Club

Carol Burnett may have been a hilarious smash hit, but the broad style of comedy she performed on her show didn't reflect the edgier sensibility that was bubbling underground, and it didn't probe the uncomfortable depths of modern womanhood. Although sitcoms of the 1970s were giving the country a peek into the inner lives of these contemporary women, the late-night programs and variety shows on television at that time were slow to capture the essence of the new world order. On October 11, 1975, NBC's Saturday Night Live *changed all that. Thousands of words have been devoted to the fact that* Saturday Night Live *was a boys' club, but there's a different way to look at what happened. In truth, the* SNL *of the 1970s was the show that finally opened the door to women trying to break into sketch comedy* on-screen *and* behind the scenes. *Until* SNL *showed up on NBC, women had been scarce on every single variety program except Lily Tomlin's shows, which never got picked up for a series.* Laugh-In, *which by then was off the air, had prominent female performers but no female writers;* The Carol Burnett Show *had a cast ratio of two women to three men, and its women writers—both of them—had male partners. The* Tonight Show *had no women in the writers' room. As for* Monty Python's Flying Circus, *the British comedy series that served as inspiration for* Saturday Night Live, *half the time the female characters that appeared in the sketches were played by the five men who formed the group!*

ALAN ZWEIBEL, writer [As a variety show] *Carol Burnett* preceded us. And then, when we came along in '75, we pretty much dethroned them, because in the spring of '76 we were up against them for Emmys and we won them all. We were the new kids on the block, and it was almost like the passing of the torch, if you will. And I remember, when we would think of sketches or even beats within sketches, there would be "Oh, Carol Burnett would do it this way, we're going to do it that way." They were the standard. And when we said, "Carol Burnett would do it this way," that wasn't a dig, but their way was usually broader, and a little more traditional. At the opening of the show, *SNL*'s logo was spray-painted on the marble walls of what was then called the RCA Building [now 30 Rock]. We were the upstart, we were the counterculture thing. *That* was the culture, if you will.

MARILYN SUZANNE MILLER   I remember when we went on the air the network thought that everybody in the cast of *Saturday Night Live* was horrible-looking except for Chevy Chase and Jane Curtin. Why? They were blond, blue-eyed WASPs. And you wanted to go to them and scream, "Excuse me, we all date each other and have sexual intercourse with each other and find each other attractive. We men and women you think are so ugly." It was just so unbelievable. That's also a way I think that *Saturday Night Live* broke through. I know physical appearance is still an enormous problem, but back then it was like nobody counted but blond-haired, blue-eyed, turned-up-nose people.

MERRILL MARKOE   *Saturday Night Live* was amazing when it started because it was the first television comedy being written and performed by people who had grown up watching TV. It had a sensibility that took the TV form and the language of commercials and the clichés of sitcoms and used them all to make fun of the bullshit of TV itself.

MARILYN SUZANNE MILLER   I met Lorne Michaels [on the Lily Tomlin specials] and Lorne asked me to go to New York and write for *Saturday Night Live*. But I kept thinking I should marry this guy I was living with and stay in California and so I'd send him writers: Michael O'Donoghue and other people. When I finally managed to break up with this guy, I said, "You know, Lorne, maybe I'll just come to New York," and so I knew everybody there.

When I got there, there weren't really offices. There were desks with typewriters. I had been in Hollywood where there was a *Variety* and *Hollywood Reporter* delivered every day. Not at *SNL*. If somebody got a phone call, someone would just answer the phone and they'd yell out, "Gilda, it's in your room!" *Your room*, like it was your house—not your office. So it was like we all lived in this big, rent-style house, seventeen stories up in Rockefeller Center. And it was the most fun ever.

Also in those days there was no writers' room. And there was no phrase *writers' room*. We worked separately and we did whatever we wanted. And if we wanted to work with somebody else, we did, and nobody fucked with what we were doing. Lorne really let us do what we wanted. We weren't rewritten. We rewrote ourselves. We produced our own segments, we talked to the set designer, we talked to the costume designer. And at NBC, they didn't know what was going on.

ANNE BEATTS, writer I've always said that I got into comedy the same way that Catherine the Great got into politics: on my back! Basically, I started going out with somebody. I was fixed up on a blind date with a guy named Michel Choquette. I was in Montreal working as an advertising copywriter, and I met Michel and then Michel started asking me to help him with his work. And meanwhile, Michel had gotten hooked up with Doug Kenney and Henry Beard, who were these two Harvard grads who were in the process of starting a new magazine, the *National Lampoon* [in 1970], which was based on the fact that they had worked together at *The Harvard Lampoon.* So Michel starting bringing me to New York, and then he would bring me to dinner with the editors. The magazine was written by a very small number of people—the editorial staff was not usually more than like five people. And they would have these editorial dinners at some of the worst restaurants in New York, like Steak and Brew and things like that. And they were paid for by the *Lampoon*, so it was a free meal. And Michel would bring me, and I would come up with ideas and then people would say, "Well, whose idea was that?" So I started writing for the magazine. I started demanding a byline. Meanwhile, I had switched boyfriends mid-magazine from Michel to Michael O'Donoghue. So at that point I was doing stuff for the magazine on a more regular basis and getting fan mail. And I was still only a contributing editor, which meant that I didn't get any kind of salary. It was very hard to get money out of that organization. I was feeling like I was being treated like something of a second-class citizen. I've always said it was like being a black voter in the South, where everyone else had to spell *cat* and I had to spell *anti-disestablishmentarianism*. I had to score 110 to get 90. I got Henry Beard to go out to lunch with me and brought this up to him, and he said, "Chicks just aren't funny," the party line at the time. And I should have punched him right in the nose, but instead I cried and I lost a contact lens in my soup! Then I never did anything for the magazine again.

Anyway, by that time the *National Lampoon Radio Hour* was getting rolling and I started writing for the show. And my boyfriend was doing something called *The National Lampoon's Encyclopedia of Humor*, which I also contributed to. Then Michael quit the *Lampoon*, and took me with him.* Michael did think I was funny and that was part of the bond between us. I thought he was very funny and he thought I was funny. Also, he was a great mentor. He wasn't so good as a boyfriend but he was a wonderful mentor.

We had this year of starving and rolling pennies and taking them to the bank, and I managed to help keep us afloat by writing a lot for a sex thing, *Oui* magazine, which was a magazine that Hugh Hefner had started to kind of compete with *Hustler*. It was supposed to be, you know, a young and hip magazine, as opposed to *Playboy*. It was supposed to appeal to younger readers. Sex had been my area of expertise

---

* "[Michael quit] because of me, but it wasn't something I planned. What happened was that I was working on the radio hour and I was living with Michael, who was producing the radio hour. It was Easter Sunday and I was just coming in to work to pick Michael up so we could go out to dinner. He was finishing up the radio hour, which had to be done and shipped on Sundays to the various stations. So I came in and Matty [Simmons, who was funding the magazine] had given my desk away to his son. And I was furious, so I went into Michael and I said, "Take my material off the show!" And he and Bob Tischler, who later became a producer of *Saturday Night* under Dick Ebersol, were finishing the show, and if they had taken my material out then they would have been there for another fourteen hours and it would have really screwed things up. So this was the leverage that I had. So Michael called Matty at home, and Matty said, "If your girlfriend doesn't like it, she can quit. And if you don't like it, you can quit too." And Michael said, "I quit!"

at the *National Lampoon,* because I'd found that when I wrote about sex, they were much more accepting of my ideas. Like, I wrote a parody of *The Story of O,* things like that. Because a former *Lampoon* guy, Terry Catchpole, was the editor of this front section of *Oui* magazine, he started throwing me work. And really, the *Playboy* organization kept us going for about a year. They were great. When they said that the check was in the mail, it was. And you know how that can be. They paid you top dollar, they gave you advances, and they paid you on time. And we were able to live that way. And so I was doing this for *Oui* and then I sold a book, *Titters: The First Collection of Humor by Women,* with Deanne Stillman. And right at that point is when Lorne Michaels came into our lives because of Marilyn Suzanne Miller, who recommended Michael to Lorne. Interestingly enough, Michael kind of got that job because of a woman who he wasn't sleeping with: Marilyn. She was a big fan of his, and she recommended him to Lorne, and Lorne decided to hire him for *SNL* and then he also decided to hire me.

And when Lorne offered me a job, I turned him down, because I said, "Well, I'm doing this book!" And I was like, "Late-night television, who cares?" I thought of television as a lava lamp with sound. And so then a friend of mine said, "No, are you crazy?" And Lorne just basically lied to me and said, "Oh, you can do the show and the book! No problem!" So my first year on the show was pretty crazy, because I was trying to do both things at once.

Initially they were paying me and Michael the same and then NBC said, "No, wait, that's a mistake. We didn't mean to pay you the same." And I went to Lorne and I said, "This can't be. We have to be paid the same!" Plus, the money was gone. I'd spent it. We are talking about a big $750 a week, which to us was largesse—unimaginable largesse. And then Lorne, bless him, just told them that they had to retroactively change it and pay us the same. And they did.

ROSIE SHUSTER Lorne Michaels entered my life when I was really, really young. I had skipped a year in school, so I was really pretty young for my age, and Lorne followed me home from school when I had just hit tenth grade and should have been in ninth grade and that was it! I had grown up, was growing up, in a comedy household. My dad and his partner were world famous in Canada—they did more *Ed Sullivan*

Shows than Topo Gigio, which was the little mouse that appeared every third week or something. And they were also live from New York on the weekend and everybody watched, so there was something in that whole formula that definitely caught Lorne's attention. And he got a real major mentoring from my dad, who loved to talk about show business.

So I just want to let the record show that a lot of Lorne's education came from that relationship. I certainly soaked it up growing up, but it wasn't such formal mentoring as it was with Lorne. And then later Lorne started to do UC Follies shows [at University College at the University of Toronto], just like my dad had, [and when I got to college] I found my way into doing those shows with him. We were together for at least eight years before we ever got married, but I was always trailing Lorne. We went to the same camp, we went to Europe together. In college, he always gave me his notebooks and his textbooks. He didn't want me to take psychology, he wanted me to take political science. So there was a lot of shaping going on. He had very strong opinions about me and I wasn't the most well-formed human at that point in time. So I both soaked it up and, you know, rebelled against it—a combo—all against the backdrop of the sixties and women's lib and all this other stuff.

So I did some writing [for the UC Follies], I did some performing at that point, but I was shy. After college, with a comedy partner, Lorne started doing the *Hart & Lorne Terrific Hour*, which was sketch comedy somewhere between *Ed Sullivan* and *Laugh-In* but without all the fast cuts. It was a produced show, so it was not live and it was done out of Toronto for the CBC; there were about four a year. The format was very much the same format as my dad's show, and Lorne became the straight man as my dad had been. So there was really like a template that was laid out that Lorne kind of poured himself into. I worked on those shows.

I also wrote for a CBC show called *Little People* with Jack Barry and Dan Enright—the same scoundrels that got chased out of the States for fixing the quiz show *Twenty One*. I had a few odd writing jobs, including writing comic vignettes for a dinky legal game show called *This Is the Law*. And then I joined Lorne to write several episodes of *The Hart & Lorne Terrific Hour*. As a child bride in L.A., I snuck a few monologues into *Rowan & Martin's Laugh-In* that had Hart and Lorne's initials on them. I was unpaid and uncredited, but when they aired, I felt

The "mothers of invention" of the late fifties and early sixties: Phyllis Diller (*above left*), who believed that "to refer to oneself in a negative way is always a good way to say hello to an audience"; Joan Rivers (*above right*), whose early stage persona focused on the perils of dating; and Elaine May (*left*), whose improvised routines with Mike Nichols had a more intellectual bent. (Above left, courtesy of Phyllis Diller; left and above right, Photofest)

Testing the notoriously conservative waters of network TV: Marlo Thomas (*left*) created and starred in the sitcom *That Girl*, which aired from 1966 to 1971. "We couldn't say 'pregnant!'" writer Carl Reiner remembers. The variety show *Rowan & Martin's Laugh-In* debuted in 1967 and blended political comedy with sillier fare—Goldie Hawn (*below*) played the ditz. The show boasted an impressive female cast, including (*bottom*, from left to right) Teresa Graves, Hawn, Judy Carne, Ruth Buzzi, and Jo Anne Worley. (Left, courtesy of Marlo Thomas; below and bottom, courtesy of George Schlatter Productions)

THE SCUM ALSO RISES BY HUNTER S. THOMPSON

ROLLING STONE

ISSUE NO. 171   OCTOBER 10, 1974   75¢ UK25p

In this issue,
the first of two parts:

JIVE
TIMES

The Comedy,
Theater and Routine Lives
of Richard Pryor and
Lily Tomlin.
By David Felton

LA BOWIE'S RETURN
THE MOODY BLUES'
TRIAL SEPARATION

Lily Tomlin, another *Laugh-In* alum, came out of a different scene; she honed her craft in the clubs of downtown New York. She and Richard Pryor gave a sharp voice to the counterculture and ushered television into the modern era. In 1974, David Felton wrote in *Rolling Stone*, "They have introduced a version of comedy which goes way beyond laughter . . . It is real theater, a theater of the routine, the blemished, the pretentious, the lame—the common affairs and crutches of common people." (Annie Leibovitz/Rolling Stone, LLC)

In the 1970s, *The Mary Tyler Moore Show* loosened network strictures and expanded the role of women in the creative process. The sitcom, which starred Mary (*above,* left) and Valerie Harper (*above,* right), riled CBS brass by openly discussing the life of an unmarried, independent thirty-year-old, but the show garnered critical acclaim. It also consistently hired female writers, like Treva Silverman (*left*), who was the first woman to win an Emmy for Writer of the Year (Series), and female directors, like Joan Darling (*below*). (Top, courtesy of Allan Burns; left, courtesy of Treva Silverman; below, courtesy of Joan Darling)

Above: The men of *The Mary Tyler Moore Show* helped to defend the show's characterizations, especially against the conservatism of network execs. From left to right: Treva Silverman, John C. Chulay, Walter Cronkite, and two of the show's guiding forces, James L. Brooks and Ed. Weinberger. (Cronkite was to appear on the show that week.) *Left*: In 1967, Carol Burnett, pictured here with Don Knotts, became the first woman to host her own variety show. *The Carol Burnett Show* was one of the most beloved shows of all time— and the last of its kind. (Above, courtesy of Treva Silverman; left, Photofest)

Improv groups proved to be valuable training grounds for female comics. Barbara Harris (*above left*) was a founding member of the Compass Players and later was the first female member of Second City, both in Chicago; Maya Rudolph (*above center*), Kathy Griffin (*above right*), and Lisa Kudrow (*below*, with Patrick Bristow) all began their careers in the Groundlings, based out of Los Angeles. (Above left, Photofest; above center, above right, and below, courtesy of the Groundlings)

Lorne Michaels (*left*, with his then-wife, Rosie Shuster) created and produced *Saturday Night Live*, which changed the face of sketch comedy in the 1970s; Rosie Shuster was one of three women to write for the show when it began. Among her many memorable creations was Uncle Roy (*below*)—"a lovable pervert, if you will," says comedy writer Alan Zweibel—played by Buck Henry. (Left, courtesy of Rosie Shuster; below, NBCUPB)

Elayne Boosler became known at the New York Improv in 1973, where her confident, sexy stand-up defied precedent. The comedian Tom Dreesen remembers, "She was talking about hookers and she said, 'How can they do that? Go to bed with a perfect stranger without dinner and a movie first.'" (Elizabeth Wolynski)

like I was getting away with murder. And then, if I was embarrassed about a show, like I was about *Keep On Truckin'*, then I wrote under the pseudonym of Sue Denim. I also wrote for Lily Tomlin and got nominated for an Emmy.

By the time *Saturday Night Live* started, Lorne and I had been married seven or eight years. We were together and apart, and together and apart. We were not particularly together when the show started, but he still wanted me to do it and we had to discuss how that was going to go, because it was a show that, on one level, was what we had been talking about all our lives. I felt like it was my birthright, like I have to show up and do it. We were not divorced but the future of our relationship was *very* much up in the air. I didn't come do the show so that I would be his wife—it was clear to both of us that that was undetermined. But in terms of my sensibilities, I felt very, very invested in what that show was, and where it was going. It just felt so right that I would be part of that. And Lorne wanted me to be part of it, and he was very clear about that.

I met Anne the month before the show went on the air. Michael O'Donoghue and Anne Beatts were like this fixture at the *Lampoon*. I had heard that they were going for this Scott and Zelda form of comedy. I don't exactly know what they were going for, but she used to wear these secondhand outfits and there was some self-mythologizing going on and it was kind of cool. And then I think Anne and I started working together by the fourth show, because Lily came in and hosted, and then Candice Bergen came in, and when there were girl things, we were just thrown together by Lorne—I don't think Marilyn Miller came until later that year—and I think he thought we would mesh together and complement each other. And because we were women—I think that was definitely a piece of it! Definitely. There were mostly guys and it was mostly guy hosts, but we were the girls, so a lot of stuff fell to us.

ANNE BEATTS We didn't start as friends. In fact, I think that there was a little bit of competitiveness—definitely competitiveness—and problems between us initially. But we ended up as friends; more than friends, in a way. Not lovers, which was what people used to always think, because we spent so much time together and slept at the office. Rosie was always irked by it and I would always go, "Well, let's just embrace it, you know?" I would just go, "Well, you don't think we spend all that time writing, do you?" So we became like army buddies. We really collaborated on everything. Rosie and I formed a combination where we played to each other's strengths and weaknesses. Rosie has a very unique and original sense of humor, which sometimes tends to be more whimsical than mine, whereas I am more logical, a structure person. So I think that sometimes she was able to give an element of absurdity to our humor that I think we really benefited from. But we wrote everything—line by line—together.

MARILYN SUZANNE MILLER I wrote absolutely alone except for the musical numbers, which I originated and forced them to do despite their fearing that they would be too Carol Burnettish. I ended up working with Cheryl Hardwick and Paul Shaffer a lot and they were not Carol Burnettish. They were the rock and roll that we all grew up with. That's the only time I wrote with somebody.

None of this is to say that sexism at Saturday Night Live *didn't exist. To survive—and succeed—the show's women needed a thick skin and firm resolve to push through the nonsense of the men. Which is exactly what they did, creating some of the darkest, most eye-opening sketches ever to appear on the show. Their scenes weren't overtly feminist as skits had been on the Lily Tomlin specials, and they didn't always mean to make a feminist point. In fact, the women writers had no intention of just writing for women. But by creating scenes with strong female characters and caricatures, and by tapping into their personal observations and experiences, they opened audiences up to the world of women, offering a sharp point of view on topics that had previously been ignored or taboo.*

ALAN ZWEIBEL On SNL the only credo we really had was "Let's make each other laugh. And if we do that, hopefully there's an audience that will also find it funny, find us funny." We were confident that you didn't have to spoon-feed the audience. Don't try to predict what they know and what they don't know; assume they do know. It makes for a smarter form.

ANNE BEATTS I think there are things women know about that men don't, because women are immersed in male culture but men aren't immersed in female culture. So if a man sees an ad for a $500 cream in the magazine, he turns the page, while a woman wonders, "Oh, is this better than the $200 cream?" So there is kind of a subculture of female culture. There was a lot of opposition a lot of times to ideas [tapping into that knowledge]. I did this piece called "Angora Bouquet" with Jane Curtin and Bill Murray during the second or third year of the show, and it was about a soap that washes your brain. "Hi, I'm stupid but beautiful and I found a soap that helps me stay that way." No one thought it was funny. It was like, "Ugh! Not funny." And then finally it played in the studio and people laughed. And it was like, "Oh, okay."

ALAN ZWEIBEL   Guys make mistakes when they write for women. They think every other line has to be about periods or breasts, as if this is all women talk about or think about.

ANNE BEATTS   There was a pervasive attitude of sexism. And I would say that Lorne was the counterweight against it in a lot of instances, although I guess in some cases he implicitly tolerated it. But he was an equal opportunity employer.

ROSIE SHUSTER   It was a boys' club and that was just how things were. And you'd try to make inroads by letting the work talk for itself, and you just couldn't curl up and die because you didn't have somebody's approval.

ANNE BEATTS   John Belushi used to regularly ask for us to be fired. "Fire the girls!" You know, the chicks-aren't-funny school. And he refused to be in stuff we wrote. We wrote something for the Lily Tomlin episode called "Hard Hats" and it was about female hard hats. And they were being taught how to heckle men and how to yell at men from construction sites. And John was supposed to be the demonstration model. He refused to do it. I think because he felt self-conscious wearing a tank top, partly, so we had to get Danny Aykroyd instead.

Another interesting piece of casting was when John was supposed to play the nerd character to Gilda's nerd in a piece that we wrote called "Nerd Rock." I was inspired to write it because of Elvis Costello—I thought, "He's not punk rock, he's nerd rock." And we had Billy Murray doing the DJ, because he had this sleazy DJ record-business Jerry Aldini character that he used to do. And so we had him being this sleazy DJ and we had John as one of the nerds that had joined this nerd rock group. And John refused be in it. So we had to switch it all around and we had to make Danny the DJ and Billy the nerd character. Even Dan, when we first pitched the nerds idea, said, "Nerds are *Laverne & Shirley.*" Which was not a compliment. Anyway, Billy and Gilda became the nerds and that became a big thing, which actually played into their whole relationship. That was one of the examples where John's refusal to be in our sketch turned out to be a blessing.

John was a law unto himself. If he didn't want to do something, he wasn't going to do it. Lorne wasn't going to make him be in it.

ROSIE SHUSTER Belushi was very strange. Jim Downey and I would team up and there were a couple of things we wrote and Belushi had no idea I wrote them. So he would go to Downey and say, "Write more of that!" And so when he didn't know I was on the sketch, suddenly he wanted more! Yeah, he definitely had a misogynist streak in him. He definitely did.

MARILYN SUZANNE MILLER He would decide "I hate Jane," because I think Jane intimidated him and seemed too proper and too—you know, who knows? John was nutty. But yeah, there were guys who would go around saying, "Women aren't funny." Al Franken would say it. All right, fine.

ALAN ZWEIBEL John didn't want to work with Jews at one point! There was a sketch that I wrote, it was in the news that Elizabeth Taylor choked on a chicken leg, and somebody had to come along and give her the Heimlich maneuver. And I wrote this piece for Weekend Update. And I knew that John was mad at me that week and he wouldn't do it. So we put another writer's name on it, a guy named Brian McConnachie. I'm not saying that's why John said he would do it, but my instinct was if he saw my name he was going to be prejudiced against it for whatever reason. We all took our turns being in Belushi's crosshairs. The women much more. John was a big fucking bear, and he would be an asshole one day to all the women, and he would put down their ideas when they were being pitched. Or he would purposely not deliver them during read-through, so he basically would sabotage their sketches. And then the next day this big fat Belushi would come in with six bouquets of roses for people that he offended, for the women, and he put them on their doors.

I don't have a strong conviction about what the office politics were. I know there were complaints, and I'm sure they were real. All I know is, if I ever look at one of our old shows, there are certain sketches that I know Rosie wrote with Anne, and that I know that Marilyn Miller wrote. Lorne was the ultimate arbiter as to what went on and what didn't, and when we first started the show, Lorne said, "This is a comedy variety show," and he explained that that means there are a variety of different kinds of comedy.

MARILYN SUZANNE MILLER I will tell you that if there are boys, there will always be a club, but it didn't do anything to me. It had no effect on me. Maybe I was spoiled, maybe I got applause at read-throughs and I did what I wanted, and it worked and I accepted an Emmy for the staff. Look, I refuse to focus on this boys' club stuff about how they sat at the table. The real thing is, who's running the show? Lorne believed that all of the girls that were actresses should have something substantial to do on the show.

The first sketch I wrote that made a big splash was the slumber party sketch with Madeline Kahn. And what was great about Lorne was that Lorne got what each of us was about, which was very difficult to do in a room full of Danny Aykroyds. You're pitching stuff and then there are these guys imitating chain saws. And you can't quite compete in humor and energy level with those guys. And I just very quietly said, "This would be about some girls at a slumber party describing what they thought sex was going to be like for the first time." And in about one minute Lorne said, "Okay, put that card at the top of the show."

ANNE BEATTS Rosie Shuster and I really felt that we had this obligation to cover the women on the show. We were sort of expected to pick up the pieces, as it were. But we did feel a strong obligation to make sure that the women were well served on the show and were not left playing these subsidiary roles.

ROSIE SHUSTER We wanted to get Gilda and Jane and Laraine on the air and do some female-identified stuff that was fresh. And it was coming right out of feminism and women's lib, and nothing on television really reflected the fact that there had been a cultural revolution. Music and movies were vastly ahead of television. Certainly *Carol Burnett* was never going to do that, and *I Love Lucy* didn't rock that boat. The few Lily Tomlin shows that went out, maybe they did, but that was pretty limited viewership in terms of addressing a bigger culture.

ANNE BEATTS Gilda, Laraine, and Jane all had to share a dressing room for the first two or three years. Also, they were always called "the girls." And Lorne would come around to us, me and Rosie, at two in the morning and say, "Well, what have you got for the girls?" And then he would sometimes say, "Can you put Garrett in it?" [Garrett Morris was the lone African-American in the cast.] It would be like, "No. No! It's set in a convent, he can't be in it." Somehow it became our responsibility to write for *the girls*, like we had to cover them, because if we didn't then the guys would just write stuff for them that said, like, "Well, Mr. Jones will see you now." You can bet that if they wrote a sketch with a doctor in it, it wasn't going to be for one of the women. Even when Lily Tomlin was hosting, Franken and Tom Davis had written a sketch about the monopoly of AT&T and the line was like, "We don't care. We don't have to. We're the phone company!" And they had written the line for a male spokesperson. And I said, "Wait a minute! We are going to have Ernestine here. Why don't we have Ernestine do it?" But it's that institutionalized sexism that spokespeople, doctors, lawyers, airplane pilots, whatever—hardhats—are men!

ALAN ZWEIBEL A lot of the girl sketches were written by the girls, and that doesn't mean they weren't funny. One of the funniest sketches we'd ever done was something called Uncle Roy. Buck Henry played this perverted uncle babysitting for his nieces—I think it was his nieces. Laraine and Gilda played these very young, pigtailed nieces, and they loved it when Uncle Roy came over and babysat. But he would make them do all these things where you could see their panties. You never thought that they were in danger, don't worry about that, but that was something Buck Henry was able to pull off: a lovable pervert, if you will. They were very funny in their enthusiasm—"Oh, Uncle Roy." You'd see their panties, or you'd see them sliding down the banister for no reason whatsoever other than Uncle Roy wanted to take a picture of it.

ANNE BEATTS   Uncle Roy was about the lighter side of child molestation. Dan and Rosie were living together at the time—not throughout the whole show, but in the middle part of the show—and Dan would play around with that character with Rosie at home, you know, pretending to be Uncle Roy.

ROSIE SHUSTER   And when we did Uncle Roy and gave it to Buck Henry, Danny was upset that I didn't have him do it. The guys did lobby to be in things. When Chevy was a doctor in the National Uvula or National Pancreas Society—I used to do some bogus public service announcements—the guys would come to me and say "Why didn't you put me in it?" Belushi might have been the only one who didn't come to me.

MARILYN SUZANNE MILLER   I wrote the Czech brothers with Steve Martin and Danny, and the reason was because Danny came to me and said, "Hey, you know how those guys hit on you and they were cabdrivers and they ran from the tanks in Czechoslovakia and now they're here and they think they're really cool?" Now, that translated to me, because, as a woman, yes, I had been hit on by millions of those guys. So that's how I got brought into that. It was a guy-girl thing. But I always wrote from the point of view of being a woman.

While the writers worked behind the scenes, it was up to the performers to bring the female characters to life on-screen. Of the three female cast members, Gilda Radner made the deepest impact. There is hardly a female sketch comic today who does not claim Radner as an inspiration for her comedy career. Radner was discovered at the Toronto outpost of Second City and she was the first cast member hired for SNL. The roster of diverse female characters she developed included caricatures of some of the most visible women of the day—Barbara Walters, aka Baba Wawa—and original characters conjured out of her own head—newscaster Roseanne Roseannadanna, the deaf schoolmarm Emily Litella.

Her female costars—Laraine Newman and Jane Curtin—struggled for the same kind of attention. Newman, whose first television appearance was on a Lily Tomlin special, had been a member of the Groundlings, another popular incubator for SNL comics. She was just twenty-three years old when she joined SNL, making her youngest of the three women (Radner was twenty-seven; Curtin was twenty-eight), and most certainly putting Newman at a disadvantage. While she had her successes, the on-screen pressures combined with the sex-and-drugs-fueled lifestyle behind the scenes took its toll, and Newman became anorexic and started snorting heroin. (Radner, it should be noted, was bulimic.) Curtin's problem was that she didn't party enough. She came to the show a married woman and went home when the day was done. She didn't stick around and lobby for sketches like the rest of the cast, so she didn't build the necessary alliances that helped propel the other players to the air. That said, the three women were integral members of a legendary cast and their diverging sensibilities added important feminine flavors to the mix.

MARILYN SUZANNE MILLER You've gotta have the fire in the belly as a female performer to even get them to look at you. It stinks, but that's the way it is. To use Gilda as an example, one night she had nothing in the show and she went on the air and she said at the beginning of the show, "Mom, you can go to bed. I have nothing on the show tonight," and she walked off. Yes, it takes a lot of balls and a lot of charm and a lot of talent and a lot of staying up late and a lot of getting Lorne to look at you, not as a big pain in the ass, but as somebody with a lot of talent to get on the air.

Gilda wanted to be on that screen a lot, and I'm sure you've heard the story about how we were up writing in the middle of the night and some people called her—this is an Anne Beatts story—and said, "We need your help, please come over." "Oh, I'm in bed. I'm in bed." And then she came over, and in fact she had been fully dressed but she put on her pajamas to come over to the building to make people feel sorry for her. Each of them pushed for what they did. I won't say that Gilda didn't push the hardest, because she did. But that's part of how it works in showbiz.

MAYA RUDOLPH, SNL cast member, 2000–2007 I don't think there is a comedy girl that I have worked with whose first comedy girl crush wasn't Gilda. There was something about Gilda. She had a light about her. She had this unbelievable smile—unless she was doing something serious, like the dancing thing with Steve Martin. And then the nightlife quotient of *SNL* in the seventies, it was like the most delicious era of New York nightlife. And in comedy, there were these cool people having fun together, they went out after, and you know that they were sleeping together, and, God, how glamorous.

ROSIE SHUSTER   Laraine was quite brilliant in her own right. Originally we had seen her in the Lily Tomlin special and I remember Lorne and me going to the Groundlings and seeing Laraine. And she really stood out, because she had this ability to nail a nuance. But Laraine, as she later realized, was really averse to repeating things. She didn't want to be like Marty Allen going "Hello, there," just reduced to some catchphrase. She didn't want to repeat certain characters that would have gone really strong and big, and she would have made a much bigger impact, I think, had she made her peace with that. She's completely aware of that now. She flubbed her lines a few times and I think too much was made of that, but writers would go with whoever could sock it home and make them look good too.

ALAN ZWEIBEL   Everybody wanted to write for Gilda, because as a writer, you aligned yourself with somebody who the audience wanted to see, and it was easier. If I wrote something for Gilda, there was a pretty good shot that it would get on the air.

MARILYN SUZANNE MILLER   Laraine was unbelievably gifted with voices, and she was the first person ever to do that Valley Girl voice and the first person ever to do the Newswoman, which I think is hysterical: "I'm standing, Chevy, here in so-and-so place."

GARY AUSTIN   Laraine went to New York and had a miserable time. She called me up crying all the time. I said, "What's wrong?" She said, "They're not writing for me." I said, "Well, write for yourself. You're a great writer. That's why you got *Saturday Night Live.*" She said, "It won't help. They're the writers. I can't write for me." I said, "Go to Lorne." She said, "He's the producer." And I knew what she meant. I knew he would turn a deaf ear.

ALAN ZWEIBEL   Jane Curtin was a supreme straight woman. Very, very funny that way. There was a Vivian Vance thing going on. You take a two-shot of Gilda and Jane on Weekend Update and while Gilda would do Emily Litella or Roseanne Roseannadanna, there was something about Jane's slow burn. She was brilliant at it, maintaining protocol while somebody else is breaking protocol, until she finally has just had it and blows up. If you go back to the Marx Brothers, Margaret Dumont used to do that, although her character wasn't as smart as Jane Curtin. Jane Curtin knew what was right, what was wrong, what was acceptable, what wasn't. Her patience was being tried, and the fun was, when would she finally explode?

ROSIE SHUSTER   Jane was just solid and stable and could deliver. She often was the straight man of the women, though she could do some pretty funny characters. I remember writing this thing once, the Dating Zone, and she played this very blowsy barfly called Iris de Flaminio, and she cracked me up so much. She just did this blowsy slattern kind of voice. I thought she was hysterically funny.

MARILYN SUZANNE MILLER   I did a piece with Danny and Jane about two people meeting in their old hometown after college. She was a captain of the cheerleaders and he was the head of the AV squad, a total nerd. And it was about how he thought now they were equal and he could just ask her out or anything. And of course it ended up that he couldn't.

ROSIE SHUSTER   I suppose Jane wanted a life that was outside of the show. She alone, of the original writers and the original performers, didn't hang around the show. She went home every night and kept a stable relationship going. The rest of us were personal disasters that way. I guess some of the guy writers had stable relationships to go back to, but we didn't. We'd spend two or three nights sleeping on the couch there—we would camp out there for three weeks.

I think if she wanted to develop more quirky comedy roles, she probably would have had to campaign for them a little bit more. Instead, Jane found niches where she had a good presence. She was always the consummate professional, and she often surprised us with her versatility, but like I said, she wasn't campaigning for it in the same way that I guess Gilda and Laraine, to some extent, were. Of all of them,

I guess, Gilda really showed up the most, late at night, and would work with us and collaborate.*

MARILYN SUZANNE MILLER Gilda punched Woody Allen in the stomach once. He would like suck all the air out of a place. He'd go into Elaine's and he had his own table and he would only talk to the people that he knew. Anytime you were in a room with him, everybody wanted to run over and talk to him, but he wouldn't talk to anybody. So we were at a party one day. Jean Doumanian and Woody were standing in the corner of the room, and there was Woody sucking all the air out toward him.† And none of us were allowed to talk to him and he wouldn't talk to any of us. And Gilda, in her usual way of just getting a message through her heart of what was wrong and having some completely unusual way of expressing it, just turned around and punched Woody in the stomach. He basically recovered, ignored it, and went back to talking to Jean. But what Gilda was saying was "Why don't you come and talk to us? We admire you so much." It was great that she did that.

ROSIE SHUSTER I had first heard about Gilda from a mutual friend of ours, Peter Gold, who had always described this unbelievably darling girl that I guess he had a crush on. I finally saw her in *Godspell* in Toronto and Gilda was just so winning onstage. She had a little face stuck in the middle of all this hair and there was something that just leaped out about it. She was just an incredibly accessible person, really brave, and she could really hold her own on the stage with guys.

JOYCE SLOANE, executive producer, Second City Gilda had the ability to embrace the entire audience every time she went onstage. You just felt like she was putting her arms around all of them. Andrea Martin

---

* Ironically, Curtin had the most accomplished post-*SNL* career of all three women. She had a tremendously successful run on the sitcoms *Kate & Allie*, for which she won two Emmys, and *3rd Rock from the Sun*, costarring with John Lithgow.

† Doumanian was an associate producer on *Saturday Night Live*. In 1980 Michaels left the series—he would return five years later—and Doumanian took over the top job. She lasted just a year, and the season was considered a disaster. Doumanian eventually became a producer of Allen's films.

[then of Second City, later a star on the sketch comedy show *SCTV*] was a little concerned about Gilda, because she used to say, "You really like Gilda better than me." And I would deny it. She would say, "Gilda's around every corner."

ROSIE SHUSTER She was just a very, very, very lovable character; a very winning and funny female. She didn't have that "count your balls" thing when she would leave the room. In those days it was hard to be funny and sexy, and yet Gilda somehow was able to be soft and winning and not threatening.

I always think of Gilda having the daddy that just doted on her and she really entertained for him. She knew how to get love through performing. That was just something that was second nature for her. But she was also immensely talented and smart—smart in an intuitive way. She wasn't a cold technical impressionist. That always blew my mind at *SNL*. You would sit there for the auditions and usually someone would come down the pike who was a flawless impressionist. They were just technically wild. And at first you were so excited because it was like, "Oh my God, we've got to get this person." And then you would recognize that the person didn't really have a funny bone. You would just watch with your mouth open rather than sitting there laughing. Gilda found an element of caricature where she could zoom in on some aspect that made the caricaturization come alive in a funny way.

ALAN ZWEIBEL Gilda may not have been as good a technician as Laraine was. I think that whoever Gilda was playing, her personality came through the character. So it was Gilda with the funny wig, Gilda with the funny accent, Gilda falling down. No matter who she called her character, you felt you knew her. I think that's why, when she died, people felt that they had lost somebody they had known, even if they'd never met her. There was a part of her that came through the screen.

I was producing the Weekend Update, and there had been a public service announcement that Rosie Shuster had written—I believe she wrote it—that had been on a month before. It was called Hire the Incompetent and in it were three vignettes with three different characters, all talking about why they'd been fired from their job. In the vignette that Gilda did, she put on this wig and had this Hispanic dialect and she talked about how she got fired from Burger King for using hamburger patties under her eyes. It worked all right. About a month later, we were out to dinner, and I said, "Listen, that character you did, why don't we move her into Weekend Update? Let's give her a name and let her do consumer reports." And there was a local newscaster here in New York in the late seventies, her name was Rose Ann Scamardella, she was on WABC. And I said, "Let's let her do consumer reports, not unlike Rose Ann Scamardella." And Gilda said, "Okay, can we call her Roseanne Roseannadanna?" She didn't even take a breath. And I said, "Where the fuck did you come up with that?" Well, there was a song in the sixties that was called "The Name Game." It was this silly novelty song where you took somebody's name and you put all these syllables in front of the name—like, take Johnny. This woman sang, "Johnny, Johnny, bo bonny, banana fanna, fo fonny." And the singer kept doing this, with different names. And somehow, if you were to sing that song with the name Roseanne, you'd get Roseanne Roseannadanna. It came off the top of Gilda's head. I'm going, "Fine, fuck, I could do that." And it just evolved.

"Well, Jane, Mr. Richard Feder of New York City writes in and says, 'Dear Roseanne Roseannadanna, I got no heat, what should I do?'" She looks up. "Well, Mr. Feder, I want to help you, because I know how you feel. Once I didn't have no heat and I was afraid I was going to come down with the flu. I had a temperature, I had the chills. I didn't have too many blankets in my apartment. So I went outside to get some soup, 'cause it's supposed to be good for you if you're clogged up. I go to the restaurant, and I ordered soup. Well, I got it, and wouldn't you know, there was a hair in it. Can you imagine that?" She extends her two index fingers about a foot apart: "It was about this long." She continues: "I thought I was going to die. Now, let me ask you this. Did you ever eat a hamburger and there's a hard thing in it? You know, it's like a toenail, and you know it's not part of the hamburger, but you separate the meat and the pickle and the lettuce and the tomato all on one side in your mouth and finally you get on your tongue that little thing and it's like a bone but it's not a bone. I keep asking myself, 'Roseanne Roseanneadanna, if they can make a coffee you like without caffeine, why can't they make a hamburger you like with no toenails?'"

ALAN ZWEIBEL   Richard Feder was a guy from Fort Lee, New Jersey, who was my brother-in-law, married to my sister. So I had him writing these long dumb letters that she would address. It evolved into a formula where he would write a letter, and she would start addressing it, and get on a rant. I'll give you an example: There was something called the Great American Smokeout where everybody was supposed to stop smoking for a week. So I'd sit with Gilda in a restaurant and I'd say, "Okay, what's the issue?" So the Great American Smokeout is happening, I'll have Feder write you a letter saying he stopped smoking, and he gained weight, he started to sweat, he started to fart, he started to do this, and started to do that." And she'd read it and say, "Sounds like an attractive guy, you belong in New Jersey." [Then I would say to Gilda] "Where did you go to lose the weight?" Oh, she joined a health club.

"Okay, what do you like about health clubs?" I would sit down and I would write everything that she would quote. I would navigate her: "What kind of machines do you work out with?" "What's it like seeing other people naked?" And I would just write and take notes. "What celebrity would you see in a compromising position?" She would say Joyce Brothers. "All right, where'd you see her?" "Sauna. Joyce Brothers had a little sweat ball hanging out her nose, it was dangling and it just wouldn't fall all the way." Now we had the letter, which was the issue, and we had how it related to Roseanne. And those became our beats, if you will. I would have these legal pads, nine, ten pages of stuff. Gilda would go home or on a date, into the night somewhere. I'd go back to the office and I just started connecting the dots and giving it form. I'd be up all night writing it, she would come in noon the next day when the actors came in, Saturday, the day of the show. I would have waiting for her nine pages of this Roseanne Roseannadanna that I wrote, connecting these dots with my own jokes, some of my own things that we hadn't discussed. She would take a red pen and just start looking at the pages, crossing shit out and making arrows and changing words. I'd get pissed off. I was up all night, God knows where she was. I'd go upstairs to my office and I'd look at what she did and I'd go, "Fuck. She made it better. Oh yeah, well, I'll show her." So I took my pen and edited what she edited. This went back and forth all day, until we would do it in dress rehearsal, and then edit it some more, and put it on the air.

MARILYN SUZANNE MILLER   I'll tell you another story about Gilda so you understand what I mean about being charming. One time Gilda had a date for Christmas at the home, in Brazil, of a guy she knew. She was real excited. She flew to Brazil, a million hours. She got taken from the airport to the mansion, which was out in God knows where. She got out of the car after traveling for a thousand million hours. She was so excited. The guy met her at the door. He said, "Gilda, I'd like you to meet my girlfriend or my fiancée, blah, blah, blah, blah." Well, Gilda went, "How do you do? May I use your phone?" Called a cab and within three minutes was on her way to the airport to get on a plane to go to New York. And you know what? When she went home, she had a date with Elliott Gould the next day. Now, let me just say what that takes. Now, true, Gilda had an endless supply of money—and not from work, from her family. But she got on a plane, she went back to New York, she wasted no tears over this guy. Gilda just had that flying-above-the-earth-in-your-mind determination.

ALAN ZWEIBEL   I don't know about body image. Gilda was bulimic, everybody knows that. I'm sure bulimia has other psychological roots. All I can tell you is that Gilda once told me that if she'd had her choice, she would prefer to be a ballerina. I said, "Why?" She said, "Ballerinas have control of their bodies. They're at one with the world around them and their environment." It's poetic, the movement, in control. It's poetry in motion. Whereas comedy, she said, was what was wrong with the world. You laugh because something's too big, too small, too fat, too thin, it's things that go awry. I guess, as somebody that struggled with food, and who had her own demons, she just wanted to be at peace. Gilda's tombstone says, "Gilda Radner Wilder," her dates, and "Comedienne–Ballerina."

5

. . . .

I Am Woman

At the same time that Saturday Night Live *started transforming sketch comedy, a revolution started hitting stand-up comedy. Until the 1970s, there was no such thing as a club designed exclusively around comedy acts—comedians had shared the stage with musicians, singers, and magicians. But the transformation of the New York Improv into a venue for comedians, and the addition of clubs like Catch a Rising Star on New York's Upper East Side and the Comedy Store on Sunset Boulevard in L.A., opened a whole new chapter in comedy. It was the era of the comedy club. Richard Lewis, Andy Kaufman, Jay Leno, and Richard Belzer were the hot young comics making their name at these clubs in the early part of the decade. And then there was Elayne Boosler.*

When Boosler emerged at the New York Improv in 1973, she was the first female stand-up to make waves since Joan Rivers and the first to evoke the women's lib attitude of the time. (Lily Tomlin, remember, was not a joke-teller.) Boosler set the tone for the women of the decade, and by the end of the 1970s female comics were descending on comedy clubs, pushing the limits of what women could confront onstage with their acts. And while no woman would achieve real success until the 1980s, when stand-up comedy exploded, the women of the 1970s indisputably broke new ground. They unshackled themselves from the old-school comedy conventions of Diller and Rivers (self-deprecation, husband jokes) and began the process of multiplying and amplifying the female voice—even if the glass ceiling they faced was harder to crack than the one faced by their sketch and sitcom peers.

JAN WALLMAN [In the late 1960s and 1970s] nightclubs started to split up. The folk scene was really the first thing to move out of regular nightclubs and into folk rooms, jazz moved into jazz clubs, American popular song music stayed in the cabarets, and in comedy there began to develop actual comedy clubs.

CHRIS ALBRECHT Stand-up comedy is a very different art form than anything else in the entertainment business, because you have to go and practice it every night—if you can, if you're lucky. Nobody's going to pay you to do that; you're your own writer, your own editor, your own actor, your own producer, your own director. And the only way you're really going to get any better is to get someone to put you on-stage in front of people—paying customers. So there needs to be business derived around that, and that was kind of the advent of these showcase clubs, of which the Improv was the first one.

JOANNE ASTROW, comedian When we started at the Improv in New York, it wasn't all stand-up. It was stand-up and singers. So you did not have to be a stand-up at that time.

MARK LONOW, co-owner, Improv Comedy Club The way the Improv transformed into an actual comedy club was that there was a comic sitting in the house. It might have been Bernie Travis, and he went over to a comic named Dave Astor, who'd been performing at the Improv, and said, "How'd you get up there?" and Astor said, "I just asked Budd [Friedman]." So Benny got in a cab and went downtown to the Village and told all the comics who were working at the Bitter End, or Café Wha?, and all those little clubs downtown, which also weren't comedy clubs. The next day, Budd shows up to open the room, and there were fifty comics waiting for stage time. So he gets a little overwhelmed. Initially, what Budd did was set it up so that it was single comic, singer, and it went all night, so he could absorb eight, ten, twelve comics, because at that time we were open until four in the morning. And over the years it actually stayed that way. The singers became less and less of the night and the comics became more and more of the night, and by the time Budd moved to Los Angeles, which was in '74, it was all comics.

RICK NEWMAN, owner, Catch a Rising Star I opened Catch on December 18, 1972. At that point there was virtually no stand-up comediennes. You had your Phyllis Diller on TV, and Joan Rivers, and there was Totie Fields at that point. They were like, your father's comedians or your mother's comedians. They weren't *our* comedians.

Elayne Boosler stood at the mic like a woman who deserved to be there. A waitress turned singer turned stand-up from Sheepshead Bay in Brooklyn, Boosler was confident, sexy, and gentle in tone. She didn't crack jokes about husband hunting or marriage, and she didn't endear herself to audiences with self-deprecating slights. Boosler, who was Jewish, the youngest child and only girl in a family of seven, was, more than anything, a product of her time and she focused her humor on subjects like religion ("The Vatican is against surrogate mothers. Good thing they didn't have that rule when Jesus was born"), sex ("What do hookers do on their nights off—type?"), and politics ("When women are depressed, they either eat or go shopping. Men invade another country"). When she first embarked on a career in entertainment at twenty-one years old, Boosler didn't set out to be a comic. She had aspirations to be a musical theater actress. She got a gig at the Improv as a waitress. At the time, Budd Friedman had a policy that all waitresses double as singers so they could perform between comedy acts. In the meantime, Boosler got to see performances by some of the hottest up-and-comers in the industry: Richard Lewis, Andy Kaufman, Richard Belzer, and Jay Leno. She fell in with the boys pretty quickly, and after only a few weeks Andy Kaufman took her aside and told her she should drop the singing and do comedy. So she prepared an act, the two became an item, and Boosler quickly rose to be the queen of comedy.

RICK NEWMAN When Elayne Boosler started as a comic, she had such a simple routine. Barbra Streisand had that hit "The Way We Were," and Elayne, who used to be a singer, would get up on that stage and go [hums song]. And then she would take a long break and then she would go [hums again], and she would just do it again. It was so silly, but her timing was impeccable and it killed! And that was the way that she opened her act, and then she would go into her material. This was early Elayne Boosler, '73 Elayne Boosler. It was a lightweight piece of material but it gave her something at the beginning to anchor her.

JOANNE ASTROW   In 1974 or '75, I would say there was really only one woman and that was Elayne Boosler. She was in her early twenties and she was the *queen* of New York comedy—first of all because she was the only one.

RICHARD LEWIS   I recall in my class of '71 coming up with Elayne Boosler. And I was sort of in a fog of comedy war there; I just didn't realize what I was getting myself into. No one really did at twenty-two or twenty-three. And Elayne was one of the few comedians who was female, who was getting good spots, and who was really strong, if not stronger than a lot of the men who dominated the scene at the time.

CHRIS ALBRECHT   Believe me, there weren't a lot of women waiting in the bar to go on. Stand-up wasn't something that women were gravitating toward at this point, because there weren't the role models for them to follow. In order to have a lot of the women after Elayne, you had to have Elayne.

CAROL LEIFER, comedian   I think a new generation really started—for me—with Elayne Boosler. Watching her is like, "Wow, there's a woman like me who's not doing stand-up from the reference point of us versus them. Women versus men." She wasn't doing an act that was like, "Am I right, ladies?" And I was just very inspired by her. She was only a couple years older than me, and the summer when I started to audition I saw her at Catch a Rising Star in New York. She was talking about the concerns of a young single woman from the city. And it wasn't what female comedy had largely been up to that point, which was "Oh, my husband this . . ." You know, Phyllis Diller with Fang, or Joan Rivers talking about being a wife and a mother. This was comedy coming from a young single woman. She had a lot of material that didn't have anything to do with sex or sexuality—they were just funny, funny jokes. I remember, she had a funny joke about "soup for one"; she had another about how she had nothing in her apartment, because, being a single woman, it wasn't very well decorated, so anytime she brought a guy over, she'd open her door and go, "Oh my God, I've been robbed!"

TOM DREESEN, comedian   There was a line that I never forgot. She was talking about hookers and she said, "How can they do that? Go to bed with a perfect stranger without dinner and a movie first."

CHRIS ALBRECHT   She was a young woman talking about dating and sex. I remember one joke: "Men want you to scream, 'You're the best,' while swearing you've never done this with anyone before." Well, gee, a young woman saying that she's had sex multiple times and not being coy about it. People weren't even talking about it offstage, let alone on-stage.

ROBIN WILLIAMS   It was amazing to see a woman stand-up, girl stand-up, and a beautiful one at the time—just gorgeous, sexy, and yet still pretty gutsy. And her jokes were sort of veiled—it seemed kind of "Oh gosh, oh golly"—but at the same time her jokes were really tough. As Letterman would say, she's funny like a guy. Being tough, but yet at the same time being beautiful and sexy, and at the same time not using that as a ploy. She would be up there just performing, telling jokes. Like she talked about the right to life and two fishermen who'll throw the fish back, but they're for the death penalty. Tough stuff but said really sweetly.

MERRILL MARKOE   She was doing the unthinkable. She combined "I'm a sexy, smart, funny woman" with a lot of political opinions, and things to say about stuff other than "I'm so flat-chested my husband won't sleep with me," which was the traditional theme of a lot of women's stand-up before that. Women's stand-up tended to be very self-deprecating. She was like a feminist crossover. She wasn't a feminist polemic, she was a smart, funny woman who was a stand-up, and that was new.

CHRIS ALBRECHT   There was no set lineup at the Improv. Budd would just decide who was on next, and while someone was onstage, he'd come and go, "You're next." And if somebody great came in to do a set—somebody like Freddie Prinze or Richard Pryor—nobody wanted to follow them. And Elayne would volunteer to follow, because she would get a better time slot in front of a bigger audience. She would take a spot that no one else would want to take. Budd would say, "Hey, you want to go on after Pryor?" and someone else would go, "No, put a singer on or do something else." And Elayne would always take the tough spots. That's how she got stage time. More stage time than she probably would have gotten had she not been willing to put herself in that position.

RICHARD LEWIS She had dated Andy Kaufman for a while. Everyone dated everybody. It was like a rock-and-roll scene, it really was.

RICK NEWMAN Andy and Elayne's relationship was always interesting. And it was fun in the sense that everyone knew it was going on. She also dated Ed Bluestone. That was a weird little triangle that happened. I think she was dating both Andy and Bluestone simultaneously. As a matter of fact, there's a story that goes around that Elayne was on the phone with Andy Kaufman and somehow or another she was in a hotel. And Ed Bluestone called in, and somehow or another he heard Elayne and Andy talking on the phone. And he got really pissed, really upset. He didn't realize that they were still seeing each other.

CHRIS ALBRECHT Elayne's the one who introduced me to Robin Williams and got Robin to come to New York for the first time—probably like in '77 or '78—and talked me into putting him up onstage.

ROBIN WILLIAMS She was a girlfriend. I came to visit her in New York, or went with her to New York, and then I started doing sets at the Improv. And she had been Andy Kaufman's girlfriend [and they remained friends] and so I went with her and Andy to see wrestling in Madison Square Garden, with [professional wrestler] Chief Jay Strongbow, who was one of Andy's favorite characters. And it was great to have her introduce me to the New York stand-up world. She kind of hit me to the fact that there's a whole 'nother world. 'Cause in San Francisco [where I had been performing] you were kind of naïve and like, "This is comedy!" and you come to New York and people go "Get off!" The moment you walk onstage, "No, I don't want to hear you! Fuck you!"

CHRIS ALBRECHT Elayne was a very up-and-coming comedian when we first met—"up-and-coming" meaning not starting out but certainly in the "looking-for-the-good-spots" stuff. She had been doing it for a couple of years, which is not a long time. Then Elayne moved to L.A. and followed Budd out when Budd opened the club, because she could get decent spots and good spots.

Since the 1960s, The Tonight Show Starring Johnny Carson *had been the country's biggest vehicle for up-and-coming stand-ups looking for an entrée to Hollywood. Comedians made the rounds on* Merv Griffin *or* Mike Douglas *but the* Tonight Show *was where stars were born. In 1972, Carson, the all-powerful host, uprooted his operation from its studio in New York and headed for California. And there to feed comedy talent to the show was the Comedy Store.*

The Comedy Store opened on April 10, 1972, a few weeks before Carson arrived at NBC headquarters in Burbank. It was founded by Sammy Shore, a Vegas comic who'd made a name opening for nightclub musicians, most recently Elvis. He opened the Comedy Store as a place for comedy friends like Redd Foxx, Jackie Vernon, Flip Wilson, and Buddy Hackett to hang out and do some sets. Shore wasn't looking to turn a profit and he certainly wasn't looking to be a tastemaker. That would be his wife, Mitzi.

In December 1973, Sammy Shore got a call from a Tonight Show *producer asking him to put on a comic named Freddie Prinze, a half–Puerto Rican, half-Hungarian nineteen-year-old from New York so they could check out his set. They loved him and a date was set. Prinze made his* Tonight Show *debut on December 6, 1973. Carson introduced him as "a young comedian who's appearing here in town at the Comedy Store." After a killer set, Carson gave him the almighty thumbs-up and invited him to sit on the couch. A few weeks later, Prinze was signed to his own sitcom,* Chico and the Man.

The combination of Carson's move to Los Angeles and Prinze's sitcom stardom was a call to all comedians to go west. And Carson's on-air announcement of the Comedy Store as a showcase put that club on the map. Comedians arrived at the Comedy Store in droves, Boosler among them. (Even Budd Friedman wanted a piece of the action, moving to L.A. and opening a West Coast outpost of his Improv in 1975.) By then, Sammy Shore had abandoned the Comedy Store and turned it over to Mitzi Shore, who transformed the business and became one of the most powerful tastemakers in comedy ever.

ARGUS HAMILTON, comedian Johnny Carson is sick and tired of coming out here twice a year to look for guests, so he decides in May of '72 to move the *Tonight Show* to Los Angeles. So what does that mean? Suddenly, to get on the *Tonight Show* you had to be in Los Angeles. So this huge migration of comics immediately came out to Los Angeles and they needed a place to work out, and the Comedy Store was right there waiting for them. Steve Landesberg, Michael Preminger, Jimmie J.J. Walker, Elayne Boosler, Jay Leno, all the comics. They all just immediately came straight here and this place took off.

CHRIS ALBRECHT One of the defining moments early on was when Gabe Kaplan and Jimmie Walker and Freddie Prinze got the sitcoms out of the clubs [after being on Carson]. There were shows based around comics. And that was kind of a clarion call—"Oh my God, there's gold in them there hills." And the clubs became the focus of people who had reason to put energy in that direction, because there seemed to be careers that could happen out of that.

SAMMY SHORE, comedian I founded the Comedy Store on April 10, 1972. I had finished working with Elvis. I wanted a place to hang out— you know, to get up and do some time when I wasn't working on the road. And I wanted a place where the guys could come and hang out— some of my comedian friends. Money was not involved. The guys, the comics, would go behind the bar and pour their own drinks, get the beer. It was an open bar for everybody, anybody that wanted it. And I got the door a little bit. But we never made any money. After I'd finished with Elvis, I had a year's contract in Vegas to work the lounge there. And it was like, "Who's going to run the Comedy Store?" And Mitzi said, "Well, I'll run it. I'll take it over." She said, "I know how to do it."

When I came back after four weeks I walked into the Comedy Store and it was like, "What's this?" Plants hanging; everything was moved around, she painted the whole thing black. It was like, "Hi, Mitzi, I'm back." "Yeah, Sammy, will you stand aside? I'm busy. I'll talk to you a little bit later." I was like, "It's my Store!" And she was like, "Sammy, can't you see I'm busy?! The place is packed! Would you just stand at the back, please!" It was like, "Wait a second. This is my wife! I let her run the Comedy Store and she's all of a sudden taken over the building. Come on!" I couldn't believe that. But what you saw was the beginning of something that was going to be something.

After we got divorced, three or four years later, that was it for me. I gave the Store to Mitzi, because she wanted it and because I was going to go work in Vegas, and to lower my child support. Which was really stupid. But she came and ran it like a business. You had to pay for your drinks. She was like a storm trooper. She was so businesslike, and I didn't like that. But it worked.

TOM DREESEN Mitzi revolutionized comedy. [When her husband was running the Comedy Store] he would let Redd Foxx come in and do forty-five minutes or an hour, and then another guy would come and do an hour. When she took over the club, she gave each one a fifteen-minute set, she did two shows, and all of a sudden she had what we in show business call continuity. It flowed. It was a good evening. It was smart programming and so the audience wanted to stay more. She was brilliant in that respect.

ARGUS HAMILTON Picture a Midwestern Jewish Scarlett O'Hara. That's Mitzi. Steve Landesberg, her boyfriend in the seventies, used to do a joke about her being the only Jew in Green Bay. He would do an impression, "Yeah, there's that Jew over there!" And so she had that sense of feeling different. When she was a little girl growing up in Green Bay, she lived catty-corner from Lambeau Field, and she would be in charge of selling the parking spots in front of her family's house. And she wouldn't let just anybody park there. She charged $10 during the Great Depression, and she only let cute guys from Chicago with big cigars and Packards park on her lawn because she knew she could get $10 apiece out of them. This was when she was seven, eight, nine years old. So it was like Scarlett O'Hara taking over the wood mill after the Civil War. Natural savvy, got it?

JOANNE ASTROW She was also a nurturing mother figure. She *loved* stand-up. She adored it. Of course we all could imitate her: "Wonderful!" Because you know she had that *Fargo* accent from Wisconsin—deep Midwest.

TOM DREESEN   If she didn't like your act, she was like, "No, you're not right for the Comedy Store." Today, you would say, "Oh, big deal, I'll go somewhere else." In those days, that was the only game in town. It was on Sunset Boulevard and if you got into the Comedy Store every night, every night talent coordinators from *Merv Griffin, Mike Douglas, Dinah Shore,* the *Tonight Show,* came looking for new comedians. We all had their names. So you had to get on at the Comedy Store. That's where all the action was.

ARGUS HAMILTON   She went by charisma. Mitzi only picked people with star charisma. Monday night she would basically watch two sets of comics. Brand-new comics that she hadn't seen, who had been lined up outside since four o'clock—that would last till about ten o'clock—then from ten o'clock till twelve, she would be monitoring the progress of comics that she had passed and sent on to Westwood [a second Comedy Store outpost], where she would send her Anglo-Saxons and her young African-Americans to develop while her New Yorkers held the stage here on Sunset.

DIANE NICHOLS, comedian   I showcased for Mitzi Shore to be a regular on November 7, 1977. I don't think I even technically met Mitzi when I showcased for her. She was just around. She was sitting with Tom Dreesen, and Dreesen said to her, "This girl has got potential." And whoever it was, Argus or whoever, came up and said, "You've passed, you're in." I didn't actually talk to her that night. Mitzi sat in that booth back then with all her little gang and it was hard to get up close.

LOIS BROMFIELD, comedian   The night I auditioned, Mitzi was just, "You're funny. Call on Monday." And that was it! She doesn't say a lot. She was pretty much a minimalist when it came to comics. I don't think I had a longer conversation with her than ten sentences, the whole time I knew her.

JOANNE ASTROW   Mitzi was pretty much a formidable dictator, impresario. She ran the club and her life like a small queendom. She had courtiers, jesters, lovers, and an entourage that surrounded her. There was this loyalty and it was literally like a court, and in that court there was a tremendous amount of scheming and plotting. But on the other hand, she nurtured and she praised and she built that club and it became a place where careers were launched.

ARGUS HAMILTON The Comedy Store was where the comics did all their hustling. Inevitably, Mitzi's booth had Jim McCawley, the *Tonight Show* talent coordinator, or Buddy Yorkin would sit with Mitzi. Or Redd Foxx would sit with Mitzi. Or George Schlatter would come in; he hired all of us to be on the new *Laugh-In* show. Everybody *loved* Mitzi. That's what you have to understand. And Mitzi loved comics. Mitzi fell so in love with Shirley Hemphill, the next week Mitzi had Norman Lear come see her, and Shirley Hemphill got her sitcom instantly. I mean, like, one month Shirley was a maid, next month she had a pilot with Norman Lear, which was *What's Happening!!*

SAMMY SHORE Budd and Mitzi didn't get along at all. Mitzi didn't allow anybody to go and work the Improv. If you worked the Improv, you were not going to work the Comedy Store.

JAMIE MASADA, owner, Laugh Factory The poison between the two clubs was unbelievable. I don't want to say one person was making it happen—it was both of them. But one time Mitzi lost her lease and Budd Friedman bought the lease from underneath her and she had to borrow money from a bunch of people—Don Rickles, Jimmie Walker, everybody—to buy the building. It was very ugly. And then Mitzi tried to do everything she could to lure all of the comedians from the Improv to her club. It got to the point where they both had spies. The comedians would go, "Oh my God, how did Budd know I was working the Comedy Store?" Or "How did Mitzi know I worked in the Improv last night?" Budd Friedman was a little bit more diplomatic—he was more diplomatic about everything: "Well, you work here, you shouldn't work there. I'd really appreciate it if you don't work there." And the next time you wouldn't get a spot at all at the Improv. But Mitzi was kind of like shrewd: "You won't play again, no, get out, you can't work in here."

CARRIE SNOW, comedian Pauly [Shore, Mitzi's son] was a little boy and he didn't have a driver's license yet—I believe he was fourteen or fifteen—and he would go to the Improv during the day and see their lineup printed out for the night and go back and tell his mother that I was working at the Improv. And I went into the kitchen in Westwood, when he was doing the catering, and I said, "You little Nazi bastard. You pay my rent. You tell me where I can work." It was such a little weaselly thing to do.

ROBERTA KENT, comedian During that time comedians were not making any money. And [in 1979] there was a strike and I was part of it, but I was just one of the mice being led by the pied pipers, and the pied pipers were Elayne Boosler, Tom Dreesen, Jay Leno, those guys who had been doing it a long time. [The idea to strike came up] on a New Year's Eve, when they were all over at Canter's Delicatessen, and the waitresses from the Comedy Store came over to the comedians and started showing them how much money they'd made on New Year's Eve. And the comics had made nothing. What happens is, when you have a cover charge and a two-drink minimum, the two-drink minimum goes to the house, and the cover is supposed to go to the talent. But people were keeping everything—at the Improv too; all of them.

ARGUS HAMILTON But the comics used Budd Freidman's Improv as a union meeting house, making Budd the good guy even though Budd wasn't paying either. That hurt Mitzi's feelings really bad and there was bitterness about that. When Budd appeared to be on the side of the comics when he wasn't paying either, Mitzi felt slighted.

PAUL MOONEY, comedian It's a man's world and it's very sexist and racist. That's why they hated Mitzi. They hated Mitzi. It's a man's world and Mitzi was doing what they were doing—she was screwing. Listen, Mitzi was taking care of them like they were her sons. She was supporting them. The ones she wasn't screwing, she was taking care of like they were her children. And it was okay for the men to do it, but it wasn't okay for the women to do it. I used to tell her all the time, "They hate you because you are female."

Stand-up comedy clubs were still in their infancy and already barriers to women had been put up. Mitzi Shore may have institutionalized the idea that you could put two stand-ups back-to-back, but she also believed it would only work as long as no two comics were alike. And that meant women comics would have to be split up. It's not that the women were actually so similar. They weren't. How could one compare Sandra Bernhard to Elayne Boosler to Marsha Warfield? But there was more bias against a female point of view. And the fact that there were so few women comics from the past to emulate made it difficult for women to figure out where they fit in.

JOANNE ASTROW   When Budd Friedman used to be the emcee, he would say, "In comedy university, you never put two women on after each other." The common enemy is the club owner and at times the drunk audiences.

PAUL MOONEY   One time Sandra [Bernhard] was at the Improv and I'd come by the club and she was crying because of the male comics and I said, "Let me tell you something—you go home and you cry and do any of that. But don't you ever, ever, let these motherfuckers see you cry."

JOANNE ASTROW   How self-deprecating is she going to be? How objective is her humor? How political? I don't think you heard many of the men asking, "How handsome is he?" And also comics had to choose lifestyles that were very hard to build relationships around, and that was something that a woman had to choose.

MERRILL MARKOE   In those days, I remember wrestling with ideas like "How can I be a girl and not have men hate me onstage?" because there was a lot of discussion of how women stand-ups could be "threatening." That's actually the word they used to use. *Threatening!* What were they so threatened by? Girls in their twenties making wisecracks? It seems even crazier now than it did then. Elayne Boosler used to get that word hurled at her a lot. It was a big issue, so I remember trying to figure out how to work around it. Did I need to wear a dress so I would look sufficiently vulnerable? Or would a dress make me too vulnerable and therefore insubstantial and not funny? Or if I wore pants onstage, like I usually did, would that make me too masculine and therefore make the old "threatening" alarm bells start to ring? I approached the whole thing with caution. I kind of thought for a while maybe I'd be a female Woody Allen type, because he was *the* big smart guy writer-performer at the time, and he had started as a stand-up and a TV comedy writer, then gone on to totally control his own comedy destiny. But that didn't really fit me and neither did the dirty, slutty, potty-mouth party girl. I was just sort of this former-art-student girl with a bunch of material I hoped was smart or original or something. Nowadays I don't have any problem figuring out how those pieces fit together, but at the time it seemed confusing because I really didn't see any smart, silly women making it big in comedy anywhere. Of my contemporaries, Elayne Boosler was the one who had the best angle on doing smart material. She was basically state-of-the-art. But I wouldn't have wanted to appear to be emulating her, so I needed something else. It was a conundrum.

RICHARD LEWIS Back in the day, these women were very strong, strong acts. Make no mistake about it, they were groundbreakers. There I go again, but it's impossible not to call them that, because the audience would go into a club, and I'm sure these women have described it, but they had to overcome this ridiculous sense of "Hey, oh, what is a chick doing up there?" It was bullshit, the swearing and "Hey, get 'em off the field" and the cursing and the expletives. They had to overcome that. They had it much harder than we did.

MERRILL MARKOE My act was mostly one-liners that were probably somewhere in between a kind of female Woody Allen and maybe Robert Benchley, who was my hero but obviously not a stand-up. I was really struggling to find my voice. I was also suffering from an insane amount of naïveté. I had started dating David Letterman, who was a big shot at the Comedy Store at that time. It was like I was a freshman nerd girl dating a really cool senior jock. Once that started, it didn't take me long to get caught up in the care and maintenance of what appeared to be his much more important career. He started guest hosting the *Tonight Show* very soon after, and watching the enormity of the effect that had on him, it was clear to me that he needed my help. So I started writing jokes for his ever more frequent appearances, because now there was an always-hungry beast to feed. Then I went the extra mile and started "loaning" him any jokes that I had in my act that were working, thinking that I was too new at stand-up to be going on TV anytime soon. My feeling was that by the time I was good enough to be booked as a stand-up on TV, no one would remember those jokes anyway, so I could just take them back and use them again as needed.

I know that sounds insane. I've since learned that behind my back, a number of people thought I was out of my mind. Mavis Leno once told me something Jay said, about how he could see that I was really undervaluing myself. As it turns out, he knew more about me than I knew. At the time, stand-up was really a man's world. Women were trying to forge a way in but there wasn't much in the way of a welcoming committee.

One would think that having a female comedy impresario like Mitzi Shore would have translated into more opportunities for women. Not necessarily. Stand-up comedy was still a boys' club and Mitzi Shore was a divisive character. She has her defenders: Diane Nichols and Lois Bromfield (sister of Valri Bromfield, the first person to perform stand-up on Saturday Night Live). *But other women felt she ghettoized them, and they resented the close relationships Mitzi forged with the young male comics she mentored.*

SANDRA BERNHARD, comedian   I don't think Mitzi ever really liked a lot of women. She might have had a couple of favorites but she liked to be like the queen bee. So there was always like a lot of young male comics who she liked and kind of took under her wing and had little flings with.

ROBERTA KENT   She was a strange woman, a very strange woman. Sad. And fucking a lot of the guys. We used to kid, "Maybe if we were fucking her, we'd get the ten o'clock time slots."

TOM DREESEN   There were several comics she went out with. She dated Steve Landesburg, she dated Argus Hamilton, she dated Steve Lubetkin. She had parties up at her house that everybody talks about, and there was cocaine and dope. I didn't do drugs, but everyone was getting loaded and getting high and it was almost like the hip thing to do if you were a stand-up. But I don't know of any girl that went up there. Every time I ever hear the stories of who went up there, it was usually Mitzi and a lot of guys.

ROBIN WILLIAMS   Oh, there were parties all the time up at her house; it was pretty crazy. Especially in the drug years, we would all go up to

her house after the shows. It was pretty crazy, but it was—she was—
fun. And it was also weird that her kids were backstage at the Comedy
Store, and all these people [were engaging in] pretty crazy behavior,
drinking, doing blow, and then "Hi! There's Pauly. Hi, how are you?"

ROBERTA KENT The guys had an advantage, then all of a sudden she
took a liking to the women. But she didn't give them as much respect.
The ones that treated her like crap were the ones she seemed to have
the most respect for. I think she liked the ballsy ones.

LOIS BROMFIELD I didn't get invited to Mitzi's house but I did take
care of her kids for two years—me and Steve Moore. We were legal
guardians to Peter and Pauly Shore. Mitzi came to me and to Steve, my
best buddy in the world, and said, "I need somebody to move into
my house and take care of my kids for two years so they can go to Beverly Hills High School." I was twenty-five or twenty-six. She must have
trusted me, for sure. I didn't sleep with her. I didn't go to her house and
sit with her and rub her feet. I didn't do anything for her. I went
and did my stand-up and I went home. And it turns out, I was the worst
guardian. We had a two-bedroom house on Doheny Drive in Beverly
Hills. They lived in the guesthouse that was attached to the main house
and I would lock the door at night so they couldn't come in. They were
like, "We are gonna tell our mom." I was like, "All right, tell her." I
would take Pauly in my car, in my bathrobe, chain-smoking, to school
and just kick him out of the car. I wouldn't even slow down. Mitzi
would come over on the weekends every couple of weeks and she would
say, "Are they okay?" And I'd say, "Yeah." And I'd say to Pauly, "Don't
say anything, I won't get any time slots if you open your mouth and tell
her." And he would start laughing. It was terrible. I was the worst. I
got good time slots for a few months, but then I would get bad time
slots because Mitzi would say, "I heard that Peter didn't get to school
yesterday." And then I'd get like a one o'clock time slot in the Original
Room.

JOANNE ASTROW She could turn on you.

ROBERTA KENT I spent a lot of time with Mitzi in Palm Springs, together, alone. We went for Yizkor services, the two of us. I mean, she

came to my mother's funeral. And then she turned. It was the strangest thing. The schmucky kid who did the booking—I said, "I'll be around New Year's," and he didn't book me. So when I was talking to her, I said, "Jim didn't book me for New Year's." And she goes, "Well, what are you telling me for?" I said, "You should know that he's doing that." And she goes, "Well, don't tell me!" She'd turned. It was never the same.

One of the few female performers to play regularly at the Comedy Store was Marsha Warfield, a stately five-foot-eleven African-American woman from Chicago's South Side. Warfield was twenty-one years old when she arrived in Los Angeles. She got the itch performing amateur nights in Chicago, and after two years dumped her husband and moved to California with $100 in her pocket. She canvassed the Comedy Store for two weeks before she got the nerve to try it herself. After her first set, Letterman and Leno went up and told her she was funny, and she was set. She hung out with the guys at Canter's Deli, where the Comedy Store crew would go to hang out after sets.

TOM DREESEN I put Marsha onstage for the very first time at a little comedy room I started in Chicago. I had one section called the "virgin spot" that was for somebody who had never been onstage ever before. Marsha came in one night, she had never been onstage before, and she asked to go on. I actually thought she lied to me after I saw her do her set, because she was so smooth, so calm—and she really got big laughs. Afterward, she told me she'd been a nervous wreck. But she had this composure about her; she was very good.

CLAUDIA LONOW, comedian One of the funniest comedians— funniest in terms of laughs—was Marsha Warfield. She was really dirty. She would go up onstage with a glass of Courvoisier and do this stuff about how she masturbates so much that if she had a baby it would be born with one fingernail sticking out of its head. She did this whole thing about girls who go, " 'Sometimes I forget to eat.' Girl, you forget to eat, you don't deserve to eat." And she would do this thing about how her underwear was *this* big.

ROBERTA KENT She had a bite to her, *whoa*, she had a bite to her. She drank a little. Not embarrassing, but a little nip before the show. A lot of them did, especially the guys who had a line of coke whenever they wanted.

MERRILL MARKOE Marsha was a *brave* performer. In addition to being hilarious, I really admired her delivery and I wondered how she had the balls to be so aggressive and serene at the same time. Or I wondered how I could ever learn to do that. I used to think about her when I was beating up on myself, because she had this very unintimidated timing. She would deliver a punch line, and then just stand silently and *stare* at the audience, deadpan. She would *wait* for them to laugh. Usually they did, but if for some reason they didn't, she never looked shook. She just kept standing there, saying nothing, staring at them, like, "Well, I did *my* part of this. I'm in no hurry. You either come across with your part or I'm not going to continue. I'll wait you out. I've got no place else to be except here."

ARGUS HAMILTON She was doing stand-up all over the country, headlining everywhere, and then she became a star on TV, on *Night Court*, and it seemed like they tried to turn her into something she wasn't built to do. Then, and this was before *The View*, they tried to do an afternoon women's talk show, and she wasn't free to be herself. That persona you saw on that talk show—the softened, muted version of her—that's not Marsha. So that sat flat and drifted off, and I don't know what she's doing now.

In 1978, Mitzi Shore gathered all the women—Marsha Warfield, Diane Nichols, JoAnne Astrow, Roberta Kent, Lotus Weinstock, and Lois Bromfield, among them—for a big announcement. She had transformed the small room on the second floor of the Comedy Store into a stand-up space exclusively for women to work out their acts. She was calling it the Belly Room, and it would give women an alternative space to hone their craft. The comics were divided. Some worried that it ghettoized the women by keeping them off the more regular stages of the Original Room and the Main Room. Others felt it was an opportunity to work out their material in a friendly environment.

JOANNE ASTROW Mitzi called us into a room and said, "I have a wonderful thing that I am doing! You gals are gonna perform in your own room!" Elayne immediately said, "Not me!" She was the most vocal. Elayne and Marsha Warfield.

SANDRA BERNHARD   It was a smaller room, and it was upstairs, which of course was kind of sexist and weird.

ARGUS HAMILTON   Mitzi felt bad because her baby boom guys were so good now that there was only room on her stage for women like Marsha Warfield when she was in town. Diane was always at Westwood, Roberta Kent was always out opening for Barry Manilow, Elayne was down at the Improv, and Mitzi had an itch to develop women. She and I were driving back from San Diego, when she decided she was going to open the Belly Room upstairs and make it for women only. And she made me pull out a legal pad and write out a mission statement for the Belly Room. She got Lotus Weinstock and some people to perform there. She pushed it and pushed it and pushed it, as hard as she could. But not a lot came of it. The women resented it; they felt marginalized.

DIANE NICHOLS   Listen, the Belly Room is so creepy. It's up between the main room and the kitchen and you go up these narrow little stairs, carpeted, and there's this big door open, but inside there's this tiny room, with a bar to the right and a little stage against the wall.

MERRILL MARKOE   Occasionally I got the Original Room, but usually I got the Belly Room, which was the weird little area where Mitzi was shoving all the women. She was making it seem like "Oh, it's a great place for women," but it was really, if you can believe it, it was a place for people waiting to catch a train. It was this tiny little room, and the people that she brought in there were waiting for a seat downstairs, so if some seats became available somebody would come into the middle of your show and go, "Okay. I can take seven people now." And then seven people would get up, with a lot of commotion . . . So that's what it was, and it was a pretty awful place. I don't have any fond memories of the Belly Room, other than becoming friends with a few of the women.

DIANE NICHOLS   In my opinion, at this point, comedy was becoming very popular and there was a lot of competition, and a lot of the women weren't as strong as they thought they were. Some of the women thought they were being ghettoized, but she wasn't trying to force women into a ghetto, she was just trying to take advantage of that room. In some cases, I think some of the women got the better of the deal. They might not think so, but they did.

EMILY LEVINE, comedian   I liked the Belly Room because what Mitzi did was once in a while let you commandeer the room for your own weekend. So you could do Thursday, Friday, Saturday, your own forty-five-minute-to-an-hour-long show, which I thought was wonderful.

WHOOPI GOLDBERG, comedian   Very few women got in the Original Room or the Main Room. The first performance I did in Los Angeles was in the Belly Room, and it was an industry thing. Then Mitzi and I became friends, and she said, "Whenever you want to come here and do something, you can come." I never wanted to put her in the position of saying, "Listen, I can't really put you in the Main Room because the guys will have their little mini freak-out. So would you do the Belly Room?" And the Belly Room was always convenient because there weren't a lot of people performing in it. I would just do my hour-and-a-half or hour-long show, then go down and see who was downstairs.

SANDRA BERNHARD   You wanted to get up every night and hone your craft, so it was better than nothing. From there I had a jumping-off place because I was really getting to perform consistently, four or five nights a week. But it was definitely a different vibe. Women could be more themselves, and they weren't under the pressure of following a man who was doing really tacky, sexist, racist humor. Or a lot of drug-reference humor. There was always a lot of that going on in the male world.

Two women made the most of the Belly Room: Lotus Weinstock, who seemed to run the place, and Sandra Bernhard, who Weinstock co-mentored with Paul Mooney. Weinstock was a kind of cult celebrity as the ex-fiancée of Lenny Bruce. She actually got her start in the mid-sixties, at New York's Bitter End, but she quickly quit, headed out to California, changed her name to Lotus Weinstock (from her first stage name, Mau-rey Hayden), and met Bruce. By the time Weinstock arrived at the Comedy Store in the mid-seventies, she was a cross between the spiritual poles of her invented name: the California space cadet (Lotus) and East Coast Jew (Weinstock). She guided Bernhard, the five-foot-ten, 106-pound redhead with the improbable Mick Jagger lips. The two of them set the tone for the tiny room upstairs.

JOANNE ASTROW Lotus Weinstock was a great force in the early community. She was very, very unusual as a comic, and very much, in her own way, like Mitzi. She had this background of being Lenny Bruce's last girlfriend, so there was a glamour about her. Lotus was looked upon as a spiritual person and a philosopher, and she worked well in a New Age situation. Sandra loved her very much.

We didn't do labeling in the seventies, but if we did, I would call her one of the first alternative comics. She was half stand-up, half performance eccentric. But very skilled. One year I think she only dressed in yellow. Lotus would get on the stage, and if people were not responding immediately, which they often didn't, she would say to the audience, "Wait one second." She'd pick up a tape recorder that she had next to her, and she would turn it on and put it up to the mic, and then a voice would come out saying, "You are a very lovely girl. Your mother loves you. The fact that they are not getting the humor is not you!" Nobody had ever seen anybody do anything like that.

DIANE NICHOLS Lotus and Sandra did some kooky stuff together on that stage, and that helped Sandra form as the person you know now onstage as Sandra Bernhard. They did a crazy thing where they had a knock-down, drag-out fight. Of course, it was fake, but they did it every night and sometimes it scared the audience, but for the most part it was a great success.

JOANNE ASTROW Sandra's a stand-up, but she's even more a performance artist stand-up. She always had her own agenda. She was destined to be what she is: unique. You wouldn't think of her as you would Elayne. Elayne was brilliant, but Elayne falls into the mode of a traditional comic. Her role models were Robert Klein and the great observational comedians. Sandra wanted to bring in music—did bring in music. We were important to her but she didn't think of herself as solely a stand-up comic. But she did think, "I'm going to be famous. *That* is going to happen." And there was no doubt about that.

SANDRA BERNHARD   Two of the women I drew a lot from at the time were Lily Tomlin and Bette Midler. They're from the early seventies, mid-seventies. But over the years, I drew a lot from everybody from Carol Burnett to Carol Channing to Mary Tyler Moore. It was just observing people that I thought were funny as actresses.

When I started, it was kind of the post-hippie era, and the beginning of disco. I was eighteen going on nineteen, I had moved to L.A. and had become a manicurist in Beverly Hills, and I started going around to some of the little funky clubs. One of the first nights I got up, I was at a club called the Ye Little Club, where Joan Rivers was at that time, getting up every Monday night and breaking in material. But they had an open mic night and I met two people there that kind of took me under their wings—Paul Mooney and Lotus Weinstock.

PAUL MOONEY   Sandra was eighteen, and when I saw her, it freaked me out. I'd never seen anybody like her. She was like a singer who had come to life. I told her, "You're gonna be famous." I said, "But you have a lot of hard work to do because they are gonna hate you, because you are skinny and you have those big lips." They used to call them nigger lips. They used to make fun of her and talk about her and it would make Sandra cry. I told her, "Someday big lips are gonna be in." I said, "You're thin." The one thing I taught her is what a prostitute taught me. The prostitute told me, "You think I'm beautiful, don't you?" I said, "Yeah." She said, "I'm not. I make you think I'm beautiful." She said that it's an illusion. She said, "If I don't think I'm beautiful, you won't think it. If I believe it, you'll believe it." It's a trick, and I taught Sandra that trick.

Sandra didn't make fun of herself. She didn't put herself down. She was honest about her sexuality. That's what fascinated me about her. And her look! So I just took her under my wing. I liked her, I liked her personality and I liked what I saw. I knew she would be famous. I told her, "When those gays get ahold of you in New York, they are gonna go *fucking crazy.*" And they did. Everything I told her came to pass.

CLAUDIA LONOW   The person who had the biggest influence on me was Sandra Bernhard. I have never seen anybody like that, ever. She was so confident and confrontational and sexual and just offbeat. *Off-*

beat! I thought she was the goddess of all time. The first time I saw her perform, it was at the Improv and it was a really small crowd and she started to focus in on one guy at the front, and then she started singing to this guy, and she's talking about how when somebody is touching your nipples at first you really like it but then it gets so irritating you just want to sandblast them off!

SANDRA BERNHARD   I never really did jokes. I always did stream-of-consciousness reflections on my life and culture and pop culture and music. And very early on, I also interspersed my act with singing, which was also very weird, because it wasn't really singing like in a lounge show or something. It was singing somewhere between a Broadway musical and a rock-and-roll revue. So that made it very different and set me apart from most of the other performers in general.

CHRIS ALBRECHT   I remember going to see Sandra one night at the Comedy Store in Westwood, because as an agent you'd go and see your clients all the time. She was running a really rough set, and there weren't a lot of people in the audience, and I was sitting in the back, going, "Oh boy." Because at some point as an agent, you wonder, "How am I going to get these people shots?" Because you can recognize the talent, but you can't necessarily figure out how guys looking to cast people in a TV show can see what's special about them, especially if the audience isn't laughing a lot. Then she stopped, and she pulled the stool up against the wall, and she just held the mic and sang "Desperado" a cappella. And she had a terrific voice, and she had everybody completely attentive, and I remember thinking to myself, "This is why I represent her, because she's really talented." Not a lot people could be up onstage and shift from trying desperately to connect to the crowd with comedy to singing a top-ten song and figuring out a way to get the crowd with you because you needed to get off the stage with applause.

ROBERTA KENT   Sometimes I'd have to follow Sandra Bernhard, and people would get up and walk out. So then there'd be like two or three people left.

SANDRA BERNHARD   Just getting up and doing something that was more musical and more overtly sexual as a woman kind of took people aback, because they were used to seeing women being self-deprecating. And so it was kind of like "Uh-oh, what is this?" And they'd be kind of freaking out and intimidated, and that was sort of the objective. Sort of. You just wanted people to be smart enough to get the nuances. Unfortunately, the comedy club scene was not very nuanced on any level—for men or for women—which is why, as soon as I could, I got out of it. But it was certainly a convenient place to hone my craft.

ARGUS HAMILTON   Paul Mooney adopted her and she became his protégée, which really enhanced Sandra's personal feeling of importance. But it made her into the chanteuse she was born to be. Mooney had that effect on people. You're around Paul Mooney for ten minutes and everybody's in Paris in the 1920s. So that's exactly where Sandra belonged.

PAUL MOONEY   I took Sandra out of L.A., and I took her to soldier camps. I took her to all the black clubs where Tina Turner worked. I said, "You can make black people laugh, you can make anybody laugh." They used to love her. Black men were *crazy* for Sandra because of those big lips. You don't see big lips on a white girl, and she had them. They loved her. Everyone loved her. She would sing and do all that shit. She used to almost cause riots, because the men, they weren't used to women like her. I took her *every*where. I used to push Sandra down their throats. I took her on *Make Me Laugh*. I put her on *The Richard Pryor Show*. I did it. I held her hand; I said she'll be fine. When I did *Letterman*, first time I did it, I took her with me and I told Letterman, "Put Sandra on, Sandra's perfect for the show." I'm the one that made him put her on. And then I took her to *The King of Comedy* too.

SANDRA BERNHARD   My friend Paul Mooney was the head writer on *The Richard Pryor Show* on NBC, a short-lived show but one that was nonetheless pivotal for a lot of people. So I did that. And then I got some movie roles and then in 1981 I got cast in *The King of Comedy* and by the time the movie came out in '83, I was able to segue out of the comedy club scene and start touring. I started doing my one-woman show at rock-and-roll clubs and theaters, so I was able to get out of that scene. I mean, there's nothing appealing about waiting at a comedy club to get on, and with the exception of my friend Lotus and Paul Mooney and Richard Belzer, these were not people I cared to hang out with.

Elayne Boosler refused to play the Belly Room. In fact, she refused any attempt to differentiate herself from male comics. She wanted to be equal—not special—and, like the guys she came up with, her influences were Lenny Bruce, Robert Klein, and Richard Pryor, not Phyllis Diller or Joan Rivers. As she told New York *magazine in 1976, "I'm a woman who's a comic. Not a woman's comic." In 1987 she told* The New York Times, *"When asked if I'm a feminist, I've always said I'm just a human being trapped in a woman's body . . . For my generation, the ones who really changed things were Robert Klein and Richard Pryor. They changed the role of the stand-up comic into that of a town crier delivering the news about life and growing up. Like all the young men who were starting out at the same time—people like Andy Kaufman and Jay Leno and Richard Lewis—I picked up from there. I never bravely set about to change things."*

JOANNE ASTROW The gender discrimination always bothered Elayne. It was painful to her to be classified not as a comic first, but as a woman. It always angered her. And Elayne has a legendary anger.

RICHARD LEWIS Decades ago, I was quoted as saying that "to me she was like the Jackie Robinson of stand-up in my class," and I meant it out of tremendous affection and respect. There was, like, a guy, a guy, a guy, a guy, and "Ladies and gentlemen, Elayne Boosler!" And she would come on and rip up the joint, and I just found it astounding, because she had to overcome so many obstacles. I just spit out some hyperbole, but I understand why the Jackie Robinson quote disturbed her—she didn't want to be put in a class by herself. She was in our class.

CAROL LEIFER I remember she went on the *Tonight Show* with a guest host, Helen Reddy, who said to her, "You are really an inspiration to so many women out there. It's great to have a young female comic on." And Elayne said something like "Well, I hope I'm just an inspiration to all comics."

JOANNE ASTROW   These are always complex stories. There's another side to it. Elayne Boosler has what I would honestly call anger management problems. And Elayne has an obsessive craziness about material being stolen from her. Bordering on crazy. Elayne was raised in Brooklyn, as was I. And I wanted Elayne to think I'm good! She came down to see me and it really, really meant a lot to me. And I did a joke in which I imitated my mother. So when I got offstage Elayne was waiting for me, angry, not supportive in any way, and she said, "You cannot use that voice! You stole that from me! My mother sounds like that!" And I said, "Elayne! We're two Jewish women from Brooklyn. How else are our mothers' voices going to sound like?!"

CLAUDIA LONOW   Did she have a chip on her shoulder or was she a creative person who was being driven crazy by bullshit? That's what I think. She was systematically being driven crazy. My stepfather was the super of a building and we had a duplex and Elayne lived on the floor for a while with Robin Williams when they were going out. This was before he was famous. They slept on the floor in a sleeping bag on some pillows. And that was cool, there's, like, this young couple in a sleeping bag on the floor who would crash at the apartment for about a month. But I also remember that in order to make money—because there wasn't really a network of money at that time—Elayne would sit with a yellow pad and write two hundred jokes a day for Dial-A-Joke. It was a thing where you would call a phone number and hear a joke. She would sell jokes to Dial-A-Joke.

In the world of comedy clubs, Boosler rose to the highest level, but breaking out as a national star continued to elude her. The Tonight Show *was still the biggest credit a comic could get, and yet, despite Joan Rivers's success, Johnny Carson held antiquated views about women comedians. In 1979, he told* Rolling Stone, *"A woman is feminine, a woman is not abrasive, a woman is not a hustler. So when you see a gal who does 'stand-up' one-liners, she has to overcome that built-in identification as a retiring, meek woman. I mean, if a woman comes out and starts firing one-liners, those little abrasive things, you can take that from a man. The only one who's really done it is Joanie Rivers . . . I think it's much tougher for women. You don't see many of them around. And the ones that try are*

*sometimes a little aggressive for my taste." The women who suited Carson's
taste were, for the most part, blond, buxom, and willing to play dumb.*

SUZANNE SOMERS, actress I needed work. I was a teenage mother
and a single mother and I needed money. I first started doing commercials and it seemed like every time I would do extra work in a movie, I
would get upgraded to get a line. And then I got that one line in *American Graffiti*. When I was doing *American Graffiti*, I was writing a book
of poetry called *Touch Me*. So when *Touch Me* was published and
American Graffiti was out, I read about a role in a sitcom called *Lotsa
Luck* with Dom DeLuise, and it described me: small-town, naïve, you
know, everything that I was. I thought, "Boy, I could play that one." So
I mustered together the thirty-five bucks it then cost to fly from San
Francisco to L.A. And naïveté is bliss. I don't know how I got myself
into the interview; I just went to NBC Studios and they said, "What are
you here for?" I said, "Interviewing for the Dom DeLuise show." Again,
ignorant, I had no agent, no manager. So they sent me over to the Dom
DeLuise office and the receptionist said, "Sign in," so I signed in and
then they called me in and after I read, they came out and they said you
have a call-back. I didn't know what a call-back was. And she said,
"Well, that means we're going to call you back." So I said, "Well, so
where do I go while I'm waiting for you to call me back?" And she said,
"I don't know, go wait in the commissary." So I go sit in the commissary all by myself at about two in the afternoon and Johnny Carson
and Fred De Cordova, his producer, walk in. And I was the only one
there, so they came over and talked to me, and I remember Johnny
said, "Hey, little lady, what are you doing here?" And I said, "Well, I'm
waiting, I have a call-back on the Dom DeLuise show, and I wrote a
book. I'm an author." And he said, "Well, good luck to you." So that
afternoon, I sent Fred De Cordova and Johnny Carson and their secretary copies of my book of poetry and that was on Wednesday. And on
Friday night of that week, I made my very first television appearance
with Johnny Carson. "We're all wondering who the blonde in the Thunderbird was in *American Graffiti*; well, we found her." I thought I was
booked on the *Tonight Show* because they loved my poetry, but they
booked me because of what they read on the back flap of the book, which
was that I was the mysterious blonde in the Thunderbird in *American*

Graffiti, and at that time it was the number one movie in the country, although I wasn't aware of that. And I went on the *Tonight Show* and I think I was so naïve and so green that Johnny Carson just loved me, and he started having me on once a month, reading him poetry. And he would do all these facial takes.

VICTORIA JACKSON, comedian I started doing comedy at clubs all around town in '80, '81. I was a cigarette girl at night at the Variety Arts Center, selling cigarettes in a French maid miniskirt. I said, "Can I do an act?" [The guy who ran the place] said, "What do you do?" I said, "I do handstands and say poetry." He said, "This I've got to see." So I started doing my little routine between my cigarette duties. I did it every night for two years and honed it in front of his adoring audience. They were all older people, and they were so sweet to me. It was like a thirties club. They played thirties music, no rock, no disco. Anyway, one night the *Tonight Show* talent scout, Jim McCawley, came into the club to see this other comic, this Australian named Maureen Murphy. She told dirty jokes, and I never liked dirty jokes because of my Baptist upbringing. So the *Tonight Show* saw the dirty comic and then saw my act, and then came up to me and said, "Would you like to be on the *Tonight Show*?" I was like, "Yes!" It was very exciting, because all the comics knew that if Johnny liked you, you would have a career. I went on *Carson* in February '83. After I finished my act, he looked over and clapped. Then he put his thumb up in the "okay" sign.

I was on *Carson* twenty times, and every time, McCawley would preinterview me. He would listen to me ramble for an hour and a half. He would take out little gems, arranging the questions to make me look funny. Then Carson would interview me while arranging everything to make me look funny, not himself. He would let me get the laughs and tap his pencil to get an extra laugh. The beauty of Carson was that, unlike many present-day interviewers who might say, "So, you're married to a fire-eater, ha-ha-ha" so the audience laughs at them, Carson would say, "So, Victoria, you're married. Who are you married to?" I would say, "I'm married to a fire-eater," and I would get the laugh. Then Johnny would tap his pencil and make a funny face and he would get a laugh. That is so beautiful and brilliant. I think that's why he was the best. But McCawley really did arrange the questions so well so that I looked ditsy and funny. I thought I was just brilliantly funny, until I went on other talk shows.

CLAUDIA LONOW   There was a woman that Carson liked the best at that time. Her name was Maureen Murphy, she was Australian, and she was very pretty, pretty in her thirties or forties. She would dress extremely feminine and do I'm-a-dumb-blonde jokes.

CARRIE SNOW   Maureen Murphy was one of the girls in the Belly Room in the Comedy Store but she had a relationship with Jim McCawley from the *Tonight Show*. She would do these cute little jokes, "Da da da da da," and have these little three- or four-minute sets which did well on the *Tonight Show*, with a nice mainstream audience.

Elayne Boosler made a mistake—she was actually quoted in the *L.A. Times* claiming that the only reason Maureen Murphy did well was because she was sleeping with the talent coordinator and they had packed the audience with NBC employees, which really wasn't the smartest thing at the time to do.*

That did not bode well for this new generation of female comics, Boosler in particular. Sandra Bernhard appeared on Carson, *but that was as an actress after she had appeared in* The King of Comedy. *Boosler got her first shot on the* Tonight Show *when Helen Reddy was guest-hosting on August 9, 1977. But Boosler still needed Carson's blessing to truly take the next step. She got it a few weeks later, on September 15, 1977, but it did not go quite as she would have planned. As she told* The New York Times *in 1987, "I went in to do the* Tonight Show, *I had a beautiful set all prepared, and they put someone on my case to write jokes . . . I remember the first joke I was handed went, 'I'm so ugly, I can't make a nickel on a battleship.' I just refused to do it."*

* On April 17, 1983, Elayne Boosler told the *Los Angeles Times*: "It's no secret that his personal relationship with Murphy has made him partial to her at the expense of others." Both the talent coordinator and Murphy denied the relationship in the article.

PATRICIA BRADFORD   At the time, my title was talent coordinator. They are now basically called segment producers. And what you did was, you booked the guests and then you produced the episode. When I first started working at the *Tonight Show* [in 1969], I was the second or third woman who ever worked as something other than as a secretary. We were not allowed to wear pants to the office. They hired women over their dead bodies. They just didn't want them there. The prejudice was astounding and that was true for almost all of television.

TREVA SILVERMAN   After I interviewed at the Johnny Carson show, they called my agent: "We really thought she was this and this and this. But he'll never hire a writer who's a woman. Carson would not feel at ease having woman writers." They said they'd never hire a woman, just never hire a woman. That was my first time thinking, "Oh, I guess they're seeing me as a woman, not what my work is like."

PATRICIA BRADFORD   He had a lot of prejudices and that was just how he felt. There were certain people you could book and there were certain people you couldn't book. Totie Fields could never get booked on that show and she was one of the funniest people in the world. She would come on the show if Jerry Lewis or Joey Bishop or someone like that was guest-hosting. I think we got her on the show once with Carson, and she was hysterically funny and he laughed his ass off, and then never wanted her back again.

JOANNE ASTROW   Elayne suffered from being an early woman and not being, quote unquote, "feminine enough and pretty enough." I was very close friends with her when she did the *Tonight Show*. And unfortunately Johnny Carson was a man who was part of his era; to him, women were broads! Somehow Joan Rivers got into the inner circle because I think she was traditional enough; that was, until she got too arrogant herself.* But Elayne did the show and the quote that went

---

*Joan Rivers made a few powerful enemies throughout her career, not least of all Johnny Carson, the very man who gave her stardom. In 1986, Rivers announced that she would launch her own late-night show on Fox to compete against the *Tonight Show*. For Rivers, it must have seemed like an enormous opportunity—Fox was still just an idea then, and its founders, Rupert Murdoch and Barry Diller, wanted Joan

back to the comedy booker was "I don't ever want to see that waitress on my show again." So it was tragic, that rejection was tragic.

MARK LONOW   She wasn't a lady, and that was a big deal. Carson was very old-school: women have their place. And I don't know what his concept of what a female comic was but Elayne didn't fit it. She wasn't playing the dumb big-titted comic; she wasn't playing the ugly, deformed comic; she wasn't playing the haggard housewife. She was just a woman—average looks, nice-looking, nothing wrong with Elayne—telling jokes, and Carson couldn't do it, he just couldn't do it. That's a big deal.

CLAUDIA LONOW   Elayne was the comic emblem of women's lib: "I'm not Joan Rivers, I'm a liberated woman! Yes, I'm having recreational sex! I'm not going to get married! I'm making jokes about men and it's not my husband!" But she came out in that period when there was such a big left–right divide and there was no other outlet except for the *Tonight Show* and that was certainly right-wing.

MARK LONOW   I still think there were other elements to Elayne's personality that hindered her career. So it's not quite so simple. It's not like "Oh, Carson didn't do it and therefore it didn't happen." Well, yes, that's true, but not quite. She was a very angry woman. At that time there was a lot of resistance to young women doing stand-up—a lot. So there was that, but it meshed with her anger. Elayne Boosler did

---

Rivers as an anchor for their new network. It didn't help that NBC had not even considered Rivers as a replacement for Carson once he retired. According to Rivers: "A friend of mine who was the vice president at NBC got an internal memo saying when Johnny leaves, here are the ten people to replace him. And I wasn't on the list. It was all men. And here I was permanent guest host: how insane, it should have been handed to me. And he wrote across the top of the letter, 'Darling, there's no home for you here.'"

To Carson, Rivers's departure was the ultimate betrayal—he never spoke to her again.

The Late Show Starring Joan Rivers debuted on October 9, 1986, to moderate ratings but ultimately was a flop. Behind-the-scenes fighting with Fox brass led the network to insist Rivers fire her husband, Edgar Rosenberg, as executive producer. She refused and the network canceled the show. Rosenberg committed suicide three months later and Rivers didn't appear on a late-night show for the next twenty years. No woman has ever hosted a network late-night show since.

very well: we're talking seven figures. She never made it on TV, she never made it to superstardom, but she did make quite a nice living.

DIANE NICHOLS It didn't make sense and it scared me, because I really firmly believed what my parents taught me: if you are good you will succeed. Now, contrary to what I just told you, the truth is if you are good and somebody doesn't like you, somebody else will hire you. We always just assumed that you will still go up the ladder and the ladder at the time was the *Tonight Show*. There was no more Ed Sullivan. No more Jack Parr. Very few to no variety shows. The only one on was Johnny and that he could take the best woman stand-up and say, "No"—well, I kind of went, "Wait a minute—doesn't he understand?"

MERRILL MARKOE

It's rare to see a woman writing for late-night; even rarer is a female head writer of a late-night talk show. Merrill Markoe was one of the first, though that is hardly the only reason she is notable. As co-creator and head writer of Late Night with David Letterman, *which debuted in 1982 on NBC, Markoe was instrumental in reshaping late-night TV for a younger, edgier audience, adding bite to Letterman's cynicism and irreverence, giving structure to his subtle disdain for the trappings of show-biz. It was Markoe, for example, who created the now-iconic segment* Stupid Pet Tricks. *But at the time, Markoe was also Letterman's girlfriend, and when their relationship soured, this arrangement proved toxic. She left the show in 1988.*

MERRILL MARKOE I was doing stand-up when I met Dave. We began hanging around together a bit in the back hallway of the Comedy Store. Next thing you know, we started going out. I had just wrapped up about a year of writing for the new *Laugh-In* (a failed sequel to the big hit *Laugh-In*) and was going out on job interviews at the time, so when I got hired for the writing staff of a brand-new Mary Tyler Moore variety show, I was pretty excited. She was an important female comedy icon in that moment because of her huge hit sitcom. She was truly beloved. Oddly enough, Dave never bothered to mention to me that he was going to be part of the cast of that show, even though we were now spending a lot of nights of the week together. I didn't find out until the first big writers' production meeting after they distributed a printed list of the cast members. I still remember how loud the echo and reverb were on the *boing* that sounded in my brain when I realized that the guy whose apartment I had spent the night in was in the cast of the same show for which I was writing and, oh yes, he hadn't bothered to mention it.

So there we were: working together and dating. And pretty quickly we both realized that the show was in trouble creatively but there was nothing we could do about it. Neither of us had any real creative power. But me being me, I felt his agony trumped mine, since he was on camera, so I started to try to make things better for him by attempting to get sketches that were tailored to his abilities into the scripts. Soon he and I started throwing ideas around for things that would work for him, and I succeeded in getting the best piece he had ever done on that show on the air. It was Dave explaining via a complex chart how a magician actually executes that rabbit-in-a-hat trick. In the chart, the hat was on a stool, and the stool was on a stage, and then a trapdoor beneath the stage led to the Stanford linear accelerator, where the rabbit was put through a series of molecular changes that allowed him to be reassembled particle by particle, then teleported from one place to another.

After that turned out to be a big hit, I started trying to influence everything else that was being written for him on that show. Because now that I was a girl in love, I was hard at work in the trenches of psychology, broadening and deepening the definitions of codependent by trying to protect Dave from having to do anything I knew was going to make him miserable. I was extremely interested in his happiness levels. So I would be going around to the various writers' rooms at work, trying to find out what the other writers were writing, and if it was something I knew would make Dave miserable, I would casually mention, "Hey, just curious: Who did you have in mind for that funny punk rocker sketch? Oh, really? Dave in a purple Mohawk? Because, you know, Michael Keaton would be so great in that sketch." Dave always had an extremely specific sense of boundaries about his comedic abilities. Even when he was thirty, he didn't want to wear a clown hat and clown shoes or do things he thought made him look foolish—he had lines that he wouldn't cross.

So I started to be in charge of writing him sketches that worked inside these very particular guidelines. Eventually the whole Mary Tyler Moore variety show didn't last long enough for my covert work to be much of an issue. But I set a precedent in our relationship as being a person who knew how to write for him. And I kept it going in this direction by writing him jokes for his *Tonight Show* appearances, which were getting more and more frequent. I had begun to think it was my job to do what I could to help out creatively and therefore make both our lives a happier place in which to live. This turned me into kind of the resident expert on how to write for Dave. And as he began to get pilots for his own show, I became his head writer.

First we did a very peculiar pilot for a syndicated talk show that never saw the light of day called *Leave It to Dave*. And then next thing you knew, we were asked to do a *live*, on-air, ninety-minute-a-day morning talk show out of New York. It was basically the time slot that turned into Regis and Whoever. But it was before Regis ascended. It was called *The David Letterman Show* and it was meant for the audience of housewives at home. Fred Silverman was the head of NBC. And he saw Dave as a young Arthur Godfrey, who was someone that neither Dave nor I knew much about but who had been very successful in the early days of TV with the same audience. So, using Godfrey as a template, he wanted Dave to have an "on-air family" and a lot of self-improvement segments like beauty makeover segments and an astrologer. He wanted the bandleader to be a singer like Julius La Rosa, who had been a personality in his own right on the Godfrey show. He would come out and tell a few stories about what had happened the night before and then do a song.

This was not remotely the show Dave and I had been preparing. Our thought was "This is our shot. We have a chance now. Let's do what we think is funny." We were under the influence of a whole new wave of absurdist comedy that had just started to be on TV. *Saturday Night Live* was new and kind of revolutionary. *Fernwood Tonight* with Martin Mull was new and very funny. We were not thinking about beauty makeover segments, except to maybe make fun of them. This eventually led to a network meeting with me, representing the show, and a group of male network executives who explained the research they had done about what women wanted to watch on TV in the morning. And me being me, I of course said something like "Hey, wait a minute, how can *you* guys tell *me* what women do and don't want to watch? Unless I'm reading this wrong, *I'm the only woman here.*" I didn't think women should have to be limited in their choices to having to watch shows full of fashion and makeover segments. I thought there might also be an audience for weird absurdist comedy. But looking back, I now see that actually I had no clue what women did or did not want to see—I was just an eccentric former art teacher/stand-up comedian who didn't have a single bone in her body that wasn't surreal or indie. I didn't know what women did or did not want to see, I just knew what I loved and respected in comedy. So we went ahead and did things we related to comedically, and we got canceled. We were a bad match for that morning audience. But our attempts at being original eventually succeeded in that we won a few Emmys, gained a college audience, and it all led to the late-night show. One thing you really shouldn't do in comedy is try to second-guess an audience. We might not have been pleasing the people at nine a.m., but it turned out we were in fact doing stuff that people late at night wanted to see.

So about a year later the night show started. At the very beginning I was in charge of hiring the writers, and there's been some discussion about why weren't there any other women on the staff. And I think my only excuse is because on the morning show, which had failed rather spectacularly, we hired a few of my friends and everything ended up badly. Although I think we actually did a very hilarious and interesting morning show that was certainly unlike any other morning show, ever, anywhere. (And don't forget *it was live*, which made everything about our eccentric content even weirder.) We hired Valri Bromfield to do her really funny, extremely bizarre characters and also Edie McClurg to play housewife character Mrs. Marv. They were both writer-performers. So that was a sizable women's contingent on the small staff of the morning show. When the night show started, we were reeling from the bad memories of the morning show cancellation. Dave was humiliated and furious and terrified and did *not* want to get canceled again. He kind of held me responsible for the morning show being so full of off-the-wall comedy. I also made some mis-hires on the morning show, which I couldn't foresee, since we were inventing the show as it went along. (And another story, too long to tell: the producer of that show, a game show guy, had quit the show over creative differences and we hit the air *live*, with only *me*, who had never even worked at a talk show before, at the helm.)

Anyway, by the time the night show started, there was a serious mandate for me to learn from what had gone wrong and not make those mistakes again. So I started looking for a writing staff full of Dave alter egos, thinking we needed to come out of the start gate with a unified field theory of Dave. I felt like I had a gun to my head not to make even one mistake again. And I succeeded in this quest by finding a bunch of writers, a lot of them from Harvard, who wrote with the perfect combination of the elements that Dave liked in his comedy material: cerebral but goofy, using traditional structure while at the same time making fun of it. Smart yet stupid. It's still what I like best in comedy—that combination of cerebral and ridiculous. They were a bunch of mostly brilliant guys who I don't regret hiring at all. I'm still friends with lots of them. So the truth is that I was never really taking a position for or against women. I didn't think gender equality was the battle in front of me right then. I was just obsessed with trying to put the elements in place to get this show right this time so as not to be canceled, then killed. Failure was not an option. It never occurred to me for a single second that if the show had a life, decades later there would still be an issue about hiring more women on the staff. I just didn't want the show to get canceled before it succeeded.

I was there on and off through '88. And I left because every aspect of our relationship was coming apart. Badly. We were in an impossible situation in a million ways, and since then I have learned that the circumstances were a great deal more impossible than I had any way of knowing at the time. I actually had stopped being head writer way sooner than made any sense, and voluntarily hired my own replacement, because I was under the impression that the deep craziness of our untenable situation might have been the result of a built-in unavoidable conflict that came from being the big honcho of the writing staff as well as the girlfriend in real life. In my youthful dopiness, I thought if I could whittle the problem areas down to just one area of conflict, instead of two, somehow there was a win in it for me. And leave it to me to pick the most problematic area of the two: the one that didn't have a prayer. It was a completely insane piece of thinking, and had I been remotely as smart as I pretend to be now, I would have advised myself, from the beginning, to forget the girlfriend bullshit, since that showed signs of trouble immediately. In retrospect it seems too bad I couldn't just have written for him and never gotten involved with him personally. But in our case, the writer *and* girlfriend thing started pretty much from minute one. Plus, to cloud things further, I had that young girl's view that everything is fixable and there's always tomorrow, and you never know, everything might change for the better. All those dopey things that girls believe when they don't want to see the truth. I guess you might say that I see things differently now.

6

The Boom Years

While the first wave of stand-ups started hitting the comedy clubs in the 1970s, it wasn't until the 1980s that any began to emerge as bona fide stars. Even then, stand-up remained a boys' club, but the rapid expansion of comedy venues hungry for talent, cable television outlets hungry for easy-to-produce programming, and network executives hungry for stand-ups with sitcom potential created an unprecedented opportunity for women. It wasn't without qualification. On the one hand, never had there been such a variety of female voices in stand-up. But on the other, the most successful female comics tended to be tough, husky, or androgynous, as clear a signal as any that the Diller-era ethos had yet to disappear. Part of the brashness of the women was a response to the rough-and-tumble atmosphere of the comedy clubs. Part of the asexuality was likely a result of the 1980s Dress for Success spirit that favored women in men's clothing. But there is also a deeper, more culturally ingrained explanation: joke-telling—the art of punching out hard, aggressive quips and one-liners—is, as they say, "doing comedy like a guy." In other words, it isn't feminine. The bias against "women's humor"—humor about relationships or body issues—would hang like a cloud over women comics throughout the decade.

SUSIE ESSMAN, comedian   Comedy was the rock and roll of the eighties. I mean, every weekend, lines around the corner to get in for every show. You could feel it. It was a hot, hot, hot place to be.

RITA RUDNER, comedian   It was a boom of comedians—we didn't

156 • WE KILLED

know why, we just wanted to do it. It wasn't because you were going to get fantastically wealthy. We just all loved comedy.

ROSEANNE, comedian   It was very loose; fun, actually. It was just so exciting as a comic to see other comics get up there and push it as far as they could push it. We loved pushing the boundaries, and seeing each other push them, too, and just having a blast before it got so corporate and Dane Cook–ized.

MARK LONOW   The clubs started to open big-time after we went on the air with *An Evening at the Improv*. After that, every guy who had a room was like, "It's no expense, all you need is a microphone and a stool, and you're in business." [In the beginning] none of the comics got paid. Within five years, hundreds and hundreds of clubs opened.

RITA RUDNER   The boom was also the result of cable TV coming into being at the same time. Cable didn't have any money, so if they put a microphone in front of a wall and hired someone that they didn't have to pay any money to, they had very cheap television.

JOY BEHAR, comedian   There was a period in the late eighties when HBO was giving a lot of specials to people and the women were among them. In fact, there was one show called *Women of the Night*. Susie Essman and I were in that; Diane Ford and Lizz Winstead and some other people were too.

Comedy sort of opened up for everybody—there were more slots, so there were more jobs. The more people opened clubs, the more time they needed to fill, and that was an opportunity for us.

RITA RUDNER   I did Broadway for ten years. There were fewer and fewer roles for dancers on Broadway, and I just sat there one day, and I said, "Let's travel a runway that isn't backed up." And I thought, "There aren't many female comedians." I only knew of Joan Rivers and Phyllis Diller. I admired them both tremendously but there were only two of them! There were lots of male comedians, so I thought, "Let's try and be a female comedian."

ELLEN DeGENERES, comedian Looking back now, I was so young! I was in all these small towns and getting picked up in these horrible cars and getting driven to some comedy condo to share with two men that I didn't know. It was just unbelievable what I did for so long. They're not the cleanest places, and [at the venues] you'd get an appetizer if you're an opening act; if you were the middle act, then the main meal was half-price; and you got a free meal if you were the headliner. It was a crazy life.

PAULA POUNDSTONE If I were to start out today, I would fail so miserably for a lot of reasons. For one thing, there's a lifestyle that surrounds it. But the other thing is I was as old as the audiences that were coming in. I started in Boston, and I hacked around there for a little while, and then, because comedy clubs were starting up all around the country, I decided to take a Greyhound bus and go see some. I went to a bunch of places. I went to Toronto and the guy there asked if I wanted to work at his place in Montreal. I took the Greyhound to Denver; there was a club there. I went to Zanies in Chicago.

CLAUDIA LONOW There were comedy hubs in Boston, Chicago, San Francisco, New York, L.A., and that's when there started to be comedy competitions—there was a Boston competition, a San Francisco competition, and every place had this person who came out of it.

PAULA POUNDSTONE One of the things about San Francisco is that on a Monday night I could go to three nightclubs and perform. I could do my five minutes or my ten or whatever it was in three different places, if I could manage either to get a ride or get public transportation quickly enough to scurry from one place to the next. There were enough audiences to do that. And it was people who were paying maybe a buck to get in. Most of the places didn't have full-fledged liquor licenses; they were mostly beer-and-wine places, so people could stay and drink for a long time, because they didn't get that fucked up. There was a pace about it, and a way about it, and there were people who were just starting their adult lives and their careers—not as comics, but in the community of San Francisco—and they discovered this really fun thing to go out and do at night. I think people had a feeling that they were getting in on the ground floor of something as well.

MARK LONOW   In general, Boston was Irish, so there was a lot of story-telling, and it was a little bit odd—that's where you'd get your Steven Wrights. Chicago was more blue-collar: Tom Dreesen, Marsha Warfield. San Francisco was a little bit more intellectual, effete; and New York, very college-educated upper-middle-class, a little bit more refined. Los Angeles was a mélange of all of that, because they were all trying to get on TV. And everybody kind of migrated from wherever—from St. Louis you'd go to Chicago; New England, you'd go to Boston; East Coast, you'd go to New York.

The gush of female comedians in the 1980s represented a major turning point for women in comedy. Never before had so many different women with so many unique points of view been given an opportunity to test their chops in front of live audiences. The solo nature of stand-up comedy offered them not just crucial visibility, but also a chance to bask in the glory of pulling off their own jokes. More important, with the advent of cable television—which had evolved into a voracious purveyor of cheap talent once it evolved into a 24/7 operation—these female comics finally got a shot at the national exposure they'd had a hard time getting on network stalwarts like the Tonight Show.

ZANE BUZBY, director   When I directed the *Women of the Night* special on HBO, the women on the show were each uniquely different. No one was just an observational comic that said, "Hey, did you ever notice at the airport . . ." They weren't like that at all. It was Ellen DeGeneres, Judy Tenuta, Rita Rudner, and Paula Poundstone. Now, start with Ellen. She was just, like, America's sweetheart. She was totally likable, great-looking, and she had a couple of unique bits where she spoke to God on the telephone—that was the big one—and she didn't do much personal material. Paula Poundstone did the personal material: her growing up with her parents, her dysfunctional household. And Paula had this odd body language; she would sprawl all over these stools. Rita's was more observational, and packed with jokes, really well-crafted jokes. Rita was known as the joke machine: she was a really good writer. And Judy Tenuta's was a free-for-all, and her act had music. At one point she spit her gum at the audience and she destroyed the place, just destroyed it.

PAULA POUNDSTONE   I don't really work like joke, joke, joke, joke. My act is kind of a loping pace. Sometimes I'm telling stories. My favorite part of the night is just talking to the audience, and I'm pretty good at it—there's a lot to be mined there in a particular evening. But part of the reason that I think it works, when it does work, is that I just leave my line out there longer than most people would. And my crowd has the patience for that. They're there for the long haul. They're not really sound-bite kind of folk.

ROBIN WILLIAMS   Paula used to do this incredible thing sometimes where she would just lie on the floor—it was lie-down comedy. She would just free-associate and lie on the floor, doing her act lying down, just to change perspective. And she could talk about anything, but it was always Mensa-quality stuff. It was always this feeling of genuine and weird, almost like Lake Wobegone stuff: the minutiae of everyday behaviors.

CLAUDIA LONOW   Paula was the pinnacle of up-and-coming women comics who would be as funny as a guy. And she really was a road warrior. She had a place in L.A. with Taylor Negron, who's also a comic. And she also lived in Robin Williams's house in San Francisco, like in a guest room or something. And she'd drive back and forth in this old car that was named Dave.

I remember I wanted to go with Paula to San Francisco because I thought that would be fun. So we met at a diner in Hollywood—a Denny's or something—and we were going to drive to San Francisco. It's a seven-hour drive and we were listening to music and talking. She was the funniest person by far and she was so nice. I worshipped her. And we get to San Francisco and the first thing we do is stop off at a club, because she's a comic. She walks into a club and they immediately say, "Do you want to go on?" This is 1984, 1985. She gets on and she doesn't do any material. She does ten minutes where she's like a fucking computer: she remembered every funny thing that happened that day. She improvised ten minutes of material based on a funny thing she said in the diner, a funny thing she said in the car, a funny thing she said here, a funny thing I said in a conversation. And I thought to my-self, "I am out of my fucking league."

CHRIS ALBRECHT   Ellen has that rhythm about her that became part and parcel of her humor—she wrote to the rhythm. And it's not that Ellen was self-deprecating, because she wasn't self-deprecating, but there was a certain kind of humility to Ellen that was very endearing and made you laugh at the same time. Ellen was very not in-your-face.

MARK LONOW   Ellen's act was very bright then, and it was completely acceptable, middle-of-the-road, with a few surprises. "I'm driving along and my headlights shine on a beautiful buck, an eight-point buck. I al-ways think, 'Boy would I like a gun now.'" That was one of my favorite jokes of hers. It's a surprise. It's also before she came out. So you had this pretty, nice, middle-class woman wishing for a rifle to kill. You go, "Whoa, hey, funny line." So it was always a little skewed.

ZANE BUZBY   Joy Behar was a teacher in a terrible school, and she had a joke in her act, something about correcting papers and writing, "It's not *who* but *whom* do you kill." So her persona was a really smart New York Jew—except she's not Jewish.

CLAUDIA LONOW   Joy had a bit about having been a teacher and a kid would go, "'Mrs. Behar, Mrs. Behar, he said F! He said F!' And it would drive me crazy until I said, 'Okay, who the fuck said F?'" She had an-other bit about how if you have nipple hair men freak out.

ZANE BUZBY   Joy went from politics, to the news of the day, to a little bit about her personal life. But Joy never really talked about the dating scene except to talk about the kind of man that everyone wants—the kind of man who would hold your purse while you went shopping. Su-sie Essman was more into the dating scene. She had some joke about being in bed with a guy who was, shall we say, in the rear and she's go-ing, "What are you doing back there?" She was a single girl.

ROBERT KLEIN, comedian   I think Brett Butler's important. I met her in Atlanta: she opened for me at the Punchline, and more than once. She was the intelligent-white-Southerner-woman-abused-by-drunken-redneck humor. And it seemed quite different and intelligent and substantial. This was "I was an abused wife," and she was funny. She represented something that was more realistic than Roseanne. It was more truthful.

WHOOPI GOLDBERG I didn't do stand-up. Stand-ups traditionally do joke, joke, joke, joke, joke, and they have to be funny. I always knew I wasn't that. I could be amusing, I could be funny at times, but I don't have the wherewithal to do traditional stand-up material. But people kept telling me I was a stand-up, and I kept saying, "No, no, I'm an actor." And they would go, "Oh, please, you're a stand-up." And I'm like, "No, I tell stories."

Here's what I knew: in order to get the part that I wanted onstage, I would have to do lots of monologues to show people what I could do. And it seemed simpler to just do the characters that I had created, because I wouldn't mess up the lines. So I wrote these folks and performed them in Europe and California and all over the West and got an invitation to come to New York and do this festival that David White put together at the Dance Theater Workshop. And the first day there was nobody there. I was like, "I'm reeeeally sorry." And he was like, "All right, no worries. People will hear and if they're interested, they'll come." And several days later, a gentleman named Mel Gussow wrote an amazing review of my show. If I'd been having sex with him I couldn't have had a better review. And it came out in the morning and, literally, that evening I was sold out for the rest of the run, and then extended. And I think once people heard the name and saw this funny picture of me that was on the flyers, they went, "Oh, I have to see this."

ROBIN WILLIAMS The thing that touched me [about Whoopi] was that it was the first time I had seen a black woman do great white characters. But it was also the range of different characters that she would do and the stuff she was talking about: like she had a story about a little black girl who wanted to be white. She took the towel, put it around her head, and said she had blond hair. It was just like, "Wow, she's turned that one on!"

And years later, when we were doing Comic Relief together with Billy Crystal, she brought a certain kind of honesty to it, because she had been homeless. She had been there, she had raised a child out in the welfare system. For her it was real. That's why you compare her to a female Richard Pryor. She would get down on people, sometimes get really angry, and talk blunt. Well, fuck, she lived it, so why not?

Stand-up is arguably the hardest form of comedy. There are no props, magic tricks, partners, or music to fall back on. It's just the comic, alone, in front of a microphone under the spotlight. When comics fail, they "die"; when they succeed, they "kill." To thrive, they have to get through many a five- or ten-minute set dying, night after night, with no pay, chasing the rush they felt the first night they got up; in front of a live audience, aspiring comics work out their material and design a persona.

JOY BEHAR   Fifty percent of stand-up comedy is persona and confidence, so: who you are and how confident you are. And the one thing that you don't have in the beginning is confidence. The men would come off and they would bomb, and they'd go, "Oh, I had a good time." That sort of denial that the men have serves them very well, because they can go on and on until they get better at it. The women would be more easily crushed. So when the women didn't do well, or even if they did pretty well, they'd say, "Oh, they hated me, I bombed."

CAROL LEIFER   The thing that I've always loved about stand-up comedy is that it's not a very complicated process. You want to be a comedian? Okay, well, you line up during the day, you get a number, and that night, guess what? You're a comedian. But to really get good as a comedian, you gotta do it every night for a long time. I always say it's kind of the conundrum of stand-up comedy. You gotta suck to get good. You really have to die and eat it a lot to figure it out.

JOY BEHAR   I was divorced—a single mother—and I had no career goals at that point, because I had done my job as an English teacher, I had worked on *Good Morning America* in production, I was an unemployment counselor, I worked at a mental hospital. I had run the gamut of jobs, and none of them really suited me. Well, this may sound immodest, but I was very funny. And so it's like when a girl is very, very, very pretty, she knows it, and when somebody's funny, they know it too. So you know what you can do. And so you want to be able to translate something that you are good at into a moneymaking operation—

isn't that the secret? Do what you love and the money will follow, as they say. So that's what I did.

MARGARET SMITH, comedian When I was trying to pass [an audition to perform] at Catch a Rising Star, I would be so devastated by the rejection that I would leave Catch—and I only lived around the corner and down the block—sit on the stoop on my way home and I would cry. I wouldn't even make it home, I would start crying the minute I left. I knew that the material was good, and I just didn't know who I was up there, and I was nervous and I would get up there and my mouth would get dry. And then I would get done crying and then I would walk another half a block home and go to sleep, because I had to get up for work in the morning. And then I wouldn't be able to do it for two weeks, because I wouldn't be able to feel that bad if I didn't pass. I was very thin-skinned. And then, over time, it became a joke: "Okay, where do I sign for more rejection?" So I guess I was getting thicker skin. And then, even though it still meant something to me, it wasn't affecting me like it did in the beginning. And then I started doing two auditions in a week, open mics, and then three, and whenever I could find time.

RITA RUDNER The first time I got onstage, people just stared at me. I stared back. And I said, "This isn't going to be easy." People laughed between the jokes that I told, so I knew I had a comedy persona, I just had to figure out how to write jokes to fit whatever persona it was that I was portraying. And I started to work at it. I watched people every night after my Broadway show. (I was in *Annie*.) I would go and sit in the audience and watch the comedians and see how they did it. And then during the day, when I didn't have auditions, I would go to the Lincoln Center library and read books about comedy, whatever books I could find. I would listen to comedy albums. I would go find film festivals in New York, because I had the benefit of living in a town that had Jacques Tati film festivals. And Buster Keaton, and Charlie Chaplin, old Bob Hope movies, whatever it was, I would just go do something related to comedy, where I felt I could learn something. You have to learn how to become a comedian. You get better and better, you say something funny, you leave it in. If something's not funny, don't say it again. You get up again, you try to put two funny things together. And then you build an act.

SUSIE ESSMAN I always wanted to be a comedic actress like Carol Burnett or Lily Tomlin, sketch kind of stuff. Stand-up never crossed my mind—never crossed my mind. I was just taking acting classes and floundering and didn't know what to do with myself, and I was in a deep depression. And friends kind of forced me to get up at an open mic night. And that's just what happened. I had never been to a comedy club. I wasn't familiar with the stand-up world. The only thing I knew about stand-up was these guys telling jokes that I used to see on *Ed Sullivan* when I was a kid. I mean, they were funny, but it didn't seem to have anything to do with what I wanted to do.

The first night that I got up—this was in 1984, maybe it was 1983. And I got up and I just did these characters—members of my family, street people, whatever was on my mind. And there were these guys there that were opening up a comedy club that came over to me afterward. It was Paul Herzich and Bert Levitt, and they were opening up this club called Comedy U, on University and 13th Street. And they invited me to come work in their club. So if they hadn't been there, I don't know if I would have become a comedian. Because the whole process you had to go through in those days, of standing on line and auditioning, was kind of humiliating and horrifying. And here are these guys, the first day that I ever got up at an open mic, offering me to come work in their club. I gave them my number, and then I didn't get onstage again.

Then, a few months after that first time, they called me and said, "We're opening up the club; will you come work for us?" And they said, "We want ten minutes." I was like, "Ten minutes? I don't have ten minutes." And I sat down and I wrote some stuff. I wrote five minutes of material that I did probably in about a minute and a half. 'Cause I was so nervous. Oh God, it was just—I remember, I was just rocking back and forth with anxiety, sitting on my living room floor. It was horrible.

But the great thing was that this club—every Thursday night they had female comedy night. Now, in my later years, I hate the whole concept of separating female comics. But in those days, it was really great because there was a bunch of us that worked there on Thursday nights, and we developed this kind of camaraderie, and sisterhood, in a way.

ROSEANNE I started at a local club in Denver called the Comedy Works. I did great the first time: I just talked about the sexism in stand-up comedy. "How to Become a Stand-up Comic" was my first routine and I was mostly making fun of men comics. The first time it just really killed, too, 'cause I had followed so many of them doing the penis jokes and fart jokes and body fluid jokes. But the second time I think they all had their hackles up, and it didn't go so well, and I got banned from that comedy club. So at that point I started to work in Unitarian churches and lesbian coffeehouses, 'cause I couldn't get on at the club for a long time.

PAULA POUNDSTONE   I lived in Boston. I was busing tables for a living. I had seen street performers in the Boston Common or the park area, and had kind of fantasized about doing that. But I'm not very much of a self-starter in that way, quite honestly. And fortunately, as luck would have it, I was at a nightclub one night, the Ding Ho, watching a friend of a friend's band, and there was a flyer up that said that on Sunday nights in that club, or every other Sunday or something like that, they had stand-up comics! And so I went to watch, and I was nervous as a cat from the moment I saw that flyer, because I knew that this was the thing that I was gonna do. And I went to watch, and they were pretty terrible. Come to find out, most of them had only started a couple of weeks before this show. And it was billed as a show; it wasn't billed as an open-mic night, or an amateur night. But back in those days, if you had two weeks' experience, by golly, you were a headliner. So that was 1979. And the Comedy Connection didn't own a building and they didn't rent a building, but they sort of took their show on the road from club to club in Boston. I guess I called them up and they said, "Well, we have these auditions." And an audition was in the basement of—I can't even remember the name of the theater anymore. But you were in the basement of this theater with the other comics, and they gathered around and listened while you told your jokes. Which is, of course, the absolute worst idea that anyone has ever had. I couldn't adjust to the idea that you knew what you were going to say ahead of time. So I just went and mumbled in front of these people, and was totally humiliated.

One day, they called me up anyway, and said, "Oh, we were going to have a show with just women, so we thought we'd have you." I had no act. But I guess I figured something out, I wrote something to go do—by that time I had gathered that it would be a good idea to know what you were going to say. So I was a table-buser at the time, and the menus in the restaurant I worked at were on the place mat.

And when they would change the prices, which was fairly frequently, all those place mats that they had stacked up in the basement of the restaurant would be just wastepaper. So I'd take the menus home and type my act on the back of them, and then I would spend days memorizing my act. My lips would be moving the whole time I was busing tables, because I was memorizing my act. And then, generally, well, my recollection of the official first time that I was on was that I was somehow brilliant. Every comic will tell you this: they always remember that their first time, it was just the greatest thing. And the second time was unbelievably bad. There's a couple of reasons for that. One thing is, there used to be this thing before you went onstage for your first time—I don't know whose bright idea this was—but they would make a big deal about the fact that it was your first time. And so the crowd was sort of sympathetic. And the fact that it was your first time was almost part of the joke. But since there weren't that many of us at that time, after you'd been onstage one time, it was like now you're a seasoned professional!

ELLEN DeGENERES   There was no comedy club when I started [in New Orleans], and it was kind of a fluke how it happened. I actually wanted to be a singer and a songwriter, and I was just doing odd jobs and making enough money to pay rent. But I guess my friends thought I was funny, and they were holding a really small benefit—not well organized—to raise money for someone who had some legal problems. And I was eating meat at the time—I don't eat meat any longer—and I got onstage, and basically I made fun of the way people start to tell a story, then take a bite and make you wait until they finish the bite, and then they start the story again, and then they take another bite and it takes forever for them to tell a story. That's what my entire time onstage was. Then I started doing some colleges and some coffeehouses and making maybe like $12—sometimes not even $12. And there was a banner hanging along a balcony in the French Quarter that read "Clyde's Comedy Corner Opening Soon." It was just in the construction stages and I went in, and I met Clyde, and he was just a business guy. He had no idea about comedy, he just knew that the comedy boom was happening and he was opening something that was going to make him money. That's all he knew. So I played some audiotapes for him and he listened. Here's a guy who has no clue what is funny or who's talented. But I'm walking in and saying I want to work there, and he hired me to be the emcee six days a week. So I started working as the emcee there and I got to watch every comedian that came in from New York and L.A. and study them. I worked two shows on Friday, three shows on Saturday, and got more comfortable onstage, and I built up some material.

Eventually Clyde's closed and I went to work at a law firm. [And while I was working there] I heard about Showtime's Funniest Person in America contest and I entered and won for Louisiana. Then I was in the top five. And then I won the entire contest, and I moved to San Francisco. I was sort of an outsider there. There was a little bit of resentment from that crowd. San Francisco was kind of snobby. There was a clique where the more alternative you were and the weirder you were, the better. Then, all of a sudden, I come in and start headlining and middling and I hadn't paid my dues in their eyes. I'd won this stupid—and I agree, it was a stupid contest. To be called the funniest person in America and not really have the experience behind me. But I did have a set. I had time, I had material, and that title earned me a slot to pull a crowd in. It's business. All that mattered was that people came in and paid money to see me. But a lot of comedians resented me for that because they had been working really hard and here's this girl who has this stupid title, and it really backfired on me a lot. And my stuff was quiet, like the conversation I did with God; that leaves lots of room for yelling out. So when I bombed, the emcee would walk back onstage and go, "That was the Funniest Person in America, everybody! She's the Funniest Person in America!" I got a lot of shit for being called that.

PAULA POUNDSTONE The audience of the Boston comedy scene were friends of Lenny Clarke's. That's how that came into being. Lenny's a very funny man. And he's a local, born and raised in Cambridge. Actually, I don't know if he was born there, but he was raised there. I assume he graduated from high school, and I know he even ran for political office at one time—he could have been a politician in the sense that he knew everyone. His style of comedy was what people came to listen to. He ran the open-mic night at the Ding Ho, which is the club where I first saw the flyer. It was this funky little Chinese-restaurant-slash-nightclub in Inman Square in Cambridge. Well, back then, the open-mic night was the biggest night of the week. It was Wednesday. People don't do it this way anymore, but back then, audience members came in for free—I think eventually, they started charging a buck—but they came in for free, and they watched this long night of comedy. And anybody who wanted to could get up and do five minutes. And Lenny was the emcee, so he controlled who went on and when. And a lot of us were terrible. Terrible! So Lenny was really what people were watching, for the most part. That kind of emcee job allows one a good deal of freedom, so he really kind of set the style, and if you fell into that sensibility, then you were going to be well liked. Now, Lenny's a really, really, really funny guy, but very crass. There's nothing he won't say. And it's funny, too, because he's such a funny guy that it almost didn't matter what he was talking about. Whereas in the hands of somebody else—somebody less charming, somebody less Lenny—the same type of subject matter was just gross and stupid. Yet it appealed to a lot of people there. So it could also be a bit of an upstream swim sometimes.

All comedians face the challenge of coming up with a viable act. But the women of this era also faced a distinct set of challenges their male counterparts were spared: sexist club owners, hecklers, and cultural dictates on what was and wasn't acceptable, ladylike behavior. In many clubs, female stand-ups were restricted to "women's nights" or special rooms at the club that were separate but decidedly not equal.

JOY BEHAR   You'd go on the road and you'd have two men and I'd say to them, "Why can't we put another woman on the show?" "Oh, no, you don't want to have another woman, you want to be the only one." They had this idea they were doing me a favor. They were not doing me a favor; they were not doing any women a favor. Can you imagine saying to a man, "Oh, you should be the only man on the bill, it'll be good for you"?

MARGARET SMITH   At the Comic Strip in New York, I wasn't passing in the beginning. I was talking about my family and growing up. I said, "I grew up in a family where everyone was fat but me. I used to have to hide in the bathroom to eat. They'd all be at the door, trying to get in to get my food." Or "I wore a neck brace for a year. I wasn't in an accident, I just got tired of holding my head up." I would do stuff based on my personality. The guy told me, "Talk about things that women talk about." I said, "Like what?" "You know, stuff women talk about." I said, "Well, it's not hard to get a guy, so I'm not going to talk about that. I feel good about myself, so I won't be saying I got dumped." It was like he wanted me to talk about someone else's life. He also told me not to wear the sleeveless blouse that I was wearing. So I never did pass there. I just stuck to the Improv and Catch a Rising Star, and then eventually I just started calling in and getting spots at the Comic Strip. It's like they forgot that I was inappropriately a woman.

MO'NIQUE, comedian To be black is the challenge in American society; then to be a woman is a challenge in American society. Now, to be a black woman and to be a comic? I guess that some people saying Mo'Nique is so blue, she can be challenging. But I never looked at it as hurdles. I never looked at it as "This is a challenge." I looked at it as "You know what? This is just part of the journey."

I would say maybe for the first fifteen years of my career, I had an all-black audience. Now you'll see black, Hispanic, Asian, white, at my shows. You'll see people who are twenty-one to ninety years old. You'll see straight, you'll see gay, you'll see in between.

And I don't get up on that stage and say, "Oh God, if I say this, will white people like me? If I say this, will black people like me?" I'm gonna say what feels good to me. Now, whoever likes it, come on and play. But what happens is, some white people may feel like "I can't go to that show because I won't be able to relate to what they're saying. They're black." And black people may feel the same way—vice versa—when it comes to a white comedian. But you'll see that when you're funny, like Ellen DeGeneres, Rosie O'Donnell, or George Lopez—when you're simply funny, it's colorless.

THEA VIDALE, comedian The first time I came to the Comedy Store [in L.A.] it was in the afternoon so I could meet Mitzi Shore and see if I could get some stage time. I happened to know the doorman from the road, and I had just moved to L.A., and I told him I wanted to meet Mitzi. He said, "First you gotta take that nose ring off, because Mitzi doesn't like that." I said, "I'm not taking the nose ring out. What the fuck is that about?" He said, "Mitzi won't like it. I can't introduce you to her." And I could see that he felt that he was in a position of power over me. And I said, "Well, I'll think about that, but anyway, I just wanna do some stage time." He said, "Let me tell you something: if you really wanna get onstage, what I ought to do is take you upstairs to the mansion and let you get on your knees and do something for me and I'll get you onstage for Mitzi." I said, "Oh my gosh." You know I had heard about this shit, but I didn't think anybody that knew me would ever come up with some shit like that. I said, "Motherfucker, you know what? You lucky I ain't got my gun with me, because you know what? I got a trick for your monkey ass. If I was you, I wouldn't ever think about putting your dick in the mouth of a woman like me, because I would bite that bitch off. You would bleed to death."

CAROLINE RHEA, comedian   I have a famous joke about blow jobs: "Why is it that during regular sex a man can have an orgasm in like ten seconds, but if it's oral sex it's five and a half hours?" I was inspired by the fact that people would say to me, "Women shouldn't talk about that onstage." And that just fueled me to absolutely talk about it onstage. Nobody should tell a woman that there are things she can't talk about.

DIANE NICHOLS   I'll tell ya, the prejudice against women comics . . . Men can get up there and talk about sports and their morning boner till you wanna puke and we're supposed to think it's funny. But if you talk about female stuff, they think you're not a real comic.

LIZZ WINSTEAD, comedian   There's this disconnect—people always said about women [that they are more self-deprecating than men and they make a lot of PMS jokes]. Yet none of the women I knew did that sort of comedy. It seems that people like to make this stereotype, but how can they keep saying that's what women comedians do all the time when a bunch of successful ones don't?

JOY BEHAR   I never talked about my period or anything like that. And the women—I came up with Susie Essman, who did the characters based on her family, and Rita Rudner never did a period joke. Maybe audiences heard one or two women do it and they extrapolated from there. I mean, you could say that men only want to talk about masturbating because I saw several men talking about that. That didn't mean that Jerry Seinfeld was doing that; he wasn't. So I think that it is just a prejudicial remark and a stupid remark.

What women were criticized for was self-deprecating material.

Joan Rivers and Phyllis Diller took a lot of the heat on that one, because they were considered to be self-deprecating. But then again, Rodney Dangerfield was the one who kept saying, "I don't get no respect." The women seemed to get the rap for that, but plenty of male comedians would come out and talk about how shlubby they were. Or they would *be* shlubby, and it would be obvious. But they would do jokes on how macho they were to show you the opposite of what they looked like. So all of that is rather self-deprecating, but no one really got on the men for it, only the women.

SUSIE ESSMAN   There would always be a late show on a Saturday night. And you got a lot of drunk people and a younger crowd—they were tough, those crowds. And there would always be some mediocre guy emceeing or something who would come off and say to me something like "You know what? You might not want to go on, they're really rough." And that would just give me so much motivation. "Oh, really? Watch me."

CAROL LEIFER   I had a lot of trouble early on, being one of the first women comedians. If there was a group of three or more guys, I was pretty sure I was gonna get heckled by them. It was just par for the course. And I had a lot of trouble with that. Another comedian, a male, gave me a really good idea for when I got heckled. He said, "With guys like that, you have to go for the jugular." So when guys would heckle me, my inevitable response would always be "So, guys, where are the girls tonight?" And it would turn the whole discussion around, because it was like, "Oh, you're guys who have no dates." So that would spin it around, and then: "Oh, I guess they're parking the car, huh?" And that would shut them right up, because I went to the part of their ego that they didn't want to be magnified at that point, which was "Oh, you're guys here alone, with no dates. Okay, so that's why you're picking on the female comedians." What I came to see is that when you perform, the audience is very fair. The heckler gets as much room as you do, which I'm surprised about, but they want to see that gladiator kind of atmosphere. They enjoy that. So I had to learn to let the heckler have his day—and then squash him.

JULIE BARR, comedian   There are a couple different kinds of hecklers.

There are the guys who just want to see what you're made of: "You're a chick and you think that you're funny?" They would, like, hint that the microphone was a dick. And those were guys I was playing to, the Boston blue-collar drunks. So Irish, Italian, working-class, where women don't have any power or say and men rule the roosts. And I would just be rough with them. I remember I wrote this line: "I have a comedy book, and it tells me what to do in the event of hecklers, 'Sir, what is your name? And what do you do? And how old are you?'" And then I would pretend to look it up in the book, and then I would say, "Oh, the comedy book tells me to tell you to SHUT THE FUCK UP." And if I would come at them hard like that, the group of hecklers would sort of dissolve, because they would see that I can handle myself and I wasn't afraid of them. Then there is the next group of hecklers: the people who want attention. They think they're funny and they think, "Who do you think you are? I'm funnier than you are." And I learned that if they said something funny, just give it to them, let them have their one time, or their two times, and then the audience would get annoyed with them. The whole point is you want to get the audience on your side. Then the third group of hecklers are passive-aggressive; women fall into this category a lot. They would be the kind of girls who weren't getting any attention, so they would just talk loud to their friends. So you would just call them out on that. But you can't really attack them, because they're not *really* heckling. The guys will confront you or heckle you; women will be like, "Oh, no, I think you're funny."

WENDY LIEBMAN, comedian   I've only been heckled in the true sense twice. People talk to me when I'm onstage all the time, but they're not mean. I was doing some college show and I used to do impressions of famous people's girlfriends, like I'd do Picasso's girlfriend. And I made a funny face, and it was ridiculous. But some guy yelled out, "Do *your* girlfriend!" I had never been heckled before then, and I said something like "I'm not gay but I could get more girlfriends than you." Another time a woman was talking to me when I was onstage and she said, "You know, I'm a comic too!" And I said, "Oh, that's interesting." Then later in the show she said, "You know, I could have written a funnier punch line." And at this point I had been performing for like ten years and I was burned out and I just wanted to cry. But I just said, "Well, where are you working tonight?"

MO'NIQUE The only time I really noticed a difference [between male and female comics] was when we did the Kings and Queens of Comedy [comedy tours]. And the Kings of Comedy, all those guys were such gentlemen, they were our big brothers, but there were times that we would see the imbalance and we would see the unfairness with the promoter. They can't have a room full of food and all we have is a cheese tray; they can't all have limousines and we're all in one town car.

SUSIE ESSMAN These days the emcee is like the low man on the totem poll. But at Catch, the emcee was the star of the show. It was like your show, and then you just put the lineup together by whoever was out at the bar. I was talking about this a couple of months ago when I ran into Chris Rock. There used to be a spot at Catch called the standby spot, and on the weekends they booked the show—an emcee and four comics—and then they'd hire the standby, who had to sit at the bar, and got twenty bucks in case somebody didn't show up. And Chris Rock used to be the standby. I remember when I was emceeing and Chris being the standby. We all paid our dues. Male and female. It was tough for all of us to get stage time and to get spots. Nobody just walked into it easily.

PAULA POUNDSTONE I don't know that women were deliberately shut out. I followed a man one night—Steve Sweeney, who now is a radio guy in Boston, I think, and I'm sure still works clubs there. Very funny guy, very interesting guy, lot of talent. I think the joke became "How low can I go?" during this particular set that he was doing. And the last thing Steve Sweeney said was "So I was eating out the cunt of a bear." And the crowd went nuts. Funniest thing they'd ever heard in their lives. And now, the emcee goes on—I think it was Lenny Clarke—and he kind of gets them back: "All right, the fun time's over. And now, please welcome Paula Poundstone." But you know, it's very hard to follow. It's like some guy unsheathes a big, huge sword and I realize I have a rubber band in my pocket. So did anybody deliberately exclude women? No, definitely not. And if I had wanted to go on and say, like, "I know that bear"—if I had wanted to join in on that in a particular way (and I think there were times I probably did try to, just in that sad elementary-school please-accept-me-on-the-yard kind of way)—[I could have,] but I knew it wasn't where I lived. And it wasn't where I was going to thrive.

ZANE BUZBY   You had to be able to get up onstage, and you had to be able to make it through the comedy scene, and I think that's why they had tough personas. It was not easy, it was not easy at all, and it was a very solitary, lonely existence out there. Rita had her manager then, and he was her best friend and then he became her husband, so she had someone in her corner. But a lot of these women were out there alone. They had to have tough personas to make it in the business. Rita is a lady, but there aren't too many ladylike comedians out there. If you're out on the road awhile, you're subject to a lot of horrible stuff, because you're a woman in a nightclub alone, you get hit on, you get treated really poorly. Not a lot of people are really made for that.

Depending on who you talk to, women comics either felt aided by fellow females or royally snubbed. Regardless, a boys' club atmosphere prevailed in the clubs, and were it not for the support of several men, many of the women would never have survived the experience.

ROSEANNE   I had a lot of support from men comics who were from Los Angeles and came through Denver and saw me. Sam Kinison, Louie Anderson, a guy named Allan Stephan, and Richard Belzer. And they really did a lot to help me. They told club owners to put me on. It wasn't the comics in Denver who were supportive; it was the ones passing through, the good ones.

SUSIE ESSMAN   Belzer was always a very early supporter. He was not a sexist male. He was Mr. Catch a Rising Star. I still was not working at Catch a Rising Star, but Lenny Belzer, Richard's brother, had seen me at Comedy U and he told Belz about me. I guess I'd been in the business just three, four, five months, something like that. So Belz wanted to see me perform and he got me on to do a couple of minutes at Catch a Rising Star. But I still wasn't a Catch act. Then he asked me to open for him at Caroline's—that was the old Caroline's on Twenty-eighth and Eighth. Great club, but they were a headline club even then. So I opened for Belz there, and Caroline and everybody there saw me, and then asked me to open for them. Gilbert Gottfried was gonna work there the following spring; they asked me to open for Gilbert. Jerry Seinfeld saw me open for Gilbert, and asked me to open for him. That was a very, very prestigious thing in those days, 'cause these were guys that were very well established and everybody in the business came to see them. So it was great exposure.

ADRIANNE TOLSCH, comedian I passed my first audition, at the Comic Strip. I auditioned three times, they finally passed me, and at the time, the show went till four in the morning. So after I passed the audition, my first spot was 3:55 a.m. There were like four people in the audience, two of them with their heads on the table. This was '78. Then I had a friend, one of the emcees at the Comic Strip, who was friendly with an emcee at Catch a Rising Star, so I got a late spot there without the audition and I started hanging out there. And what happened was, I was hanging out there, trying to get onstage, hanging out at the bar like all the other comics, and who was emceeing that night? Kelly Rogers was emceeing. Great comic. Kelly was the house emcee and he was just great. And he'd been doing it for a long time, and he was starting to get bored—he'd show up on roller skates and with animals, anything to keep himself from being bored to death. And one night he came in and said, "Fuck those other Jews, you're emceeing." So I got up and emceed that night. It was not the first time I'd ever emceed, but it was the first time I'd emceed there. And it was either that night or the night after that that Richard Belzer saw me, and picked up the phone and called Rick Newman, and said something good, because from then on I was emceeing regularly. I did it for five years. Richard Belzer was king of Catch a Rising Star, and he was my mentor. There was nobody better than Richard Belzer. There was nobody faster, there was nobody funnier, there was nobody savvier than him. He was—and still is, for my money—the best.

ALLAN STEPHAN, comedian I was a big act in Denver in the early eighties and so was Louie Anderson. I got to the club early one night—and Roseanne was onstage. I was fascinated by her. I thought she was very original. And her closing joke was "A lot of people say I'm not feminine. Well, they can suck my dick." And I said, "Wow, I have to meet this woman." I went backstage. I thought she was delightful; she was funny. I said, "When do you work here?" and she said, "Oh, they won't put me on." And I said, "What are you talking about?" She said, "Well, they don't find me funny. They're very difficult on women here." And I go, "Well, you'll just have to be on the show with me." And that was the beginning of our friendship. And I fought for her there. And I said, "No her, no me."

ROSEANNE They called me a "girl." Allan Stephan went to the club owners and was like, "Why don't you put that girl on? She's funnier than all the guys that you're putting on." He and Louie Anderson, they went right to the club owners on my behalf and got those rules changed for me.

Life at the comedy clubs wasn't just a struggle. There was a lot of late-night fun, fueled by drugs and heavy drinking, and the camaraderie among the comics—once established—developed into long-lasting relationships. More than just friendship, these associations gradually formed a network of funny people who circulated in Hollywood as a pack, often appearing on each other's sitcoms or behind the scenes in each other's writers' rooms.

PAULA POUNDSTONE I remember I used to go watch—I watched a lot back then, for a couple of reasons. One being, you needed to kind of show your face to stay in people's memory—because there were only a handful of bookers—so that when they went to make their schedule, they would go, "Oh, you know, let's get Paula Poundstone." So you needed to be a part of the group in that way. You really did need to hang around and drink with them, and schmooze, or whatever you want to call it, just so you'd be one of the guys and get on the list. Therefore, I went to the clubs even if I wasn't working. I went out and I watched and I hung out.

JOY BEHAR You had to hang out. You had to go there at around, let's say, eight o'clock, nine o'clock, and you had to hang out at the bar. And you sat around and talked to other comedians at the bar. And then there'd be a show going on in the next room. And at that time the emcee was in charge of picking who was going to get on. And so they'd come out to the bar and they'd see who was there, and then they'd ask you if you wanted to do five, ten minutes. And you'd be petrified—and you'd just do it.

CAROLINE RHEA Joy was just the queen of Catch [when I came to New

York in 1989]. There was a bar at Catch a Rising Star and she was the queen. She knew everybody.

CAROL LEIFER   People always have this image of comedians being backbiting and competitive, but it was a very rare time that I feel lucky to have been a part of. People would watch each other and give each other notes. They really became my surrogate brothers and sisters, like a family in a lot of ways. And you'd go on every night.

BOBBY SLAYTON, comedian   Paula Poundstone moved to San Francisco from Boston, and I was a headliner at the Punch Line, which is the big comedy club. And I always chose my opening acts. I was one of the first people to really help Paula. She hadn't been doing comedy very long, but I thought she was really good. And I remember at the time, she would come over to our house and she'd be in bed with my girlfriend watching television—nothing sexual, she was like a little kid when she'd come over. And after the shows, if the comics would hang out we'd go to a diner, like to Denny's, four or five of us. And Paula would sit there downing packs of sugar. The rest of us were doing coke, so I guess sugar is better for you. But she must have had some sort of chemical imbalance, 'cause she'd suck down like five or ten packets of sugar.

RICK NEWMAN   Waitresses were sleeping with comedians and comedians were sleeping with comediennes.

SUSIE ESSMAN   I never took time off. None of us did: that's how we got good, 'cause it was also our social life. We'd hang out, we'd all be at the club, Catch a Rising Star, we'd all be working, and we'd all go to the diner afterward.

ADRIANNE TOLSCH   We'd go to the Green Kitchen, a diner, which was a little funkier than it is now. It was open all the time! We had our pictures on the wall: it was a real pseudo–Stage Door. And we were eating crap at one or two in the morning.

RICK NEWMAN   You would wind up at the Green Kitchen at three in the morning talking about everyone else's sets and sharing lines with each other, written lines and other lines. There were two kinds of lines!

ADRIANNE TOLSCH   Coke was everywhere in the clubs. And now that Catch is closed I can say this. This was early eighties, you'd go down to the basement and there was a fluorescent light fixture and tucked inside were a million little half grams of coke and a straw for you to use. Yeah, it was ubiquitous. I don't remember doing a line before I went onstage; maybe I did. But I was around the corner in a stupor under a car, toking up with other people. There were comics that didn't touch the stuff. There were comics who touched the stuff but you didn't know, who were kinda cool about it. Then there were slobs like me and the rest of us who just dove right in. And I ran into trouble.

I would get a line as a headliner on the road and have to do an hour. And I would do fifty minutes and come offstage thinking I had done an hour. "Hey, I killed!" "No you didn't, no you didn't, and your nose is bleeding." So that had to be taken care of. [Drugs] became such a distraction, I eventually became homeless while I was working at Catch. I never actually slept on the street, thank God. When comics went on the road, they would let me stay in their apartments two, three nights, or stuff like that. But I lost my apartment; everything I owned was in two plastic bags. I would show up at Catch, put my plastic bags in the coatroom, go onstage for the night, then grab the plastic bags and ride the kindness of other comics and stay at somebody's house. I did have to sleep on the stage at Catch one or two nights because I had no place to go. One of the bartenders locked me in for the night. It was a distraction, and yes, if you're in that kind of head, you're not gonna make follow-up calls: "Oh, did you see me last night?" "Can I have work?" and all that stuff. So I guess that really got in the way.

LINDA SMITH, comedian   Boston is a very heavy drinking town, absolutely. In those days we didn't pay for alcohol, because a lot of the times you were working for nothing, so instead of paying you they'd say, "Yeah, go drink." And then things started to change, but still, a lot of it was free. It didn't matter. I'd pay for it. I wanted to drink and I'd stay out all night. I mean, the guys and gals in Boston—it was mostly the guys—they were a lot of fun. But you know, we were all drinking too much.

There was also a ton of coke. And I did that too. I don't do it anymore. There were two coke clubs. The interesting thing about Boston was that the coke guy, the dealer, he would show up just as you were getting paid. How interesting—I'm getting my cash and "Oh, there he is!" And there goes your money. And then we would be out all night. And then a lot of times you wound up at somebody's apartment and carried on. But listen, it was a ton of fucking fun. And I know we were snorting coke and I knew I shouldn't be, but I was having a ball!

JULIE BARR   I was never paid in cocaine. But I know at a couple of the comedy clubs you were paid in cocaine. I had never even done cocaine until I came here [to Boston], and I thought, "What is this, L.A.?" I couldn't even stand it. But I mean everyone was doing it, and Nick's Comedy Stop would pay headliners part cocaine and part money.

PAULA POUNDSTONE   The truth is, I was not as big a drinker as many people that I know, but it sure did fuck me up. And so I would just have to say that I didn't handle it as well as the others. I would still be an enormous advocate of a one-or-two-drink high. My problem was I just kept overshooting it. I could never remain at the really good spot that you hit. And even now as I describe it, I'm not sure if it's a one- or a two-drink. I don't know if it was one and a half or one and three-quarters. But what would happen is, once I went past it and I was no longer there, I would think, "Well, maybe it's a three-drink high. I can't remember anymore." In terms of going onstage, I didn't necessarily get drunk onstage but would have a glass of wine before I went on. I think it was like Dumbo's feather. I think it made me feel more confident. I was more relaxed—or I thought I was. I couldn't say that everyone did it, but I would say it was fairly common. I know a guy who locked himself in a club and drank himself to death. I certainly know guys that fell prey to that. I think the percentages would be the same whether you went to a comedy club or you went to a church. The only difference may be—and may I rot in hell for this ever being true—that I probably had a certain sense of entitlement. I think I told myself that it went with the territory. I think I thought that this was to be expected, and that's probably where the real trouble existed.

Among the comics who were getting ahead—nods on the Tonight Show, *television sitcoms, starring and costarring roles in movies—there was one attribute the female comics who had tasted success all had in common: they were brassy, overweight, or sexually ambiguous, and none focused their acts on dating or sex. The one barrier this new crop of women could not knock down was the old exception that pretty isn't funny.*

LILY TOMLIN   When I was at the Upstairs at the Downstairs in the late 1960s, I wasn't knowledgeable enough to know that there's an ingénue—a leading lady—and a character woman. I thought everybody could do anything and, of course, I was probably always the character woman. And so the girl who I suppose was the ingénue was horrible onstage, I mean totally boring onstage, as ingénues are. But in the dressing room this girl was so damn funny, I would just be doubled over. She would tell me some story or characterize it or do something, and be very funny. And I'd say, "Oh God, you've gotta do that onstage." And literally her hair would balloon out, get twice as big just on its own, and she'd pull herself up and she would always wear a fur coat to the club. And I remember her looking in the mirror and pulling herself back together. And she said, "Oh, I wouldn't want anyone to think I was unattractive." Literally, she said that. That was the prevailing sentiment.

LOUISE LASSER   Woody [Allen, Lasser's ex-husband] always used to say to me, "You should do comedy." And I'd go, "Don't say that! That's horrible! I don't want to do comedy!" And he said, "Why don't you want to do comedy? You're so funny." And I said, "It's a disgusting thing to do." I thought of it as a very masculine thing to do. I thought of it like the old-broad comedians. I had a prejudice against it. So I'd say, "No, I'm not doing that! I don't want to do that."

ZANE BUZBY   There's a thing called "Comedy isn't pretty," and when you're casting, everyone's always looking for the beautiful female comedic lead. And except for people like Jennifer Aniston and Mary Tyler Moore, that does not exist. There were very few in history who were ever considered beautiful, ladylike, and funny. Because beauty isn't funny. The reason people are funny is because they're usually overcoming some kind of personality flaw or physical flaw, so they become the funny one in their family, or they become the class clown in school. That's why they're funny. Very beautiful people don't have to try very hard to be liked, so they don't have to develop their comedy timing to be liked or be considered cool and hip and fun. Beauty is not funny.

MARGARET CHO, comedian I think for women in comedy, it's really hard if you're pretty. If you're pretty, you just can't work. It sucks, because people just don't care. They're like, "We don't want to hear anything from you." You can see how much resentment people have toward people they think are privileged, and on the top of that list are, naturally, really beautiful girls. I remember going to see beautiful girls trying to do stand-up comedy and it was just a disaster every time. Not only were people gonna not listen to you because you're a woman, if you're good-looking, then people *really* don't want to listen to you.

When I was younger, I was really fat. So that was good, because then you just automatically get some kind of weird authority. If you're fat, people go, "Oh, she's cool." But I also wore a lot of Madonna-wannabe old lingerie kind of stuff. And it was really upsetting to people that I was fat but also being super-flirtatious in the way that I dressed. I kept being told I was too sexual, even when I didn't think I was doing anything.

MARGARET SMITH None of the women were wearing dresses onstage back then. Possibly Rita Rudner was wearing a skirt. But most of us wore jeans and blouses. I didn't wear a lot of makeup. I was young and I really didn't need makeup. But then I had a manager who said, "You really should wear lipstick." I used to talk about it in my act. I said, "Well, what if I'm not funny and it's coming out of these big old red lips? Aren't they going to notice it more?"

ZANE BUZBY Funny will always win in terms of getting the industry's attention. So if a female comic was spotted in a club and she was truly funny—she killed—she would get noticed and be brought to the attention of agents, managers, networks. Because funny is funny. It's undeniable. But if her persona was "a single woman's sex life" or the dating scene where she could be perceived as promiscuous, it was a turnoff for TV executives and their sponsors. So people like Susie Essman, who were undeniably funny in the clubs, would get a shot to be seen by the networks or HBO and even maybe get a special; but in terms of a series, even if they managed to get a development deal or even shoot a pilot, the persona of the strong, independent, single female was still as threatening and "unattractive" to the networks and the advertisers.

For Roseanne, who was brash and strong and not particularly attractive—well, that could all be tempered by making her a working-class *mom* struggling like so many families across the U.S.A. were. They could surround her with something familiar—a family—and make her totally relatable, not some sexpot that would be totally unrelatable to the demographic the advertisers were trying to capture.

CINDY CHUPACK, writer I definitely remember, before *Sex and the City*, that trying to sell a show to the networks that was just about dating was nearly impossible. It always seemed that could be part of a story, but it had to be like a *Mary Tyler Moore*, where it was a workplace as well. Love didn't seem like enough of a topic to hold a show. And certainly dating. And then, after *Sex and the City*, it felt like there was a lot of demand for that. It just sort of opened the doors to the things that women talk about, that we've always talked about and joked about with our friends but that weren't necessarily considered legitimate topics for television and for comedy.

JANEANE GAROFALO, comedian Of course, in mainstream television and mainstream film, the nature of that beast is that the women still have to be good-looking. Men can be funny and look however they want to and be any age. But women have to be young and beautiful, which knocks seventy-five percent of the talent out of the box to be funny.

WARREN LITTLEFIELD, former president, NBC Entertainment One of the—I am reluctant to say a rule, but one of the broadcast observations that you can make, [from] many shows across a long period of time, is, female audiences are very comfortable looking at funny men, and male audiences will look at men doing their own shenanigans, the things that men do. And an exclusive female comedy—it is much more difficult to get men. You know, it's damn near impossible.

WHOOPI GOLDBERG [When I was doing movies] they never gave me a guy to interact with. And when they did, they said, "Oh, no, you can't be having a big old love affair. We'll hint that there's one but we'll never see it." It broke my heart, too, because I would have loved to have kissed Sam Elliott. But a lot of it had to do with what one director labeled my "fuckability factor." And basically he said, "You have no fuckability factor. No one wants to fuck you." Literally. And I was sitting in a room with the fabulous Sam Elliott and before I could really snap, Sam said, "Number one, that's the rudest thing I've ever heard anybody say to somebody else, and number two, what are you talking about?" And he said to the director: "And who wants to fuck you?"

LISA KUDROW, actress   I had an agent a long time ago who said, "You know, we don't know what to do with you. You're not, you know, gorgeous, so you don't really fit in anywhere." Because those were the only roles for women on TV. I think there's still a pressure to be as attractive as you possibly can. And it's not from outside, it's inside too. They start feeding into each other. You see yourself on TV and it's like, "Wow, I really should lose; I really should be ten pounds underweight if I can manage it."

KATHY GRIFFIN, comedian   After *Suddenly Susan*, and I swear to God, may God strike me dead if I'm lying, I went to every network and I said, "What if you put four funny chicks together?" And these are four women that are proven in television, not even newcomers. But what if you did a show with me, Jennifer Coolidge, Megan Mullally, Cheri Oteri, Molly Shannon, pick names. Four chicks in comedy. You do the show with the four of us." And I would have network people say, "What about Carmen Electra?" And I'd be like, "Four *funny* women, don't you understand?" And I had this one meeting and this guy goes, "What about Lara Flynn Boyle?" And I go, "Okay, great on *The Practice*, but are you fucking kidding me?" Four comedians. Roseanne-funny, like women who are comedians professionally. And nobody would touch it. Then *Desperate Housewives* comes on and they're like, "Girl power!" I'm like, "Okay, Nicollette Sheridan is in a bikini half the time. Teri Hatcher is from *Lois and Clark*. Felicity Huffman is a David Mamet dramatic actress, and Marcia Cross is from *Melrose Place*. I'm sorry! I like that show, it's a great show, but they're not Jennifer Coolidge. They're not Lisa Kudrow. They're not Kristen Wiig. They're not comedian funny."

RACHEL DRATCH, cast member, *Saturday Night Live*   I kind of think maybe I should have gussied up a little more—which is frickin' sad to say, because that's not what I want to be thinking about with comedy—but I have to say, maybe there's something to that. I don't think [it was an issue at *Saturday Night Live*], I'm just saying the vibe was to play it up or something. There's no vanity in comedy. But maybe that kind of bit me in the ass. Because sometimes people see me on the street, they're like, "You look so much prettier in real life." And I'm like, "That's 'cause you only saw me playing like old ladies and with an arm out of my head." And maybe I shouldn't have taken that so far? Not that I would ever. I have no regrets. But I just mean, like, it definitely influences how Hollywood thinks of you.

PAULA PELL, writer   I wrote a sitcom. My pilot that got picked up was about fat and it was about weight. So it was about two sisters and they grew up fat. One lost a bunch of weight and became gorgeous, and the other one was still fat. But the one that was thin now was insecure and was lost at sea, and the fat one was kind of this sexy, funny, sassy young girl that didn't care. She was of that era now [when some] young girls are becoming less crippled by being a bigger person. And she was more confident. So it was one of those things where on paper and where you're pitching it, "Oh, we love this. We love the subject." NBC was so excited about the subject of fat and women talking about fat. And there was a Weight Watchers meeting in it and all this stuff.

When you get to the reality of it and the casting of it, you start hitting those walls that the person that I think is the funniest person for this, they think is too fat. And God knows, over the years in sitcoms—there are all those dudes that play [in shows like] *The King of Queens*, giant gut and then the cute wife. You know, it's such a double standard of body.

So we were trying to find the fat sister, and to find girls that have a résumé and that are fat are few and far between, because they had to be young. So this girl comes in and they say to me, "Did you audition so-and-so?" And they named this one person. And I go, "Yeah, we auditioned her for the thin sister." And the person went, "And you couldn't pad her?" They wanted to pad her to be the fat sister. And I'm like, "First of all, that's ludicrous. Like you'd know immediately that that person wasn't a fat person. But how sad is that, to suggest like that would somehow be more palatable?"

And the girl that ended up playing the [heavier] sister was hilarious—I loved her, I was so happy with her—but she was not as heavy a girl. The first girl that I found was like, you know, bells went off. I went, "Oh my God, this is exactly the voice I want this girl to have," because she was kind of smart-assy with her sister and intolerant and funny. And she just came in and killed it. But she was this super-short, super-big girl. And I just watched the network people staring at her body as she was auditioning instead of listening to how funny she was and just kind of doing the up-and-down, like, "I don't know if people wanna see that on television." Meanwhile, *The Biggest Loser* was one of their biggest hits.

MARCY CARSEY I can't stand that there are no loud-voiced women in comedies on television anymore. Where are the big, brash women? Where is the Lucy and the Maude and the Roseanne? I mean, all these women in these comedies are mildly funny and they are all size zero or size two. Am I forgetting anyone? 'Cause it really has been ten years of this!

Given the so-called masculine nature of stand-up, many female comics found their sexuality under scrutiny, and accusations from peers and audiences that many of these female comedians were lesbians were hard to avoid. In some cases, rumors that certain female comics were gay were true (Lily Tomlin, Ellen DeGeneres), but in others women were unfairly singled out. Not that being gay necessarily hurt these female comics— lesbians were among the comics who were most easily finding success. Ironically, though, the repercussions of coming out were not so clear-cut.

ILIZA SHLESINGER, comedian Paula Poundstone and people like Ellen, their comedy was never about sex. And maybe it's because they're lesbians—well, I'm pretty sure Paula [is a lesbian]; it would be weird if she wasn't a lesbian. But their comedy was never about being a girl, it was about being a person, and everyday things. I remember taking that with me and thinking, "I respect that they did that and that they didn't acquiesce to the influences of society that 'girls have got to be girls.'" And I always liked that about them, their seeming asexual.

ROBIN WILLIAMS Years ago Paula did this great joke about this guy tried to pick her up, saying, "A lot of people think you're gay, but I don't." And she went, "Well, now I want you—big-time." She would just turn it on its head.

LOUISE LASSER   I went to see Lily's one-woman Broadway show. This was '76. I was in her dressing room, and her publicity agent, Pat Kingsley, who was also my publicity agent, was there—she was a big publicity agent at the time. And I'm in the room, listening, and Lily wanted to let people know that she was gay. And Pat kept saying, "You can't do it; you're going to ruin your career." And Pat would only have her best interests at heart—she really was a great publicist—but she was insistent. You could imagine believing that it's going to ruin her career.

And then, after, we had to go outside to the car, which was in front of the theater. There was a huge audience, and when we got in the car, her fans were rocking the car back and forth. And the idea that somebody's career could actually be ruined and that their lives could get ruined was astonishing. I remember, it just struck me. To go from that to "You can't let out that you're gay or they'll hate you" struck me. It really struck me.

LILY TOMLIN   I mean, there were many instances where lots of different things happened—everything from people saying, "I don't think you and Jane should drive to work in the same car" to any number of silly things that I just ignored.

In '75, *Time* magazine offered me the cover if I would come out. Because they just needed a gay person. And they later put a soldier on the cover. I think it's September of '75 or something. And we were recording [my comedy album] *Modern Scream*. And the conceit of the album was that I'm being interviewed for a fan in *Modern Scream* magazine. We were in the studio at the time when I got the phone call, so we put this in the [fake] interview [where the interviewer asks silly questions about heterosexuality—for example, "I want to talk to you about your frank film about heterosexuality. Did it seem strange to you, seeing yourself make love to a man on the big screen?"].

ELLEN DeGENERES   I definitely wasn't wearing dresses and talking about [traditionally female topics] but I had longer hair and I was definitely—look, maybe I was delusional and it was obvious that I was gay. I think it was obvious I was gay when I finally came out. But when I was doing stand-up, I don't know that many people knew that I was gay.

WHOOPI GOLDBERG People would come up to me and say, "Are you gay?" And I'd go, "No." The interesting thing about me is, no one ever felt like they needed to be careful about what they said to me. You would never think someone would have the cojones to walk up and just blatantly ask you.

MARGARET CHO With women, there is so much more permission to be queer than with men. Imagine a male bisexual! That would be so outlaw. Comedians are so homophobic in that way. I think women have a much easier time. There is certainly a lot of fluidity that women are allowed sexually. And I was interested in men too. But I didn't find animosity about homosexuality coming from the male comics, mostly because the guys love that and are very curious about it. I did feel a little bit of it from women. And then a lot of lesbians were freaked out—*that's* who didn't like it. Lesbians were like, "Well, you're not completely gay, so you don't really count. You can't be one of us unless you are all the way one of us." That to me was much more of an issue.

With the stand-up boom of the 1980s leading to the sitcom boom of the 1990s, certain biases against funny women were illuminated, most glaringly by the very writers brought on to write for women and by the network executives who preferred adorable women over flawed ones.

JANEANE GAROFALO There is a prevailing myth in some men's minds that women aren't funny. And unfortunately, that myth can be perpetuated by the way mainstream entertainment writes for women. There are a lot of males who will say, "I can't write for women." I don't know why they say that, and I don't know why it's different writing for one human being to another human being. But they tend to—when they write scripts or a sitcom, they write women as the straight person and guys as the funny person. Like the classic paradigm in sitcoms is the heavyset, funny husband and the hot, not-as-funny wife.

LISA KUDROW I've known a lot of guy writers who are extremely successful, and every one of them would say, "Look, I have to apologize, but we just don't write women well." And a couple of them would even say, "Well, because women aren't funny. They're just not as funny as men, they're just not." And it was shocking, because this would come from men that I thought were pretty sophisticated. But if the only funny thing they get to do is knock over her glass of water, or in romantic comedies where the only funny thing a woman can do is say, "Why can't I get a man?" and she trips, then yeah, women aren't as funny as men.

GAIL PARENT I can tell you that twenty-eight-year-old males could write menopause jokes. If you're good, you're good. Mitch Hurwitz wrote a joke that was—I guess Blanche said something like "My little friend is late." And Dorothy said, "You haven't had your little friend in a long, long time," you know, indicating it was menopause. And then somebody else said, "Isn't it amazing that women who live in the same houses get on the same schedule?" I loved that, coming from a young writer who's male.

ZANE BUZBY I've directed about two hundred sitcoms. There was always one woman and six men in them—usually, not always, in an ensemble—because they could barely write the woman's part. God forbid there should be two women. Oh my God, how could you ever have that happen! Unless one's sloppy and one's neat, those were the distinctions.

LISA KUDROW Depending on who the director was, when we would rehearse stuff [on *Friends*], I know that there was a feeling sometimes like, "Wow, they're spending a lot of time on the guy scenes, figuring out how to make it as funny as possible." And sometimes with the girl scenes, we'd run it and like, "All right, well, that's good." Sometimes it felt like there was a little more enthusiasm to figure it out with the guys.

MARTA KAUFFMAN, writer There was a story that I very often tell about the pilot of *Friends*. There's a thing where Monica is dating a guy and he feeds her a line and she buys it, and she sleeps with him and she's very upset. And the network executive's comment was "Well, she got what she deserved." And literally, I think my head exploded. I was just stunned to be dealing with that kind of a comment and that kind of outright misogyny. Nobody deserves that kind of treatment, but he was basically saying, "She's a slut and she got what she deserved."

The network handed out a questionnaire during one of the nights when we were doing dress rehearsal and I swear to you, one of the questions was something like "For sleeping with guy on the first date, do you think Monica is (a) a slut, (b) a whore, (c) easy?"! It was the funniest thing. And we discovered from this question that people didn't care that much. They weren't shocked by it.

When we did the lesbian wedding episode, they were very concerned. They didn't ask us not to do it, but they were very concerned and they put on, like, forty operators that night, because they thought that they were going to get phone calls and the affiliates weren't going to air it! They got four phone calls that night, that's it. Four, out of the millions of people who watched it. And then, about two months later, we got a whole slew of letters—clearly the Reverend Wildmon, who has a very right-wing organization, they sent out letters, and actually none of them had actually seen the episode—they had just heard about it and didn't want it on the air.

ZANE BUZBY The great thing about Joy Behar was that you could build a show around her real persona. So for Joy, I looked at all of her stand-up and saw that she was a teacher. And there was one line—she was teaching in the South Bronx or something, she was teaching these tough kids English—and it was like, "I had to teach them, '*Who* or *whom* do you kill?'" She just made me laugh. Then I realized we could sell her, because that's the only line we need, and we could just run down the halls at CBS and go "It's the teacher in the school from hell." Bingo, she had a real, real persona, which is what's necessary for the emotional center of a show.

We had a great pilot, right? It starred Joy Behar, Dan Hedaya, Paul Sand, and Hank Azaria. I mean, it was a great cast. So at that time CBS was going through 150 of its changes. And CBS had traditionally been the women's network. It was always the women's network, which was why we went to CBS. The day we went to the table reading on this show, they changed the head of CBS—his new mandate was, he wanted to get the young men in, eighteen-to-thirty-five-year-old males. We said, "This is never going to happen." And we were right; they changed their programming in ten minutes and we got caught in that. But it was a great pilot.

RITA RUDNER The absolute truth is that women in comedy on television is different from women in comedy in clubs, because when you get to the level of sitcoms, the network executives will always pick a model over a funny woman. To them, Brooke Shields was hysterical. I'm sure she's a very nice woman and she's a very talented actress, but I wouldn't say she's a great comedian. The criteria for a female were much different from a male. Which is why many more men got shots at sitcoms than women, and the women who did were Roseanne, which is a certain kind of classic female comedian who's kind of aggressive.

It's Friday, August 23, 1985. Roseanne Barr is making her debut on the Tonight Show Starring Johnny Carson. *She stands in front of the gray curtain, her chin-length hair slicked back so it looks almost like a mullet. She's wearing a black button-down, a black-and-yellow-patterned jacket with a corsage pinned onto her chest. She tells the audience, "So I'm fat—I thought I'd point that out," and the audience laughs. "Have you ever noticed that fat people don't think like skinny people? We have our own way of thinking. Like, did you ever ask a fat person for directions, because that is where the difference in thinking really shows, you know. 'Cause you go up to the street and ask them where something is and they tell you like this: 'Well, go down here to Arby's'"—the audience erupts in laughter, and she starts to laugh with them, her mouth open wide—"'and go right by Wendy's, McDonald's, Burger King. It's that chocolate brown building down there.'" The audience laughs and it's clear that they like her. "But it's good that I'm fat, though, 'cause I'm a mom and fat moms are better than skinny moms. 'Cause what do you want when you're depressed? Some skinny mom: 'Well, why don't you jog around awhile and that will release adrenaline in your blood and you'll better cope with stress.' Or some fat mom: 'Well, let's have pudding, Oreos, and marshmallows.'" This time the audience roars with screams and whistles. "When you wake up from that sugar coma, it will be a brand-new week." Roseanne killed.*

When Roseanne Barr emerged on the Tonight Show *in 1985, she became—amazingly—the first female stand-up to hit big since Joan Rivers. As a fat mom who talked about her weight, raising her children, and married life, she seemed conventional enough to get past Carson's cen-sors. But as a modern woman, she flipped those old tropes upside down: her weight was an asset, her children were a pain, and her husband was incompetent. Unlike her predecessors, these problems weren't her fault; they were just her reality. She returned to the* Tonight Show *again and again, landed her own HBO special, and within three years was starring on her own prime-time show.*

MARK LONOW   Roseanne developed in Denver. And Roseanne came on the scene—on the big scene—full-blown with the character, and her *Tonight Show* appearance really broke it wide open. When she became the domestic goddess, that was a big, big statement, and that was a definitive moment. It was like when Rodney came up with "I don't get no respect." That's a big deal, because it defines what we're looking at in the person, and when that gels, usually the comic becomes a star.

LAURA KIGHTLINGER, comedian   I remember watching Roseanne do stand-up on the David Letterman show in 1988—I remember because I was watching with a male roommate and we were equally engaged and blown away by her. She was so unapologetic and genuine, so com-pletely herself without pretense or artifice—and her material was obvi-ously based on her own experience but was concise enough and well written enough to include everyone.

LOUIE ANDERSON, comedian   We toured twenty-five cities together—the Vast Wasteland Tour—[and on the road it was] Travel. Eat. Check out the show. Eat. Go to bed. Eat. We found out what the best restau-rant was in town and asked them if they would stay open for us. And we ate, ate, ate, ate.

Roseanne and I always loved each other, so I was not affected by her stuff. I would do an impression of her going, "Pick me up. Now put me down." She was a big baby—I'm also a big baby—and she could be a real grump. But we were comedians getting up early and traveling. I think I made the tour better for her. I hope I did. I'm more of a people person than she is, so she would really be happy that I would meet and talk with people and she wouldn't have to. It was hard for her because she has a bit of a social anxiety around people. She's a very shy person, actually.

ROSEANNE   I did feminist comedy. It was a response to all the comedy by guy stand-ups that I'd been seeing since I was a little girl. I definitely had an ideological point of view that I was putting across. It was very left-wing radical and it took me about two years to kind of restructure it so that I was able to work in the regular comedy clubs. I had to make it less political and more mainstream. So I was reworking it, going to various places to try it out. There were usually three or four of us that went out, and we went everywhere from luncheons to biker bars. So we got a very broad spectrum of reaction and that kind of helps you to bring your acts to middle-of-the-road. And at the Comedy Works, which was like the only comedy club in Denver, we'd all do ten minutes.

LOUIE ANDERSON   Roseanne was doing satire and commentary on the plight of the American housewife. Her act was lined up exactly where society was and she [represented] women telling their husband to shut the f—— up. Phyllis Diller was not interested in any social commentary. There's social commentary written all over Roseanne. And even though Roseanne was a character to a lot of people, I think she was really herself. She's completely authentic. You never saw Phyllis Diller have to lift a finger. I didn't, anyway. She had a big cigarette holder and usually some sort of fur on. She was very well dressed. People related so much to Roseanne because she was just who she was. She wasn't a character. Roseanne thought those things about her kids; Roseanne thought those things about men. But Roseanne really liked being a mom and I think she really liked being a wife. I think she always got kind of a raw deal with the guys that she was with.

LOIS BROMFIELD   Roseanne came on the scene and she was just a funny, dumpy girl who was so smart. She was different from everybody else at that time. There was no one like that who was doing the housewife, fuck-you kind of attitude to the men. There was nobody like that. Her delivery was great, she wore funny outfits—the first time I saw her she was wearing overalls and her hair was completely messed up—her voice was nasal, and she was just completely confident, unshakable. That was what was so wild.

LOUIE ANDERSON   She's a really good joke writer but her timing was almost perfect. And her attitude was beyond perfect. I had a similar throwaway, deadpan thing myself and so I related to it a lot. "Here's what you think you're gonna get, and here's what I'm gonna give you." Some sweet little remarks, but then you got the brutal honest truth. That's what she's so great at.

ROSEANNE   I stayed in Denver till 1985. If I wanted to be on Broadway, I would have gone to New York. And there are a lot of great clubs in New York—Catch a Rising Star, Dangerfield's. I'm probably forgetting some, but that was a different kind of a career. I wanted to be on television.

ALLAN STEPHAN   We did some traveling together on the road. Then she befriended Louie as well. And I think at some point we kept saying, "You have to come to L.A. You have to come to L.A." We made some calls. We went to the Comedy Store and Mitzi took a look at her and I think put her on that night.

DIANE NICHOLS   It was the domestic goddess: "Hey, when you come home and your kids are still alive, I've done my job." It was different from the rest of us. It was more like Phyllis Diller. But it was refreshing, because we knew who she was the minute she walked onstage. That's why Mitzi loved her.

ARGUS HAMILTON   When I first saw Roseanne I was standing by Mitzi. And Roseanne presented herself as a working-class feminine heroine. No one had presented themselves as a white-trash queen since maybe *The Beverly Hillbillies*. But nevertheless, it was fresh in the mid-eighties. So anyway, Roseanne did her set. Mitzi had Jim McCawley in the next Monday. And just before you know it, Mitzi set Roseanne up with a big management company.

DIANE NICHOLS   She was everything Mitzi loved. Somebody was there who watched them meet, said it was absolutely hilarious: *"Hi!" "Hi!" "We sorta have the same voice a little bit."*
   She was not self-deprecating at all. Roseanne was like, "Screw you, I'm fat. So what?"

ROSEANNE   It's because of Mitzi Shore that I have a career. Really, that was like the hugest break. Not to undercut going on the *Tonight*

Show, but to be seen at the Comedy Store on the Sunset Strip was a huge goal that I reached. That was where the *Tonight Show* scouts used to come and see people. And that's where they saw me. That's where Rodney Dangerfield saw me. Every break I ever got was because they saw me there.

JAMIE MASADA   After the Comedy Store, Allan Stephan brought her to my club, the Laugh Factory. And he said, "Jamie, you've got to watch her." I said, "Okay, I'll watch her." And Paul Mooney was in the audience. Paul is a very sharp, sharp, sharp guy. And Paul used to go back and forth with Richard Pryor, with Jimmie Walker, everybody. And Paul was too quick for them. But with Roseanne, she trashed him so fast, it was amazing. *Amazing*. I never saw anything like that in my life. And I said, "Oh my God, she's going to be a big star."

ROSEANNE   [My success] was overnight, actually. The first time I performed at the Comedy Store, I was seen by scouts for the *Tonight Show* and I was put on the following week. It was incredible. I had a killer ten minutes. I had a laugh every fifteen seconds and it was a huge laugh. That takes a long time and a lot of skill to put that together. I was a frequent guest. I don't know how many times—but at least ten. I was on Johnny Carson's last week on television. Then Rodney Dangerfield also had a show called *Young Comedians* on HBO and he picked me to play his wife. And between that, George Schlatter's show called *Funny People*—that was about women comics—and the *Tonight Show*, I had three great things happen for me at the same point. But the *Tonight Show* was the biggest one.

CARRIE SNOW   We really thought that when Roseanne got on the *Tonight Show*, it was going to open it up for women comics.

LOUIE ANDERSON   With Roseanne, it seemed like it was being handled by a higher power. Just watching her go through one show business wall after another without her hair getting messed up. You know what's so really brilliant about Roseanne Barr? She knew exactly what she was doing, she knew exactly what she wanted, and she never backed down one inch. And it hurt her and saved her. Her legacy's intact but it did hurt her. I don't think the industry liked being held hostage by a woman.

Not only was Roseanne the first female stand-up of her generation to write for and star in her own half-hour comedy, but her television program, which debuted on ABC on October 18, 1988, was a comic tour de force. Hailed as one of the funniest programs of the 1980s, it also broke new ground as the only program to turn its eyes on working-class families living day-to-day in the Midwest. It focused on the travails of working mother Roseanne Conner, whose home was a radical departure from every other home depicted on television: a shabby plaid couch decorated the living room; strewn papers littered the kitchen table; Roseanne Conner, schlubby and 215 pounds, was the hardworking mother of three in a financially strained household.

Certainly working mothers were nothing new on television. The Cosby Show's Claire Huxtable was a lawyer, Family Ties' Elyse Keaton an architect, Growing Pains' Maggie Seaver a reporter, and Who's the Boss's Angela Bower an advertising executive.* But these were pretty, secure, upwardly mobile mothers with pristine homes; they seemed to have no trouble balancing their professional and personal lives. Roseanne changed all that. Within weeks of premiering to rave reviews, the show leaped to the top of the ratings chart, where it stayed in the top ten for the next seven seasons.

BRANDON STODDARD, president, ABC Entertainment 1985–1989
Roseanne was really the pivotal show. The rest of the shows may have had working women, but Roseanne was the nuts and the guts of it. It was a real show with real people and not all pretty and lovely and handsome and everybody's hair done. It was the real dilemma of a working woman juggling five different roles and really having a very difficult time doing it. And it just seemed to us that that was something that women were going to identify with.

---

* According to Stu Bloomberg, ABC's vice president of comedy development from 1982 to 1989, the original title for *Who's the Boss* was *She's the Boss*. The title was changed after ex-*Taxi* star Tony Danza was cast in the show.

MARCY CARSEY   I didn't really set about doing shows about and starring women. What we did do, my partner and I, was whenever we decided on some area to develop a show, first of all we looked at the television schedule, both ours and other people's, to see what wasn't being talked about on the air in comedy form, because we just wanted to explore new territory and we also wanted to, in most cases, touch on something that was really going on in American society. My partner, Tom Werner, and I were raising kids—separately, obviously—but we were both parents and we hired parents whenever we could and women whenever we could, because it just seemed that we were doing a lot of family comedy. And you know [the saying], "Write what you know and produce what you know." Well, in the case of *Roseanne*, before we knew about Roseanne we wanted to do a show about the plight of the working mom—the working-class working mom in America—because it just wasn't being dealt with on the air.

We went to NBC first, because that's where our hit [*The Cosby Show*] had been. I did get "No" on *Roseanne*, [because executives worried] who's going to want to watch her? NBC didn't believe that she would be appealing to America: the loud voice, the less-than-thin body, whatever it was. The whole package was just too brash and unappealing in their eyes.

So we went to ABC, and ABC had been taken over by very wonderful people. Between the time I was there as an executive [in the late 1970s] and the time I was pitching *Roseanne*, ABC had fallen into the wrong hands. But by the time we were pitching *Roseanne* it was being newly run by the Cap Cities guys, who were very smart and open. And they, too, said, "I don't know." We had given them the pilot script and just a tape of Roseanne and John Goodman sitting at a table, reading a scene together. That's all they had.

STU BLOOMBERG, vice president, comedy development, ABC, 1982– 1989   Carsey-Werner pitched *Cosby* to ABC first but we didn't make the deal—that went to NBC—and it was always a huge disappointment. So we were talking about the fact that not everybody comes home to that gorgeous Cosby house and has a new beautiful sweater every week, and they pitched that concept, *Life and Stuff*, with Roseanne.

In Los Angeles, Mitzi Shore (*above*) booked shows for her husband's club, the Comedy Store, which opened in 1972. With Shore as its tastemaker and Johnny Carson regularly drawing from its talent, the Comedy Store quickly became one of the nation's most popular clubs, though some female comedians felt ghettoized there. *Below*: Shore poses with (from left to right) Richard Pryor, David Letterman, and Robin Williams. (Above and below, Mitzi Shore and the World Famous Comedy Store)

Sandra Bernhard (*above*) emerged from the Comedy Store scene to have a thriving stand-up career; after years as a dancer on Broadway, Rita Rudner (*right*) tried her hand at comedy around the same time, at the beginning of the eighties. She remembers the time as "a boom of comedians—we didn't know why, we just wanted to do it. It wasn't because you were going to get fantastically wealthy. We just all loved comedy." (Above, Mitzi Shore and the World Famous Comedy Store; right, courtesy of Rita Rudner)

Among the household names minted in the 1980s comedy boom were Ellen DeGeneres (*above*) and Roseanne (*below*). Both women developed comic personas that flew in the face of conventional femininity; both met with derision or confusion from early audiences; and both leveraged their stand-up routines into title roles in groundbreaking prime-time sitcoms. (Above, courtesy of Ellen DeGeneres; below, Elizabeth Wolynski)

Paula Poundstone (*above*) and Joy Behar (*below*) were vaulted to fame by their stand-up performances; specials on cable TV helped them reach a national audience. Whoopi Goldberg (*left*) took a different tack, attracting attention as an actress and a storyteller: "In order to get the part that I wanted onstage, I would have to do lots of monologues to show people what I could do." (Above and left, Photofest; below, courtesy of Joy Behar)

Cracking the late-night-TV boys' club: Merrill Markoe (*above left*) won multiple Emmys for her work as head writer on *Late Night with David Letterman*; Anne Beatts and Rosie Shuster (*above right*) thrived as writers on *Saturday Night Live* despite rampant fraternalism; Joan Rivers (*below*, with Johnny Carson) was the *Tonight Show*'s regular guest host through the mid-eighties, and many believed she was being groomed as Carson's successor. (Above left, courtesy of Merrill Markoe; above right, courtesy of Rosie Shuster; below, Photofest)

Though she eschews the label, Janeane Garofalo (*above left*) became the poster child for alternative comedy, an early-1990s reaction to the collapse of the mainstream club scene. With Margaret Cho (*above right*) and others, she cultivated a tone that was unabashedly smart, self-conscious, and postmodern. By the end of the decade, comics like Sarah Silverman (*below*)—sweet-faced but deliberately lascivious and bigoted—had further ironized stand-up, subverting audience expectations for big laughs. (Above left and below, Photofest; above right, Kevin Lynch)

In 1994, Beth Lapides (*above left*) and her husband founded Un-Cabaret, a Los Angeles organization that gave shape to the nascent alternative comedy movement; later in the nineties, Lisa Sundstedt started Pretty, Funny Women, a showcase designed to disprove the notion that sexiness and comedy are mutually exclusive. On *Saturday Night Live*, younger writers like Paula Pell and Emily Spivey (*below*) kept writing strong character pieces, holding their own against the conceptual Harvard-guy set. (Above left, courtesy of Beth Lapides; above right, courtesy of Lisa Sundstedt; below, courtesy of Paula Pell)

The 2000s saw the rise of a new generation of comedians, such as Anjelah Johnson (*above left*), a former NFL cheerleader who at the close of 2009 had an hour-long Comedy Central special; Whitney Cummings (*above right*), who had two sitcoms, *2 Broke Girls* and *Whitney*, debut simultaneously on network TV in the fall of 2011; and Natasha Leggero (*below*), a roundtable regular on *Chelsea Lately*. "Whereas I used to think that looking pretty or sexy would alienate women, now it's the opposite," Cummings says. "Now I feel like when I embrace my femininity, it makes women relate to me more, because they go, 'Oh, she's just like me, she puts on makeup and she tries to look cute, and she wears Spanx and she wears heels.' "

(Above left, courtesy of Anjelah Johnson; above right, courtesy of Whitney Cummings; below, courtesy of Natasha Leggero)

BRANDON STODDARD They had done a little demo tape and stuck a stupid little camera into a room and John and Roseanne were talking together, and you could see there was really a nice chemistry together, and balance. And you could see then that John was—is—a superb actor. So he was a kind of an anchor for the show. You just know that John would be able to deliver at all times, and as a result Roseanne felt comfortable with him, which was good. And I thought Roseanne the actress was worth a gamble. And I thought Tom and Marcy could handle her, and we went ahead and did the pilot. And it is interesting, some of the changes that we made in the pilot included a speech that, I think, came out of Roseanne's act. It was about her frustration with trying to fulfill all of these roles. And of course it was accentuated by her husband, who was a lovely man, and a nice husband, but not too zippity-doo-dah in the workplace.

STU BLOOMBERG It was very blue-collar, and yet really smart. And Roseanne, I mean, you just didn't hear that voice, you didn't see that person on TV. As soon as they pitched the idea and talked about Roseanne, it was a no-brainer to me.

MARCY CARSEY When the pilot was shot, they had doubts again as to whether to put it on the air.

BRANDON STODDARD Of course I was terrified, everything we did about this show was against the grain. It wasn't so much Roseanne in particular, it was the whole show. I mean, the set design: the couch was a wreck, the place was filthy, the dishes never got done. It was realistic. And no show had really been done that way. It was the way the language was, the looks of the people, the clothes, the room, the dirty dishes: the entire tone of the show was intended to be quite opposite of any other comedy that had been on air. And so of course that is a huge risk, because it can be repugnant to some people.

MARCY CARSEY I just said to the newly terrific Cap Cities management, "Just do me a favor and take the pilot home to your wives and watch it with them and see what they think." And we got it on the air.

BRANDON STODDARD   We showed it to the affiliates, which was about two thousand people or something in this room, and I remember when Roseanne did the speech about her frustration with "They want me to do this, they want me to do that, I can't be a mom, I have to go to work," there was an extraordinary audible reaction by the women in the room. They totally connected to it, and I thought, "Oh my God, I will be able to keep my job for another week." And then I thought maybe we were really onto something—and you know what happened to the show. It became a smash hit for a number of years, and made a whopping amount of money for ABC.

During the first year, Roseanne's star and the head writer, Matt Williams, collided in a spectacular power struggle that ultimately led to Williams's ouster and concern for the series' survival. Roseanne had earned a reputation as a ballbuster prone to fits of violence—she once threatened a producer with a pair of scissors—and sick-outs. A second head writer, Jeff Harris, was brought on to replace Williams, but he barely lasted a season before he, too, quit, taking a parting shot with a full-page ad in Variety: *"I have chosen not to return to the show next season. Instead, my wife and I have decided to share a vacation in the relative peace and quiet of Beirut." (Lebanon was in the middle of a civil war.)*

The conflict between Roseanne and the show's writers and producers stemmed from two very different takes on who created the series: Roseanne believed that she was the show's chief architect, and that the story and plotlines were based on her life and her stand-up; Carsey-Werner and Matt Williams held the position that the show had been their idea, and that Roseanne had been brought on as an actress with just the right sensibility. ABC just wanted to keep their hit show. In essence, the conflict between Roseanne and her producers was more than just the diva versus her boss. It was a fundamental dispute over whether Roseanne deserved credit not only as the star of her series but as the creative genius behind one of television's highest-rated and most groundbreaking series.

ROSEANNE   The Carsey-Werner Company, they had seen me on the *Tonight Show.* They wanted the show to be based on my stand-up.

MARCY CARSEY   It had nothing to do with her stand-up. Her talent obviously infused it, and her style—the way she delivers a line—

obviously both influenced the writing and was a huge part of the success of the show. But her stand-up was really about being a domestic goddess and "Hey, if my husband gets home and the kids are alive, I've done my job." So we had to turn that a hundred eighty degrees around to being a working-class heroine, really. She was the glue of the family. She had to earn money. She had to take care of the kids. Obviously we always wanted it to be very funny, the characters have to be very funny, because you have to laugh. And very smart. There was no adopting her point of view, but there was an accommodation to her talent and her strengths and weaknesses.

TED HARBERT, president, ABC Entertainment, 1993–1996; chairman, ABC, 1996 Roseanne, more than anybody ever in my opinion, as a female, delivered a point of view. And Matt Williams said, "Okay," and Carsey-Werner said, "Okay, if I can go take this domestic goddess—that level of confidence, that level of brashness—and transfer it into the kitchen and living room of a sitcom, we've got something here." And it's not easy to do, but they did it. Because you still have to come up with who's John Goodman, who are the kids, who's her best friend. That's all very, very difficult work. It's never just one person by themselves. In fact, Brett Butler [of *Grace Under Fire*], which became the number one show in television as well for a brief time, that show was really more on Brett's shoulders. I mean, there was Julie White, who was fantastic around her. But we didn't have the rest of the cast, the way the rest of the cast of Roseanne was just genius, and really helped Roseanne bring her point of view to the forefront.

ROSEANNE I was a strong woman writer, okay? I was a writer, not a character. I was a strong woman writer with an idea and a whole act. I wasn't the character—I was the writer. So I knew what I wanted and I just held out for it. So I was able to write. I wasn't at the whim of a writer defining me or what I wanted to say or defining my character or, as a matter of fact, any of the characters on the show. I oversaw all the writing for the entire show, like Tina Fey does now. I wasn't in any of those little boxes they're continually trying to put me in. I was bigger than all of that. And my ideas were bigger than all of that. But that was the battle of the powers that be always trying to put you in a little box, take away your power, and take credit for your work. That was what I lived through for nine years. I didn't let it stop me, but there's definitely damage to my nervous system from all that fighting.

TED HARBERT   There was tremendous tension. There was tremendous tension with Roseanne, Brett Butler, and Tim Allen [of *Home Improvement*]. And I think there was a very good reason for that. Even though the public didn't know them very well, they had spent years out on the road as stand-ups. And when you're a stand-up, you're the damn boss. You're out there and you're onstage and you have one hundred percent control over what you say and there is no one in the world who can give you a note, can give you an adjustment, can give you new script pages and tell you, "Here, go do it this way." They are artists. They are pure artists, and artists have creative control.

The problem is none of them—and I love them all—could write a script themselves. That's a different job. They couldn't write a script. It's all been written about Roseanne and the twenty-seven writers with twenty-seven T-shirts all numbered one through twenty-seven. Yeah, she's a writer. She wrote a fantastic stand-up comedy act. It's just a different form of writing than a script, and she didn't end up having much respect for the people that do that for a living and do that quite well.

LOIS BROMFIELD   I mean, she was tough! She was tough. And a lot of the guys in the [writers'] room were pretty nasty about her. And she was right and wrong. She would come into the room and she'd go, "I hate this fucking script, rewrite it," and you would look at it, and really, you would have loved to have had some specific points of what she hated. When you start to look at the script, you would see, yeah, there were things about it that were wrong and it did need to be rewritten. I would say she was right about eighty percent of the time about the writing. And it didn't come because she was a writer necessarily, it would come because it was her. And the show was about her, so it was from her gut feeling. If something felt dishonest or something, she wouldn't do it as a character.

ROSEANNE   I was always pretty clear about what I wanted. I never went around asking other people's opinions, 'cause I didn't care what they thought. And that's why it worked. Also they didn't know how to write anything about working-class people, 'cause they were all from Harvard.

LOIS BROMFIELD The main people were Harvard grads—they came from Harvard and were people who had written on tons of shows before. So the main group was that. But after a couple of years it was comics [like me] who got hired. And Roseanne also made a point of hiring women, and she really injected the writers' room with strong women. But there was huge conflict [between the Harvard guys and comics]. On the one hand, I didn't blame the head writers and the writers who had had experience for having to deal with comics who had never written. The key was really to listen and shut up. The first year I was there, I literally said nothing. If you opened your mouth, you were probably wrong. So I didn't say anything, and then of course the next four years I talked constantly and wrote scripts, but you had to really learn it.

The best example of the writers' room and the difference between the Harvard grads and the comics was this moment. I won't say the writer's name, because I don't want to do that, but when we were writing a scene, there was something about lunch meat written in the script. And our head writer said, "What is lunch meat? What do you mean?" And I was like, "Lunch meat—you know, for lunch sandwiches." "What is it? What are you talking about? Is it like sliced steak?" "No, no, no. Bologna. Like bologna, salami, whatever, cheese, that's lunch meat." And he's the head writer, he's writing for a blue-collar family, and he doesn't know what lunch meat is. So that was really—for me that was the defining moment where you go, "Okay, I get it. I'm glad I didn't go to Harvard so I had to learn what lunch meat was!" It was pretty funny.

BRANDON STODDARD I was always concerned [about the problems on the show]. If you got an unhappy star and it is hard to replace her, but she is screaming and yelling about the writers, "I can't say these words," and "I am not coming out of my dressing room . . ."

I think her major concern was about the writing. And we read every draft, and we read every word that was written on that show, and it was good. The writing was good on that show. But it is not unusual for actors to have difficulties with the writers. And the writer, unfortunately, can't have difficulties with the actor. It wasn't an unusual problem, to tell you the truth. And it isn't to say that sometimes the actors aren't right, and the writers suck. But in a lot of cases, here is what tends to happen: as the star power increases, and they become more and more popular and bigger and bigger stars, they tend to take on the battle over the writers. I am giving you a general truism. Actually, I think Roseanne started screaming quite early. In general they are not screaming in year one. They are still happy to be working on a show. But as their power increases, and their knowledge of the show increases, their sense of being indispensable to the show makes them pretty powerful.

ROSEANNE One of the biggest problems on the set was that there was a whole point of view that they tried to foist on me. There was sexist and offensive and stupid stuff in the script all the time. And I changed it, 'cause I was able to write. I'm a comic and I can write a joke and I'm pretty damn good at writing a joke. If I had not been able to write, it just would have been a big bomb.

It's hard to talk about [the conflict], because there's so many angles to it. They were trying to stop me from controlling my show. So it's not just the stuff they wrote for my character. There's just layer and layer and layer of it.

MARCY CARSEY This is not a gender thing. This is a personality. We steered her, obviously, in a terrific direction and she came to realize that at some point. And it was a hit show and it was a wonderful show—both qualitatively and from a ratings point of view. That show worked. It was what we needed it to be. It stayed that way as long as we could keep her showing up and kind of being professional. But no, that had nothing to do with gender.

ELLEN DeGENERES

Ellen DeGeneres never intended to become a lesbian icon, nor was she interested in effecting social change through her comedy. When De-Generes started her career as the house emcee at Clyde's Comedy Corner in New Orleans, she just wanted to focus on performing the kind of hu-mor she found funny: clean observations about our everyday lives. As she transitioned from local comic to national television star, DeGeneres earned a reputation as a female Jerry Seinfeld. All that changed in 1997 when DeGeneres, under pressure to give narrative focus to her struggling ABC series, decided, finally, to come out. Ellen DeGeneres's on-screen counterpart, Ellen Morgan, wasn't the first gay character to appear on television, but she was the first to lead her own series. Forty-two million viewers, triple the regular number, tuned in to see the now-groundbreaking "Puppy Episode" in which Ellen Morgan confessed to her therapist (played by Oprah) that she was gay. While her career suffered in the immediate aftermath, Ellen was anointed—ironically and unwittingly—the most prominent lesbian entertainer ever and remains so to this day.

ELLEN DeGENERES When I started as a stand-up, I didn't want to be the stereotypical female comedian. I wasn't going to stand there and talk about men or different kinds of female problems. I never wanted it to be gender-specific. I like pointing out obvious things that people don't pay attention to: for example, if you taste something bad, you'll always want somebody else to taste it immediately; or when somebody writes "over" on the bottom of the letter, as if they have to put that or else [the recipient] won't turn it over.

It was important to me to make people laugh at our human behavior, and that was my kind of humor. I also remember at Clyde's Comedy Corner, Clyde would tell me that for the one a.m. show on Saturday that I needed to curse more, because that was the X-rated show—and it was never important for me to curse, either. It was such an education to be an emcee and watch these different people from New York and California come through. At first I was so impressed at how they could make people laugh, but then I noticed that they were just adding *fuck* before a punch line and that would make people just laugh hysterically. I found that to be really lazy and formulaic. I didn't want to be that kind of comedian. And then I watched people get laughs for being mean-spirited or making jokes at the expense of other people, and I just never wanted to do that either.

When I finally got a spot on the *Tonight Show* in 1986, I was ready. I had already done HBO's *Women of the Night* and the *Young Comedians* special. I had auditioned for *Letterman* at the Holy City Zoo [in San Francisco] and had not been accepted. I was disappointed about that but I was scared at my audition, because I wasn't ready. But I was ready by the time I did *Carson*. I was at the Improv in L.A. and Jim McCawley was the guy who booked the *Tonight Show*. I was doing a set, and Jay Leno had worked with me, and he told Jim that I was somebody to watch. So Jim McCawley booked me that night and "you'll be on next week"—it was that quick.

And if you went on *Johnny Carson*, it really meant something. So for me to be booked on *Carson* was a huge deal. And then for me to be the first and only woman ever to be called over to sit down on his couch after my first set, that was an honor in itself. It changed everything. It changed the venues that I played, it changed the audience—all of a sudden they had respect. When I was doing my phone-call-to-God routine, it was quiet instead of loud. And I got more money. I started doing theaters and I was able to make $5,000 a night.

The problem is, people still didn't know what to do with me. I wasn't going to be the lead in a sitcom, because I wasn't the pretty girl, and so they just didn't know what kind of show they were going to build around me. And I say this to people all the time when they're different: the good news is, you stand out because you're different and unique; the bad news is, no one knows what to do with that until you find your own niche.

I got a part on *Open House* [in 1989]. That was a tiny role but it grew a little bit and it became an important role. But it was certainly not my show in any sense. After *Open House* I did a very tiny part on something called *Laurie Hill* [which aired in 1992]. I was a receptionist who answered the phone and my only line was "Hello" to someone walking in. And this was at a time when everyone else had their own shows. I was touring, I was headlining, and I remember my brother and some friends going, "You're seriously going to go in to read for 'Hello'? Why not hold out for your own show?" But I just thought, "Work is work and you never know where it leads." I think they only aired three episodes, but [during filming] I said to Neal [Marlens, creator of *Laurie Hill*], "If this show doesn't go, will you create a show for me?" And three weeks later he called me and he said, "The bad news is the show got canceled; the good news is that we want to create a show for you." And they created *These Friends of Mine*. But it was not in any way my show like Roseanne's or Tim Allen's shows. It was called *These Friends of Mine*—it was not *Ellen*. It was an ensemble show, and then slowly it became my show. Anyway, we shot the pilot and it sat there forever and it finally aired mid-season, like a year later after the Super Bowl, [and in the time slot] after *Roseanne*. It got huge ratings and we were off.

These Friends of Mine was troubled from the start. Although it finished its first season with top ratings, by the fourth—when DeGeneres would come out—the show had been through several shake-ups, many of which sent its ratings into free fall. The original creative team had been dumped; a new cast had been brought in, twice; and the show had been rechristened Ellen. *Rumors started to swirl: Was there more to* Ellen *than its producers, writers, and star were willing to let on?*

JOYCE MILLMAN in *The San Francisco Examiner*, March 30, 1995
"Like DeGeneres, Ellen Morgan favors androgynous trouser outfits, minimal makeup and short, no-fuss hair. She's good-looking in a clean, sturdy, gym-teacherish way. Every so often, Ellen Morgan takes a stab at a relationship. She and Adam, her pal since college, try making out to see if their erotic dreams about each other are worth acting on. Nope—no chemistry. She goes out with Nitro from 'American Gladiators,' but quite suddenly he calls it quits—no chemistry. She dates a guy who thinks the world of her and wants to get married, but she breaks it

off—no chemistry. Ellen Morgan isn't the first sitcom single woman who has had trouble finding Mr. Right. But Mary Richards and Rhoda Morganstern didn't throw off the, um, gender-neutral vibe that Ellen Morgan does. As a single gal sitcom, 'Ellen' doesn't make any sense at all—until you view it through the looking glass where the unspoken subtext becomes the main point. Then 'Ellen' is transformed into one of TV's savviest, funniest, slyest shows. Ellen Morgan is a closet lesbian."

ELLEN DeGENERES For a long time, coming out hadn't been important to me because I was able to live my life. Everyone knew I was gay, nobody had a problem with it, and my show was successful. But I was always in fear, during every interview, about what to do if they asked me about being gay. And that's a horrible way to live: to constantly try to hide your relationship and to fear that if they know I'm gay, I'll lose my career. I'd been doing lots of soul-searching, and it sounds corny, but I wanted my work to be honest, I wanted to feel good about myself, and I was having these dreams—I had a very specific dream one night that just made it so clear to me that I was living in a cage. It was a beautiful cage but I was living in a cage. But, absolutely, [the network] did not want me to come out.

TED HARBERT There was a series of long, painstaking discussions and meetings that led up up to my going to Michael Eisner [at that point the chairman of Disney, which owned ABC] and selling him on it. Either Ellen called me, or her manager, or maybe the head writers at the time came and said, "We talked about this." It was long in the making.

ELLEN DeGENERES It was a nightmare convincing them to let me. And then, once I did, everybody just threw their hands up. Advertisers backed off, and the network and the studio just backed away like, "I'm not trying to help her." Everybody let me slowly die.

*In 1998, nearly all of ABC's top sitcoms—*Grace Under Fire, Home Improvement, Roseanne—*had taken a beating in the ratings.* Ellen, *which had been renewed for a fifth season, was no exception, and the show was canceled soon after. At the time, DeGeneres accused ABC of homophobia and claimed that the network killed off the show by failing to promote the series and giving it a bad time slot.*

ELLEN DEGENERES   I didn't even have a chance to prove that the show was gonna [pick up], and actually, I think the season after I came out was even better, because it was dealing with someone who had come out late in life and that hadn't been seen before. It dealt with what happened at work, it dealt with what happened with my friends, and I think it was a really good season that no one got behind. And so my nightmare, that if they found out I was gay I'd lose my career, came true.

STU BLOOMBERG   I found [the accusations about homophobia] very painful and hurtful, because I was such an advocate for her and for the show. I completely believed in it, as did ABC. [The cancellation] had nothing to do with that. It was about the ratings, and at a certain point you just can't support it. But honestly I found it hurtful. I felt a very strong attachment and history with Ellen DeGeneres the person. I spent a lot of time with her back in the days before that show and felt I had a relationship [with her], and the end was not pleasant, let's just put it that way. She was really upset and took it out [on ABC], but as far as I am concerned, it was about the ratings.

ELLEN DEGENERES   By the time I came out, I had stopped doing stand-up. The only reason I started up again was because I lost my show and I lost my income. There were no other offers coming to me. I sat for about a year, year and a half, waiting for the phone to ring, and finally I was like, "This is ridiculous—I started my career, I know how to write, I know what to do, I just have to remind them that I'm the one that got me here." I realized the only thing I could do was go back on the road and start over again, which is why I named that special [which aired in 2000] *The Beginning*, because it's how I started. And when I went on the road to build up for the HBO special, I would say that ninety percent of the audience was gay and ten percent were straight. I lost all of my straight fans because everyone thought I was going to be some militant lesbian comedian and talk about rainbow flags. They were the same people that had been on tour with me all those years, they were the same people that saw me get to where I got, and then all of a sudden they were gone. Then I think a lot of gay people that came to see me were expecting the show to be all about some movement. And that's why I made the joke "I'm your leader," because there really was a lot of frustration on my part. I never intended to change anything other than living in truth. The only thing I wanted to do was be honest. And then I lost my straight fans and all of a sudden I gained all these gay fans who were then disappointed that I wasn't gay enough. It took a while for me to slowly get the audience back to what it was, which is everybody.

I would say it took three or four years [before the industry started to look at me again]. What helped was during that time I got *Finding Nemo* [2003]. The guy who wrote it, Andrew Stanton, said he was writing it with me in mind. And so the only thing I was doing while I was on tour was the voice of Dory. Then Les Moonves at CBS was kind enough to give me a shot at another show with Mitch Hurwitz but that only lasted one season. Then the talk show idea came along and it seemed like the ideal thing because I wasn't trying to play a character, I could just be myself.

At first we couldn't sell the show. There are people that own several different stations and there were a lot of them who wouldn't buy me. There were a lot who blatantly said, "This is housewives at home during the day; who's going to watch a lesbian during the day?" That was really their response when they were trying to wrap their head around my show. Somehow, all my words had *lesbian* woven through them. The show had nothing to do with sexuality, and yet it was a hard sell. But there was one guy that took a chance and bought in five different markets, and that gave a few other people [the impetus to buy the show too]. So it's pretty sweet success that it's doing so well and that audiences have proven them wrong by saying that all success comes down to is whether the show is entertaining or not.

7

· · · · · · · · · · ·

Janeane Garofalo and Friends

By 1992, Johnny Carson had retired; the comedy club wave was crashing, leaving a stale Hollywood business in its wake. Independent showcase clubs were shuttering across the country. What remained, mostly, were national chains, which charged a cover at the door and a two-drink minimum. For the stand-ups of Generation X, it was harder than ever to get a spot on a lineup. Even if a young comic landed a slot, audiences who could afford a night out were not always looking to hear new voices. If they wanted to prosper, comedy's underclass had to find alternatives.

More than any other comic of that day, Janeane Garofalo, a five-foot-four Gen Xer who came to the stage in red lipstick and combat boots, became the poster child for a new generation of comics, disdainful of the predictable set-up punch line style that had come to define club comedy. What came to be known as "alternative comedy" was an effort by Garofalo and other twentysomethings to take comedy out of the club cartels and into the coffee shops, bookshops, and Laundromats—any place that would have them. This do-it-yourself approach also marked a stylistic shift reminiscent of the 1960s, with comics tossing out polished acts in favor of looser, more improvisational delivery, often blending spoken-word and character work. The joke became less important than the identity of the person telling it, and comedy transitioned from aggressive, joke-based stand-up to more fluid and oblique storytelling. Storytelling is considered to be a feminine form of comedy, and without a need for the balls-out, brassy-broad persona seemingly required to carry a joke, ladies in shoulder-padded power suits gave way to softer-looking women in corduroys. In the variety of their material, these women covered a lot of *ground, from bawdy (Margaret Cho) and catty (Kathy Griffin) to sexy but filthy (Laura Kightlinger and, eventually, Sarah Silverman). By the 2000s, the old stereotypes about women and stand-up had evolved.*

JANEANE GAROFALO   In my senior year of high school in Houston, I started going to comedy clubs. There was a great comedy club called the Comedy Workshop, which you could go to even though you weren't the legal drinking age. So I started going there a lot to watch stand-up. Then, when I was a junior at Providence College in Rhode Island, I went to a club called Periwinkles, which was close to school. It was 1985 and there was a night when you could sign up to do stand-up, so I signed up to do it that night. The first night went great, maybe because I was so naïve and fearless the first time, and I was kind of drunk, and it just worked out. I had written some bits on my arm, so I could look at it like a cheat sheet, and people in the audience thought that was part of the act and thought it was funny. And yet nobody ever thought the cheat sheet was funny again. I started bombing from there. I don't know why that happened. Some people say there's a myth that if you do really well your first time, you're meant to do it, so I moved to Boston when I graduated in '86, got a day job, and then thought, like everybody else who's just starting out, "You'll have your day job and you'll do stand-up at night."

Play It Again Sam's, which was a bar/restaurant that had stand-up downstairs, was a particular favorite (a) because I got time there, and (b) because it was literally right across the street from where I lived. I also enjoyed the Comedy Connection, Stitches, and then Catch a Rising Star, which opened in Cambridge and was really great. And then there were one-nighters in the outlying suburbs at restaurants and things like that.

DAVID CROSS, comedian   There were two very visible factions of stand-up comedy in Boston. I wouldn't say people like me and Janeane struggled, but we clearly weren't the standard-issue comics at the time, and we were able to get gigs simply because there were so many colleges, country-western bars, biker bars, pizza places, and Bennigan's that had comedy nights. But it was all very, very male dominated. If you didn't fit into that working-class, blue-collar, male-centric comedy mold, then whatever you did was kind of alternative, in a sense. And for a woman to be intellectual was even more off-putting and difficult, I think.

JULIE BARR   Janeane was in the Dennis Miller school. She would do offhanded references and very obscure references. I remember one of her jokes was "Hester Prynne lettered in high school." And that's a very funny joke, but only if you've read *The Scarlet Letter*. And she would just stand there and look at these people and think, "You're just idiots, why do I even stand there and talk to you?"

BARRY KATZ, comedy manager   Denis Leary hosted his own night Thursday at Play It Again Sam's, and Janeane Garofalo is somebody that Denis Leary put on every single week. And in my opinion— probably not her opinion or maybe not Denis's opinion—but in my opinion she was bombing every single week. She was doing very smart material but the crowd was just not laughing. And after about, you know, four weeks I turned to him and I said, "Denis, you know she's bombing every week. Don't you think we should try somebody else in the show and take her out for a few weeks? Give her a breather." It was the only time he ever got mad at me in his entire life. He stuck his finger in my face and said, "Fuck you, Barry. She's funny. She will work my show every fucking week, and if you don't like it, I'm out of here."

LINDA SMITH   Janeane used to do my show at Catch a Rising Star [in Boston]. I remember her as one of the newbies and I thought she was good. She was younger than me, and I was like the elder comic. It was my show and all that shit, but I liked her. And she was pals at the time with Laura Kightlinger. So the two of them were the ones introducing a new brand of comedy, which was interesting, and it was kind of un- comfortable, too, because I used to always think they were looking at me and going, "Oh, old-school. Yuck." You know, I'm, like, "Hey, new- school, yuck." What the fuck? There's room for everybody.

CLAUDIA LONOW   [Later, in L.A,] she was famous for not doing her full time. When she would go on, she'd say, "Stay in the room, I don't know how long I'm gonna last." If she was a dud or if she didn't like the crowd, she'd walk off the stage.

BARRY KATZ   Laura Kightlinger was from Emerson, and Anthony Clark—who I managed later on in my life and still do—loved her, and he used to put her on the Sunday shows. She had more of a huggability and lovability. But she was inconsistent. Like, she'd do okay one week and then the next week she wouldn't. But she had this lovability about her and this really bizarre, quirky humor. And I remember I had her go on Anthony's show and there was one night where it just all came together for her and she killed so hard, I remember taking her back and saying like, "You get it, you crushed it."

JULIE BARR   I would never really question a booker. They would only put one woman on any show and they would say, "Look, we already have a woman on that show." I would just be like, "Yes, sir. No, sir. Whatever you want. That's fine. I just want to work." But when Janeane Garofalo came in, she used to make a big deal out of that. She used to really argue with club owners.

JANEANE GAROFALO   You only want one woman or one black comedian per show—at the time, club owners would actually have the nerve to say that out loud. Or they would say something like, "Well, we just had a female comic last weekend headlining and she bombed, so we're not going to have any more women." Or "We had a black comic who we didn't like, so we're not going to have any more black comics." The first few times it happened, I was shocked. Then I would say, "Do you say, 'We had a white man here'?" Sometimes they would say, "No, I would never say that, and that's a good point," or they would go, "That's ridiculous." There would be no point made.

BARRY KATZ   At some point, I was booking a ton of shows. I had like fifty one-nighters all across New England that I was booking. And I was booking a lot of comedians, giving them a lot of work, but I would never really book Janeane, because she never did that well for me. And I remember one night she came down the stairs at the club and she sat on the stairs and she said, "Can I talk to you?" And I said, "Sure." And she was crying. And she said, "I just want you to know you're the reason why I have to leave Boston and I'm moving to Houston, because I can't survive here because you won't give me any work." And I was like, "I'm the reason you're leaving? Am I the only guy in town that can give you work?" Janeane was one of the first people that I just didn't have a connection with. She really let me know that women are funny; who said, "Book me, and I can do this." But I just didn't feel it with her.

JANEANE GAROFALO   I had to go back to Houston for family reasons and also I knew I wanted to start saving money for Los Angeles, so I thought I would move back home and save money for my big move to L.A. I didn't think of it as leaving Boston, because that wasn't my style. I both bombed a lot and did well a lot in Boston. But I figured I could bomb or do well anywhere. I thought of maybe moving to Minneapolis or San Francisco, but then I met a manager named Jimmy Miller who had said, "You should try L.A.—just skip Minneapolis and San Francisco and just go directly to L.A., because you're gonna wind up there anyway." And as it turned out, he kept his word [about helping me once I got there]. He set up some open mics for me when I got there, which was very surprising, and he didn't have to do that. And he hooked me up with my first manager, Rick Messina, who was very encouraging. And that's how it started.

I did the Laugh Factory and the Improv. I didn't pass my audition at the Comedy Store. It took me five auditions to pass at the Improv. Actually, Dennis Miller put in a good word for me—you know, shocking when you think of today's incarnation of Dennis Miller. He's become a very nasty right-wing person. I guess he always had that nasty side of his personality; now he just hides it beneath politics and pretends it's politically oriented. But in the beginning he was quite supportive. His brother is Jimmy Miller and I think he saw me do stand-up. My first TV show was *The Dennis Miller Show* and then the MTV *Half Hour Comedy Hour.*

But my stand-up never took off. What happened was I met Ben Stiller at Canter's Deli and he cast me on *The Ben Stiller Show.* Then I met Garry Shandling and he cast me on *The Larry Sanders Show* [HBO's smart satire about late-night television starring Garry Shandling]. So that's actually where a lot of breaks came. I never had a huge stand-up break. It's the acting that started first and that enhanced people knowing that I did stand-up and coming to see me do that.

DAVID CROSS   Janeane was a pioneer in going out west and settling the landscape for the rest of us. Janeane was the first woman out of that

214 • WE KILLED

scene who really made it and made it big. I mean, she skyrocketed. She moved to L.A. and then she was on *The Dennis Miller Show* and all kinds of stuff happened for her. My whole foray into Hollywood and the entertainment industry outside of stand-up was basically through her, because she was on *Ben Stiller* at the time and—I don't mean physically—on *The Ben Stiller Show*, although I think she did fuck him. I had my sketch group in Boston and it had started getting some renown outside of Boston, and she got me hired on *The Ben Stiller Show* as a mid-season writer's replacement, so quite literally she's the reason I went to L.A.

MARGARET CHO Janeane invented this idea of alternative comedy. And what was popular in the late eighties/early nineties was a kind of observational humor where the joke-teller didn't have an identity—anyone could be the joke-teller. Alternative comedy was more about the identity of the person telling the joke. And Janeane was a really big pioneer in this idea of identity versus observation.

Janeane basically taught me how to do comedy. I used to think, "Oh, you've got to think up all these jokes, and you've got to really work hard on your craftsmanship, and it's really about how the jokes are." She was like, "No, they just want to see you. They just want to listen to you, they want to know what you're thinking, they want to know what you did that day. That's much more valuable than all the jokes the boys are working out." Janeane brought me the idea that people are interested in *me* and that they're interested in what I have to say. They don't really care about how well I can craft a joke.

And when you look at the people who are popular now as comedians, they're all people who would have been considered alternative comedians—Sarah Silverman, David Cross, Tenacious D, Kathy Griffin. Janeane was very influential for many people.

DAVID CROSS I would have to qualify that statement; I don't think it's right to say an individual invented alternative comedy. The label came later. The thing that we now look at as alternative comedy was just generational and it was a bunch of people who at the right place at the right time got together. We were all kind of like-minded—not that we all did the same kind of material, but it was about not doing the kind of material that had a familiar kind of subject matter, patter, and delivery [as was popular in the 1980s]. I'm not saying that those comics weren't good joke writers, but [their humor] wasn't that personal.

There was no concerted effort to make an alternative scene. It just sort of happened, and Janeane was at the forefront of that group. She was responsible for putting a show together in L.A. at a place called the Big & Tall Bookstore, which kind of presaged the post-alternative boom where all of a sudden people were doing stand-up at Laundromats and coffee shops. It was kind of going back to this sixties folk thing of doing comedy wherever you could. So she's very responsible for what we now see as an almost calculated idea, but that really wasn't.

JANEANE GAROFALO The comedy boom [of the 1980s] lasted until about '92, '93. Then, one by one, comedy clubs started closing, and fewer and fewer people were seeing it as an entertainment option during the week or on the weekend. But out of that comedy bust, if you will, came a kind of interesting, "other" comedy scene in the early to mid-nineties. Some people call it alternative. Others bristle when the phrase *alternative comedy* is used, because they don't understand that it just means performing in a place that's an alternative to a comedy club. So out of the comedy bust started springing up a scene of venues that would do spoken-word and stand-up comedy nights that were not comedy clubs proper. They weren't chains, like Funny Bone or the Improv, and they didn't charge an arm and a leg to get in the door and then have a two-drink minimum. And there were more thoughtful comedians performing in them.

GREG BEHRENDT, comedian What was really cool was that in that particular scene at that particular time, it was very pro-woman. I remember I came down to visit Janeane when she was living with Jeff Garlin, and we were lying on her bed listening to a Juliana Hatfield record. You had Lilith Fair and a lot of corduroy pants. And the women were the ones who really made the alternative scene unique. The alternative scene was really an umbrella that fell underneath Janeane Garofalo. And the girls were the ones who were getting famous, remember that. It was Janeane and Margaret Cho and Kathy Griffin. Those were the girls that could fill the rooms.

JANEANE GAROFALO   When the music scene shifted for that wonderful, brief time—when Nirvana busted the doors wide open for different kinds of music, and there were [women-dominated] bands like Hole, Veruca Salt, the Breeders, Liz Phair, and Juliana Hatfield—it seemed like a shift really happened in the comedy scene too. In the way that the music scene had that wonderful renaissance at that time, it seemed like comedy did, too, when it came to women and comics of color.

While Garofalo's stand-up career never quite resonated with audiences, her string of television successes culminated in a star-making role in Reality Bites, *Ben Stiller's Zeitgeist-defining 1994 film that captured the apathy plaguing a group of Generation X postgrads. (The screenplay was written by Helen Childress.) That movie, plus Lorne Michaels's subsequent high-profile decision to hire Garofalo as savior of the sinking ship that was then* Saturday Night Live, *completed Garofalo's transformation from underground comic to icon. (A lesser-known Laura Kightlinger was also brought on as a cast member that year.) In stark contrast to those successful female comedians who came before her, Garofalo used the influence she wielded to prop up fellow funny females.*

GREG BEHRENDT   If Kurt Cobain is the male voice of the generation at that point, Janeane sort of holds down the female end of it. They both sort of embodied that, quote unquote, slacker idea that was forming at the time.

MARGARET CHO   I remember there was once a time when Janeane was doing a few movies and she got to interview Eddie Vedder. It was, like, a really big deal. Can you imagine in the nineties she gets to have dinner with Eddie Vedder? And interview him! It was so exciting. And then I remember one time Weezer did some photo shoot for some big magazine and I think it was Matt who wore a shirt that said "I Love Janeane Garofalo." It was such a big deal. So this was like the mid-, late nineties when alternative really started to become cool.

The boys were always super-supportive of each other. Whenever a new guy comic was coming into town, everybody would go see him. And the girls didn't really have that until Janeane Garofalo came to San Francisco. When she came out, all the girls went to go see her. Finally, we had somebody that we could look up to. We just thought she was this little rock star. She was this punk-rock girl, she had really black hair, and only wore red lipstick. And this was the '90s, so she knew a lot about music, and all these bands, like the guys from Weezer, were really into her. She was this hero because she had one foot in indie rock—because all these indie-rock boys were really in love with her—and then one foot in comedy. She thought I was cool, and I taught her how to smoke cigarettes, which is really bad, but it was all I could do.

And one of the first trips I made to L.A., I did *Star Search*—our version of *American Idol*, many years ago—and that was probably a big turning point. I was nineteen and scared. I didn't know where anything was, and I'd just learned to drive. And I remember Janeane spent the night with me.

KAREN KILGARIFF, comedian The first time I saw Janeane, I was like, "Oh my God." She was wearing her black tights with her cutoff denim shorts over them and her Doc Marten boots. And she walked out and then starts doing all this brilliant, amazing observational comedy. I had just started to do comedy three weeks before, and after I watched her, I realized that I was speaking in a really high register onstage, almost in a baby voice, like "Be nice to me, I'm the girl!" After I saw Janeane do stand-up, I immediately talked much lower and did much more of a pulled-back, too-cool-for-school character.

But she was one of the first female comics that I ever saw that was so self-possessed and so "This is how I am." Up until that point, the only people I ever saw were like, "I'm Rita Rudner, I'm the sexy ditsy mom," or "I'm wearing a pantsuit."

KATHY GRIFFIN I'm always going to be grateful to Janeane. When I first started, I called Janeane and said, "I can't get a break. I've been in the Groundlings forever. Everybody is getting on *SNL* but me." Janeane said, "Okay, look. I think that we should do something called alternative comedy. I don't think we should even try the clubs. Fuck the Comedy Store. Fuck the Improv." This was when Janeane was in *Reality Bites* and she was the hottest thing in the world. So I started renting a theater myself and I would go to Kinko's and print out flyers that said: "Comedy night with Kathy Griffin and Janeane Garofalo." We would charge $1, because we were convinced nobody would come if we charged more than that. It was called Hot Cup of Talk, and the show was only an hour, and we promised we wouldn't be taking up people's nights. And then we would get celebrity guests: one week Lisa Kudrow would come and do fifteen minutes; another week Quentin Tarantino would come do fifteen minutes—people who weren't even comics. And it was full every single week. One night Jodie Foster would be in the audience and industry people would hear that celebrities were going and then they would come. That night changed my life.

DAVID CROSS   I met Bob Odenkirk, who I created *Mr. Show* with, through Janeane. It was definitely a casual meeting, but I was there in L.A. probably for like a week, week and a half. And I was bored and I wanted to play basketball. And she said, "Oh, my friend Bob, he likes basketball." So I had a basketball in my hand, I don't know where I got it from, and Janeane and I walked over to Bob's house, and the door was open and there was a screen door, and he was inside watching TV and writing. And she goes, "Hey, Bob, it's Janeane." "Hey Janeane." "Uh, hey, this is my friend David. He was just wondering if you wanted to play basketball." I felt like I was ten years old. And he just sort of looked over his shoulder. He's like, "Oh no, I'm busy." And then I stood there at the screen door, and after about five or six seconds just sort of turned and walked away. That was our first official meeting.

As is true with many grassroots efforts, alternative comedy started largely from necessity, a way to get out from under the controlling thumbs of comedy club bookers. The first attempts to get stage time outside these clubs were in L.A.'s growing number of coffeehouses, where many of these comics went to work. Soon, shows at coffeehouses led to shows at bookstores and, later, in theaters. Women in particular played an important role in setting up comedy nights at these alternative venues.

MARGARET CHO   In the early nineties, there was a coffeehouse boom, and there was this one called the Ministry on La Brea. Ben Stiller was there, and Judd Apatow and Colin Quinn were writing in their notebooks, so Janeane was like, "Oh, we've got to do that too. We've got to work." So everyone would just get together and sit and write. It was like comedy study hall. It was the greatest thing, because you could try to be a girl and try to flirt with these guys, but they were just super into what they were doing and just didn't care.

JANEANE GAROFALO Sometimes we would meet at around eleven or midnight. There were a couple of places where we thought we would just sit and write in our notebooks! For me, it was a way to combat my sense of inertia, because I just wasn't working enough and making enough strides. And Margaret would go, and Moon Zappa, Dana Gould, Colin Quinn. We weren't getting enough stage time at comedy clubs, so we thought, "What if we talked the owners of these cafés into giving us a night to do stand-up?" It evolved out of that.

LAURA MILLIGAN, comedian The alternative stand-up scene started with Janeane doing shows at the Big & Tall bookstore. The Big & Tall bookstore was a bookstore, and it was in no way organized to do any kind of show. There was no PA so it was kind of horrible, because people would be there to just be at a bookstore, and suddenly they would be assaulted by this guerrilla comedy show. Janeane would organize them with her friends, Kathy Griffin and a couple other people starting out. Colin Quinn would do it. And, actually, Janeane was going out with Ben Stiller then. He would get up and do stuff. I think she made him do it. She was like, "You just gotta get up and just tell a story." Like, he had told a story about candy or something that day in the car, and she said, "See? Just get up and tell that story. Just get up and tell it exactly like that. Don't think about it, don't write it down, just get up and say it." For her, that's what it was about. She was sick of seeing people with an organized act.

KATHY GRIFFIN Janeane came to see me the very first night I ever did stand-up. It was in a bookstore and of course I bombed. Number one, I was in a bookstore and fighting these cappuccino machines; number two, I didn't do conventional jokes. I did these rambling stories. And I was kind of honest about whatever run-ins I had with celebrities or my own crappy dating life. And Janeane was helpful to me, because she said, "Don't change a thing that you do. Don't try to become a joke-teller, don't try to become whatever is the stand-up comic du jour."

DAVID CROSS   I did two [Big & Talls], as a matter of fact, when I was out there visiting. Before I was on the *Stiller* show I went out there, I can't remember why—I think it was to do some showcase-y thing. I had *no* money and I think I was auditioning for stuff. But [while I was there] I met with Janeane and Ben Stiller at this bar called the Snake Pit when he was getting his show together. He didn't have it yet. And we hung out and had a couple beers. And we all got along and it turned out to be, obviously, a fruitful meeting. I think Janeane was acting like my dad and I was a bit of a debutante and we were having our coming-out party. She was introducing me to high society and she was very instrumental and helpful that way. And while I was out there I did a couple sets at the Big & Tall and loved it. It was right up my alley.

JANEANE GAROFALO   It wasn't segregated at all. In these, quote unquote, alternative scenes again—and I say *alternative* only meaning not in a comedy club proper—there was no ghettoizing with men and women or comics of color, if you will. And that sounds like I'm ghettoizing to say it that way, but what I mean is that there were none of those issues: "Oh, you only want one woman per show, one Asian per show." That's never been an issue in the alternative comedy scene, with the audience or with the people booking it.

GREG BEHRENDT   The other thing is we booked these rooms. If you were around, somebody would give you a set. These were our rooms. There wasn't a "guy." You didn't have to audition for anybody. You didn't have to go through any of that horseshit or any of the fake patriarchy that's there. Comedy club owners, some of them, are among the worst people on the planet. And the horseshit that they make people go through is just ridiculous. Comics will lick boots to do work. I think so many of us just said, "Fuck that, there's a microphone, a PA, here." Or: "There's a rock club and it's empty on Monday nights, let's do this, let's call your friends and let's do sets." I think people just wanted to put on a show. It was that mind-set, which is very much a music mind-set: "Fuck them, then we'll go do it in a Laundromat, I don't need the Improv." I don't think anyone cared about being on the *Tonight Show*.

BOB ODENKIRK, comedian   The traditional stand-up comics saw alternative comedy as sloppy and unprofessional and too hit-or-miss compared to their very well recited stand-up comedy bits. But I mean, why would they like it? It's the opposite of what they were doing. But it's way more interesting. I could never do traditional stand-up and still can't do it, because I just don't like any joke enough to want to tell it eight hundred times.

MARGARET CHO I always stayed firmly within the conventional comedy clubs—I never left. I didn't have the luxury of just being an alternative comic. I had a lot of gigs on the road, I was doing a lot of universities and a lot of shows at comedy clubs all over the world at that point, so it wasn't like I could safely stay in alternative comedy. It wasn't where I learned to do comedy.

LAURA KIGHTLINGER I've performed in both classic and alternative comedy clubs and I always do better in alternative spaces. I don't think the audiences in the more generic places are as willing to "go with you" on personal anecdotes or conceptual, out-of-the-ordinary topics. They're thinking about fucking their dates or getting home to relieve the babysitter and aren't too keen on long setups. The dick jokes need to be fast and plentiful and I generally don't have the energy for it.

A note on the self-deprecating tendencies of female comics of the nineties: While critics tend to scrutinize self-deprecation along gender lines—often pointing to Phyllis Diller and Joan Rivers as the progenitors and ultimate examples of this style of humor—not all women who cut themselves down can be linked to these comic ancestors. For the female alt-comics of the nineties, self-deprecation was less a device used to gain the love and acceptance of an audience than it was a reflection of the cynicism these women had about the world around them and where they fit in it. In fact, self-deprecation was largely generational, a sensibility shared by women and men. While comics of the seventies and eighties revered Johnny Carson, comics of the nineties looked up to David Letterman, whose persona was built around his own self-loathing. It was that point of view—plus Gen X's own disillusionment with their lot in life—that set the tone.

BOB ODENKIRK People make self-deprecating comments, and there is a strain of artificial self-deprecation that is really grotesque and strange. I can't name names but I've seen friends of mine do it, and it's an attempt to gain the audience's sympathy because you're calling yourself names and saying that you're a loser or you're a nerd. And this is from people who I know think very well of themselves, and they know it's just a ploy. It is just a trick to sound humble and to attempt to win people's affection. But with Janeane, it's all too real. That could be said of her act sometimes—it's all too real. She genuinely beats herself up and she doesn't think too highly of herself.

Janeane's cynical—cynical and intelligent. She sees different sides to things that aren't the obvious points of view. She's extremely self-deprecating. It can be hard to take sometimes as an audience member, to watch somebody rag on themselves so hard. "Enough, all right, we like you. We feel bad that you don't like yourself." Yeah, she's self-deprecating—sometimes to a fault.

And she certainly didn't get a big head. It probably would have been more healthy for her head to grow. It was probably part of her all-too-real self-deprecation that she did not change at all. She was vehemently alternative and down with the unknowns and the undiscovered far too much. I mean, she probably didn't make nearly enough of her big break. I know she didn't. She just didn't because she just doesn't associate herself with success at all. Anything successful is something she's not interested in being a part of. That's not a good thing in the long run. You should have some little modicum of appreciation and ability to accept success a little. And maybe make something out of it. She really rejects that, but that's Janeane.

GREG BEHRENDT   She'd make a movie and then talk about how shitty she was in it, and then when she'd go to promote it she'd say it was horrible and she was bad in it. There is a little bit of a game—a bunch of people put up a bunch of money to make that movie—but that's Janeane.

DAVID CROSS   Joan Rivers has funny, silly, self-deprecating punch lines about her looks but it's encapsulated in ten words and it's jokey. Whereas Laura and *especially* Janeane will sit there and talk about what they find are their faults with themselves in relation to whatever the subject matter is in a self-analysis, analytical, contemplative way that's still funny and still sharp. And that's a generational thing. Comics just didn't do that until relatively recently. You see somebody like Louis C.K. who's just brilliant, and that's what he does. And we all came up together. We all kind of do that to a degree.

LAURA KIGHTLINGER   I don't think of my stand-up as being self-deprecating. I think of it as being self-aware. I'm an awkward person who, for some reason, needs to forge a connection with strangers by sharing true, intimate, humiliating events from my own life.

One by one, comedians descended on Los Angeles to take part in what was by then transforming into an actual comedy movement. Many of them arrived from San Francisco, where they formed a tight-knit group who lived and partied together, performing comedy at what was then a nascent little show, the Un-Cabaret.

LAURA MILLIGAN   When I moved to Los Angeles, I lived with this musician Gere Fennelly, who was in this band Redd Kross, and then Margaret Cho came down and it was the three of us. We had a studio apartment and it became the comedy condo and everybody slept on our floor, so we ended up getting a house on Curson Ave. While I lived there, Janeane lived there, Laura Kightlinger lived there. Later Laura and Jack Black lived there when they were a couple.

KAREN KILGARIFF   It seemed like everyone moved to L.A. at the same time. There was just this huge San Francisco posse that kind of moved down and this was almost like your halfway house when you moved to L.A. It was in the hills and everyone was drunk on tequila all the time. And it turned into this big codependent posse that ate every meal together and then went and did comedy and then stayed at a bar all night together.

MARGARET CHO   Janeane also lived in another place on Curson, which was a similar situation, and which may have been the precursor to the Curson house. It was a big house up the hill, and that was the place I hung out [at] before I moved into the big Curson house, and that was where you would see Judd Apatow or Colin Quinn or Ben Stiller.

LAURA MILLIGAN Janeane ended up going out with Greg Behrendt; that's why she moved into our house. But at that time she was having *way* more success than anyone else, because she had just done *Reality Bites* and she was in *The Truth About Cats and Dogs* with Uma Thurman. So she was shooting that while she was going out with Greg and staying at the house. And that's when everything was just mayhem. There was a lot of incipient alcoholism, and a lot of people not being able to deal with emotions properly. When I started with Janeane doing the alternative thing, we weren't drinking really at all. There weren't that many drugs that I saw. But people started drinking more, and by the mid-nineties there was a lot of drinking.

MARGARET CHO I never slept very well there. There were so many people around all the time, it wasn't just about living there, it was like people were just there. It was a centralized place for a lot of comedians to hang out. That was where I met Sarah Silverman for the first time.

LAURA MILLIGAN There was always a party happening there. There was this one night where we all were doing this one-nighter down in San Diego. And we came back and Janeane was there and she brought Kim Deal [of the Breeders] over, and Jack Black was in the yard with his beat-up acoustic guitar and his pants falling down because he didn't have a belt. David Cross was, like, passing out in the corner. That was a typical night.

We *all* hung out together *all* the time. Like breakfast—you would never consider going to breakfast just by yourself, you had to be with this group of people. I think that is the comedy mentality: you just have to be around this group of people to feel validated. There's some fear of being alone, I think. And it was like a family. Everybody was totally welcome. And I think that's what inevitably led to it all just going south in the end: no one had any privacy, which was a wonderful thing at first, because you never had to be alone—and then you desperately wanted to be alone.

GREG BEHRENDT We were like this gigantic, massive crew. You'd get up around noon, recover from your hangover, maybe take a hike up Runyon Canyon, which was a few feet away, go to the Farmers Market or walk around the mall and plot what you were going to do next. We'd all go to the movies together: thirty-seven of us would go see *Speed*.

Quentin Tarantino—he was around a little bit in those early days—and Moon Zappa and Kathy Griffin. Then you'd figure out where you were going to party that night or where you were going to do a set. Nobody was working. And we all were in love with what everyone was doing.

LAURA MILLIGAN All the bedrooms were so tiny and there was no air-conditioning and it would get so hot in there in these tiny little rooms, it was just gross. And the bathroom was in the hall, and if you took a shit it was just lethal. No ventilation. I know Jack Black was telling me when he lived there with Laura the water in the toilet was just boiling hot for about a month and they couldn't fix it. It was like this boiling cauldron. Even before then, that's what this house was like: a boiling cauldron of emotion.

GREG BEHRENDT There was a lot of love around those times. Everybody was very supportive, and if you didn't have a boyfriend or girlfriend, there was always one if you needed one.

MARGARET CHO Kathy would come over and tell us that we were like animals, and she would judge us. That was her role. And even though she wasn't older, she would act older, and constantly judge everybody for sleeping together. She was a mother hen even though she was really our age. Kathy lived in Santa Monica in a tiny apartment, so she was very defensive about living in Santa Monica; she's still very defensive about how she felt she was in the gang even though she lived in Santa Monica.

DAVID CROSS Kathy and I had a couple of tiffs and arguments, and believe me I'm one of dozens who had them. Nothing that I would ever consciously start, but somebody would go, "Man, Kathy Griffin is fuckin' pissed at you." "What? Why? What did I do?" "Well, apparently last month you were talking to blah blah blah and you said something about her pants." You know, one of those crazy things. And there were several times during an Un-Cabaret set where she'd say something and I'd fuckin' write down my responses, and I go up after her, or a couple people later. Sometimes she was right. There were certainly occasions when you'd have to step back and go, "Eh, I guess she's got a point." But that was the great thing. It's not in a vacuum. She goes up and says that stuff or it's published, and then, you know, five minutes later I'm on-stage refuting it. It's kind of fun in a way.

GREG BEHRENDT   Kathy Griffin just started to come out and give these monologues about her career in show business, and about the way she felt about people, before she became a person who just went after celebrities. I'm not trying to boil her down to just that. But that's sort of what she's known for now. But in the old days, literally she'd go out on a date with Jack Black and then talk about that. She was incredibly confessional and personal. Kathy did a lot of apologizing after those shows; she would have to do a lot of apologizing.

BETH LAPIDES, cofounder, Un-Cabaret   When Kathy did Un-Cab she was *much* more personal. It was a lot about finding love, and career flameouts, and wild stories. It wasn't quite as celebrity, but, you know, her life has changed, so of course her stories have changed. She was a little more girl-next-door.

GARY AUSTIN   Kathy Griffin had no taste and she somehow funneled that into a great career. But I didn't like it. One night, for the improv show [at the Groundlings], she says to me, "Can I do a monologue to-night about a date I had last night?" Sure. I go, "No problem." She gets onstage and she talks about this one-night stand. She had a guy the night before and they had sex. She describes the sex in detailed and embarrassing terms, but what was worse about it than that was she was making fun of the guy. And it was just ugly and awful. And I'm sitting there thinking, "These people paid tickets to see a show and they're listening to True Confessions from somebody who has no taste, who's just totally ripping apart some guy and talking about their sex that they had." Ick. I didn't like it. The company I created didn't do that kind of stuff. I'm not saying we censored ourselves and avoided sexual topics. That's not true. But bad taste is bad taste.

DAVID CROSS   Kathy more than those other women is nuts. She's got a couple of particulars about her. And I think she's also, I don't wanna say paranoia, but there's a bit of defensiveness to her that those other women in that community don't have. You wouldn't necessarily know it from her stage act. I don't know what it is, I have never really thought about it, but maybe there's a competitive sense. And, you know, Kathy's one of those people who, like every cycle of friends you go through, you seem to have one friend or acquaintance who gets very dramatic about stuff that is not important to you, or you wouldn't expect them to have this dramatic reaction. Like, "I'm not talking to you for six months." Like, "What?" "You didn't answer my e-vite." And just weird shit like that. And, I don't know, the difference for me, speaking just for myself, between Janeane and Laura and Margaret and Julia Sweeney and Laura Milligan is that I really don't care about the stuff that Kathy talks about and I never did. I think she's funny and she's really cutting and she's honest, but I just don't give a shit about Ryan Seacrest or her take on the Oscars or fashion or this gay guy or whatever. I just don't give a shit about pop culture. So I recognize her talent but I don't give a shit about anything she seems to care about. She made a career out of it. I mean, nobody would have heard of Kathy Griffin if she didn't talk about celebrities. Ever.

LAURA MILLIGAN   Kathy was exactly as she is. She was really fun, but she'd freak out all the time. She's your friend and then she's freaking out at you, and you have no idea why. Just her whole thing revs up from zero to a million really fast. Now she has enough world subjects and her world's a lot bigger. But back when all her worlds were smaller, it was pretty much emotional. It wasn't pitting people against each other, but she knew what she was doing. She was bored probably, so she'd stir shit up, make sure all the plates were spinning. At first I thought it was the greatest thing, and I was really good friends with her. Then it drove me crazy. It's like, "Knock it off, tone it down." But it's great that she didn't tone it down, because now it totally makes sense: it became this great vehicle for her with her Bravo show [*My Life on the D-List*]. That wasn't an act, that's her.

Beth Lapides opened Un-Cabaret in 1994. It was the first established alternative comedy room and ground zero for Los Angeles's cadre of young talent. It drew to its stage the biggest names in the alternative comedy business: Janeane Garofalo, Margaret Cho, Kathy Griffin, Andy Dick, Patton Oswalt, David Cross, and Bob Odenkirk. And although Un-Cab was not at all set up to appeal specifically to women, it was originally designed as a female-friendly show. The fact that Lapides had rules requiring comics to be personal, spontaneous, and conversational also made the show particularly accessible to women, since the style played to their strengths as comedians. Margaret Cho, Kathy Griffin, Julia Sweeney, and Laura Kightlinger were among the comics who best exemplified the Un-Cab style, and the stories that they told onstage helped forge the idea that identity was tantamount to joke-telling in comedy.

During Un-Cabaret's run, comedians took it upon themselves to start up even more shows in venues across Los Angeles. At Tantrum, created by then comedian Laura Milligan, comedians had more latitude to use character and music in their work, giving people like Bob Odenkirk and David Cross their first opportunity to perform their comedy sketch Mr. Show; and Jack Black, his mock rock band Tenacious D. Kathy Griffin created her own show, Hot Cup of Talk, at the Groundlings; then in 1996, Mark Flanagan opened the doors to Largo, until then a music venue, thus transforming Monday nights into the most visible time for comics to see and be seen. It was these comedians, in these rooms, that began to shape stand-up for the twenty-first century.

BETH LAPIDES   I was working in New York as a performance artist in the eighties. And at one point I just got this little flash that was very much like "Oh my God. We get older, we learn about life, and then we die. It's so tragic." And then I was like, "Oh my God, or maybe it's really funny." And then I just got this idea that I could be doing exactly what I'm doing but it could also be funny and that would be so much better. So I just shifted my work into the comedy clubs and I started to learn what it took to be funny on purpose. And then Greg, my partner and husband, wanted to move to L.A., so I started to work at the comedy clubs in L.A., and I was horrified at how showcase-y it was. Everybody had what was called the "tight ten," which was ten minutes that you could do over and over again in showcase situations for producers and casting people and agents. So I would keep doing my one-person shows off to the side and then two things happened simultaneously. The first was I was at the Comedy Store one night and I followed Andrew Dice Clay. He was doing his usual woman-hating shtick and I was hating him and I was hating the audience for liking him and I was kind of hating myself for being there. Then shortly thereafter I was doing my one-person show, Globe-o-Mania, and I was about to tour it in London, so I wanted to retool it. So I did it at this well-known art venue called the Women's Building and they were like, "We're women and we're artists and we're lesbians and we can't go to comedy clubs because they just make fun of us." And I said, "I am going on my tour; when I come back, I'm gonna make a show especially for you. It's gonna be unhomophobic, unmisogynist, unxenophobic. I'll call it the Un-Cabaret." And literally that's how the Un-Cabaret was born. And this was in 1990. So I did that and then three years later I opened at Luna Park.

At Luna Park you would enter the club upstairs, then you would walk down this long staircase and look at yourself in these mirrors and then let go of that and walk down into this dark room. So you sort of saw yourself and let go of yourself. The room itself was small and packed. And it was very womblike and close in. The ceilings were very low. There were couches. It had an intimate feel. And we always felt like that worked for the show. It was very much about the subconscious. Also, we did the show every Sunday, so it had sort of a Sunday vibe, which meant that it was after the weekend, people read the paper, and even if industry did come, they weren't in suits. You're just in that churchy kind of head. So there was a Sunday-ness about it, which was great.

The rule of the Un-Cab was that you weren't allowed to repeat yourself. That was sort of the shortest version of the rule. But what it meant was: Don't do your act. This was a place of discovery. This was a place of being able to experiment. This was a place of being able to go as far as you could go. And we had other strict rules, too, like no characters. It was just really about you. And the audience came along for the ride. In all the years of Un-Cabaret, I can literally remember only two instances of heckling.

GREG BEHRENDT Beth Lapides wasn't saying, "This is the way comedy must be done"; she was saying, "In this room, you have to come with new material, and we'd like you to be personal. We'd like to see people mine their personal lives, and take a risk." It felt like the show was based on what Janeane was already doing on some level, which was a very confessional, I-try-not-to-repeat-my-material, this-just-happened-this-moment, that's-why-I-had-to-write-it-on-a-piece-of-paper type stand-up. But suddenly people were saying, "That's what the scene is." I don't know if that's specifically true, because you go back, everybody has their own version of the truth. Certainly there were joke-tellers and certainly there were storytellers.

ANDY KINDLER, comedian Beth was like, "Don't tell jokes, don't tell jokes." But I always told jokes, and she always let me tell jokes. I got along with her really well. She used me all the time, she laughed at me, but in general she would tell other people it's not about jokes.

MERRILL MARKOE When I was recuperating from leaving the *Letterman* show and the breakup and everything, I wanted to get back into stand-up but I couldn't figure out how because I didn't have an act anymore. And you can't just get out in front of a crowd without some tested material unless you're an improv person. It's much too risky in the world of straight stand-up, where everyone is doing their act. So my friends George Meyer and Maria Semple kept telling me about the Un-Cabaret. Finally they took me to see it. And instantly I was overcome with performer lust, because the rules of it so appealed to me. By definition it was a level playing field: you weren't supposed to do any repeat material. If nobody was doing repeat material, then whatever I came up with for that set was exactly as prepared as everyone else's set. She had managed to attract an audience to Un-Cab who were happy to listen for wordplay. The audiences who liked the Un-Cabaret actually responded to funny descriptive phrases, or word use. They liked ideas. They liked stories. They liked character description. It wasn't all about punch lines, necessarily, although you still needed those too. The Un-Cab was also about context and nuance and tiny details.

And another great innovation that was utterly freeing for me was that you could bring up a sheet of notebook paper onstage! Everyone did! In the old days, that was verboten. The only person I ever saw do that was Richard Lewis. He was always waving a piece of paper from a yellow legal pad with his act on it. But at Un-Cab everyone brought their notebook and after they finished a thought, they'd look through and say, "What else? Oh! I got arrested for speeding on Tuesday." And then go into that material. I was thrilled that I had permission to write bullet points of what I wanted to say and words I didn't want to forget, and then, if I got stalled, I could check to see what I'd forgotten. That was heaven for me. It also taught me how to relax.

GREG MILLER, cofounder, Un-Cabaret The early days of the Un-Cabaret were great, because there was such a pent-up need of a lot performers to do comedy that wasn't fitting into the mainstream comedy clubs. So there was this initial wave of people that had been doing work in the clubs but weren't that satisfied with it. There were people like Julia Sweeney and Kathy Griffin who never did the clubs who just came right from the Groundlings. And there were some TV writer people who had once done stand-up but then quit and were now like, "Oh well, if I can really talk about what I want, then I'll come." And that was part of what gave it a good mix. People were coming from different places. It wasn't all like *stand-up* stand-up.

MERRILL MARKOE Sometimes it seems to me that a sweeping generality can be made about the central difference between men's humor and women's humor. Obviously there's lots of crossover. But I think it might be true that women prefer relating to things more personally— personal anecdotes, storytelling, character-driven stuff, weird little details. Un-Cabaret was set up so that everyone did this kind of material, men and women.

GREG BEHRENDT My first comedy special was called Mantastic, and it was written entirely there, based on my understanding of who I was as a person. I got sober during my run at Un-Cabaret. And as soon as that had happened they started having me come every week, because they wanted to hear what that journey was like. It definitely had to be funny, but I talked about what I was going through. Everybody knew that I had been dating Janeane, and my dealing with that. So it became that people followed your story line there. That's why they would come back: because they were interested. If you were good enough at telling those stories.

DAVID CROSS Sometimes Beth would have, I don't wanna say themes, but suggestions for what you might talk about. Then occasionally you'd say, "Oh my God, Beth, this crazy thing happened, can I go up next week and talk about it?" But mostly you just had an idea and then you went up. You just sort of riff, but it was all personal, anecdotal stuff. So you had a true story to talk about and reflect upon. And I guess my favorite stuff, the stuff that I kept going back to because particularly at the time I was doing Un-Cabaret in the mid-to-late nineties, there was a lot of crazy shit happening in my family. So I would talk about that because they were really just crazy, jaw-dropping stories. It was very therapeutic in a way too.

MERRILL MARKOE   Julia Sweeney was so naturally good at telling the stories of her life. I didn't know much about her before Un-Cab except for the Pat stuff from *Saturday Night Live*. And watching her at Un-Cab was a real object lesson in the way a spot on *SNL* could be incredibly limiting to someone. Because here she was at Un-Cab, not only so much more than that odd one-dimensional sexless character she was famous for, but a fully realized, extremely brilliant storyteller and detailer of her own consistently hilarious, always carefully thought out, very female point of view. I watched her with awe as she repeatedly did what seemed impossible: translate bleak, terrifying, and utterly unfunny topics like the death of her brother and her own bout with cancer into truly hilarious comedy. Seriously. Hilarious.

GREG MILLER   I believe that we met Julia through Kathy Griffin. They knew each other from the Groundlings, I think. It took her one or two shows before she was, like, "Okay, well, I guess I better tell you why I am here: my brother has cancer! Ha-ha hold for laughs." That was her great way of defusing the tension immediately. Then she just launched into it. And that really opened our minds to the possibilities of what could happen when people are telling the ongoing story of their lives. We started having a repeat audience, so that created [a desire for] episodic storytelling: "Well, you've already told the first installment; now let's hear the next installment." I remember laughing really hard at one incident Julia told about her brother having a stent put into his brain. Somehow she made it not just *kinda* funny but really *really* funny. It was revelatory to me. It explained that virtually anything could be made into humor if you meshed it in with the details of your own consistent humorous point of view.

Korean-American comic Margaret Cho was just fourteen years old when she got a taste for comedy while performing with her high school comedy troupe at a local San Francisco club called the Other Café. By sixteen, she was performing stand-up on her own, and what followed was a string of successes: opening for Jerry Seinfeld, performing the college circuit (which led to a nomination for "Campus Comedian of the Year"), frequent appearances on The Arsenio Hall Show, *and eventually a Bob Hope special. In 1994, when Cho was twenty-five years old, she debuted in her own sitcom on ABC,* All-American Girl—*about a Korean-American family—that was, at the time, touted to be the first show to focus on being Asian in America. Within a year, the show tanked and Cho was left to pick up the pieces of her career by returning to her stand-up comedy roots.*

MARGARET CHO   It was the nineties, and people were looking for comedians to build a TV show around. And if you do comedy in L.A. and you're working at comedy clubs, people come see you. And I was doing comedy, and I got noticed by people. I was head-hunted right away because I was so different from anybody else out there. I was funny, and people thought they could build a show around me because I was Asian-American and it seemed like the right thing. But basically, what I was doing as a stand-up comic couldn't be made into a television show: you couldn't put my sensibility on TV at eight o'clock in the early nineties. I was too off-color and way too out there for television. So they kind of tried to do their own idea of what a television show about me would be like, and it didn't work. I couldn't really fit into the show that they had planned for me when I was doing *All-American Girl*, because it was so family-oriented. It was basically *Hannah Montana*, but my character wasn't singing.

And when I first started stand-up, being fat was very, very helpful. And then later, when I got to Hollywood and started to do stuff on TV, I was freaked-out because I thought I was thin—because I was so much thinner than I had been—so I was like, "What do you mean, I'm still fat? I'm thin now, so I could be a TV star." But I wasn't, by TV standards. That's when I had a lot of hard times too.

BETH LAPIDES   When *All-American Girl* went down, Margaret Cho was really ready to reinvent herself and to tell the story. Margaret goes all the way and she did some very dark, very wild, and very introspective stuff. She dished it out. I mean, Un-Cabaret wasn't the only stage she played by any stretch of the imagination, but I feel like it was one of the places that she did it.

GREG MILLER She did some very intense work. She really used to use it as comic therapy. After *All-American Girl* was canceled, she was redefining her whole sense of herself, and that involved talking about what happened with the show and all the pressures of looks and body image. And then, from that, out came stuff about her family and some of the darker past material which doesn't work in the comedy clubs, obviously.

GREG BEHRENDT Margaret had a way of being incredibly brassy. She was able to get up and tell you she gives the worst blow job in the world—and be really be funny about it—and then at the same time be really overtly sexual. So you're not sure: Did she mean that? Did she not mean that? She seems really sexual, she seems really interested in sex, but then she would take herself out.

MERRILL MARKOE I love when Margaret talks about her mother. Her mother is one of the great comic characters of all time. But I will never forget the time I heard her do a set about her father. He was apparently pretty rough with her when she was a teenager. She gave quite a few frightening details. Her set was so frank and such a stark look at another side of her life that I can still see, in my mind, the lighting and Margaret onstage when she was delivering it. The room was silent. For a while she just left comedy behind and was simply telling the truth about something painful, it seemed. And then she made a left turn and went back to her comic side and everyone was laughing again.

EMILY LEVINE When I first saw Margaret Cho—with all credit to Sandra Bernhard—I was like, "Oh my God. This is like the quote from Muriel Rukeyser, the poet: 'What would happen if one woman told the truth about her life? The world would split open.'" To have that kind of bravery and just put it all out there. I was blown away. I still am.

MARGARET CHO I think it gave me a lot of freedom to expand on what I was doing, and it gave me a lot more confidence, but I had to modify it too. You couldn't just take that into the mainstream comedy rooms at the time; you still had to have jokes. That was really important. I had to make money, which I was doing at the time, but I still wanted to be hanging out. You never make any money in alternative groups, so you would go to the alternative groups for hanging out, and go to the rest of the gigs for making money. But then it was structured so that the alternative groups happened on Monday, Tuesday, Wednesday, and then the rest of it happened on a weekend.

MERRILL MARKOE Laura Kightlinger was one of my first friends at Un-Cab. She's extremely funny, a great performer, relaxed and playful and hilarious and gorgeous and smart onstage. She's also a great joke writer and prose writer too. Laura's got this combination of comedy strengths that in an odd way always reminds me a little of Eve Arden. It's the deadpan delivery, the amazing good looks, and the wisecracks all working together in a way that says, "Don't fuck with me. I know what I am talking about and I just might be the only sane person here." But where she's nothing at all like Eve Arden is in her unique dark, frequently bleak angle on things. Laura manages to find a really surprising, unexpected, original perspective on almost everything she writes about. She's got great imagery, great wording, and the weirdest sharp edges and odd angles. You think she's going in one direction and she heads off in the opposite direction. The first time I really noticed this was when I saw her do a joke that went "I was asked to do a benefit for babies addicted to crack, I said, 'All right, I'll help you raise money for them, but I think we both know what they're going to spend it on.'"

GREG BEHRENDT Laura is one of the unsung heroes of stand-up comedy. She's one of the best comedians ever. She was just provocative and interesting and dirty, a good writer, and really pretty. She had a different aesthetic than Garofalo. She'd go up there in a miniskirt and boots, but she was also far more provocative than Janeane—and dirtier. She would talk about fucking, and masturbating, and coming, all that stuff. She would really get graphic, but funny! And self-eviscerating, and lonely and dark. She's just her own thing. She'd have jokes like "I saw myself on TV, and it's so interesting, because really when I watch myself it only takes me a few minutes to come." Wow, that isn't what I thought you were going to say at all. She always had this way of delivering something and you're like, "Oh, wow, you're going to go there." She was great.

GREG MILLER Laura is the dark princess. She talked a lot about her crazy family. Her father sort of had two families and she and her mother were the wrong-side-of-the-tracks family growing up, so that was fascinating. Also, she had insane dating and relationship material. You've got to love Laura, because she is so dry and dark at the same time, and beautiful. And when we booked Un-Cabaret we would think about balancing any given show with lighter and darker people. Dryer and wetter, more explosive and more magnetic. That was our booking criterion. So each person, we would think about "What are they?" And Laura is definitely dry, dark, and, I don't know, intense!

MARK FLANAGAN, owner, Largo nightclub Laura Kightlinger was dating Jack Black, and for quite a long time. Jack had become very famous and his duo, Tenacious D, started pretty much at Largo [another alternative club that opened after Un-Cabaret]. Everybody knew them through the Largo scene. We did stick to stand-up, but every so often Flight of the Conchords, Tenacious D, or some really funny comedic music would start the show with a song and then we would start the show. So the comedians definitely knew Jack Black. So one night, Laura got up and said, "You guys I'm so excited to be here. It's like home for me. I think you all know my boyfriend, and I'm really excited, because I haven't told anybody, and I hope it stays in this room, but we're pregnant." The place went nuts, clapping and everything. She goes, "Whoa, whoa. Don't get too excited. I'm not sure I'm gonna keep it." And the energy of the room was just like *holy fuck*.

8

. . . .

Saturday Night Live: The Girls' Club

In the thirty years after Lily Tomlin and Gilda Radner bounded onto the small screen as some of the most iconic characters of all time, female sketch comedians had been mostly overshadowed by their stand-up counterparts. This was largely because stand-up was de rigueur in the eighties and early nineties, and comedy audiences came to regard it as their preferred form of comedy. But another reason female sketch artists were overlooked: Saturday Night Live—*the biggest, most successful of all sketch comedy shows—had become the worst kind of boys' club. To be sure,* Saturday Night Live *has always had a woman problem. But the degree to which women have had to fight for airtime has varied from cast to cast, a fact that is usually evident in the quality of the show at various points in history. The years between 1986 and 1990, when Jan Hooks and Nora Dunn were prime players on the variety series, were a bright spot; the years between 1980 and 1985 (when Lorne Michaels was not helming the show) and between 1990 and 1995 (when stars like Adam Sandler, Chris Farley, and David Spade ruled the roost) were generally regarded as the worst periods for female players on the show. And perhaps not coincidentally, the years when the women were least visible were also the years when the show suffered from its poorest ratings and reviews. By March 1995,* Saturday Night Live, *the variety series that had once surprised and delighted television audiences with its uneven originality, was on the brink of cancellation. But all that would eventually change.*

238 • WE KILLED

MARY GROSS, cast member, 1981-1985* At Second City [where I had trained], I did not feel I was underused or mistreated because I was a woman. But once I got to *Saturday Night Live* I felt like I was really in a battle for my dignity. In fact, there was a moment in 1982 when we were doing a show, and I was dying inside because of the characters I was playing on that particular show. I can remember at least two of them: one was a zombie whore and one was a game show lady who just points at things. None of them had any dignity or depth, and in the course of the show I just couldn't stand it anymore. It was like my head was going to explode. We were doing the live show and at one point I walked into this room where the writers were and I said, "I just want you to know it's 1982 and women are judges and they're lawyers and they're cops." And then I just walked out of the room. I'm sure they were all like, "Oh, man, she must be on the rag."

NORA DUNN At any given time there were never more than maybe two women on our writing staff, sometimes three [out of at least fifteen writers]. And when I was there for those years, every meeting was "What's your sketch about?" "It's about a guy who . . . It's about a

---

* In 1980, Lorne Michaels left his perch as executive producer of *Saturday Night Live* to turn his focus to making movies. NBC executives wanted to keep the show and, without consulting Michaels, named Jean Doumanian, an associate producer, to take his place. The ten months under Doumanian are widely considered to be among the worst in *SNL* history; her only accomplishment was the hiring of Eddie Murphy.

In the *SNL* oral history, *Live from New York* by Tom Shales and James Andrew Miller, Doumanian defended herself: "I had to get an all-new cast and all-new writers in two and a half months. When I took over the show, the first thing they did was cut my budget . . . I don't know this for a fact, but it would seem to me that if a woman could actually mount a show and get it done in such a short time, it minimized the importance of those who preceded her. And nobody liked that. So I was attacked viciously. How dare I take this job? How dare I think I can do the show? Most of that was said by men. You have to remember, the show had been biased against women for a long time."

In 1981, NBC named Dick Ebersol—the former vice president of late-night programming at NBC who hired Michaels and who had originally helped him conceive *Saturday Night Live*—to take over the series. Ebersol's background in comedy was thin—his interest was always in sports—and during his tenure the show remained uninspired. Yet he stayed with the series through 1985. Ebersol became president of NBC Sports in 1989.

guy who . . ." And there was so much controversy among us about why the writers could not write for women, why they would freak out when there was gonna be a female host—"I've got this great sketch but I have to hold on to it in case we ever have a female host"—because they just couldn't come up with the material for women. So I was baffled by that. But a lot of these guys came from one place: it's called Harvard.

CHRISTINE ZANDER, writer, 1986–1993 You can't deny the fact you're there to help the women get stuff out there, because you understand where they're coming from. And a lot of what you write comes from what you are experiencing in the daytime, during the week, like in delis or on the street, in the news or on television. And women are drawn to women things. I didn't have a problem feeling like I was supposed to write for the women. It wasn't like "She can't write for men." I wrote plenty of stuff with the guys. Mike Myers and I had a nice relationship, and when he first started, we collaborated on a few things. We did something called Handsome Man. And I produced a lot of sketches that were universal, meaning they appealed to both sexes. I think the only obstacle was that as a woman, sometimes, you really felt like what you had written would appeal to women *and* to a broader audience but that the men didn't think that. But I made great male friends who would help me with writing and who were also really supportive. And if you came up with something that was female-centric but accessible to men, they were thrilled. Nora Dunn had this thing called Attitudes. It was this parody of a female talk show and they loved that.

NORA DUNN Ultimately I feel like Jan Hooks and I were very bonded. We were very similar. She's really an actress but she's also a comedian. The person we didn't work well with was Victoria Jackson. It was an uncomfortable association for all those five years. Look, if you're gonna work with somebody, you have to click. My friendships are always based on humor. That's how you get along with somebody. What is your sense of humor? But Victoria didn't get my sense of humor. I didn't get her sense of humor. Jan and I did work a lot together and I think Victoria felt left out. But Jan and I understood each other. Victoria is a right-wing, evangelical person. So clearly I'm not gonna have a lot in common with her. I think we got blamed for the fact that she didn't feel she was doing enough in the show. And the guys said, "Well, you deserve that. You don't work with her." My point is, you're the writers, you write stuff for her. Why do we have to be lumped together? I feel like if we had a stronger person in Victoria, we would have done more work. And that's what they didn't understand. It's not just "Oh, we're working together because we're females." That's not what makes it. She's a girl, that doesn't mean I get her.*

VICTORIA JACKSON   I thought the *women* were very difficult. I just think women and men compete differently. I would watch the men, and they were competing against each other, but in a friendly way, and I just noticed that women made it really hard. There was a time when one actress got someone to take my joke away, because it was a great joke and I got a huge laugh. She was friends with the writer. Now, that's pretty scary, when you go to work every day and do your best and you have to deal with that. I guess that's in every business.

It was a very difficult atmosphere. It was competitive and high-adrenaline. We had to write our own material. Nobody was going to write it for us. I mean, Jan Hooks had two writers flown in and hired to write just for her. They were Terry and Bonnie Turner, who then wrote *3rd Rock from the Sun* and *That '70s Show*. She'd worked with them before. I didn't have anybody writing for me. Lorne said, "Victoria, just find some writers who you click with, and that's your key to getting on the air." I tried: I couldn't find anyone to click with me. I knew how to write things that were like monologues, so I would get on the Update desk often because I would write those myself. Jon Lovitz, Dana Carvey, and Kevin Nealon were really nice to me, and they would try to write me into their sketches. They wrote me into a Pump You Up—you know, Hans and Franz—as Roseanne Barr getting liposuction, and I got to do my first impression.

---

* When Nora Dunn caught wind that Andrew Dice Clay, a brutish, misogynistic stand-up comedian, was scheduled to host the season finale on May 12, 1990, she exploded. Dunn was offended by Clay's woman-hating bravado and even more offended that Lorne Michaels had offered him the gig. She refused to perform with Clay and gave Michaels an ultimatum—it was either her or Clay. Michaels chose Clay. In response, Dunn boycotted the show, the second-to-last episode of the season, which was also Dunn's last.

CHRISTINE ZANDER   [After I left *Saturday Night Live* in 1993,] those years were I guess bumpy for those guys. I know Julia Sweeney stayed on after I left. She was finding it difficult, and then they kept adding people. [In 1993 there were sixteen cast members. The women were] Melanie Hutsell and Beth Cahill and Ellen Cleghorne. They were all lovely people who tried really hard to get things on, but it takes a lot to break out. Melanie did "Oh my God" [with a Valley Girl accent] in the Delta Delta Delta sketch and that was about it. I don't want to criticize them, but sometimes it just doesn't work out. You got to be more flexible. You're not going to exist there if you can only do one thing or only have one look. And I feel like that might have been all of the women's problems.

MELANIE HUTSELL, cast member, 1991–1994   Those guys—Chris Farley, Adam Sandler, David Spade, Rob Schneider, Chris Rock—they had a real bond with each other. And I think those kinds of bonds just happen. You can't control it. People either have chemistry with each other or they don't, and those guys were definitely a group. And I think that when you are on a show like *SNL*, that's what people can feel and see and respond to. As far as how they interacted with the older guys [like Dana Carvey and Kevin Nealon, who had been held over from the previous cast], I think they had great respect for them, but it really did feel like two different camps. And then there were the girls.

I never felt like the guys didn't like what I did. But looking back on it I feel they really sort of saw me as the little sister that they loved but didn't want around. Like whenever I would come into the room and they would be doing that extremely dirty fraternity thing, or if I would try to get in on it and say something, they would all just get quiet and look at me like "Oh." I just remember feeling like they just wanted me to stay away so that they could do their guy thing. Tim Meadows used to say, "Oh, it's okay. They don't really feel that way." And I was like, "Oh, yes they do."

I do look back on [my experience on *SNL*] and say, "Maybe it would have been better if I'd had a little more life experience under my belt in order to take the blows that come your way." Sometimes when my sketch didn't get on, I would cry—I would never do that now. But I really thought that would help me—"I'll show them my emotion." No, not a good idea.

CHRIS SMITH in *New York* magazine, March 13, 1995 "Standing in the darkness just beyond the set lights is a glum Janeane Garofalo. As *SNL* tried to rebuild from its disastrous 1993–'94 season, hiring the smart, sarcastic 30-year-old comic actress seemed perfect. Besides being funny—she is widely beloved from HBO's *Larry Sanders Show* and became something of a generational mini-icon in the movie *Reality Bites*—Garofalo added two qualities in short supply at *SNL*: She's hip and she's female.

"Right now, though, Garofalo looks like a forlorn child trapped at her parents' dinner party . . . Garofalo watched *SNL* as a kid (she was in fourth grade when it premiered), and after she signed on last summer, she called it a dream come true. Now her mood is as black as her fingernail polish.

"For the first three months of the season, Garofalo's largely been stuck in dull, secondary wife and girlfriend roles. In 'Uncle Joe,' she's a waitress, with a single line near the end of the sketch, and the scene keeps breaking down before reaching her cue . . .

"None of the outside critics, however, has pinpointed why the show that two decades ago revolutionized TV comedy continues to fall on its face. Four weeks spent recently at *SNL* offered up a rare portrait of institutional decay—the gargantuan exertion of sweat, blood, fried food, and bluff self-denial that yields, for example, a mind-bendingly awful sketch about space aliens and rectal probes . . .

"The choices are often hard to fathom. Michaels frequently rejects pieces that he thinks are over the heads of *SNL*'s teen and frat-boy demographic. His preference is for the broadest likability, not the sharpest bite."

JANEANE GAROFALO People always just paint it with a very broad boys' club brush. And yeah, it was a boys' club. But that was the least of the issues. It just wasn't funny. It is not even worth discussing, it was such a nonevent when I was on it. It was not even gender-related. It just wasn't funny that year. It was bad enough if you were a white guy, even worse if you were a black guy or a girl.

LAURA KIGHTLINGER I had been a writer on the *Roseanne* show, which was a huge break. I was on a staff with writers, most of whom were stand-ups, and I had a blast. We'd get in at ten a.m., eat breakfast together, and make each other laugh trying to outdo one another with bits every morning, and then go into separate writing rooms to work. It was one of the best shows on television and I had such a great time there. One of my biggest regrets was leaving a show I enjoyed working on and most everyone respected, to go and work on a show that was being eviscerated by every publication imaginable, and no one enjoyed being there. I will not go into what an anxiety-producing, misogynistic soul-suck place that was.

In October 1995, at the beginning of SNL's *twenty-first season, the show was in dire need of reinvention. Lorne Michaels replaced nearly his entire creative team with fresh blood, and by the fourth episode of the new season, in a scene starring Molly Shannon as overeager Catholic schoolgirl Mary Katherine Gallagher, it was clear that the situation for women was headed in a new direction. In many ways, that sketch—which introduced the first breakout character of a new cast—was a brilliant, riotous prelude for* SNL's *next chapter. In short order, women became a dominant force on the show.*

PAULA PELL   Tina Fey is a very old friend of mine and I adore her. But I think there's a little bit of a fogginess about what came before her. And it's always bothered me, because I was here before Tina came, and [starting in 1995] there was an amazing female presence at the show. The *Rolling Stone* cover that we did during that time featured Molly Shannon and Cheri Oteri as Mary Katherine and the Cheerleaders [respectively]. They were stars, and I think those women set the tone. They were so determined. The three of them—Molly, Cheri, and later Ana Gasteyer [who came in 1996]—were headlining three-quarters of the show.

MAYA RUDOLPH   I remember, very clearly, watching Molly on TV doing Mary Katherine Gallagher. It was the Gabriel Byrne show. She was in the school gym and she ends up falling back on all the chairs. At the time, I was playing with a band, and we were all on tour and we were watching the show and I remember going, "Holy shit! What is *that*?"

MARCI KLEIN, coproducer   I saw Molly in Santa Monica. Her manager, Steven Levy, knew that I was looking for people—I am always looking for people—and he said, "There is this woman that I have that I think you are going to love, and you have to come see her do her show here." And he picked me up at my hotel and drove me there. And when I saw Molly, I mean, I had never seen anything like her before; I completely flipped out. I was like, "Oh my God." I immediately saw three or four or five characters that I knew could go on the show like that. And she had a following. People were obsessed with her. There were so many people at the theater that night. What you saw was just raw talent.

PAULA PELL There was something about Molly being this weird loser-y girl smelling her pits and mumbling to herself that just made people come to her. I think Molly is a really great actor and she was really coming at it from the inside out, as opposed to just applying a silly wig and saying, "I'm doing this character." But also I think she had a fearlessness. She wasn't a druggie or someone who was like, "I just wanna cut myself!" but she had the kind of guts that said, "To get the laugh, I will do anything." And she didn't talk about it a lot. She'd just set her scene up and say, "I want the chairs like that." And then, on the live show, she would just run into them. I mean, those folding chairs hurt when you fall into them. And she frickin' bruised the shit out of herself but she would get an applause and people would go apeshit.

MAYA RUDOLPH When Molly came back to host the show, I got to work with her. I was still new on the show, and when I watched her blocking stuff, I was sitting in the costume room. I think we were talking about the time—we were worried that the dress rehearsal was running over, and we didn't know what was going to get cut. And they said, very matter-of-factly, "Don't forget with Molly's pieces; when she goes, she goes." And Molly kind of just established this thing that she does, that it is just a very raw, instinctual behavior. And you could see it in her eyes: she looks like she's just like a fucking lion ready to pounce.

CINDY CAPONERA, writer, 1995–1998 When Molly and Cheri and Ana joined the cast, that was when the women became way stronger than the men, initially. I mean, nobody does sketches like Jan Hooks, but Jan Hooks was not the star of the show. But here we had three very,

very, very strong women that everybody wrote for. They were aggressive. They were ambitious—and rightfully so. I also think they succeeded because they all came in at the same time. It wasn't like somebody was hired as a feature player on a kick-ass cast. That wasn't the experience. Everyone was in a position to make changes. It was a level playing field.

PAULA PELL   Cheri was very determined, too, very determined to write and take care of herself and make sure that she was getting stuff on. I always called Cheri "the terrier" because she has such an adorable little frame, and when she would play that druggie lady [a character who was hopped up on prescription medicine that first appeared on an episode hosted by John Goodman], she used to make me laugh so hard. She also had guts—I don't know how to describe it except that it's like that old school of comedy where you're just balls-to-the-wall. If it's not going well, you're gonna make sure you amp it up so when you leave the scene, you're gonna get a huge laugh. She always used to do that. She'd leave a sketch with her little part and do some little butt jig or something and just get a huge laugh.

CHERI OTERI, cast member, 1995–2000   We all really bonded when we got there, even the writers. It was like we were all going into first grade at the same time. There were a couple of people who had been there that were still there, but all the cliques had been broken up. Eventually hierarchy forms, and [office] politics, but when I went *in* there, everybody was so happy to be there and so excited and so nervous.

ANA GASTEYER, cast member, 1996–2002   We had so much airtime. Those first three years were crazy. It was me, Cheri, and Molly. And every single week each of us had a heavily featured personal character, which by comparison to the men was a lot, if you figure that there's like eight scenes a night. Every week each of us had a major scene—it was like a given that each of us would have one. So the takeaway for so many people was, like, the women, the women, the women.

Don't get me wrong, everybody played plenty of whores and wives. My first time on the show, I was in a G-string. It was this Caribbean Essence commercial parody with Tracy Morgan being a Rastafarian. I don't even know what the hell it was. Anyway, we were all supposed to be in a big hot tub covered with bubbles. And we were in G-strings and practically nude and covered in bubbles, the three of us in the tub as these, like, body girls. I remember Molly being really mad about it. It was the first thing I'd ever done, so I was kind of like, "This is icky and embarrassing," but it's also part of your job to represent America. You're a sketch comedian!

CHERI OTERI I remember when we were auditioning for *Saturday Night Live*, they told me, "Oh, and they want you to do at least one impression." And I was like, "I don't do impressions." I was so nervous about that. So I remember, Lisa Marie Presley and Michael Jackson had just been on Diane Sawyer's special, and everybody had watched it. Everybody. It was so topical. So I did Lisa Marie Presley, sitting there as if Michael was there. I don't think it was necessarily good. But it was topical and I made her tougher than she was, and I kind of blew how she acted out of proportion a bit.

Then, when I got to *SNL*, it came down from the authority up above, "Lorne wants you to do Barbara Walters." And I'll never forget, I said to the head writer at the time, Tim Herlihy, "Oh, um, I don't do impressions." And he let it go. And then he came back and said, "Lorne wants you to do Barbara Walters." And I was like, "I wouldn't want to tackle that, let somebody else tackle that, because I don't do impressions." And all I thought about was, I don't want to be compared to Gilda Radner. And then the next day he comes and goes, "Cheri, when Lorne asks you to do it, *do it*."

I had watched Barbara Walters all my life, but then I started watching her from a different perspective. And I just watched her over and over and over, because I felt so much that I needed to have a different take on her. I always enjoyed people's *take* on a character, not necessarily their dead-on impressions. So when I would do Barbara Walters I would think [does a Barbara Walters voice], "This. Kissed. Wissed."

The first time I did her it was me and Darrel Hammond as Hugh Downs from *20/20* and it was written for me. Then I started writing her. And then they did a [parody of] *The View*. So, yeah, I resisted doing Barbara Walters, but it turned out to be the best thing they could've made me do.

LORI NASSO, writer, 1995–1999 I knew as soon as I saw *The View* [on television] that it would hit [as a sketch]. Tina and I had seen it during the summer and when we came back from hiatus we said, "Oh my God, we've got to do something on *The View*," because it was so crazy and everyone was talking over each other. And half the people we worked with didn't know what it was. But Tina and I were like, "Oh my God, it's gonna be, like, it's hilarious and crazy." And then I also wrote Judge Judy. I'd seen her and I thought, "Oh God, this is great, we could easily get Cheri to do this."

I actually liked writing parodies, because it was kind of half written for you, and then you could make fun of it.

MAYA RUDOLPH I certainly had never done Oprah, but you learn very quickly that if someone comes up to you and says, "Can you do Oprah?" you say, "Yes, yes I can."

ANA GASTEYER Lori Nasso handed Celine Dion to me. She came to me and said, "You should do her; you kind of look like her." Things like that would happen and they were gifts from God, believe me.

LORI NASSO During the whole *Titanic* phenomenon, Celine Dion was driving me crazy with every interview she was doing. I thought, "Ugh! I have to do something." And the sad thing is, I felt so bad. Oh God, I felt so bad sometimes. I'm not really a mean person and I would write these sketches and then I'd think, "Oh my God, that person's real!" And then Celine Dion had Ana and me come to Madison Square Garden as her, in front of thousands of people, rising out of the stage. And I just felt bad. I said to her backstage, "I just want you to know that this is all in fun." She was like, "Oh, yeah, yeah, yeah." She didn't even get [that we were making fun of her]. And I thought, "Oh God, this is horrible."

PAULA PELL I think, as a woman, you have to *really* make sure that you're taking care of yourself and make sure that you're covered and you have enough material written for you. It's true for all people new to the show. But it's especially true for the women, because the guys don't tend to write the women's character sketches. So you really have to make sure that you're bringing stuff to the show and getting people on board with it, or creating it with people here.

RACHEL DRATCH   Before I got on the show, I was always like, "Why do they do all these recurring characters?" But Lorne likes to do them, so if you get one that recurs, you're like, "Oh my God, I finally have one of these." And whatever character gets on the air, that immediately becomes your favorite. Forget "Oh, my precious babies." What matters is "I'm on the show!"

Over the next decade, a stream of new blood joined the cast, very funny women with bold ideas who amped up the visibility and dominance of women on the show. Among them: Amy Poehler, Maya Rudolph, Rachel Dratch, Kristen Wiig, all of whom quickly proved themselves to be comedy powerhouses who could deliver a sketch and drive home a joke. Meanwhile, Tina Fey, who had been a writer on the show since 1997—and who became the show's first female head writer in 1999—was finally given a chance to move in front of the camera. By 2000 and beyond, it was clearer than ever that the women were equal to if not better than the male players. That's not to say that what they did was the same. Tension continued to exist between the guys and the girls, only during this era, it had less to do with outdated notions that women weren't funny, and more to do with stylistic differences. To put it most simply, there are two kinds of sketches: character-based scenes, in which the performers design the skits around the eccentric antics of a funny person; and concept-based pieces, in which a writer creates a funny scenario and plops characters into the skit to help drive the premise. The character-based style is generally considered to be a more feminine approach to comedy, while the concept approach is considered more masculine.

PAULA PELL   To give you a sense of the difference between character- and concept-based pieces, let me give a real simple example: it's a funny situation versus a funny person. So when you have Kristen Wiig's Target lady character, she has a little comedy game in that she likes the things she's checking out and she'll walk off and say, "Well, where'd you get this?" But the crux of the humor is this funny person—you're laughing at how she's interacting with her customers as opposed to a funny situation. [In terms of a concept piece] I remember a sketch where the writer wanted to re-create a disaster movie on an escalator. So the idea was that there were all these people stuck on an escalator, and they could easily walk down the escalator, but they don't. So the jokes are all about the people being dumb as a group, and they're kind of collectively serving an idea.

ANA GASTEYER The women, at least in my generation, tended to come at it almost entirely from a character standpoint. Certainly Molly Shannon, Cheri Oteri, me, Rachel Dratch, Maya Rudolph, and Amy Poehler—well, Amy's maybe a little more intellectual that way—but pretty much all of us would start with a conception of the character and then find the situation or the conceit that would drive the comedy thereafter. [The alternative is for a sketch to be] premise-driven—a joke that starts the whole idea.

EMILY SPIVEY, writer, 2001–2011 I wish there was a way that character pieces weren't perceived as feminine and concept pieces weren't perceived as more masculine, but that's just the way it is. Perhaps I'm speaking out of turn, but I feel like a lot of the character stuff is generated by women. Paula is responsible for a lot of great characters, and I hate to say it, but it is sort of the realm of women and gay guys—they write all the character stuff. Maybe that's because women are more emotional. I sound like an asshole, but women are just more emotional and they're gonna notice the softer, more emotional side of things, and that's really what a good character is. There's always a sadness and a more rambling emotional quality than a real concept-y piece. But then again there are writers like Andrew Steele who wrote a lot of the character stuff for Will Ferrell. But Will is very feminine in his comedy. He really likes to do character stuff and he really likes to do silly stuff.

PAULA PELL I think sometimes if someone writes very dyed-in-the-wool conceptual stuff, they look at character stuff as being more loosey-goosey; they think it doesn't have a game to it. And actually it does.

LORI NASSO I don't think I wrote specifically well for that show when I first got there. I was merely trying to survive, and I found it very difficult. [After the second season] they were going to fire me. They said, "If you want to come back, you gotta call Lorne." That's what people do. So I talked to him in the summer and he was very clear about what he wanted—that this is joke-driven. I was always trying to create *moments* or the *truth* of being a woman. And he was very, very nice and very supportive and it just clicked. And I came back and ended up getting stuff on the air every week.

EMILY SPIVEY The one thing that is dicey is period stuff, and nursing, and things like that. That's where guys are like, "Ugh, that's never, ever gonna fly." I had a sketch that almost got on with Rainn Wilson about a guy that wanted to watch a lady breast-feed. It got a big laugh at the table, but I think the guys were still like, "Okay, that's a little too much into the biological areas—like, we don't wanna think of you having your period and we don't wanna think of you as a food source."

PAULA PELL I think the fear was if a scene was about some female issue, it wasn't going to have hard jokes. We don't do subtle little observational things. It's gotta have hard jokes in it and it has to have some observation with an edge. For example, I wrote a thing back in the day called Kotex Classic. It was a commercial parody for Kotex and it was commenting on "classic" things coming back, like Coke Classic. And that's where I got the idea: What if it's something classic that isn't good, like this horrible pad and belt that, thank God, we don't have anymore. So there was a concept behind it, which they like to have, and the idea was a new kind of Kotex, where they're going back to the old kind of Kotex that had the belts. And when you first pitch things like that, about a pad or whatever, there's always the worry, "Well, how's it gonna work?" And I think Lorne, because he's a sixtysomething-year-old man, is squeamish about any female thing like that, as many men are. But I think as celebrities became more like Courtney Love, and with Molly, especially, having such abandon and coming out and showing her underpants [as Mary Katherine Gallagher], we could write harsher, crazier, harder things for the women. [The Kotex Classic sketch aired on March 16, 2002.]

CINDY CAPONERA We would have arguments at the writers' table where guys would say to us, "Yeah, you'll get a laugh, but do you want that kind of laugh?" It was like, "Why the fuck are you judging what kind of laugh I'm getting? Why do you give a shit?" But the three of us [me, Paula Pell, and Lori Nasso] created more from a character background and the guys created more from a lampoony background. It was a stylistic difference, but everyone should be able to appreciate everybody's style, and you shouldn't be trying to put robots in a scene about a failed marriage.

KRISTEN WIIG, cast member, 2005–2012   A character's not me but it comes from me—it's an observation of a person in the world. It's a person that you want to sort of invent and show people.

I do a character named Aunt Linda on Update. She's like a movie critic. But that came from a woman who was on a plane with me once. I think she was watching *The Matrix* on the in-flight movie. She was so confused as to what was going on and was so loud about it and just kept looking around at everyone like "What? Where . . . where are they?" I was laughing so hard and I just kept writing down things that she was saying.

EMILY SPIVEY   Kristen's a genius. She's an amazing writer with a very unique point of view and she can pull off the weirdest, strangest characters. I would describe her characters as women who are confident but cracking a little bit; who are trying to present a brave face but have something underneath that's just boiling and raging.

MAYA RUDOLPH   The first thing I did on the show was an MTV sketch that Ana and Paula Pell wrote. I played a DJ named Ananda Lewis [who is black], which was perfect because it was sort of the beginning of my thing there. The characters I created were never really racially based, but lo and behold, the writers needed somebody to play a character that was current. So it was a lucky tiny thing, and I had one joke in it.

[As far as playing racially and ethnically diverse characters] there was never a conscious idea on my part that I was taking an opportunity to fill a hole but I think for the writers there was. Oprah was something that was written for me initially, and Whitney was something that was written for me too [both by Emily Spivey, who was in the Groundlings with me]. She brought me Donatella—and Donatella ended up like becoming the walking dead: she could get electrocuted and say, "That was fantastic." And thank God, I was definitely Emily's muse for a lot of her fucking crazy bitches characters. Over the years, we ended up writing a lot of stuff together, and these pieces really became characters—they were never really portrayals of real human beings.

Anyway, I think what happens is twofold: you have to write stuff for people to get to know your voice, and if you are lucky enough, you get handed sketches by the writers. And obviously if there was a celebrity of a darker skin tone that needed to be in something, and if she was female, there was no question that she was going to be me. I think they got tired of it being Tracy Morgan, because that just became very bizarre. I love Tracy Morgan, but not every woman that is black can be portrayed by Tracy. He didn't want that either.

EMILY SPIVEY Maya was born to be on *SNL* because she was so versatile and her background is so unique. She's part Jewish and part black. Her mom was a singer. And because she's mixed, Maya can play a white girl, she can play a black girl; she can play Whitney Houston, and she can play a Valley Girl. If you can find someone that can plug into all those parts, that's just a gift from heaven. So I think, because she was available, she played a lot of women of color. And if you can find a funny woman of color, you snatch her up, because it's always needed. That sounds bad, but just her versatility was an amazing thing to have on that show.

MAYA RUDOLPH Rachel Dratch is like this little cartoon, a tiny little animal with enormously large blue circular eyes that blink at you quizzically, asking, "Are you my mother?" She and Amy are both tiny, but their demeanors are incredibly different. They're about the same height—they are itty-bitty—but Rachel has a very gentle, soft, lovely little heart. And Rachel is a crazy solid sketch performer. The Rachel that I know is a soft, gentle little soul, but there is this comedy Dratch that is a different thing. She's just got a crazy skill set. She's a highly intelligent person. I really, really loved doing Wake Up Wakefield! [a sketch about two middle school students who broadcast a morning announcement program to their classmates] with her. We would purposely write scenes in which she could do a lot more looking and blinking. And she played this really shy little boy who you wanted to hold and rock—he was like the boy that is your best friend when you're thirteen, and he's probably not gay, but he could be. There is a little bit of heartbreak in her comedy.

RACHEL DRATCH   I don't set out to be like, "I'm gonna play a dude." Tina and another writer wrote the Wake Up Wakefield! sketches and Tina had the idea to make me her *boy*friend instead of a *girl*friend. Sometimes I'll start talking in some voice and say, "I wanna put that on the show." And then, for the Abe Sheinvold character, that was just some voice I was doing around the offices: "Does it have legs?" That's how that started. And then Seth Meyer and I wrote those.

Debbie Downer probably got me the most attention from people on the street with like, [in a New York accent] "Hey, Debby Downer!" That's probably the character I'm most known for. And that one kind of just popped into my head one day, which is how it tends to happen for me. I can't just be like, "I'm gonna think of a great character," and then sit there and then, boom, think of one. I was writing that with Paula and we were trying to figure out how to write it. And first we put it in like an office, and then Paula had the idea to put it at Disney World, somewhere really happy.

ANA GASTEYER   This is a generalization, but I think Tina was almost more of a guy in her approach to comedy and Will Ferrell was more of a girl.

CINDY CAPONERA   Cheri and Molly were old-school. When Tina came, [the show] became what I feel is less character-driven. Any given show had like two or three strong character pieces, and then you had the piece that kind of ate itself. You could see what the concept was [and it was coming from] the nerdy Harvard guys. They were really conceptual. They were all about comedy being smart as opposed to character-driven and so that was a big clash of the titans. So Cheri and Molly were more old-school. And Tina's super-, super-funny, but not big on character.

I was there for one year when she was there. And I know that she came in with permission. In other words, Adam McKay and her were good friends from Second City and Adam was a writing supervisor at the time. So she came in. When you have three writer-performer girls like me, Lori, and Paula, and then you have really young Harvard boys, we were at—not necessarily at odds, but they didn't necessarily give it up. We were women and it was very—it was separate, stylistically. And then, because Tina came through Adam, the boys who worshipped Adam kind of gave it up to her right away. So it was like, "Wow, that was really smart." The boys wanted Adam's approval because they loved him so much and he was so talented, and they were going to give it to her. So she wound up having a different relationship right away with the boys. I'm not knocking her talent. She's very talented, very funny. But she had permission in a different way to create more freely.

LORI NASSO   She was finding her way, too, for the first few months, like everyone else was. And then I think by October [1997], she wrote a giant baby sketch. And it was just really funny and weird, and from then on she just kind of took off. Then the next year she was the toast of the town. The men loved her because she was super-funny and quick. Super-smart.

Tina Fey may not have been as talented an actress as the other cast members, but she was by far the wittiest—a quality not lost on Lorne Michaels, who plucked his head writer from behind the camera (after she famously lost thirty pounds), and gave her the co-anchor slot next to Jimmy Fallon. It was 2000 and Fey was the first woman to co-anchor Weekend Update since Jane Curtin. Having a male-female anchor team was a move that Michaels had wanted to make back in the mid-nineties when Norm MacDonald was still hosting the segment. At the time, Mac-Donald objected—not surprising, considering that MacDonald's jokes about women focused almost exclusively on their sex appeal and looks. ("Yeah, Ricki Lake, you know she is, really, an animal lover. She has three cats, two dogs, and a big ass that follows her around everywhere.") But with the new era of strong women upon them, Michaels was finally ready to make his move.

PAULA PELL   Starting probably with Janeane Garofalo, and that era of stand-up ladies who were starting to be more brainy and strong and clever, guys started noticing those girls as sexy smart. I always called it smarxy. It's like that sexy smart girl who's cute but also knows how to sit and talk to me about some nerd thing or *Star Wars*. And I think Tina was one of those people: the brainiac, the nerd. She tapped into that and Liz Lemon [the character on *30 Rock*] taps into that.

KELLY LEONARD, executive vice president, Second City   Really, when you look at Tina's work, both in terms of *SNL*, Sarah Palin, *30 Rock*, and *Mean Girls* in particular, she had such insights into the female psyche that, I know from many women that I'm friends with, makes them uncomfortable. Because it's so true, it's painful and truly unique to this time, to her voice, to getting this stuff out.

After Tina had left for *Saturday Night Live* and Rachel had left the main stage here, they came back for the summer and I produced a show in the e.t.c. [a theater at the Second City] with them called *Dratch & Fey*. It was a two-woman show. It was what got Rachel hired on *Saturday Night Live*. And it was the most layered, interesting show about women. They played men, they played women. There was this one scene where Tina was a *Playboy* model getting plastic surgery and she had tape all over her face and it was just beautifully funny.

ANA GASTEYER The main thing that Tina does that's so brilliant is assessing pop culture in an uncompromising way. She will say what most people are too afraid to say on any subject in pop culture. So I think that was very much her influence on the show's writing in terms of what she was able to kind of address and take down. I don't think she had much of a feminist agenda.

PAULA PELL I think that Tina's pretty fearless on camera. She was fearless in a different way than Molly was, but she was fearless in terms of just saying it. I don't think Tina's a person that hesitated. I think that's why she did so great here too. Besides being a very talented writer, she was fearless about pushing an idea through and saying, "No, we need to say something about that." Lorne loved that about her. Also I think it helps in any comedy room for a woman to have very strong, respected convictions, because then it opens the door up a little bit for other women to have that.

ANA GASTEYER Tina definitely wrote things that she put women in that were really funny but she also wrote, honestly, as much for Chris Kattan and Tracy Morgan.

LORI NASSO She could write for anybody. And she wasn't afraid to say what she wanted to say. She could let it rip in a sketch. She always had a point of view. She wasn't careful—I was always like, "Oh, is that too mean?" But she just knew what she wanted and she was great. I also think she was fun and fast to work with. She didn't apologize. I was apologizing for being there. "Why am I here? There are so many people who are way funnier!"

I did all that stuff with Princess Diana. Remember that big interview she did about how life was horrible for her in the royal family? So we made all these jokes about her. And Anthony Edwards played her and he did a great job. He bowed his head and he had all this eyeliner on and he talked about how they would keep the head of Anne Boleyn in a jar and all this stuff. And people loved it and it got written up in the newspaper. And it put me on the map as a writer on that show. And I just feel awful about it, 'cause, I mean, she died! And am I part of what killed her? I had this horrible feeling. You know it's all in fun, but she took it pretty seriously. I've never gotten over that.

PAULA PELL   The fear that some males in the comedy world have is that females are too soft. They're always afraid that the women are gonna go, "Well, I don't know if we should do that." And then the guys will have to take the stand of "You know what? If we wanna get the laugh, we have to go all the way with it." It doesn't exist as much here, but I think, in general, there's still that worry that women's comedy is gonna be soft.

And when we were discussing who should be on Update, I remember saying, "Tina's got something to say." Lorne loves people to have opinions. He loves them to be resolute in "I like this, I don't like this, this is why I hate this, this is why I love this." And she was very much like that. Whether you agree with it or not, it was funny because it was a sharp opinion. And she provided very clear, hard comedy where the audience knew what was being said here. It wasn't muddled at all. I think she was so expert at that because she is such a good writer and she *came in* as a very good writer. And I think people were fascinated by the fact that she was writing *and* performing. She had that self-effacing thing, like Conan O'Brien, or other people who are always making fun of themselves but are still aware that they're pretty great and got a lot to offer. And she did. So the audience glommed onto that. And I think Update is when people started really falling in love with her. When you're on Update, it's always so great to have that sense of your own point of view, because then people wanna hear what your jokes are. It's not just a joke you're saying. You're saying it as yourself.

MAYA RUDOLPH To me, Tina's comedy is a combination of being incredibly bright and incredibly fierce. If we are all sitting in the room and we're watching something on TV and we're all bagging on somebody, she'll always nail it in a funny way. As a writer I always noticed, she could express exactly what she means and she can find the funny part.

In 2004, Jimmy Fallon left SNL and the Weekend Update desk and was replaced by Amy Poehler. It was the first time two women would anchor the fake newsdesk together.

PAULA PELL When they decided to have Amy do Update with Tina, there was a discussion on Tina's part about what kind of energy she wants next to her. And the question was, Who's the funniest person that could be out there with her? But Update is a delicate thing: you don't really know until you do it, and with Update you're always trying a new combination. Jimmy was a very specific kind of energy, so you didn't wanna replace that with the same thing. And I think because Amy and Tina had a friendship and a past that included years of improvising together and knowing each other's moves, they had a knowledge of each other. So the thought was that the chemistry between them was something you'd wanna tap into. They're alike in their power, and their wit, and they're hilarious, but they're both very different too. Amy was a little more goofy, and Tina played well off the goofy. And I think, when they would tap into something where they would both come at the camera and stick their fingers out—because when those girls get something going, they'd get the fingers out—the audience *loved* it. The audience loved when the two of them would start on a roll about something.

By 2008, the girls' club had been firmly established with Tina and Amy at the forefront. The boys' club of yesteryear had turned the keys over to the girls, and potential competition among the female cast members had given way to a kind of we-can-all-succeed-together camaraderie. But if there was a bona fide leader of the girls' club, someone who looked out for them, encouraged them, and inspired them, it was Amy Poehler, the assertive blonde who had cofounded the Upright Citizens Brigade Theatre in New York.

MATT BESSER, cofounder, the Upright Citizens Brigade Theatre Amy's a bit younger than the rest of the UCB [members], so she came to Chicago [our original home base] after us. We were all working out of this place, the ImprovOlympic, which was mentored and directed by this guy Del Close. We were already on what's called the house team, an all-male group called the Family. I think the shortest guy in the group is like six foot three. The only reason I point that out is because at that moment in time at the ImprovOlympic, and I would say in the improv world in general, there just were not that many women. There were very few that could hang with the guys. But within six months of being in town, Amy was turning heads. She was just starting out and everybody wanted to play with her. She was on a group right away, which is a little unusual. And her first group had Tina Fey, too, oddly enough, and they became great friends and soon dominated their group. And to have two women be the dominant force in a group was unheard-of—that just never happened. And as this was happening, my group also had a sketch group called the Upright Citizens Brigade, which had been around since 1990, '91. And we did one or two shows a year. And we asked Amy to do the show, which was new for us, too, because we had never had a woman in the sketch group.

JANEANE GAROFALO I remember meeting Amy Poehler first and foremost at a book group, not even knowing that she was with UCB. I met her at a book group that I went to one time with Sarah Thyre, Andy Richter's wife, who was involved in the comedy scene. I think it might have been a book by Kathryn Harrison, a memoir about a bizarre childhood, if memory serves. And in the circle of people discussing the book was little Amy Poehler. And I thought Amy Poehler, who I clicked with immediately, was a kid. Honestly, I thought she was a high school kid or a college kid, that's how young she looked. And I was like, "Who is this delightful, very-wise-beyond-her-years [girl]?"—not knowing she was an adult 'cause she was so tiny and cute. So I met her first even before I was exposed to UCB.

MAYA RUDOLPH If you go to eat with Amy, it's like, "All right, let's order. Does everybody know what they are going to get?" She's in charge, she's the leader, she's like, "We're not wasting any time, let's do this." And in the most loving way I can say, she's incredibly bossy. And

I fucking love that about her. And I love the combination of the fact that she is a teeny tiny person and she's really tough. I mean, she's from Boston. And she has this very sort of aware East Coast way of looking at things. I think the term *blue-collar* has been said by her many times in terms of like a way of looking at life—it's like, "There are no free rides, I am going to fucking make my time on this earth."

EMILY SPIVEY   Amy's a hero. I cannot think of anyone who's done more, in my opinion, in front of the camera and behind the scenes for ladies than Amy. If I could make a lady comedy flag, it would have Amy Poehler's face on it. She's just amazing.

Amy has a very boy energy to her. And that sounds weird but she's able to sit down with the dudes and just relate to them in a way that just makes them so comfortable with her. She's a little blond girl, but she's gonna fucking get this done. And everyone's in love with Amy. She has a way of just making everyone—boys and girls—feel so comfortable and confident in not only what *she's* doing but what *they're* doing. She and Will Ferrell are cut from the same cloth in that they're just so good and they just make everyone feel good about what they're doing. And that's important behind the scenes.

CASEY WILSON, featured player, 2008–2009   Amy Poehler's like a cheerleader—kind of like a mama bear. She wanted the other women to succeed and that's trickled down to Kristen, and then trickled down to me. I think people want there to be some sort of feud or tension, but it's like "Why can only one of us do well?" One time I remember we were doing a *Mad Men* sketch, and I was playing the redhead. And I had a funny bit where basically I came in and dropped off some papers, but I didn't have a line. It wasn't even Amy's sketch, but she piped up and said to the writers, "Let's give Casey a funny line when she comes in." She didn't have to do that.

MATT BESSER   A big criticism of the sketch world and the improv world is that it is a boys' club, and a lot of the boys would always go, "Hey, we're not kicking girls out! They're just not hanging with us on-stage. We don't not want to have a woman onstage, it's just when they are onstage they are always playing a wife or a little girl or a nun. They are always playing female archetypes rather than just playing." And I think that's what Amy and Tina both did. They would come out and play a truck driver. They wouldn't just come out and play females—they were going to be comedians. These days you don't think of Amy as a female comedian, you just think of her as a comedian, and I think that's a plus. And she didn't go for that whole notion that women are not treated fairly. She was just like, "I'm just going to do my best and not give a shit," and it worked. She didn't care about being pretty and dainty onstage, or charming, or all those things you might say about a successful sitcom actress, a prototypical one. She could be weird or nasty or ugly or whatever. Those are things that *guys* more typically do. But really it's what a comedian should do and that's what she is.

PAULA PELL I remember there being a *little bit* of time where Amy was not in a lot of stuff, but it was pretty short. You know her one-legged girl who's like, "Jealous?" The audience just eats her up. She had so many chops before she came here—she had written her own show, she'd had her own theater. She really came here so experienced, and that's strange, because it's a rare person that can come here experienced and make it, because Lorne likes to create people here.

EMILY SPIVEY Maya and Amy are good at everything—you could give them the phone book to read and they would get a laugh. Maya was really good at showbiz characters—real hard-core and obscure pop culture stuff—and she's a good singer, so we would always try to do something where she got to sing. And Amy was just really, really good at taking a subtle idea and turning it into something that just everyone can relate to. She's a real everywoman. She's real good at a good ol' blue-collar character.

I have to give props to Lorne, because Lorne really, really, really loves funny ladies and he really goes to bat for that. If you're a funny lady, he just loves you.

MAYA RUDOLPH I mean, the only thing Lorne ever said to me [that had anything to do with gender] was "If I had known that you were pregnant when you did that sketch where you fell through the piano, I would not have let you do it." But I hadn't told him I was pregnant yet.

Ana was the first person on *SNL* to ever be pregnant on the air, and then came Tina and then me. We were like these girls in high school, carrying their binders really close to their stomachs, not telling anybody about their teenage pregnancy. Amy was literally on the show until she went into labor. We were going to do a Bronx Beat on a Jon Hamm show, and she knew that her baby was due on Sunday, so she was going to do her show on Saturday and have her baby on Sunday. And we rehearsed Friday night, and Saturday I got a call that her water broke and she was in the hospital.

You know, people used to ask, "So, was it a boys' club [on *SNL*]?" And I was like, "What the fuck is going on? Why do people keep fucking saying this?" In every interview somebody would ask me that question. Amy was always the first to get mad about it; she got really mad. When she did, I figured, "Well, I guess I'm allowed to be mad too."

RACHEL DRATCH   *SNL* wasn't a boys' club when I got there [either]. It probably had been before, but I didn't feel I faced any, like, sexism, or whatever you want to call it. It was more that I faced a lot of competition. It was competitive because when I was there the number of people in the cast was so high. Then I left and the cast dropped by like five people, and I was like, "Oh my God, it looks like a dream to be there now"—and of course it's after I'm gone. It would be so much easier to get on when there are five fewer people. It's the same with the women thing. I was gonna sound all PC, but then I remembered what it was like to hear "Oh, there's another woman coming on . . ." I mean, the guys have to really fight it out, because there's like ten of them—ten white dudes.

The general vibe felt a little more ensemble-y when I left than when I got there. When I got there it felt a little bit more like every man for himself, but that could also have been a function of being the new person. There's definitely no welcome wagon; I definitely felt thrown in. When I started, I was the only new actor that year, so I didn't have anyone to pal around with. It was like, "What the hell's going on here?" It was trial by fire.

CINDY CAPONERA   My first year I did most of the monologues for the guest hosts and I had this crazy fight with Chevy Chase. We were bantering in the pitch meeting and then he got mad because I got a big laugh. And he said, in the middle of the pitch room, "Why don't you give me a hand job." Then I had a sketch picked to go, and he wouldn't be in it. So they gave it to Norm MacDonald, and it got cut between dress and air. [But the male writers and cast members] were on my side. Will Ferrell, Norm Hiscock, and a couple of other guys came into my office to check and see if I was okay. They were totally sweet and supportive.

PAULA PELL When I came, I remember, there was that thing where the go-to with a female host would be that she's hot. It's like, "How about there's this situation—but she's *HOT*?"All of the women would have the same reaction: "I don't get why that's funny." But to the guys it was very funny.

KRISTEN WIIG The boys' club thing, I don't really know. I was coming into a group of really strong, funny women. Maya was out having her baby when I started, but there was Maya, Rachel, Amy, and Tina, and I was just like, "All right, I'm just gonna sit back and watch them for a while and see what happens."

PAULA PELL I remember one time at a rewrite table, one of my female cowriters was arguing her point about a sketch. She was *really* taking a stand, which was a little rare and a little scary with all these guys. And the person arguing with her was a particularly snarky guy who tended to really try to stir it up when you'd argue with him. So he kept arguing with her about it, and then he really went into a zone and got a little jerky about it and she called him out for being jerky. Then I just watched her go into a complete fear mode of regret, like, "I just crossed him in front of everyone." It washed over her face. But it was what I think of as a characteristically female thing to do—stopping and pulling back and being like, "Oh shit, I shouldn't have done that, I shouldn't have done that, I shouldn't have done that." She turned around and sabotaged herself. I've definitely done that over the years. There are so many times, even to this day, when I'll really take a stand on something and my first impulse the next day is to apologize. I'll actually pick my phone up to say, "Hey, by the way, yesterday . . ." Now I always stop doing it. The truth is, he probably won't even remember what I'm talking about. But it comes from that little teeny bit of fear that I don't wanna be that person. But, well, they're that person many times. We're *all* that person. We're just having opinions.

The writer called me later in the night and I said, "Do you believe that your point was valid? Do you still believe in that opinion?" She goes, "Yeah." And I go, "He's past it. He's not even thinking about it. You're spending the whole night thinking about it." And I think that's true of women's inner monologue at the workplace. It's like, shut your brain *off.*

On September 13, 2008, the premiere episode of Saturday Night Live's *thirty-fourth season, Tina Fey and Amy Poehler encapsulated all the ways the show's female cast members had emerged as the show's biggest comedy stars. Their skit eviscerated Sarah Palin, the then vice presidential nominee, and poked fun at Hillary Clinton, the former presidential candidate, zeroing in on the distinct issues facing these two very different women in politics: Clinton's smarts and experience getting overshadowed by the media's unfair focus on her "cankles"; Palin's ignorance and hokey spirit. Their performances were so spot-on that they've been credited with influencing the election. The success of Fey and Poehler was a score for female comics. It was high-profile and very, very funny.*

And yet, it would not have been possible without the respective successes of Palin and Clinton, two women who captivated Americans at large. It's been said that the rise of women at Saturday Night Live *has coincided with the rise of American women in general. To an extent, that is true—there are more powerful and prominent women to satirize than ever and that has afforded female sketch comics an opportunity. But it's also true that a successful sketch requires a talented woman to write and play the part. There was a time when Chris Farley or Adam Sandler would have been cast to play the women's roles. And the truth is, back in the day,* Saturday Night Live *didn't satirize colorful figures like, say, Madonna nearly as much as they could have.*

The emergence of high-profile female politicians, business leaders, media personalities, and divas in the real world—at the same time that Saturday Night Live *was blessed with a strong female cast—created a perfect storm for women to become the show's biggest stars for the first time in its more than three-decade history.*

NORA DUNN   [When I was on the show] we didn't have enough political fodder with women in it. I did Pat Schroeder, which was fun. She ran for president. But politically it was very male-dominated—we didn't have Sarah Palin or Hillary Clinton.

ANA GASTEYER   The mid-nineties was an era when women started to blow opportunities open. Martha Stewart became this international domestic powerhouse; then, after I left, Hillary Clinton ran for president. There are more female newscasters now, so whatever the political joke is, you can throw it to Katie Couric instead of to Brian Williams. There are certainly plenty of sexist and traditional roles. There's always gonna be more male presence represented. But you have this ability to play more openhandedly with a fuller comedic deck.

LORI NASSO   [The women's success] was a combination of women rising up in the pop culture arena and the women on the show being strong enough and dependable enough so that we could give them stuff that would be considered for the basis of a sketch.

EMILY SPIVEY   Guys will ignore lady things. It doesn't matter how many lady things are going on: if they don't think it's funny and if they don't have a funny person to pull it off, they're not gonna write it. I think you pray for a hot mess like Whitney Houston or Oprah or whoever to plug those ladies into it, but you have to have somebody good there to pull it off. Obviously someone like Sarah Palin comes into the fore, you have to go, "Okay, well, somebody's got to play Sarah Palin." And then it was the perfect storm of "Well, Tina looks exactly like her," and because Tina is so good, we were able just to throw that at her. It has to work both ways.

The Palin and Clinton sketch was a collective effort. At the time of the 2008 elections we were doing two live shows a week for four weeks and so we all really had to hunker down and do it. Tina had a lot of input in that, but that was really us and Seth Meyers. But my God, that time was so crazy. We were all there late at night just poring over scripts. When McCain was on, we did a Home Shopping Network thing with Palin and Senator McCain. And the idea to give it the Home Shopping Network angle came from the girls. The guys would've never conceived of a Home Shopping Network angle. So just Sarah Palin being a female, the girls had more of a chance to get into the political arena, because the political stuff is really the guys, even still. That's the dudes. They really just want the coterie of guys sitting in the room, sadly. But they're sweet dudes.

MAYA RUDOLPH You know, there's a reason why this particular group of *SNL* women has been asked to come back [for the reunion shows]. We are part of a different kind of generation that was there as a group. There was something really solid about us as a group, and I think that's why there have been so many newspaper stories and magazine articles about us. It was like, "Hey, this is a boys' club, what are you guys doing here?"

9

. . . .

Comic Rising

During the first decade of the twenty-first century, New York had re-emerged as a major hotbed of comic activity, only this time the best venues were not on Manhattan's Upper East Side but in a cluster of small bar back rooms and loft spaces, and in an old piano shop on the gentrifying Lower East Side. As in nineties Los Angeles, the change in venue brought a change in style. No longer were tough girls with New Yawk accents banging out jokes in a room full of potential hecklers. Instead, there emerged a softer, quirkier bunch of women, like Kristen Schaal, who reflected the alternative movement's idiosyncratic sensibility. And instead of fighting for time and attention at the few established clubs still around—which by then required new comics to bring their own audiences—these women preferred artsier, more offbeat venues with far-out names like Surf Reality, Luna Lounge, and Collective: Unconscious where they could perform and mingle with the comics they had grown up with—people like Janeane Garofalo and David Cross, who had finally left Los Angeles for the East Coast.

JEN KIRKMAN, comedian and writer, *Chelsea Lately* I started in Boston back in 1997, and at that point the whole alternative comedy thing had already started in New York City. I remember there was a big article in, maybe it was the Boston *Phoenix* newspaper, about Luna Lounge. It was about Janeane Garofalo and people like Marc Maron, who were running this place and it was really cool. And that made me want to move to New York. So I kind of knew that place existed and knew that would be ideal.

KRISTEN SCHAAL, comedian   After college I moved to New York. The East Village and Lower East Side was where it was happening back then. And there was an open mic night called Surf Reality, and it was for comedians, musicians, anybody.

And I just started putting pieces up one night a week. One of the characters I had was a girl who would do, like, junior high class presentations. So I had a few of those that I would do. I had a science project where I tried to take the popularity out of a girl in school, and I did it all using voodoo but I used scientific terminology for it. Or I'd have a monologue about the dangers of marijuana. And in the end the person tries marijuana for the first time and ends up dead from it.

JEN KIRKMAN   Surf Reality was on the Lower East Side. I've actually read stuff and heard people say that it was in someone's apartment building. I don't remember that. But I do remember going up this huge flight of stairs and then going into a big room, and it looked more like a place where kids would have a dance recital than it was like a club with a stage or anything. And there was just every single kind of person that you would find in New York. There were comedians that worked the clubs, comedians that worked on TV, people who were just starting out. And then there were people who did poetry or music or were mentally ill, who needed to get up for three to five minutes and just be weird.

I remember putting my name on a slip of paper and putting it in a bowl or a hat or something. I honestly don't remember how long I stayed each time I went. But I remember I was so new that that was one of my only options. So I think I was fine with it, because it was a pretty supportive crowd. It was a lot of crazy people, and sometimes there were so many performers there that you didn't always get on. But I tended to do it when a bunch of comedian friends and I would decide to go together. After the first time I went, I rarely showed up by myself.

KRISTEN SCHAAL   I was really shy, and I took my time. I would go and watch shows. I would do the very low-profile open mic night shows on the Lower East Side, and then I would go to Eating It [at the Luna Lounge] and other shows to watch. After a couple of years of doing these underground shows here and there, I finally got the courage to give the booker a tape, and I got to do Eating It, which is a much more high-profile show. I got to hang out with Eugene Mirman and David Cross, and all these great, great people. And over time, you see them at shows and then they become your coworkers, in a way.

JANEANE GAROFALO   Luna Lounge was just a bar in the front, and then a room in the back with a stage, mostly for bands. It was just your classic Lower East Side bar. Pool tables in front, that kind of thing. And it was on Ludlow Street, which in itself was an exciting street to be on. I did not start [the show Eating It at the Luna Lounge]. I might have done the first show. And I do recall doing it quite a bit. I mean, it was only one night a week but I went a lot . . .

But there were a lot of great rooms: there was also Collective: Unconscious, and eventually David Cross, Jon Benjamin, and Todd Barry started doing a show at Piano's called Tinkle. There was also a great scene at Stella, which was [a sketch comedy group created by and] with Michael Showalter, Michael Ian Black, and David Wain, the same guys who were in [another sketch comedy group,] the State—they had a great, great show at Fez on Wednesday nights for a few years. Fez was a beautiful restaurant club underneath the Time Café, which no longer exists. So it was a very nice cabaret kind of setting downstairs. And on Wednesday nights Michael and Michael and David put on a great multimedia show, if you will—there was film, there was music, there was stand-up, there was spoken word. And there would almost be more people hanging out than performing, all the time.

Then I remember the UCB guys showed up and brought with them a whole great new scene. I mean, really, really talented people and a lot of people who had been influenced by Del Close.

In 1997, four members of the Chicago improv comedy team the Upright Citizens Brigade descended on the New York alternative comedy scene. The only woman among them was Amy Poehler, the person who would soon become the most famous of the four. While the group's goal was to land a Comedy Central series—which they did in 1998 (it lasted for three seasons)—their real legacy was the founding of a theater and improv school on West Twenty-sixth Street in Manhattan. More than any other sketch comedy school, the UCB is responsible for the spread of long-form improvisation performers throughout mainstream culture: from Saturday Night Live *and* The Daily Show *to several popular sitcoms—Parks* and Recreation, The Office, Happy Endings—*and blockbuster comedies as big as The Hangover. UCB's curriculum is based on the work of guru Del Close, a former Compass player who spent decades fine-tuning the long-form improv technique known as the "Harold." But Close didn't come up with the Harold on his own—the root of the technique was planted by the 1950s improv prodigy Elaine May.*

The Harold applies a three-act structure to a set of improv games and principles, the most well known being the "Yes and . . ." technique, which lets players build upon the characters and objectives of fellow players. Close based his philosophy on the earlier principles laid down by May, with whom he had once been romantically attached and who had played an important role in introducing Close to improv. May had developed several principles of improv (with Ted Flicker, a founder of the St. Louis offshoot of the Compass Players), which Close once described as "a tripod on which I was able to base a much more complex and probably not very much more profound theory or system aimed at the professional theater."*

---

* After leaving the St. Louis Compass, Close moved to San Francisco to join the Committee, a Second City offshoot that was open from 1963 to 1972. Close was part of the collective at the Committee that created—as a group—the first, most primitive form of what would become the Harold. While Close didn't develop this early Harold on his own, he can be credited with kneading, shaping, transforming, and disseminating the technique once the Committee closed.

At various points throughout the 1970s, Close had taught various forms of the Harold at Second City to some of its most famous alumni, including Jon Belushi, Gilda Radner, Bill Murray, and Chris Farley. And yet Close often butted heads with Second City cofounder Bernard Sahlins over the use of improv during performances. Much of the reason had to do with a fundamental difference between the two men's points of view: Close believed that improv was an art form that was meant to be performed; Sahlins believed it was simply a tool meant to create set sketches. (It should be noted that Close was also prone to erratic behavior, drug abuse, and beliefs that women were not funny.) In 1983, Close left Second City to join forces with Charna Halpern, who had cofounded ImprovOlympic in 1981 with the help of old Compass founder David Shepherd. (Shepherd left the operation within the first year.) Close, who had spent decades trying to develop a still uncertain Harold into a clear, workable performance technique, had finally found a partner with whom he could work, combining his practices with the improv games that Halpern had developed for ImprovOlympic. What they created was the long-form improv technique now known as the Harold.

*By the 2000s May had been living in New York for decades and mostly working as a ghostwriter. While her improv days appear to be long behind her, her seminal work has lived on through Close, his Chicago theater, ImprovOlympic, and now the UCB in New York. With that, improv—which had been defining Chicago's theater scene since the Compass Players was founded in the mid-fifties—was for the first time making its mark on New York.**

MATT BESSER We didn't move to New York and say, "Let's open up a theater." We moved there because in Chicago it's pretty hard to pitch a show. If you are going to pitch a show to television, you need to be in L.A. or New York. And we went to New York with a very specific goal of doing sketch showcases until Comedy Central specifically noticed us and gave us a sketch show, and that's exactly what we did.

We all found different, small ways to get by—I'd saved money myself from Chicago, Amy worked at Aqua Grill [in New York] for like a year—but we taught a lot of classes. We would flyer, flyer, flyer, flyer—go to Washington Square Park and Union Square and hand out flyers to our show, and work it, put on little skits in the park, get people's attention. We quickly became part of the New York alternative comedy scene. New York didn't really have the Chicago long-form improv, but there was plenty of alternative comedy, especially stand-up-wise. There was a show called Eating It, also known as Luna Lounge, which we were invited to do every week. We did every stand-up club, and we did our shows at Tribeca Lab and the Duplex, at Surf Reality.

So to a lot of people, that was a new thing and they liked it and we knew how to teach it. We had already taught it in Chicago. And before we got the Comedy Central show that was our job, we did classes, and

* Before UCB, there had been other attempts to bring Chicago-style improvisational theater to New York. In 1960, Ted Flicker opened The Premise Theater on Bleecker Street, which for a period starred Joan Darling, George Segal, Gene Hackman, and Buck Henry among others. It closed in early 1964. In 1962, the Second City opened at the Square East nightclub in Greenwich Village but it only lasted until 1966. In 1980, Chicago City Limits, a group of former Second City actors, opened in the theater district. (It eventually moved to the Upper East Side, where it was for eleven years before heading back to Broadway.) Though the Chicago City Limits continues to stage performances today, it never made an impact on the city's comedy community in the same way UCB did.

classes led to students wanting to do shows. And we were renting out so much space all over New York, and it became economically ridiculous *not* to get a theater.

Our first theater was, like, a lap-dance emporium before we moved in. The owner was a former stripper, so we were all a little intimidated by this New York stripper madam. But Amy went in there and turned on the charm, and everything worked out.

SETH MORRIS, artistic director, UCB L.A. When I first showed up at UCB in New York, you could see Andy Richter there, and Conan O'Brien would be in the audience.

ELLIE KEMPER, comedian I was in an improv group in college and my great friend Scott was in it with me. We spent a summer in Chicago. That was the summer before my senior year. I was basically interning at an ad agency, and taking these improv classes at night and seeing all these shows at ImprovOlympic. And that was what really made a major impact on me in thinking, "Oh well, I wanna do that after I leave school." And I spent a year in England after college not doing improv. But then I came back and my friend Scott and I were talking about which is a better place to go to: Chicago or New York? Because Chicago, with Second City, was the hub of improv, and I thought, "Well, that's where it's at its purest form." But then it seemed like there were a lot of other acting opportunities in New York. So I decided to come to New York. And UCB has just exploded since then.

Now, I don't think that saying you studied in Chicago carries as much weight as it used to; you no longer think that Chicago is the only place to do improv. I don't know if anyone ever thought that—[but I used to think] you go to Chicago to get good at improv, not New York. I was so relieved when I saw my first show at UCB, because I was like, "Oh! They do improv here too."

AUBREY PLAZA, comedian Since I was like sixteen or seventeen, I just wanted to be on *Saturday Night Live.* That was what I wanted more than anything. The cast that I was watching at that time was Will Ferrell and Ana Gasteyer and Amy Poehler, and all of those people. I remember doing research and trying to figure out how the cast members got on the show because that's what I wanted to do. A lot of them did improv, so I was like, "All right that's what I'm gonna do." I was also interested in filmmaking. So the reason I went to NYU was thirty percent to go to film school and seventy percent just to be in New York so I could do UCB and try to weasel my way onto *SNL*. That was a big motivation for me.

I started socializing at UCB first. It's a very social scene, and there's a lot of after-show hangout time. And the relationships are very important, in terms of meeting people. Then you end up writing with them or doing a sketch show with them. So I started hanging out there, going to shows and getting a feel for it before I started taking classes.

ELLIE KEMPER There were six levels of classes, so I took the full curriculum within a year. I took one after the other. And then after you've gone through the curriculum you can audition for the Harold team, which is a house team where you can perform every week.

There's a head of UCB—the artistic director—and then there's a committee of teachers and artistic directors who make the decision of who goes on what team. There are auditions and you're selected. You can't form it yourself. So people would get kicked off teams and people would get added to teams, and there was no guarantee that you would stay on a team once you were on it.

AUBREY PLAZA You have to at least get through level three to audition. And the first time I auditioned for a Harold team, I didn't get on. I was devastated. I thought my life was over. I cried myself to sleep. Because when you're really into that scene, it consumes you and it's like your entire life and getting on a Harold team is the only thing you want. But I wasn't ready at that point. They knew I was funny, but it's not just about being funny to be on a Harold team; you have to have a level of confidence and I didn't have it yet. I was a bit hesitant, so I would stay on the back wall a bit and I wouldn't come right out with a big choice. A lot of times I would be really frustrated, because I would see people get on Harold teams that I didn't think were that funny, but their confidence was off the charts so they appeared to be funnier than they were. That being said, confidence is a really big part of being funny too. And the next time around, I guess two or three months later, I auditioned again and got on.

ELLIE KEMPER At UCB every team had eight. And usually it was me and one other girl. At the most, I think, out of eight people, there would be three women on the team.

AUBREY PLAZA When I was doing improv at UCB it was definitely male-dominated. And on those Harold teams there were maybe two women on every team out of seven, so you do feel like you're in the minority. But if you were funny and you were a girl, it's a bonus, because there weren't that many girls. And there definitely weren't that many really, really funny girls.

ELLIE KEMPER I met Amy Poehler in the green room a couple of times—that's the back room where the performers hang out before a show—because it's her theater. Of course *I* know who *she* is. But then here's the thing: she knew who *I* was from watching shows.

CHELSEA PERETTI, comedian I don't know why I didn't continue doing improv after college. I kind of wish I had, actually, but I think at the time UCB seemed like this closed circuit to me. I remember feeling like it would be hard to infiltrate. It's funny, because as a stand-up I perform there all the time. And I did monologues at UCB for ASSSSCAT. And Amy used to e-mail us [the members of *Variety Shac*, which was the live show and Web series I did with three other women] and go, "I loved this short!" And then I asked her if she would do [an episode of a different Web series I did called] *All My Exes* with Fred Armisen, where she and Fred Armisen would play this couple that I dated. And they both said yes. Fred had been in some *Variety Shac* shorts before and was a friend from the comedy scene. Same with Amy. And actually, Amy had gone out with *Variety Shac* as an executive producer when we were pitching it as a show initially. The show didn't wind up happening, but we wound up doing it as a smaller-scale project with [the cable channel] Adult Swim.

CASEY WILSON My best friend, June, and I decided to do a two-woman sketch comedy show after college, and we did it at the UCB and it ran for about a year. It was inspired by Rachel and Tina's show—they had a two-woman show [called *Dratch & Fey*]—and by our girlfriends Mindy Kaling and Brenda Withers, who had done this two-woman show about Matt Damon and Ben Affleck. And so we did it. It was called *Rode Hard and Put Away Wet.* People really liked it, so we took the show out to Aspen, the HBO Comedy Arts Festival, and we thought we're gonna be huge stars—our mugs are gonna be everywhere after this show. And we got signed as writers. And I was like, "Excuse me?" Not to be insulting to any writers, but I took it as a bit of an insult. I wanted to be an actress and a comedian and they're like, "We'll take you behind the scenes, thank you."

At first, I took it as a little bit of an injury to my pride, and then I realized it's amazing to be able to create comedy for women. And then the twain kind of met when I sent in my audition tape for *SNL*, which was all about writing for yourself and coming up with characters. So for a while we got hired to write. And it all kind of just rolled in together, the last gasp being that I got hired as a performer.

ELLIE KEMPER   It was such a big deal when *Conan* was in New York. If somebody from UCB got a part on *Conan*, it was important. But the appearances were sketchy. They were so short and you were doing something that someone else wrote. Still, if you were doing that, that was a good thing. It wasn't make-or-break, but people who I knew who were regulars on that show I thought of as doing very well.

AUBREY PLAZA   When I was in New York and I was doing UCB stuff, all the casting directors started to catch on and they started coming to shows. And UCB became *the* place to go to find the funniest young people in town. A lot of times for commercials, so I was auditioning a lot for commercials.

I remember, too, there were a couple people that, through UCB and doing videos, were just getting our name out there in New York. We were on the top of all the New York casting lists. And it's like once you reach that point, then the L.A. people start to, not totally pay a lot of attention to you, but start asking you to be put on tape. At the time it was Ellie Kemper and me. We were on the top of those lists with a couple other people, too, and so I would go to callbacks and I would always see her. We'd always see each other at all the major auditions, even though we're so different. I really love Ellie, but that always made me feel better whenever I would walk into a callback and see her, because I would be like, "Oh my God, really?" I never felt bad if she got the part over me, because we're so different. I was like, "Well, they just wanted a totally different vibe."

ELLIE KEMPER   I had a lucky string of commercials, which lets you pay rent. That is your job. And if it lasts long enough, then that's a good situation to be in. But I was still writing other sketch shows and I did a couple one-woman shows. That's how I got my theater and film agent, from doing that one-person show.

SETH MORRIS   Improv is kind of like the new stand-up. When I was in high school and thinking about being a comic, it was pretty much you were gonna be a stand-up. And I think, for a lot of people, the generic trajectory was that you would do stand-up and then create a character around your stand-up persona and have a TV show. *SNL* and all those sort of careers were always there, but it wasn't the main thing. For instance, I didn't know until I went to New York that you could pursue a career doing sketch and improv. And UCB has arguably, more than anybody, put long-form improv into the mainstream.

While the Upright Citizens Brigade was spreading the gospel of improv, shock comic Sarah Silverman was putting her stamp on the world of stand-up. Girly-voiced but tomboyish, Silverman emerged as a part of a second wave of alternative comics who had started taking the stage in the early to mid-nineties, but it wasn't until more than a decade later that she would burst out, fully and disturbingly formed. In 2005, Silverman managed to secure three high-profile appearances that would clinch her notoriety on the national stage: first there was a strong and stunning appearance in The Aristocrats, *a documentary film about the dirtiest joke ever told; then Comedy Central signed her up to develop her own sitcom; and finally a national tour,* Jesus Is Magic, *in which Silverman coyly joked about rape, racism, and the Holocaust, and won accolades among critics, some of whom called her the second coming of Lenny Bruce. By the end of the year, it was clear that Silverman was prepared to dig into territory no other comic had yet to dare, deftly using her sex appeal to pull audiences in and then delivering a ballsy punch line to make them cringe.*

Silverman's impact on female-driven comedy, in the meantime, has been profound, if not unfortunate. There is no shortage of young, aspir-

ing stand-ups trying to mimic Silverman's mix of baby-voiced sweetness with shockingly dirty language. But what is lost in the copycats' attempts is Silverman's original point of view and joke-writing skills. And what is left is a sense that women are too focused on getting dirty and being raunchy than actually getting a laugh.

BARRY KATZ   When I started my club in New York, Sarah was an open-mic-er. She was going to NYU and all the comedians just loved Sarah Silverman. I mean, every single one of them wanted to go out with her, every single one of them wanted to sleep with her, every single one of them wanted to just be near her. She was infectious. And even though she might not have always been that consistent, the thing about comedy is that male comedians just wanna be around pretty girls who are funny, who they think they have a chance of fucking. So if you're a female comic who can walk that line and can navigate that, you'll get onstage anywhere you want, and your comedy will grow tremendously and you'll get more stage time and more opportunities, because the men will take you where you wanna go. If you can just hold them at bay and not have to sleep with them, you get all the stage time you want and you can have a great time and learn as well.

MARK LONOW   She did use her being a woman very well. She dated guys—and there's nothing negative about that. Guys do it with women. And she befriended guys as a woman. And it was part of how she worked the room. And she just became one of the guys—but never a guy. She's not gay. And that's part of her aura, if you will.

MELANIE HUTSELL   I will tell you Sarah Silverman was [working on *Saturday Night Live*] the last year that I was on [in 1993] and she also got [the ax] with me. And after it was confirmed to me [that I'd been let go], she called me and she said, "Let's go out." And I was like, "Go out? I don't feel like going out." And she was like, "Come on!" And I said, "Well, I'm not drinking, 'cause I'm depressed." And she was like, "Have a coke, whatever, man, just come on." So we went out that night and she had just found out that she wasn't picked up for the next year, and she got up and did her stand-up. Now we look at her and we go, "Of course; of course, she did that." But at the time, I was like "That girl right there, she's going to go all the way." She's got guts and she's got a thick skin. And I just remember sitting there watching her and just being in awe of her ability to go on. I'd have took to the bed.

GREG BEHRENDT By the time Sarah got to Largo, she had already been on *Saturday Night Live** and I think she was already crafting a pretty strong point of view. Has her comedic style evolved? Sure. Is she a better joke writer? Sure. But I think she was always cute, playful, sexy, and dirty. That's how I recall it. Most people that end up where Sarah or Zach Galifianakis are have a really strong point of view from the beginning, and it's just a matter of the mechanics catching up to them.

BARRY KATZ I think her comedy has become much bluer than it used to be. I don't remember it being as blue as it is now. But if you can have a smile on your face, have people love you, you can get away with anything, because huggable and lovable wins the race.

GREG BEHRENDT I think she joked about rape in the very first set [I ever saw her in]. Dudes liked her, and women were confused by her in the beginning. Sarah was really pretty, and I think had a tough time at the beginning, because I think some of the other girls thought that she was playing to the men. But at the end of the day, Sarah was doing what she was doing. Everybody has a judgment about somebody, and everyone's always intimidated by attractive people.

CLAUDIA LONOW She was younger than me, she was pretty, and she came out of nowhere. It wasn't like she was mean or anything. She was really nice. But we were so threatened by her.

MARK LONOW For a long time she wasn't that funny, but it was so shocking, how could you not put this woman onstage?
    You know the joke, "I was going down on my boyfriend last night and the longer I did him, the more I kept thinking, 'As I get older I'm becoming more like my mother.'" I was standing in the back and when

---

* In 1993, when Sarah Silverman was just twenty-two years old—and three years into her comedy career—she was hired as a writer on *Saturday Night Live*. She lasted just a season. Not a single one of her sketches ever made it on the air.

she cut off she passed me and said, "Your daughter wrote me that joke," and then left the room. I fell down, it was so funny. "Your daughter wrote me that joke." Well, thank you for telling me. Something I hold near and dear to my heart.

CLAUDIA LONOW   I wrote that joke, and I tried to do it and I couldn't make it work. It was "I was licking jelly off my boyfriend's penis when I thought suddenly, 'God, I'm turning into my mother.'" It was based on something that happened with my mother, but I couldn't make it work, so I said to Sarah, "Look, I wrote this joke but I can't make it work. I think it will fit in your act." And it became one of her most quoted jokes. It was in *Rolling Stone*, not credited to me, but she has told everybody that I wrote the joke.

GREG BEHRENDT   Sarah and Laura Kightlinger have a comedic style—and you can attribute it to Wendy Liebman too—where there is a lot of mislead before you get to the punch line. Sarah and Laura just happen to go dark with it. Stylistically, I think there are some similarities between Sarah and Laura, but I don't know if there is any direct correlation between the two. I mean, they are joke writers. They're not just storytellers. They write jokes and that's a style of joke-writing: there's a mislead.

AUBREY PLAZA   When [I created my audition tape for] *Funny People* [a 2009 movie about a stand-up comedian directed by Judd Apatow], I taped myself doing a five-minute set in a bar in Queens. And it was terrifying. I had never done stand-up before and I really didn't know what I was doing. And before I did it, before I wrote anything, I watched a lot of Janeane Garofalo and young Sarah Silverman. But Sarah Silverman was different when she was young. When she was starting out she wasn't how she is now. I think it took her a little bit of time to really figure that out. You could see little hints of her persona in the sets that she was doing, but it wasn't full-on, that wasn't her whole thing. Some of her jokes were just jokes, and she didn't deliver them as the character that she is now. Now she delivers the jokes as if she's a fool, which is why they're okay to say. Some of them are really shocking or ignorant, but it's funny because you know she doesn't really think that. And I think when she was younger, some of her jokes were delivered like that but some of them were delivered earnestly. But once you figure out "Oh, I get more laughs when I deliver it like this or when I have this attitude," the more it's like "I need to keep doing that."

MARK FLANAGAN   Sarah has a new bit that is just unbelievable about how she can't believe that she came out of her father's balls. And she talks about the ejaculation and everything else and she goes, "When I think back on it, it's hard to even imagine that I was once that thin." But it really is a variation on a theme.

CAROLINE HIRSCH, owner, Caroline's on Broadway   She did something very sexually explicit onstage at the comedy festival in Montreal. I went to see her at Club Soda—it's a club up there. There were three hundred people in the room, and when the audience was waning, she did something very sexually explicit with her hand down her pants. So she did it for the shock value. But Sarah always does that. Even when she talks about when she was dating Jimmy Kimmel, the things that would come out of her mouth. I'm almost embarrassed saying them. She was on a roast or something and she said something about smelling Jimmy's balls and they smelled like her grandmother's clothes, like mothballs, something like that. But she's about the shock value, no? And here you see this gorgeous woman—you know, she's really quite beautiful—and you see her refer to something like that. But that's the thing about Sarah: she's this gorgeous woman, and then what comes out of her mind and her mouth.

But she's of a generation that is no-holds-barred. So why shouldn't she say things like that? That's her persona, that's her skill, that's her comedy—to shock. And all the young kids are into her. She has this following now, all these young women in their twenties and all these young men in their twenties.

GREG BEHRENDT   I thought Sarah was funny and I never felt like she was trying to deliver you a set that you could easily mold into a television show. I never got the sense from any of these girls [of the alternative comedy movement] that they were trying to get a sitcom. If anything, all these women made it very difficult for people to be able develop something for them, because their point of view was not the generally accepted worldview at that time. There's something kind of bold and awesome about seeing anybody go onstage, and you say to yourself, "I don't see how anyone is going to develop that." They're clearly doing this because they want to be comedians, not because they want to be TV stars. The fact that some of them did, that you get something like *The Sarah Silverman Program* [on Comedy Central], is a testament to how strong that point of view is, and that it can eventually evolve into something. That's what's so great.

LINDA SMITH   I've been teaching and performing and the females tend to come in trying to be Sarah Silverman. And you know what? Only Sarah can do Sarah. Because then it comes off as disgusting. Honestly. She pulls it off—don't get me wrong, she does. But not everybody can do that. These people trying to be comics, they don't understand that unless it's in your DNA, you can't do it. And for whatever reason, that kind of stuff is right for Sarah. That's her. Not everybody's like that. And they're all coming in there talking about their vag. It's like, "What? You never talk about your vag. Why are you doing it now?" I can tell. I say, "What the fuck are you doing?"

PAULA PELL   There's a very tits-and-ass thing [going on now]. I noticed it a couple years ago. We really needed to cast some women [for *Saturday Night Live*] and there was an audition here where we had a lot of women audition. I would say eighty percent of them showed their midriff and had these *Playboy* voices: "I'm being sexy and dirty and really saying filthy, dirty things." They're doing Sarah Silverman, I guess, even though I think she's very funny. But they did that thing where it's like, "I'm gonna say the filthiest things but I'm also somebody you wanna fuck." And it was such a turnoff to me. I don't think anybody here tends to like that move. Lorne doesn't. Nobody likes it.

LISA SUNDSTEDT, comedian and founder, Pretty, Funny Women showcase   A lot of women who take my classes try to be dirty right up front. They think it's interesting to be edgy. I had one girl in my last class who wanted to do a joke about—this is going to get very graphic— but she wanted to do a joke about when a guy comes inside of you and the next day you can feel it coming out throughout the day. She wanted to talk about come. And I said, "Absolutely not. You have five minutes onstage. What do you want your legacy to be? How do you want this audience to remember you? Talking about come? Really? You're a smart twenty-one-year-old girl who's been on three sitcoms and that's how you're going to try stand-up and that's what you want people to think of you as?" And it's because it's easy. It's an easy way to get a laugh around the boys at the open mics and it's an easy habit to fall into for women if they hang out at too many open mics around too many male comics.

ILIZA SHLESINGER   On the whole, just from being in comedy clubs every night, girls think, "If I'm shocking—because it's worked for a couple of other comics, and God bless them—but if I'm shocking, they'll laugh. 'I'm a cute girl and I'm saying *cunt*, that's funny.'" It's like eh, where's the intelligence in that writing? So I think a lot of girls ride that "I'm cute but I'm dirty" wave. But it's like, "All right, what do you do when you're forty?"

JEFF SINGER, consultant, Just for Laughs Festival   I've found that there's been a trend of women who try to borrow that style. They say things for shock value or try to make off-the-cuff comments that get very crude and dirty, and it's just not funny. That style overshadows the content and the meat of the material. I've noticed that a lot with female comics. I know all the up-and-coming female comics and I've seen too much of it. They're trying too much to have that laid-back, snarky, cold, aloof attitude and talk about stuff like they're a dude and eschew their femininity and talk like a guy. It works sometimes, don't get me wrong. But too often they don't have the goods.

And I wanna say it's probably because of Sarah Silverman, who was one of these first pretty girls who was able to talk about rape and incest and more guy stuff—scatological humor, sexual stuff—with a little sinister twinkle in her eye. But listen, Sarah is a good writer. She's got that formula down. She knows how to do that twist down the road and the element of surprise, which is what good comedy is all about. And for the most part there weren't a lot of pretty female comics. You've got Elayne Boosler, Roseanne Barr, Phyllis Diller, Joan Rivers. You could go on. Those weren't considered attractive women, so when Sarah came along—I'm not saying she was the first, but she was definitely in a minority and that definitely made her different—who's this cute face who's all of a sudden got a potty mouth. And I think that made her alluring, given the historical context. And now you're getting so many more women and much more attractive women trying the same thing. It's been done. It's not a shock or surprise anymore; now let's hear what you have to say.

Sarah Silverman's shtick may have been made more accessible because of her looks, but one comedian whose attitude and appearance worked in tandem was Chelsea Handler, the pretty blond comic who managed to do what once would've been unthinkable: spin her slutty, boozy, party girl persona into a blockbuster comedy career. At the time that Chelsea Handler emerged as a full comedic force, Sex and the City's Samantha Jones had only just shattered the glass ceiling on sexual frankness. But, unlike Handler, Samantha was only a character, and her critics poohpoohed her lifestyle as being based on that of a gay man. (Even Silverman's persona is a kind of character.) Handler, on the other hand, is the real deal: a naughty, raw, sometimes scatological comic who got her first taste of stand-up at AA, has posed for Playboy, and once made a sex tape (supposedly as a joke) to nab the attention of casting agents. While sexed-up blond bombshells have certainly been popular comedic figures before, they have usually been intellectually challenged. But Handler is no dummy. And while her late-night hosting gig may feature a cleaned-up version of her act, her dry, just-rolled-out-of-bed, telling-it-to-you-straight attitude still shines through.

No comedian has branded herself with quite as much savvy as Handler: she's got a top-rated late-night television show, four bestselling books, a publishing imprint, a comedy tour, and a production company. And by fostering the careers of her rotating panel of comedians, who came to the show as relative unknowns, she is putting her stamp on a few rising stars and proving that there is a huge untapped market for women comedians who appeal to female audiences.

TED HARBERT Chelsea has a freedom—a behavioral freedom and a sexual freedom and an emphasis on a good time—that goes to a bit of an extreme, but that makes it relatable to people. Everybody's got a couple stories about a one-night stand or that time I got drunk or the time I went to this party. Chelsea's got a lot of those stories. And most of her act in comedy is based on things she's done or said.

And frankly, part of her point of view is informed by her look. It's very rare—incredibly rare—to have someone who's that good-looking have that fearlessness. Usually, people associate female comedians with not necessarily great-looking people. Chelsea's been on the cover of *Playboy* and *Shape* and gets a bunch of photo shoots.

JAMIE MASADA   Chelsea was very pretty. And the first time she came to the club, the attention was mostly on her prettiness and her face and her body. But she was a little bit of an edgy comic. She would drink one or two drinks on the stage, and she would have fun. A lot of the guys who used to come to the club were not used to seeing a pretty girl do comedy. But no matter what the audience thought, Chelsea had fun on the stage. And at the beginning it was tough. They did not want to have fun with her. But after a few minutes on the stage, the audience started laughing with her.

CHELSEA HANDLER, comedian   I'm always super-casual. Even now, on my show, half the time I'm in jeans. I guess my dad drove that into my head all the time—that it's much more about what you are reading and what you know about than the way you look. He was always saying that to me. So I was always super-conscious of not dressing up and showing off my body. I feel that it's not the thing that you want to put forward. It's just now, in the last couple of years, that I feel more comfortable being sexy.

WHITNEY CUMMINGS, comedian   When she would do those E! Countdown shows—like *101 Celebrity Oops* and *100 Hot Couples*—which all of us comedians would do, everyone would go on those shows and would have written jokes. Like I would go on and say my jokes. And she just had a different energy. She was like slouched in her chair. I remember she would be looking at her nails. And she was funnier than everyone on her own terms.

ROBIN WILLIAMS   Chelsea Handler is gutsy in a "I drink, what the fuck" kind of way, and talks about guys the way men talk about women.

Like "Nice cock!" And you're going, "Wow! So you actually are carnivores! Oh my God, well, way to go!"

TED HARBERT   The reason people come to me all the time and tell me how much they love her is that she just says what they're thinking. All of us are born with some sort of filter and some sort of reservation with saying what's on our mind. She just has less of it. When she talks about having a baby crying "Mommy, Mommy, Mommy" behind you on an airplane and the mommy isn't listening because the mommy's just tired of it or doesn't even hear it anymore, most people just sit there and take it. Chelsea turns around and says, "Hey, lady. You're the mommy, listen to your kid—answer your kid." And she does it. I've seen her do it. And by the way, some of the things she says onstage are exaggerated and a lot of the things in the book are exaggerated, but there's always a kernel of truth to them.

CHELSEA HANDLER   The way I talk on TV is the way I talk in real life— that's who I am. So when people go, "Hi, Chelsea"—like, this weekend, people were like, "Chelsea! Chelsea!" across the restaurant—they think they're my friends. And it's not like I'm an actress they don't know. The fact that people think they know me—well, they actually do. I am very vocal about the fact that I like to drink and have a good time, and I talk about everything, including my personal life. And it's been good for me to have that persona be my person.

LISA SUNDSTEDT   My showcase became one of the hottest places to be seen for women. Chelsea started my show when her manager called me and said, "I have a client, she's going to showcase for Paradigm Agency. Can you please put her up? Her name is Chelsea Handler." And she was very young at the time and I said, "Oh God, I don't know. Yeah, I'll put her up, but she has to go first." So I put her first and she did great. I just loved her and I thought, "This girl's amazing." I said, "I want you on all my shows, I think you're great, and I think you're going to be a star." So she was doing my shows every single month, probably for about five years. And her whole persona was just a drunken floozy. She talked about sleeping around, and dating, and drinking. Her act was very much her first book, *My Horizontal Life*. And it was her truth, which is why it worked. See, now a lot of girls come in and they try to do it and it doesn't work, because it's not their truth. And the reason Chelsea blew up was because she was exactly who you see she is. And I think people like it.

TED HARBERT I joined E! in July of 2004, and honestly, to my own discredit, I had never heard of Chelsea. And truthfully, I had never seen *Girls Behaving Badly* [a *Candid Camera*–type show featuring five women, including Handler, playing pranks on people]. And I think it was a month or two after being here [that I first became aware of her]. I've got several monitors on my desk here, and I was watching one of E!'s famous countdown shows—you know, those 101 Bootylicious Make-overs; those silly shows that we've been putting on for years that viewers love. Those shows feature several comedians making comments about the clips, and Chelsea was one of them. I saw her once, and then a couple minutes later I saw her again, and I said, "Who's that?" And the producer of those shows, a guy by the name of Gary Socol, had either seen Chelsea doing stand-up or maybe on *Girls Behaving Badly*. And then I watched the show and saw her, I don't know, a dozen times and said, "That's a TV star." Not that she should have her own show—that's not the first thing I thought; I thought the first thing is that she's a TV star.

Then I asked my staff to ask her to come in and talk. And if I re-member the story correctly, she came in with David Alan Grier and pitched a show. I don't think it was a reality show. It was more of a hybrid-scripted show. It was something about David and Chelsea as a fake married couple, I think, in the witness protection program or something like that. They had to act like they were married. It was sort of like a sitcom, but I think they wanted to improv a lot of it. And that show wasn't right for us at the time, but I told my staff, "Let's come up with a show for her." And we all talked and came up with *The Chelsea Handler Show*, the first show we did with her, which was a series of field pieces reminiscent of what she did on *Girls Behaving Badly*. She would do studio introductions in between the pieces and little funny com-mentary. That show did well for us, but as a weekly show it was sort of expensive and it was hard to do, because it was so production-intensive. But I knew we had to stay in business with her and I'd always wanted to do a comedy roundtable, because I had developed one of those at NBC, and gave them the idea for what is now *Chelsea Lately*.

JEN KIRKMAN My manager called me and said, *"Chelsea Lately* is looking for a writer, you should apply to it." I watched the show and then I wrote a sample and they called me in. Chelsea was there in the interview with the two executive producers and the head writer. And Chelsea can seem like she's not paying attention. So she was reading my jokes as I was in the room—I don't know if she'd read them before— and she's looking at my packet and just like, "Oh, that's funny, that's funny." Because that's what comedians do—you don't really laugh out loud when you read something, you just say, "That's funny." And I'm like, "This is weird, she's reading my packet in front of me, what if she hates it?"

Then she asked me if I was a lesbian and how old I was. And we used to have this kind of all-business executive producer lady, and she's like, "Chelsea! You can't ask someone that in an interview! Those are the two questions you can't ask someone." And I really liked that. I thought it was fun. She was blatantly setting me up so that I could say something funny. That's the weird thing about interviewing for comedy jobs—you as the comedian have to set the tone. If she hadn't been joking around, I could have gone in there and been very serious, like I was interviewing for a bank job, and I wouldn't have gotten the job. And I think she was like, "Can I see this person every day and joke around with them or are they going to drive me nuts?" I think that's the big part of comedy too: obviously you hire who you think is the best writer, but it's got to be the best writer and the best fit for the job. And then she had somewhere to be and she just left the room early. And I'm like, "This did not go well." And then I got hired.

CHELSEA HANDLER I'm pretty decent friends with everybody that works on the show. All the writers and I have hung out a lot, so we've all become friends. But they weren't all friends when we started. I'd say fifty percent are people I knew—like Josh Wolf I've known forever. Sarah Collona and I used to perform together all the time fifteen years ago—I met her when I was twenty-one and we used to do stand-up together. She wasn't working on the show, and I asked her to come work on the show. Heather McDonald I knew, but I didn't *really* know, and once I got the show, she heard about it and asked me if she could write on it—and now we're pretty good friends.

WHITNEY CUMMINGS   One of the first things I noticed when I went on her show is that her staff is like her family. It's got a real family vibe. These aren't just people she works with.

CHELSEA HANDLER   It's kind of like having a bunch of brothers and sisters. Like you fight and you argue and then you make up and go to the movies.

But if I'm going to say anything negative about the female sex, it would be about the females that don't support each other. That, to me, is the most imperative thing that I want to do, and that I will do. But I don't discriminate against men and women and only just help females. We have an even male-female staff; we have an even male-female ratio of on-air talent. There's no discrimination. If anything, I always want more women, but I'm never going to be the type of woman who hires women just because she's a woman. And I don't think it's hard to find a lot of female stand-ups who I think are funny. I think cool chicks attract other cool chicks. And yeah, it's hard for a guy to find women he thinks are funny if he doesn't think women are funny.

LONI LOVE, comedian   On the show Chelsea uses three comics a night, five nights a week. That's fifteen comics—that's a lot of comics. So you tune in to her show and you see this female, this female, this female, and wow! I would do Jay Leno, what, once a year?

JEN KIRKMAN   There's *The Daily Show* too. Jon Stewart with all his correspondents. He introduced a lot of people into the public eye but a lot of those guys aren't stand-up. They're actors. So it's kind of similar, but I think she's the only one putting on that many a night. And it's really amazing, because it's all different types of comedians. You have some more alternative-y people, you have your I-do-the-road-every-weekend kind of guys, you got girls—I mean, tons of women.

CHELSEA HANDLER   The show kind of became a great outlet for comics. It wasn't intentional, but it ended up being a great promotional tool for when they're on the road—the comics that are on the roundtable are usually promoting something. But I'd be lying if I said that my goal [was to nurture other comics], because it just kind of turned out that way.

I mean, the reason you become a comedian is so that you're holding a microphone on a stage and no one else is fucking saying anything. Think about it—it's probably the most narcissistic thing you could do. But a little bit of the spotlight goes a long way, in my opinion. I'm always just like, "Okay, enough is enough." You really have to be self-absorbed to want that all the time. And having other people share the spotlight takes the pressure off you, and it doesn't make you look so, you know, egomaniacal.

NATASHA LEGGERO, comedian All of her roundtable regulars have headlining careers now. I have to say that's definitely what moved me to the next level where I was able to headline clubs by myself and attract my own fans.

LONI LOVE What happens when you do *Chelsea*, because you only do it once every two weeks, is that it allows you to tour. She announces where you're going to be, and then you build up your audience and your fan base like that. You get a movie. You get on a TV show. Whatever. She'll let you plug one thing. That really helps, because the comedy clubs are suffering right now. But Chelsea says, "Loni's going to be at Virginia Beach Improv," and my Virginia sales—it's phenomenal. I'm booked until January next year.

WHITNEY CUMMINGS I had done *Best Week Ever* and a bunch of things and I think [the producers on Chelsea's show] were just aware of me, and so I did it once. And it went fine and I got asked to come back like a month later, and then two months later, and then I started getting called every two weeks, every two weeks, every two weeks, and got in regularly there.

LONI LOVE Chelsea gives you a list of topics, and you're able to say and do whatever you want to say on those topics. You get an hour to decide what you want to say and write your jokes. You just do it. It's taped, so if they don't like it, they take it out. It's not like the stuff you go through on other late-night shows. If they don't like it, they can edit it out right there.

JEN KIRKMAN We have to be careful about our wording, like "He *allegedly* had an affair." I can't just be like, "He had sex with fifty people." I can't say slanderous things and I can't use certain swearwords. But otherwise I can do any kind of jokes I want.

CHELSEA HANDLER   On our show, we don't get notes about anything. All they do is tell us that we need to delete—*fuck* or *pussy* or whatever, which we know. We know the rules and the guidelines, and they've left us alone because the show has been a success for so long. We do whatever we want. I walk into a meeting and say, "Oh, you know, this happened to me this weekend," and we reenact it, or somebody has a video from the weekend and we put it on the air.

In terms of writing, I have little nuances, like you like to joke in threes, or you change a number—like, someone will write "Eight hundred miles an hour," and I'm like, "No, eighty-four miles an hour is funnier." I always try to tweak things and put them in my language. There are certain words I don't like to use, like *dork* and *geek*. Not for any real reason, I just think they're *dorky* and *geeky*. So when the writer calls open for me and my monologue and I look at it and I'm like, "I never say *dork*, I never say *beaver*, I don't use the vernacular." So usually by now they have it down. But no one really ever has down your voice one hundred percent of the time.

WHITNEY CUMMINGS   When I was on the show, I also remember that she was going so off the cards. She had jokes written on cards, but she was doing her own thing.

ILIZA SHLESINGER   I did *Chelsea Lately* three times and it was great. You get an appearance out of it, and she was nice. But I didn't feel good at the end of it. I felt bad that I had made fun of people that I could potentially work with someday or be in the same room as—unless it's someone who I just think is total garbage. Like any of the Kardashians could just disappear and I'd have no issue with it. And I would tell that to their face, because they're just trash. But I remember I made a joke about the Jonas Brothers, and while I've never met them, I don't think anything bad about them. And I left feeling like "I shouldn't have said that, it didn't feel right." It's social commentary, a bit on the cattier side.

You'll see a lot of time guys—straight men that go on that show—often have trouble chirping in, because it's not really in alpha male nature to shit on Kim Kardashian for no reason. Or the Jonas Brothers.

That show is for women and gay guys. It just is. And the nature of that show is that it's very gossipy, a little catty, and people love it.

LONI LOVE   First of all, her demographic is not just women. People are mistaking that. I go to the airport now, and I have older Americans coming to me, and I'm like, "What are you doing watching the show?" The difference is, when I did my first *Tonight Show* set, they're like, "Aren't you a comic?" Now they're like, "Loni! I saw you on *Chelsea*. You're hilarious. I like when you and Chelsea argue." They know me by name. It's a big difference.

CHELSEA HANDLER   There's always a guarantee that people aren't going to like you; it's just par for the course. It's just going to happen. There are people that hate me, and I'm very well aware of it. When people are like, "Ugh," I don't blame them. I don't want to watch my show every night either, but whatever.

TED HARBERT   *E! News* was a much more established show than *Chelsea Lately* when it came on, because *E! News* has been around for a long time. So the right scheduling thing to do is take care of your strong show and put it at eleven o'clock and launch a new show at eleven thirty, even though it would be against the established late-night talk shows. I always look at Chelsea as a totally different audience than [David Letterman or Jay Leno]—and the demographics prove it. The median age of Chelsea's show is fully twenty years younger than those late-night competitors. It's a young female audience. We get a lot of men, too, but I know it's a different audience. And then it showed surprising strength at eleven thirty. So, being an old scheduler at heart, I said, "I think this show can do better at eleven o'clock than *E! News* is doing now," and that has proven to be the case. And actually, it's up against tougher competition than Jay Leno and David Letterman, because Jon Stewart has a very young audience as well. It's more male than female, but still, it's a young audience. So actually it's a testament to how well *Chelsea* does that it does so well against another show that has such a young audience.

And not only is *Chelsea Lately* one of the more talked-about programs, it's one of the more highly rated. She airs original programs on Monday to Thursday, usually. And I would say that usually, at least anywhere between two and four nights a week, it's the highest-rated show in the network of the day. It's extremely important to our schedule.

JEN KIRKMAN And then Chelsea started a tour, the Comedians of *Chelsea Lately*, so we're all touring the country. She's smart. It's a good way to be. She's almost like franchising us, like we're all a brand together.

CHELSEA HANDLER I still enjoy stand-up. But I think it [depends on] the volume of work that you're doing. It's like people think, "Oh God, you've hit it, you have to take whatever job you can get." It's like, "No, you don't." You don't have to do that. That means you're going to burn out. And I definitely got a taste of that. I was doing a hundred shows a year on top of my regular TV show. So I was flying out on a Thursday to do two shows in Milwaukee, do two book signings, then go to Pittsburgh the next day and do the same thing there. That's not enjoying what you do—that's overworking.

BARRY KATZ The country rallied around her and the network rallied around her and then Chelsea created her own production company and the ability to put other stuff on the air and the ability to do the books and these tours [with other comedians]. All those tours are sold out because of how she promotes them. They wouldn't sell out if you just put these four people on a show and said, "This is the Young Americans Tour," or whatever the hell it is. If it didn't have Chelsea's name on the tour, it wouldn't have sold out. And if you go on, you do well, and you come back in as a headliner in that city, hopefully.

She's really become an incredible businessperson by figuring out any way she can to build the brand. I think she's one of the most powerful people in comedy in terms of her influence and her scope, because the women were not being addressed by anyone else in that way. Like women power, and showcasing other women, and people with women's views. Now, granted that Rosie O'Donnell and Ellen DeGeneres are incredibly successful people, but they, for whatever reason, didn't make the effort to build the brand of women out in the world of comedy. And that's what Chelsea's been doing.

CHELSEA HANDLER I don't think of myself as a mogul. I am aware that I have influence, but I am always surprised at how deep that can run or the impact you have on somebody. I remember reading in the *New York Post* that I came into a comedy club and all the comedians were basically auditioning for me. And I was like, "What? That is so weird." I was just walking in to see a friend—I had no idea that that was going on. And I remember thinking, "Oh my God, I can't believe that."

With the success of Sarah Silverman and Chelsea Handler, it's safe to say that old conventions that pretty could never be funny are finally passé. Silverman and Handler may be the most successful hot comics of the moment, but they are by no means the only ones. If the eighties were an era defined by brassy women in shoulder pads and the nineties were characterized by nerdy women in corduroys, this past decade has been marked by an unusual, more unlikely kind of female comic: the stand-up bombshell.

LISA SUNDSTEDT   When I was starting stand-up comedy, the comics that were very famous were Roseanne, Rosie O'Donnell, Brett Butler, Paula Poundstone. They were very masculine, and maybe androgynous. But the sitcom actresses were *Friends*—it was like Courteney Cox and Jennifer Aniston. So the industry was looking for pretty and funny, that was their big thing. And so it was like they started to realize this is a gold mine right here, girls that look like this but can do comedy. But there weren't any stand-up comics who were famous and who were really attractive. It wasn't a sexy profession for women. There was no woman who women could look at and go, "I wish I could do that." If you were going to be a stand-up comic, you knew that you might have to be a guy, which is why a lot of women go toward dirty, aggressive material when they first start. They think that's what they're supposed to do. Which is what I don't allow in my classes. I make my women be clean and tell the truth.

DAVE RATH, comedy manager   Attractive women had not had a lot of success doing comedy, I think, because comedy is mostly about vulnerability. To me comedy is all about watching somebody onstage be really honest and talk about their perception of the world in funny ways. But it is about vulnerability: people have to identify with those things, and that's what everybody is laughing at. So when a hot girl goes onstage, all the guys want to be with her and all the women are like, "Why is my boyfriend looking at her that way, he's not laughing, he wants to be with her." So over the years the audience has always been put off a little bit by attractive women.

ANJELAH JOHNSON, comedian I was a cheerleader for the Raiders from 2002 to 2003—that was the year we went to the Super Bowl. And for me, personally, [the barriers] were being a woman and not being overweight or ugly. When you think of comedy, you don't think of a good-looking person up there. As soon as I would walk up onstage, you could just feel the shift in the audience like "Who is this? She's not going to be funny. Is this the joke?" Nobody thinks that you can be funny if you don't look funny. So that was definitely something that I had to work through in the beginning. And it was like the first few minutes of my comedy was like me having to break down a wall to prove to people that I was actually funny, before they started listening to what I was saying and "Oh, okay, we can laugh, she is funny."

WHITNEY CUMMINGS Going onstage before I was known as a comedian, sometimes three, four, five minutes into a set, this would happen: I would hear in the back of the room, "Fine, why don't you just go home with her!" And then a girl would storm out. It was clearly a girl who just got in a fight with her boyfriend because her boyfriend was either laughing at what I said or looking at me and she got jealous. I'm like, "I'm not trying to steal your man!" So when I first started doing stand-up, I would wear hoodies and no makeup and I would wear my hair back and sneakers. I used to self-deprecate a lot: I just got cheated on, I just got broken up with, I hate myself, to make women go, "Okay, she's just like us. She has problems too."

ILIZA SHLESINGER I remember people thinking I was the waitress at clubs instead of a comic. That's the thing a lot of comics don't understand: there's nothing wrong with being attractive, it's how you talk to the audience. I'm really good at ingratiating myself. I have a lot of self-deprecating humor, but I don't say anything I don't feel. I don't like my thighs, I say they look like deer haunches. What it does is it lets the girl in the front row who's on a date know, "Hey, I don't think I'm that hot, so whatever you think, know I have insecurities. I bet you do too; let's bond on that." And guys like it and it is the way I feel. Everybody has insecurities, and when you talk about it, when you make fun of yourself, people love you for it.

But as someone who isn't hideous, I cannot get onstage and talk about how ugly I am. I can't get onstage and talk about how fat I am— even if I feel that way that day, because I'm not. To the girl in the row who's three hundred pounds, I can't be like, "Oh, I'm so fat"—she'll hate me. There was a comic I saw one time, gorgeous girl who used to be a model, and she's talking about how fat she is, and what a loser she is: no one here's buying it, because you are a model. You have to understand what you're working with.

However, being somewhat attractive, I go onstage in a zip-up hoodie, because I actually have huge boobs. And it would be detrimental to the act to come onstage in a low-cut shirt, because that's what you're going to be looking at the whole time. And it's hard to be physical, and I get that. My guy friend's like, "Why don't you dress up?" and I'm like, "Because I've seen the way you look at me when I wear heels and a short dress." That's not what I want when I'm onstage. I also dress down, in general. I'm just very casual.

NATASHA LEGGERO   I'm four foot eleven, so that is not exactly a Hollywood standard. But I think that some girl comics who are equally attractive, they really play down their looks and talk about how they can't get a guy even though everyone wants to have sex with them. And I think a lot of people get afraid that they can't be taken seriously if they are attractive, so they will play it down. But I feel like I'm just being myself. I've always dressed up and I've always been into glamour, and I just felt like the stage should just be an extension of who you are and hopefully a little bit of an exaggeration. I don't do casual. So for me to kind of dress down and not put on my eyeliner, I just wouldn't.

I have a joke: "Aren't you a little ugly to be talking to me?" That joke is just about a particular type of male open-mic comic. And I remember I was on my way to an open mic and I think I got pulled over because my car wasn't smog-checked and I couldn't afford car insurance, so it was this big mess and I was depressed and I'm like, "What am I doing with my life? I'm just gonna go to this open mic and some talentless schlub is gonna start harassing me because I'm a woman." And then that joke just kind of popped into my head, which is kind of what happens. Like you're in a bad situation and then, all of a sudden, like something comes into your head to try to, like, make sense of it, and it's funny.

WHITNEY CUMMINGS   Whereas I used to think that looking pretty or sexy would alienate women, now it's the opposite. Now I feel like when I embrace my femininity, it makes women relate to me more, because they go, "Oh, she's just like me, she puts on makeup and she tries to look cute, and she wears Spanx and she wears heels." And I think that now, being known helps—you can get away with more.

I talk a lot about high heels—why the fuck are we wearing these, why do we wear thongs, we wear Spanx, we wear underwire bras, we put on all this makeup? I talk a lot about them in my act more and more now, and why do women have to torture ourselves with all this shit but guys are hideous and they don't have to wear any of that stuff? So I've started addressing it more and I think that those jokes are more powerful when I'm clearly a victim of all the things I'm talking about.

KATHY GRIFFIN   Chelsea Handler is hot, but I have to tell you, when I watch her show, what do I care that she's a hot blonde? I just think she's really funny and smart and quick. Do I think that it helped Tina Fey that she's good-looking? Of course it did. But man, she just worked the system in a way that she was able to let her actual material come through, more than the fact that she's a super-cute brunette.

JEN KIRKMAN   Sometimes I worry that comedy is going to a place where you will have to be a hot chick for people to be interested in you.

There were definitely tons of times where I just had ridiculous conversations with people in the entertainment industry about my place in the business because of being a woman. I remember this guy used to book the Aspen comedy festival and all the comics would, like, lose their minds and get so excited for the guy to come scout us once a year—it was like Santa Claus coming. And I remember him telling me, "You dress kind of sloppy onstage, you know you need to be pretty." Stuff like that. And I'm like, "Well, everyone looks like a slob."

And before I got my writing job, I was going on a lot of auditions and the call would always be, "We need a funny woman; there's no funny women and we need a funny woman for this role." And I'd be like, "What's the role?" And they're like, "Oh, it's this movie and it's this hot chick." I would get scripts sent to me and the descriptions are like, impossibly hot women, like Gisele Bündchen hot, in a bikini—but she's supposed to be funny. And I would get the call from these casting people saying, "We just haven't seen any funny women." And I'm like, "If the women fit that hot description, they're probably not going to be funny, because they're models and they're not comedians." So you're not going to be happy when I walk in that room. I mean, I'm cute but I'm not a model. And I would walk into the room and you would see people physically look you over and you would know that you weren't the type. And then they end up casting a model anyway.

CHELSEA PERETTI   I don't think I'm attractive by Hollywood standards. I definitely think there are prettier comedians that are probably aided by their looks more in Hollywood. I feel like even the ugly funny girl, who is the best friend of the hot girl in movies, is still a pretty girl who's not funny. I think it's incredibly narrow what is considered beautiful in Hollywood, and I certainly don't feel like I am in that narrow margin.

SETH MORRIS   I've seen a lot of people [looking for] hot funny women. You know, hot women trying to be funny. That actually really pisses me off, because a lot of them are not funny at all. But they can get away with being in a bikini and then saying something raunchy. It's frustrating, because there's all these amazingly talented funny ladies who are cut off at the knees because they don't have a bikini body.

JEFF SINGER   Natasha Leggero is a pretty girl, same for Whitney Cummings. These are the ones who are going to get more attention because they have that castability factor—they're pretty girls. That's not to take away from whether they are good comics or not, but it's just that they're going to get a step ahead because of their looks. That's how it works for females. It just does. The days of Elayne Boosler getting a shot are few and far between. Take someone like a Laura Kilmartin who's now a writer on Conan's show. She's written for Adam Carolla, Craig Ferguson, Bonnie Hunt, Colin Quinn—she's a great stand-up comic. And Laura's attractive all right, but she doesn't look like Whitney Cummings or Natasha Leggero and is never going to get a shot like that: she's a great writer who carved herself out a career. But the industry has always been that way and especially toward women. Looks count for a lot in castability. And these comics want to be actresses. Do I think that Whitney Cummings or Natasha are going to be comics like Louis C.K.?

While the proliferation of cable TV may have created some opportunity for women, YouTube has changed the game. The ability to create and share videos showcasing your talent has, more than ever, given young comics the sense that they are in control of their own professional destiny. Gone are the days when a young comic needed the approval of someone like Johnny Carson or Mitzi Shore to get noticed by Hollywood—today, comics are taking it directly to the public.

ELLIE KEMPER   It's like a puzzle: How do you break into all this? Well, you can perform all the time and write your own shows, which is what I did. My friend Scott and I were always writing sketch shows and putting them up with the hope that an agent would come and see it. The idea being that the more you put yourself out there and show you can write and act, the better. Today, people are still writing shows, but if you are putting yourself out there to get noticed, I think the first thing you say is "What video can I make?"

WHITNEY CUMMINGS   It used to be that you go on the *Tonight Show* and you're famous. Now you go on the *Tonight Show* and nothing happens. It's a good tape, maybe. TV is still very important and YouTube is very important for bookings, because you can send a link and two seconds later, they see "Oh, great, she's good." Everything is quicker and faster. But the downside is that you have to be better because something online is immediately accessible. It can be forwarded and will be on the Internet forever, so you have to be much more careful with what you post. You send someone a DVD, one person sees it. Something online will be there forever and you have no control over it. So you have to be more careful with what you do.

It's also hard in this day and age because people take camera phones, videotape you performing, and put it online. There's a video online of Sarah Silverman working on new material for her new special. And this guy's videotaping her, and she's like, "Dude, that's not cool, can you please stop?" And the guy won't stop. And she's like, "Seriously, please stop." And then she's online saying that, and suddenly she's a bitch. But it's like all of a sudden she can't even work on new material without someone putting it on the Internet. So it's a blessing and a curse.

NATASHA LEGGERO   It definitely helped to get a *Tonight Show* set on tape and to be able to send that around. But there's so much oversaturation of everybody that having even two great performances on the *Tonight Show* doesn't necessarily help—and by the way, you can't even put those on YouTube, because they take them off. So it's just hard for people to be able to see it. It helped me get a good agent.

CHARLYNE YI, comedian I started posting on the Internet because I didn't really know how to go about promoting my shows, and my friend was like, "You know, there's like this whole Internet world." And I was like, "Oh my God, the Internet is so scary." And I had been handing out flyers by hand, constantly promoting my shows, so I was like, "Oh, this is a way to save paper too." So my friend showed me how to use YouTube and then from there it was pretty simple, because it is only like three steps. And I started posting videos online, as well as information about my shows, hoping that people would come. "Oh, look at this ice-skating video! If you like it, maybe you should come to my show!" I remember doing that with my first UCB show. I was like, "Oh, I have this last-minute decision: everyone should bring a pillow, because there's going to be this big pillow fight!" And so many people brought pillows, it was so amazing.

And also, I was just bored—some things work onstage and some things don't, so I'd make videos and just post them and see if people would watch them. It's funny: sometimes I'll post a video and there's like three views, and sometimes I'll post a video and there are over a thousand views. I don't know how it works. I don't know who watches my videos.

CHELSEA PERETTI We had a website for *Variety Shac*. But getting recognition really came from a combination of the live show, where we would premier a new short every month, and the Internet. So we started to have fans who just knew us from online, and it was definitely seen by comedy tastemakers and comedians, but I never felt like I was this runaway hit on the Internet. I've certainly seen people who have that experience. My brother and I have two projects, "Black People Love Us" and the "Rejection Line," that were definitely runaway hits on the Internet. But the stuff that was more just me and my personality hadn't been.

Another project I did was with SuperDeluxe [a comedy video website]. Basically you got money to make Web stuff and I had two Web series with them—one called *All My Exes* and one called *Making*

Friends—where they ordered a certain number of episodes and then I got to hire out my own team to make it and do it however I wanted. That was a very cool project that I got to do. It didn't give me like this crazy mass audience of exposure, but comedy people saw it.

LISA KUDROW   A long time ago on TV, you were given time to find your show. It wasn't going to be canceled after one episode. Now there's no time for any show to find its legs. But the Web lets you find your show. It's a place for you to develop something. That's how I saw it. Let's see what *Web Therapy* develops into. Is it a multicamera series or do we have an objective camera? We had to bundle the episodes together for iTunes. Each episode was [about seven to ten] minutes long and it was just two people in a screen, so at first we thought, "Okay, well, no one's gonna sit and watch a bunch in a row, because who would have the patience for that?" And yet it was still watchable, even in a longer form. Showtime licensed it for a half-hour version. So we were looking at it as "Could we watch thirty minutes of this?" And the answer was "Yeah, you can."

AUBREY PLAZA   I was at UCB right around the same time that online videos were starting to get popular. And I had done this Web series called *The Jeannie Tate Show*. And it was right when Derrick Comedy started doing videos—this is before Funny or Die, before all of those websites. It was just when people were first figuring out, "Oh, if I'm a comedian, I can just do a video and send a link, and look how easy it is to get someone to see me rather than try to beg agents to come see a live show," which is really hard to do. And so I kind of tapped into that and I started doing a lot of videos and stuff. And then *The Jeannie Tate Show* was just like another video that I got involved in through [*SNL* player] Bill Hader's wife, Maggie Carey, who I was in a class with at UCB. I didn't really know her very well at all. We took a class together and were socializing, and she just mentioned that she was doing this video with a couple of *SNL* people and she needed someone that could look really, really young and play sixteen. And I was like, "Oh my God, yes, I'll definitely do that." And it was supposed to just be a onetime thing, but the video ended up being so good that she started writing more, and then it became a series, and then eventually Warner Brothers bought it. That was how I started working with CAA [Creative Artists Agency]. They were looking at the video, because they had clients in the videos who were on *SNL*, and then they saw me and they were like, "Who's that?" Once I had contacted them, I was just relentless with sending them links to everything that I was doing, and I was just calling them all the time.

ANJELAH JOHNSON   In 2007 my life changed. I was in this place where I like had no money, my unemployment checks had run out, I landed on a TV show, and the show got canceled. I still wasn't pursuing stand-up, it was just a thing that I did. And it was fun. Every now and then I would go to do a show here or there but it wasn't what I was focusing on. In January 2007, when YouTube was still kind of new, this video came out with a clip of me doing a joke about the nail salon. And when that You-Tube video was filmed, I had only been in comedy for four months, so I was so brand-new and I had maybe twelve minutes of material. I had done this one little show at the Ice House and they videotaped it, and put it on the Internet a year later. And from January to February there were like four million hits on this one video. And I remember, Myspace was very hot at the time and people started contacting me on Myspace. And somebody from the Gersh Agency had reached out to me on Myspace. And by March, I had met with everybody in L.A., all the different networks—NBC, ABC, CBS, *MADtv*. All these people had seen this video of me doing stand-up and called me into a meeting. And by the end of March I had a new agent, I had a new manager, and by May I was auditioning for *MADtv*. I booked *MADtv*, and by the end of the year I was touring. I had written about forty-five minutes of material, and I was traveling around the country with this stand-up. That was all in 2007.

And when I was on *MADtv* I did the character Bon Qui Qui. And after that, the writers' strike hit, a lot of TV shows lost writers, actors, and a lot of TV shows were canceled. We had some budget cuts on *MADtv* and by budget cuts I mean me, and that was the end of that. So I left *MADtv* and just kept on with the stand-up. And then a new YouTube video was posted with Bon Qui Qui [which has generated over 55 million views]. The nail salon had already started fizzling, but then this Bon Qui Qui video came out just in time. The funny thing is, with both of those videos, I wasn't the one who put them on YouTube. Someone else had.

The development of YouTube, meanwhile, has led to a cottage industry of comedy-based sites online, from CollegeHumor to Funny or Die. The emergence of a new Internet-based comedy industry, however, has reinforced the new set of challenges women will face in the years to come: there are very few woman writers at those sites, and videos starring female comedians are few and far between. In the meantime, women on the rise at comedy clubs and sketch comedy schools continue to face the same sort of obstacles their forebears did, all of which serves to suggest the "Women aren't funny" line will not die—even when all the evidence suggests otherwise.

ILIZA SHLESINGER   It's not that women aren't funny, it's just that there are fewer women doing comedy. Therefore, when a women sucks, she represents a greater majority of women that suck. You go to see a lineup and some girl sucks, they go, "She's not funny, women aren't funny." You're not going to remember the three guys that ate it because there were five other guys that were fine. But the thing is, it's also a stepping-stone, because when you're in a lineup of eight comics and you are funny, they're going to remember you.

CHELSEA PERETTI   Comedy is a tough industry in general and I think there are times where being a woman helps you, because people want to book a woman. What happens a lot of times is people want to put a woman in the lineup, so they put someone who's less experienced with all these people who are very experienced and then people go, "Well, women aren't funny." And that's because they are seeing someone who has two years under their belt with all these people who have five or ten years under their belt. And that's just because someone wanted to include a woman on their show. So sometimes being a woman helps you get that spot, but then it can also feed that misconception that guys are funnier than girls.

CHARLYNE YI   At open mics in Los Angeles, I remember there were just comedians in the audience. And when they announced my name, I heard them say something about me being a girl and they all walked out. And I remember having to just be there. And I was like, "Well, I drove two hours to get here, might as well do my set to the sound guy in the back; I hope he's listening." And it was so uncomfortable, so awkward, and then I realized that I can't really rely on other people's gigs to make me happy. So I figured I would have to start my own show. The UCB [in Los Angeles] had just opened up. Matt Besser from UCB saw me perform and he was like, "Hey, I've heard you're looking for a theater to perform. Here you can perform half an hour if you want."

WHITNEY CUMMINGS   I have a theory that part of the reason that there aren't more female comedians is because the life is just very hard. You have to be on the road all the time, your social life takes a hit, your romantic life takes a hit, it's exhausting, and not that women aren't physically capable or mentally capable of doing it, but we just choose not to because it's exhausting.

LONI LOVE   It's a hard lifestyle. I'm on the road 265 days a year. How can you maintain a relationship like that? You can't have kids. You can't even have a damn dog if you're on the road. You leave on a Thursday, you're back on Monday, you only have three days to get yourself together, and then you're back on the road. That's the reason you don't see a lot of females. Not because they're ugly or they're retarded or whatever you want to say. It's easier for a guy to go out on the road. Most of the comics that are in their forties are married but their wives know that they're going to come back home. For a female, it's harder to say, "I'm going to leave my husband, and I'm going to be gone." It's just different. It's harder to do that with children. You can't do that to a child. So there are certain sacrifices. I've sacrificed. I decided I'm not gonna get married, I'm not gonna have kids. It takes too much to do this. My job is to entertain America, so this is what I'm doing now. I have a good life. I don't regret not having kids, I don't regret not getting married. But I tell a lot of females coming up, "You've got to decide what you want. Because you think you can have it all? I can tell you, girls that started out with me, they're not here, they're not on the same level that I am. You can't do it all."

LISA LAMPANELLI, comedian   Big Frank D'Amico, a comic I used to date, was so strong as far as giving a good punch line. Bing, bing, bing. He had seven minutes of the funniest fat jokes ever. People were crying. And I'm like, "Oh, I guess that's how you do comedy." You do punch line, punch line, punch line. No set—hardly a setup. I loved that, because I want big laughs. The audience isn't paying for prose, they're paying for punch lines. A comedy teacher once said that to me. He goes, "Cut all that out. They're paying for punch lines." I'm like, "He's freakin' right." Whereas women, characteristically, it's like, "Yap, yap, freakin' yap." Shut up. They wanna laugh. We don't wanna hear your dumb stories. So I'm not really, obviously, a huge fan of a lot of women comics because I'm like a guy. I'm a guy comic. That's how I came up.

I don't click with women. I have a lot of women friends, but I don't really click with them as well as with gay guys and with straight guys. I think because I have a real straight-guy comedy voice. Like I did an all-woman show at Rascals for a year where I was the headliner. I did the all-woman show. And I just didn't even like to be around at the end. It's unpopular to say that I don't really like a whole lot of women comics, but I don't. I don't think they work as hard as guys. I think they feel entitled. I think it's easier being a female comic and standing out than it is a guy. How many funny white guys are out there? A million. If you're a funny chick, you're gonna stand out. But then they whine about it's harder for women. It isn't harder; it's easier to be noticed. Oh, a funny woman? Holy shit. Nobody sees that.

I always say there's three women comics I'd pay to go see: Sarah Silverman, Kathy Griffin, and me. And I'm so good, I'd pay extra to see me and I get free tickets. And I like Susie Essman a lot. I always forget her.

CHELSEA PERETTI   If you ask any male comedian, "Who are your favorite comedians? Who do you look up to?" no one is going to name a woman. It's just not cool to do that. It's never considered cool to say, "My favorite comedians are Joan Rivers and Sarah Silverman and Margaret Cho." No guy is going to say that. You have to go, "Who are your favorite female comedians?" before anyone is going to bring up these people. And it's just these little ways in which you just start to feel like you are not a real comedian. It's like you're some little subcategory.

ILIZA SHLESINGER   I always hear that girls aren't funny. And actually, I get this compliment a lot—"Can I just tell you I loved your act. You're not just funny for a girl, you're funny." What is funny for a girl? I made a lot of cock jokes, is that funny for a girl? Is that like half-funny?

CHELSEA PERETTI   I mean, people say that to me—"I normally don't think women are funny, but you are really funny." People say that to me frequently.

BARRY KATZ   In comedy involving women, there are not a lot of variables. Very few men in the world say to themselves, "I'm going out to see a female comedian."

The crowds that go to see women are gay men, gay women, straight women, and maybe their dates. And that doesn't mean Whitney doesn't have a lot of guy fans. She does. And they love her. But they also think she's beautiful and sexy and wanna go see her for that as well.

ANJELAH JOHNSON My audience is definitely women. I get groups of, like, sixteen girlfriends who all got together and wanted to come to my show. I get the soccer moms whose kids watch me on YouTube. And then I get the gays—I have a huge gay following. And it's not like Lisa Lampanelli and Kathy Griffin where they have gay men. I have the lesbian following and the gay men following. And I don't know how that happened. I have the Latino following, and the Asians—just the young professionals. It's so diverse, the only thing it's lacking is really just men. I rarely get a group of guys coming to my show. Usually the straight men that are at my show are there with their wives or their girlfriends.

[I also prefer to tour with] just men. I feel like I have worked with other female comedians on my show, where they had come and done a guest spot or something, but if someone is actually featuring for me, I like to keep it diverse. I don't want it to be an all-women show, and especially for the guys that are coming, too, I don't want them to feel alienated. But I like to keep it different, mix it up a little bit, and [include] different points of view. Especially when working with another woman—the odds that we are going to have the same point of view on something are pretty good. We both get hit on by men, so you know there is a good chance that we both have a joke about getting hit on by men. And then we are stepping on each other's material. So I like to mix it up a little bit.

KATHY GRIFFIN Thank God for women and the gays. Gay men look at Rosie O'Donnell and they think, "Funny." They don't see "overweight lesbian." Gay men come to my show and they come to hear what I say. They want to see a funny show. What do they care what I look like?

LISA KUDROW Gay men loved *The Comeback* [her former series on HBO about a sitcom actress turned has-been]. The gay men early on appreciated what I was doing. And that reminds me of what Michael Patrick King [who co-created the series] kept saying about *The Comeback*. He was like, "Look, first the gays, then the ladies, then everybody else." We only got as far the gays with *The Comeback*. But the really satisfying thing is that it's on top 10 lists of comedies and top 10 show of the decade lists, so that's pretty great, considering there were only twelve of those altogether.

JEFF SINGER I don't buy that there's been some eruption of funny women [in the past few years]. There have always been funny women. I just think that's what the industry does: a show about addiction works and suddenly there are four shows about addiction on TV. And you know what? I think it will dip and then it will come back up again. And if you look historically, that's what always happens. There's some star and then "Oh, women are back in comedy," and then it goes dead again.

CHELSEA PERETTI I think there is a huge crop of women that are coming into their own. And I feel like there is, hopefully, some momentum for creating lineups that are more mixed and stuff like that. But I always think how crazy would it be if all these guys were the one guy on lineups all the time. Would they still wanna do stand-up? You know, if it was constantly five girls and them? It's just a different reality. It's really hard for me not to feel like a subset sometimes where I just have to remind myself that I belong here. I'm in this scene and I'm a part of the scene.

The funny thing is, I used to get really outraged and worked up about these things and then I started to feel like it's better to have these conversations in private with people that you trust. I don't feel like it does any good to shine a light on it half the time. Because I do feel like most comedians have an attitude that "I don't belong" and "I'm a piece of shit." Some of that isn't about gender. It's very possible to have that feeling no matter who you are. I've heard white guys complaining that no one wants to book white guys, because they think they're all the same.

So it's a great conversation to have with your therapist or with your best friend if you are feeling down about it someday. I don't think there's much to be gained from it. All it does is alienate you from other people and set you further aside to talk about it all the time. No one wants to hear you complain about this or that hardship. At the end of the day, it's entertainment. It's not some civil rights issue, really.

Acknowledgments

There are many people I need to thank for making this book a reality, not least of which are the very comedians who agreed to speak with me—this book would have been impossible were it not for the number of voices included in its pages. A huge thanks must also go to the ladies of *Marie Claire*, the magazine where this book was born: Joanna Coles, its editor-in-chief, saw the importance of this kind of history and was the first person to publish it, as an article, in the pages of her magazine; Lucy Kaylin was the editor who helped inspire the piece, gave it the green light, and, most important, actually believed that I'd be able to pull it off; Lea Goldman convinced me that there was more to this topic than just an article, and generously shared her insights throughout the process of writing the book; Lauren Iannotti offered skillful support during the writing of the article; and Dana Stern gave me numerous introductions to the many, many publicists who needed to be contacted in order to nail down interviews.

Of course, the process of transforming the article into a book was another story, a long and demanding effort that would have been impossible were it not for the keen insights and guidance of my editor, Sarah Crichton, who shared my vision for the book. She took a chance by signing me to write it, and I will be forever grateful. And thanks to her assistant, Dan Piepenbring, for fielding the hundreds of e-mails I've sent him over the past three years and tirelessly responding to my many, many questions. And to my agent, David Kuhn, for always looking out for me. Thank you, also, to Billy Kingsland and Jessi Cimafonte for helping to walk me through the process, and to Kathy Daneman.

I really must thank my transcribers, who spent hours upon hours listening to recordings—Cassie Seinuk, Vanessa Dimaggio, Alexa Tsoulis-Reay, Jen Wieczner, and Nicole Irvin—and my fact-checker, Katie Van Syckle, for staying sharp.

An additional thanks to the following people: Maggie Bloom, Katie Feola, Russell Goldman, Jessica Brickman, John Ortved, Slade Metcalf, Colin Miner, David Miner, Christopher Farah, Mike Farah, Merrill Markoe, Treva Silverman, Rosie Shuster, JoAnne Astrow, Mark Lonow, Rick Newman, Greg Charles, Alf LaMont, Janice Mowery, Karla Thomas, and Jeff Singer. Thanks as well to Gerald Nachman, author of *Seriously Funny: The Rebel Comedians of the 1950s and 1960s*; Gregg Mitchell at the Writers Guild of America; and Jane Klain at the Paley Center for Media.

Finally, I'd like to thank my family—Wendy Capeluto, Josef Kohen, Stanley Heilbronn, Jill Kohen, Jamie Kohen, and Jesse Kohen—for their love and support. And last but not least, thanks to my husband, Michael, a lawyer by training but an editor in spirit: you spent many nights and weekends reading drafts and talking it through. Your opinion counted the most, and I could never have done it without your patience, encouragement, and unflagging sense of humor. If you laughed, I knew it was funny.